ALAN ROGERS SELEC

EUROPE

over 400 of the best campsites across Europe

alan
rogers

full page listings
comprehensive writeups
expanded UK & Ireland sections

Compiled by: Alan Rogers Travel Ltd

Cover photo: Camp Bohinj SV4110 (p395)

In memory of our friend and colleague, Jo Smethurst

Editorial & Production
Editor: Robin Fearn – enquiries@alanrogers.com
Editorial Assistant: Florrie Wood
Production & Cartography: Robert Baker
Visual Design: Ben Tully
Contributor: Karla Baker

Advertising Agencies
France: ICCS International Tourism Promotions – info@iccsfrance.com
Spain: Servicios Turisticos Heinze Latzke S.A. – info@servitur-heinze.com
Portugal: Roteiro Lda – info@roteiro-campista.pt
UK: Space Marketing - davidh@spacemarketing.co.uk
Other countries: Alan Rogers Travel Ltd - rob@alanrogers.com

Alan Rogers Travel
Chief Operating Officer: Chris Newey
Finance Manager: Alison Harris
IT Manager: Roland Greenstreet

Special thanks to our Campsite Assessors
John & Margaret Corrall
Pete Lowen & Ann Cazenave
Mike Annan
Mike & Anita Winks
Paul & Jill Bate-Jones
Paul Johnson

Published by: Alan Rogers Travel Ltd,
Spelmonden Old Oast, Goudhurst, Kent TN17 1HE
www.alanrogers.com

54th edition - February 2022
ISBN 978-1-909057-95-1

Printed in Great Britain by S&G

Stay in touch alanrogers.com/signup
Contact us alanrogers.com/contact

 facebook.com/alanrogerstravel

 twitter.com/alanrogers

 instagram.com/alanrogerstravel

Contents & map

Travelling Safely..4
Welcome To The 54th Edition...5
Alan Rogers: In Search of 'Only The Best' 6–7
Using This Guide..8–9
Useful Information...10–11
Maps..472
Indexes...488

Austria................................. 12
Belgium................................26
Croatia................................. 40
Czech Republic..................52
Denmark.............................62
France 72
Germany...........................180
Great Britain....................206
Greece...............................272
Ireland 282
Italy....................................302
Luxembourg......................330
Netherlands......................340
Norway...............................368
Portugal.............................378

Slovenia............................392
Spain..................................400
Sweden..............................452
Switzerland.......................462

Norway (368)

Sweden (452)

Great Britain (206)

Denmark (62)

Ireland (282)

Netherlands (340)

Belgium (26)

Germany (180)

Czech Republic (52)

Luxembourg (330)

Austria (12)

Switzerland (462)

Slovenia (392)

France (72)

Croatia (40)

Spain (400)

Portugal (378)

Italy (302)

Greece (272)

Travelling safely abroad

EU travel

If you're a UK resident, travel to the EU, Switzerland and Norway has changed. Some things have changed, other things have remained the same, but it is best to familiarise yourself with any new processes that have come into effect due to the UK's withdrawal from the European Union.

For the most up to date information, visit **gov.uk/brexit**

Top tip GB stickers are no longer valid. You now need a UK sticker. You do not need a UK sticker if your number plate includes the UK identifier with the Union flag.

However, you will need to display a UK sticker clearly on the rear of your vehicle if your number plate has either; a GB identifier with the Union flag, Euro symbol, national flag of England, Scotland or Wales or numbers and letters only with no flag or identifier. Use the handy guide below to identify your number plate type.

If you're visiting Spain, Cyprus or Malta, you must display a UK sticker no matter what is on your number plate.

If you have a GB sticker, you should remove it before driving outside the UK.

| GB with Euro symbol | GB with Union Flag | National Flag of England | National Flag of Scotland | National Flag of Wales | No Identifiers (standard) | No Identifiers (EV) | Post Sept 2021 (UK Badge) |

COVID-19

Restrictions may have eased, but you should remain vigilant when travelling abroad. To keep yourself and your family safe, remember to wash your hands frequently and wear a mask if required.

For the latest information, visit **gov.uk/coronavirus**

Welcome to the 54th edition

Alan Rogers Guides were first published over 50 years ago. Since Alan Rogers published the first campsite guide that bore his name, the nature of European campsites has changed immeasurably.

Back in 1968, many campsites, though well established, were still works in progress, having been converted from farms and orchards in the post-war years. Of course, there were fewer to choose from than today, and the quality levels varied hugely.

Over the 54 years since the first edition of the Alan Rogers guide, the quality of most campsites has evolved in leaps and bounds. In terms of today's facilities, infrastructure, technology and accommodation types, there is very little comparison with what was on offer half a century ago.

Since 1968 we at Alan Rogers have developed longstanding relationships with many campsites. We have worked with different generations of campsite owners and shared the trials and tribulations along the way with many of them. Typically, campsite owners are a hardy breed, passionate about their campsite, and keen to show it and their region off to every visitor.

The Alan Rogers guides have always aimed to celebrate the variety, recognise the quality and salute the unique. So read on and find the perfect campsite for your next holiday, whatever type of campsite that may be.

1968

Alan Rogers launched his first guide. It contained over 50 "really good sites" personally recommended by Alan Rogers himself.

1970s

1975 Our first guide to Britain is published

1980s

1985 Our first guide to France is published.

1986 After 18 years of development, Alan Rogers retires. The company is purchased by Clive and Lois Edwards.

1990s

1993 We celebrated our 25th anniversary.

1998 Our first guide to Rented Accommodation in France is published.

2000s

2001 Mark Hammerton buys the business.

2003 Dutch language guides are published.

2004 Guides to Italy and Spain are launched.

2010s

2010 Digital guides are launched.

2013 The company is acquired by the Caravan and Motorhome Club.

2018 We celebrated our 50th anniversary.

2019 Venturing further than ever before, worldwide caravan holidays are launched.

Founder of Selected ▶
Sites in Europe
Guide, Alan Rogers

▼ Our first guide,
published in 1968

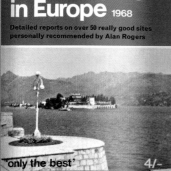

1918 Alan Rogers is born in Warwickshire.

1939 Rogers works as a wireless telegrapher for the RAF during
World War Two.

1948 After the war, Rogers devoted much of his leisure time to
his twin passions of rallying and caravanning. He spent
long periods over the summer with his wife Ruth exploring
newly-founded continental campsites and collecting
information on these sites.

1967 Work begins on compiling his first official guide to camping.
It goes on sale the following year.

1986 Rogers retires. He continues inspecting campsites until the
mid 1990s.

2001 Aged 81, Alan passes away. His legacy lives on through the
annual guides that bear his name.

Alan Rogers: in search of 'only the best'

There are many thousands of campsites across Europe of varying quality: this guide contains impartially written reports on over 400, including many of the very finest, in 19 countries. Are there more? Yes, of course, and in countries not included in this book. Online at alanrogers.com, you'll find details of many more - over 8,000 campsites.

Put simply, a guide like this can never be exhaustive. We have had to make difficult editorial decisions to provide you with a selection of the best, rather than information on all – in short, a more selective approach.

We are mindful that people want different things from their choice of campsite, so we try to include a range of campsite 'styles' to cater for a wide variety of preferences.

Those with more specific interests, such as sporting facilities, cultural events or historical attractions, are also catered for. Whether it's part of a chain or privately owned, the size of the site should make no difference in terms of quality. The key is that it should be 'fit for purpose' in order to shine and stand out.

If a campsite can identify and understand what kind of campsite it sets out to be and who it wants to attract, it can enhance its kerb appeal by developing with that in mind.

By way of example, a lakeside campsite with credentials as a serious windsurfing centre should probably offer equipment for hire, secure storage for customers' own kit, courses and tuition, meteorological feeds and so on.

A campsite in the heart of the Loire Valley might offer guided excursions to local châteaux, weekly tastings of regional wine and cheese, suggested walking or cycling itineraries to local châteaux with entry discounts and so on.

Whatever style of campsite you're seeking, we hope you'll find some inspiration here.

▶

Taken from our very first guide, Alan coins the 'only the best' term.

Alan Rogers, 1968

Alan Rogers believes strongly that there is no point in camping uncomfortably when, with a little planning, you can do so in quite reasonable comfort.

He considers too that the greatest degree of comfort is obtained by using organised camping sites and, more especially, by using only the best of these sites. Alan Rogers' Selected Sites for Caravanning and Camping in Europe 1968 enables you to do just this.

Country

Alan Rogers reference code and on-site information including accommodation count, pitch count, GPS coordinates, Postcode and campsite address.

Campsite Name

A description of the site in which we try to give an idea of its general features – its size, situation, strengths and weaknesses. This section should provide a picture of the site itself with reference to the provided facilities and if they impact its appearance or character. We include details on approximate pitch numbers, electricity (with amperage), hardstandings etc., in this section as pitch design, planning and terracing affect the site's overall appearance. Similarly, we include a reference to pitches used for caravan holiday homes, chalets, and the like.

Lists more specific information on the site's facilities and amenities and, where available, the dates when these facilities are open (if not for the whole season).

Campsite contact information

Opening dates

Below we list 'Key Feautres'. These are features we think are important and make the site individual.

 Beach nearby

 Dogs allowed

 Open all year

 Fishing

 Watersports

 Golf

This is a QR code. You can scan it with your smartphone and it will take you directly to the campsite listing on our website. Newer phones have the ability to scan these codes using the camera, but you can download an app and try it.

How to best use this guide

The layout of this edition is similar to our previous 'new-style' Europe guides but different from our old editions. We still aim to provide comprehensive information, written in plain English in an easy to use format, but a few words of explanation regarding the content may be helpful.

Toilet blocks Typically, toilet blocks will be equipped with WCs, washbasins with hot and cold water and hot shower cubicles. They will have all the necessary shelves, hooks, plugs and mirrors. There will be a chemical toilet disposal point, and the campsite will provide water and waste-water drainage points and bin areas.

Shop Basic or fully supplied, and opening dates.

Bars, restaurants, takeaway facilities and entertainment We try hard to supply opening and closing dates (if other than the campsite opening dates).

Swimming pools These might vary from a simple, conventional swimming pool to an elaborate complex with multiple pools and waterslides. Opening dates and levels of supervision are provided where we have been notified. There is a regulation whereby Bermuda shorts may not be worn in swimming pools (for health and hygiene reasons). It is worth ensuring that you take 'proper' swimming trunks with you.

Leisure facilities For example, playing fields, bicycle hire, organised activities and entertainment.

Dogs If dogs are not accepted, or restrictions apply, we state it here. If planning to take a dog or other pet, we recommend you check in advance.

Opening dates Campsites can and sometimes do alter these dates before the start of the season, often for good reasons. If you intend to visit shortly after a published opening date or shortly before the closing date, it is wise to check that it will be open at the time required. Similarly, some sites operate a restricted service during the low season, only opening some of their facilities (e.g. swimming pools) during the main season. It is always wise to check.

Sometimes, campsite amenities may be dependent on there being enough customers on-site to justify their opening. Some campsites may not be fully ready by their stated opening dates. They also tend to close down some facilities at the end of the season and generally wind things down.

We usually give an overview of the pitches, including an approximate quantity. This figure may vary year on year, so it is rarely absolute.

Accessible travel

We firmly believe that travel should be accessible to everyone. It's a wonderful thing to explore a place, journey somewhere new, instil a sense of adventure in the little ones, discover new cultures, learn, experience, and stimulate.

But for some, travel can be challenging.

With the help of Karla, a friend, member of the Caravan & Motorhome Club, writer and wheelchair user, we've rated each country against our five-point criteria.

This criteria focuses on the following five areas:

 Public buildings and services Government buildings, libraries, tourist offices, embassies, national museums, travel hubs, post offices, religious buildings, hospitals etc.

 Transport Buses, taxis, trains, trams and metro, boat services etc. Disabled parking and on-road parking.

 Street movement Pavements and pedestrianised areas. Street furniture such as benches, planters, market stalls etc. Geography of the area. Tactile paving, dropped kerbs, level access etc.

 Attractions Theme parks, swimming pools and water parks, historic, natural and outdoor attractions, museums and galleries, zoos etc.

 Rural travel Access to out-of-city areas, amenities in isolated regions, travel links etc.

We couple this criteria with government attitudes and legal provisions to give a score out of five for each country.

To find out more and to download our free mini-guide to accessible travel in Europe, visit **alanrogers.com/open-to-all**

Say hello to Karla

Karla has Spinal Muscular Atrophy, a condition characterised by weak muscles and problems with movement. She lives on the south coast of England with her partner, Stephen. They both have a passion for travel and being outdoors, so when they got their first caravan in 2017, it was one of the best decisions they ever made!

Keep up with Karla

 AdventureWheelsUK

 @adventurewheelsuk

On their travels, they've encountered a broken caravan water pump, a severe fault with her wheelchair, and becoming unwell 700 miles from home (not all at the same time, thankfully!). Although these situations are less than ideal, they managed to muddle through, which is the case for most issues that can arise.

Useful information

Low Emision Zones

Countries across Europe, including the UK, have enforced Low Emission Zones to help reduce urban pollution. These include Zero Emission Zones (ZEZ), Ultra Low Emission Zones (ULEZ) and Low Emission Zones (LEZ). Most major cities have implemented one or some of these schemes. It means some vehicles are prohibited from entering or are required to pay to enter the zones.

For further information, visit **urbanaccessregulations.eu**

Recycling abroad

We are all considering how we can be a little bit greener in our everyday lives, but it is just as important to be as environmentally friendly on holiday as it is at home. That's why we've made it easier to know what to and how to recycle abroad. We've introduced a traffic light system to show how geared up to recycling each country is.

Green Recycling is widespread and similar, if not better, than in the UK. Expect glass, plastic, aluminium and paper/cardboard to be recycled via public bins, deposit schemes or other initiatives.

Amber Recycling is a little hit and miss. Perhaps some materials are recycled and others not, or rules differ from region to region.

Red Recycling is not widespread, and/or rules are complex or unclear.

> **Keep it clean**
>
> Leave your pitch exactly how you found it. What you leave behind can have a huge impact on nature, no matter how small. And while it might not be realistic to go totally zero waste, it's important to be mindful of leaving as little a trace as possible during your stay.

Public holidays

It's always best to research public holidays before travelling. We've listed all public holidays, some have fixed dates and others vary from year to year.

Climate

We've added a climate chart to each country introduction page to make it easier to plan and prepare for your holiday. Across Europe, June to September are the warmest months, and November to February are often the coldest. You can expect the months in between to be mild. The information we've used in these charts is based on historic weather averages from each of the country capitals listed. Therefore, weather across each country will differ from the stated averages, generally warmer in cities and cooler on the coasts.

Capital Vienna
Currency Euro (€)
Language German
Time Zone CET (GMT+1)
Telephone Code +43

Shops Larger stores are open 8am to 8pm weekdays, smaller shops open later and close earlier. Many close early on Sat and stay closed on Sun. Bakeries open Sun morning.

Money ATMs are widespread, accessible 24hrs a day and have multilingual instructions. Cards accepted at transport hubs and some restaurants; expect to pay cash elsewhere. Daily withdrawal limit of €400.

Accessible Travel Generally well catered for in cities and larger towns, especially Vienna. Most, but not all, attractions and public services offer assistance.

Travelling with children Programs are usually organised for children over the summer period. Many lakes have supervised beach areas. Many museums in Vienna are free for under 18s. Restaurants will have children's menus or prepare smaller portions.

EU Travel Austria is an EU member state and located within the Schengen Area.

Low Emissions Zones in major cities, currently only applies to HGVs.

●●●●○ **Accessibility Score**
View our digital e-guide & find out more at
alanrogers.com/open-to-all

Tourism website austria.info/uk

Public Holidays 1 Jan New Year's Day · 6 Jan Epiphany · Mar/Apr Easter Monday · 1 May Labour Day · May Ascension · May/Jun Whit Monday · Jun Corpos Christi · 15 Aug Assumption · 26 Oct National Day · 1 Nov All Saints · 8 Dec Conception · 25 Dec Christmas Day · 26 Dec Boxing Day

Driving in Austria All vehicles must pay a toll to use motorways in Austria. You must display a sticker in your windscreen to show you have paid. All vehicles above 3.5t max permitted laden weight are required to use a GO Box. Dashcams are illegal. It is legal to overtake a tram (at slow speed), providing passengers are not endangered. At traffic lights, a green flashing light means the green phase is ending, and drivers should prepare to stop.

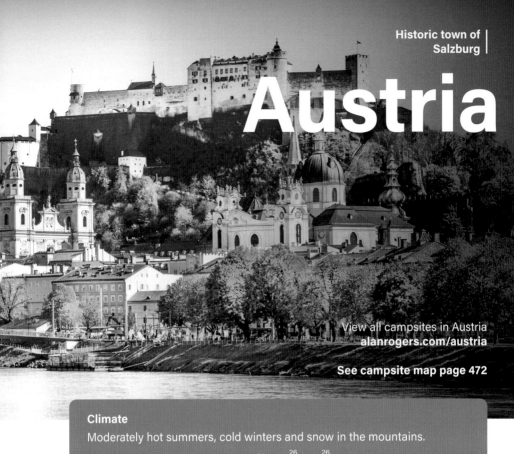

Austria

View all campsites in Austria
alanrogers.com/austria

See campsite map page 472

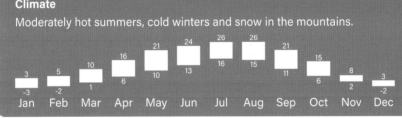

Climate
Moderately hot summers, cold winters and snow in the mountains.

	Jan	Feb	Mar	Apr	May	Jun	Jul	Aug	Sep	Oct	Nov	Dec
High	3	5	10	16	21	24	26	26	21	15	8	3
Low	-3	-2	1	6	10	13	16	15	11	6	2	-2

Austria is primarily known for two contrasting attractions: the capital Vienna with its cathedral, wine bars and musical events, and the skiing and hiking resorts of the Alps. It is an ideal place to visit all year round, for the Easter markets, winter sports and the many cultural and historical attractions, as well as the breathtaking scenery.

The charming Tirol region in the west is easily accessible and popular with tourists who flock to its ski resorts in winter. It is transformed into a verdant landscape of picturesque valleys dotted with wildflowers, a paradise for walkers in the summer.

Situated in the centre is the Lake District and Salzburg, the city of Mozart, with its wealth of gardens, churches and palaces. Vienna's iconic Ferris wheel is a must for taking in the beautiful parks and architecture from a height of 200ft.

The neighbouring provinces of Lower Austria, Burgenland and Styria, land of vineyards, mountains and farmland, are off the tourist routes but provide good walking territory. Further south, Carinthia enjoys a mild, sunny climate dominated by crystal clear lakes and soaring mountains. There are numerous monasteries and churches, and the cities of Villach and Klagenfurt, known for its old square and attractive Renaissance buildings.

13

Alan Rogers Code: AU0220
2 accommodations
97 pitches
GPS: 47.13452, 10.93147
Post Code: A-6441

Umhausen, Tirol

www.alanrogers.com/au0220
info@oetztal-camping.at
Tel: +61 5 2555 390
www.oetztalcamping.com

Open (Touring Pitches):
All year.

Camping Ötztal Arena

This is a delightful site with lovely views, in the beautiful Ötz valley, on the edge of the village of Umhausen. Situated on a gentle slope in an open valley, with a river running along one side, it has an air of peace and tranquillity and makes an excellent base for mountain walking in spring, summer and autumn, skiing in winter or a relaxing holiday.

Around 100 pitches, some on individual terraces, are all marked and numbered and have 12A electrical connections; charges relate to the area available, long leads may be necessary. The reception building houses an attractive bar/restaurant, a TV room, a fully equipped sauna, solarium and gym and a ski drying room.

With underfloor heating, open washbasins and showers on payment, the toilet facilities are of the highest quality. A small toilet/wash block at the far end of the site is used in summer. Baby room. Washing machine and dryer, drying room. Motorhome services. Fridge hire. Bar/restaurant (Closed Nov and April). No shop, but bread can be ordered at reception. Sauna. Solarium. TV room. Ski room. Fishing. Bicycle hire. Basic playground. Climbing wall. Dining hut with coffee machine. Chalets to rent. WiFi over site (charged).

Key Features

 Open All Year

 Pets Accepted

 Play Area

 Bar/Restaurant

 Bike Hire

 Fishing

Scan me for more information.

Alan Rogers Code: AU0070
100 pitches
GPS: 47.22862, 11.88603
Post Code: A-6280

Zell-am-Ziller, Tirol

www.alanrogers.com/au0070
info@campingdorf.at
Tel: +43 5282 2248
www.campingdorf.at

Open (Touring Pitches):
All year.

Campingdorf Hofer

Zell-am-Ziller is in the heart of the Zillertal valley, about as far as is comfortable for caravans, and centred around an unusual 18th-century church noted for its paintings. Campingdorf Hofer, owned by the same family for over 50 years, is on the edge of the village, just a five-minute walk from the centre, on a quiet side road.

The 100 pitches, all with electricity (6A in summer, 16A in winter; watertight 2-pin adapters and long leads required) are grass on firm gravel. A few trees decorate the site and offer some shade. Adjoining the reception area are the bar/ restaurant and terrace, games and TV room, a small heated pool with sliding cover, and a sun deck.

Good quality, heated sanitary provision is on the ground floor of the apartment building and has some washbasins in cabins. Baby room. Washing machines and dryers. Gas supplies. Motorhome services. Restaurant with bar offers special themed weeks with international dishes. Shop opposite. Swimming pool (April-Oct). WiFi over site (charged). Free organised entertainment and activities in high season. Bicycle hire. Guided walks, cycle tours, barbecues, biking, skiing. Free ski bus service (every 20 minutes). Ski room and ski boot dryer. Youth room. Apartments to rent. B&B and half-board accommodation.

Key Features

 Open All Year

 Pets Accepted

 Swimming Pool

 Play Area

 Bar/Restaurant

 Bike Hire

 Scan me for more information.

Alan Rogers Code: AU0185
110 pitches
GPS: 46.80601, 12.80307
Post Code: A-9900

Lienz-Tristach, Tirol

www.alanrogers.com/au0185
seewiese@hotmail.com
Tel: +43 4852 69767
www.camping-seewiese.de

Open (Touring Pitches):
Late May - Mid September.

Campingplatz Seewiese

High above the village of Tristach and 5 km. from Lienz, this is a perfect location for a peaceful and relaxing holiday or as a base for exploring the Dolomite region. Situated amongst giant conifers and surrounded by snow-capped mountains, the site offers everyone a view of the volcanic Lake Tristachsee.

The 110 pitches all have 6A electricity (long leads necessary for some) and the 14 pitches for motorhomes near reception each have electricity, water and drainage. Caravans are sited on a gently sloping field that has level areas although pitches are unmarked and unnumbered. At the bottom of this field is the lake which is used for swimming.

Toilet facilities are clean, heated and modern with free showers. No facilities for disabled visitors. Washing machines and dryers. Motorhome services. Shop (July/Aug). Excellent restaurant/ bar (June-Sept). Small play area. WiFi (charged). Swimming in adjoining lake. Lakeside games field.

Key Features

 Pets Accepted

 Play Area

 Bar/Restaurant

Scan me for
more information.

Alan Rogers Code: AU0212
70 pitches
GPS: 47.81664, 13.05232
Post Code: A-5020

Salzburg City, Salzburg

www.alanrogers.com/au0212
info@panorama-camping.at
Tel: +43 6624 50652
www.panorama-camping.at

Open (Touring Pitches):
Mid March - Early November &
Christmas period.

Camping Stadtblick

Panoramacamping Stadblick is superbly located for visiting Salzburg. From this 70-pitch site with excellent modern sanitary facilities, there are views over the city to Salzburg's hilltop castle beyond. The city is easily reached, either from a bus stop only a few minutes walk away, or tours can be arranged departing directly from the site. There is also a cycle route to the city.

All the level pitches are on grass-gravel with 6A electricity and are arranged on shallow terraces with a separate area for tents. Fresh bread and breakfast are available from 08.00, warm, homemade Apfelstrudel is an all-day treat, and the cosy restaurant is open from 18.00.

Salzburg is much more than Mozart and The Sound of Music, it is a city with a long and rich and interesting history and there is a great deal to see and do both in the city itself and in the surrounding area.

Excellent sanitary facilities include six spacious wash rooms with shower and washbasin. Suite for disabled visitors. Baby room. Washing machine and dryers. Freezer for cool packs. Motorhome services. Shop for basic supplies, gas and souvenirs. Restaurant (15/5-15/10). Small play area. WiFi (charged). Apartments for rent.

Key Features

 Pets Accepted

 Disabled Facilities

 Play Area

Scan me for more information.

Alan Rogers Code: AU0094
7 accommodations
110 pitches
GPS: 47.73912, 13.40082
Post Code: A-5342

St Gilgen/Abersee, Salzburg

www.alanrogers.com/au0094
camp@birkenstrand.at
Tel: +43 6494 04879
www.birkenstrand.at

Open (Touring Pitches):
Start April - End October.

Camping Wolfgangsee

Camping Wolfgangsee Birkenstrand has spectacular views over the Wolfgangsee and the distant mountains. This friendly, family-run site offers a relaxing holiday in an 'away from it all' location in Salzburg. With direct access to the crystal clear waters of the lake, the opportunities for watersports are numerous - snorkelling, scuba diving, windsurfing and water-skiing; courses are also available. There are multiple cycling routes from the site which range from flat and easy to more challenging.

There are 110 good sized pitches (90-110 sq.m), all with 12A electricity (Europlug) and some are fully serviced. They are marked, low hedges divide many, and there is occasional shade from small trees. There are several interesting resort towns along the lake, including St. Wolfgang with its historic rack railway dating back to 1893. There is a restaurant within walking distance of the campsite offering regional specialities.

The modern heated sanitary block is well maintained and fully equipped with hot showers (on payment), washbasins in cubicles, and a baby changing room. Washing machine and dryer. Motorhome services. Campers' kitchen. A small shop in reception supplies fresh bread, ice-creams and pizzas. Sauna. Playground. Table tennis. Table football. Kayak and bicycle hire. No charcoal barbecues. Communal barbecue. Dogs are accepted (max. 1). Internet access and WiFi over site.

Key Features

 Play Area

 Bike Hire

Scan me for more information.

Alan Rogers Code: AU0290
16 accommodations
120 pitches
GPS: 48.33239, 16.07275
Post Code: A-3430

Tulln, Lower Austria

www.alanrogers.com/au0290
camptulln@oeamtc.at
Tel: +43 2272 65200
www.campingtulln.at

Open (Touring Pitches):
Mid April - Mid October.

Donaupark Camping Tulln

Donaupark Camping, owned and run by the Austrian Motor Club (OAMTC), is imaginatively laid out, village style, with unmarked grass pitches grouped around six circular gravel areas. Further pitches are to the side of the hard road which links the circles and these include some with grill facilities for tents; 100 of the 120 touring pitches have electricity (3/6A) and cable TV sockets. Tall trees surrounding the site offer shade in parts. Tucked neatly away at the back of the site are 120 long stay caravans. Activities are organised in high season with guided tours around Tulln on foot, by bike and on the river by canoe.

The ancient town of Tulln lies on the southern bank of the River Danube, about 20 miles northwest of Vienna. The city can be reached by train in about 30 minutes and one can sail on the river through the Wachau vineyards, orchards and charming villages.

Three identical, modern, octagonal sanitary blocks can be heated. One is at reception (next to the touring area), the other two are at the far end of the site. Facilities for disabled visitors. Washing machines and dryers. Cooking rings. Gas supplies. Shop. Bar and restaurant. Play areas. Tennis. Bicycle and canoe hire. Excursion programme. WiFi (free).

Key Features

Pets Accepted

Disabled Facilities

Play Area

Bar/Restaurant

Bike Hire

Scan me for more information.

Alan Rogers Code: AU0302
2 accommodations
200 pitches
GPS: 48.20848, 16.44733
Post Code: A-1220

Wien-Ost, Vienna

www.alanrogers.com/au0302
neuedonau@campingwien.at
Tel: +43 1202 4010
www.campingwien.at

Open (Touring Pitches):
Easter - Mid September.

Camping Neue Donau

This is a very good site from which to visit Vienna. It is easily accessible from the Autobahn system and the city centre is quickly reached from the site by the efficient Vienna U-bahn system, line U2. Some train tickets can be purchased at reception. There is some traffic and train noise as is found on most city sites.

With 200 level touring pitches with electricity and a further 12 with water and drainage, the site has a large and changing population. The site is close to the Donauinsel, a popular recreation area.

The Neue Donau (New Danube), a 20 km. long artificial side arm of the Danube, provides swimming, sports and play areas, while the Danube bicycle trail runs past the site. This is a useful location for an overnight stop or a short break to visit Vienna and the Danube.

Modern toilet facilities are clean, and well maintained with free showers. Facilities for disabled visitors. Washing machines and dryers. Motorhome services. Campers' kitchen with cooking facilities, fridges, freezers and TV. Shop. Small restaurant (July/Aug). Play area. Barbecue areas. Bicycle hire and free guided bicycle tours. WiFi (free).

Key Features

 Pets Accepted

 Disabled Facilities

 Play Area

 Bar/Restaurant

 Bike Hire

Scan me for more information.

Alan Rogers Code: AU0502
70 pitches
GPS: 46.87558, 15.93445
Post Code: A-8344

Bairisch Kölldorf, Steiermark

Camping Im Thermenland

www.alanrogers.com/au0502
camping.bairischkoelldorf@bad-leichenberg.gv.at
Tel: +43 3159 3941
www.bairisch-koelldorf.at

Open (Touring Pitches):
All year.

Camping Im Thermenland is tucked quietly away in the hills of eastern Steiermark, 45 km. southeast of Graz and close to the borders of Slovenia and Hungary. It is a modern, well-maintained site with 70 level touring pitches, with some hedge separation, all with 16A electricity, water and drainage. As the name suggests, the site is situated close to numerous spas and thermal baths including Bad Gleichenberg, which dates back to Roman times. Nearby Bairisch Kölldorf is a town of only 1,000 inhabitants; it does however boast a fire station that takes the form of the world's largest fire engine!

Steeped in history, this part of Europe is known to few tourists, but it has much to offer, both from the past, with some superb castles perched atop rocks with steep, well-fortified approach roads, and from the present with attractions such as Styrassic Park – a must for youngsters. A regional bus stops outside the site, making sightseeing easy for those who like to take a break from driving.

Excellent toilet facilities are clean, well maintained and include free showers. Facilities for disabled visitors. Dog shower. Washing machine and dryer. Restaurant with terrace adjoining small play area. Unheated outdoor swimming pool with cover (May-Sept).

Key Features

 Open All Year

 Pets Accepted

 Disabled Facilities

 Swimming Pool

 Play Area

 Bar/Restaurant

Scan me for more information.

Alan Rogers Code: AU0505
63 pitches
GPS: 46.77888, 15.52900
Post Code: A-8430

Leibnitz, Steiermark

www.alanrogers.com/au0505
camping@leibnitz.at
Tel: +43 3452 82463
www.leibnitz.at/sport-freizeit/
camping

Open (Touring Pitches):
Start May - Mid October.

Camping Leibnitz

Near the Slovenian border, close to the small town of Leibnitz, this site is set in the rolling wine-growing countryside of southeast Austria. A small site with only 63 pitches, it is set in a lovely park area, close to an excellent swimming pool complex (some noise can be heard) which is available for campers' use (with access arrangements for disabled visitors).

A sports centre and facilities for minigolf and tennis are nearby. All the pitches are of a good size, level and with 16A electricity connections, and most have some shade. The town has shops and restaurants with weekly events held, for example, at the Jazz Club. There are marked footpaths and cycle routes to allow you to explore.

Excellent sanitary facilities are clean and well maintained with free showers. Facilities for disabled visitors. Washing machine. Snack bar and takeaway (May-Sept) but many restaurants within walking distance. Small play area. WiFi over site (charged).

Key Features

 Pets Accepted

 Swimming Pool

Scan me for more information.

Alan Rogers Code: AU0370
340 pitches
GPS: 46.61858, 14.25742
Post Code: A-9020

Klagenfurt, Carinthia

www.alanrogers.com/au0370
info@campingfreund.at
Tel: +43 4632 87810
www.camping-woerthersee.at

Open (Touring Pitches):
Mid April - Start October.

Klagenfurt Wörthersee

Set in the picturesque region of Carinthia, Camping Klagenfurt is located near the east bay of Lake Wörthersee across the road from the public beach, Strandbad Klagenfurt. The site is in a green area of more than 400 acres and has 340 pitches for mobile homes, caravans, and tents. There are three different sizes of plot ranging from standard to over 100 sq.m. with electricity (10A) and showers included in the price.

The main attraction is Strandbad Klagenfurt, a sandy beach with an especially long water slide, a 'beer island' and an area of nearly 40 acres for sunbathing. The beach is just a short walk from the campground (less than one minute). Access is with a chip card available from reception for a small fee.

Two modern and clean sanitary buildings including facilities for disabled visitors. Family shower rooms. Baby room. Laundry facilities. Motorhome services. Mini shop in reception (all season). Small restaurant with beer garden (Mid May-Mid Sept). Cinema. Video arcade. Unfenced play area. Minigolf. Bicycle hire. Entertainer offering many fun activities, reading and play. Free WiFi throughout.

Key Features

 Pets Accepted

 Disabled Facilities

 Play Area

 Bar/Restaurant

 Bike Hire

 Golf

Scan me for more information.

Alan Rogers Code: AU0475
12 accommodations
214 pitches
GPS: 46.76768, 13.64850
Post Code: A-9873

Döbriach, Carinthia

www.alanrogers.com/au0475
office@camping-brunner.at
Tel: +43 4246 7189
www.camping-brunner.at

Open (Touring Pitches):
All year.

Camping Brunner am See

This well-appointed site at the eastern end of the Millstätter See is the only one in the area with direct access to its own private beach. Consisting of fairly coarse sand, it is regularly cleaned. The 214 marked pitches (60-107 sq.m), all for touring units, are almost all serviced with water, drainage and 6A electric hook-ups, and are in rows on level grass with tarmac access roads.

The site is fairly open with some shade from bushes and trees. The site owns some land on the opposite side of the road, which includes forest walks, a dog walk, a parking area and an adventure playground. There are three play areas for children. There is access to the cycle route around the Millstätter See and the wonderful walking and hiking area of the Hohe Tauern/Nockalm National Park.

Well-appointed sanitary unit behind reception with good facilities for disabled campers, especially disabled children, plus a children's room with low-level showers, washbasins, baby baths, changing deck etc. Family bathrooms (some for rent), all washbasins in cubicles, laundry facilities. Motorhome services. Site-owned supermarket adjacent (May-Sept.). Communal barbecue. Indoor playground for children (up to 10 yrs). Internet access. WiFi over site (charged). Fishing.

Key Features

 Open All Year

 Pets Accepted

 Disabled Facilities

 Play Area

 Bar/Restaurant

 Fishing

Scan me for more information.

Alan Rogers Code: AU0405
65 pitches
GPS: 47.01499, 13.61498
Post Code: A-9863

Rennweg, Carinthia

www.alanrogers.com/au0405
info@camp-ram.at
Tel: +43 4734 663
www.camp-ram.at

Open (Touring Pitches):
All year.

Camping Ramsbacher

This is a beautiful small site set in a high alpine valley with great views in every direction. With 65 touring pitches, all with electricity, this is a great site for those seeking peace and quiet and the opportunity to explore the local area either by bike or on foot.

The site is well placed in the Katschberg Mountains and close to the Pöllatal Nature Reserve, home to the attractive Wolfsbachtal valley. Cars are not allowed in the national park in the summer so entry is via a small tourist road train.

In winter, of course, the site is very well placed for local skiing. There is a free shuttle bus, four ski schools, 14 uphill facilities and cross-country ski tracks nearby. For the less active winter visitor, there is alpine curling and horse-drawn sleigh rides.

Toilet facilities are clean, heated and modern with free showers but a communal changing area. Washing machine, dryer and drying area. Bread, milk and butter sold. Attractive restaurant/bar with takeaway. Small play area. WiFi (charged).

Key Features

 Open All Year

 Pets Accepted

 Swimming Pool

 Play Area

 Bar/Restaurant

 Scan me for more information.

Capital Brussels
Currency Euro (€)
Language
French, Flemish & German
Time Zone CET (GMT+1)
Telephone Code +32

Shops Most shops are open 10am to 6pm weekdays or until 7pm/8pm on Sat. Some shops open on Sun and close on Mon morning but check before visiting. Some close for an hour at lunchtime.

Money ATMs are widespread, accessible 24hrs a day and have multilingual instructions. Credit/debit cards are widely accepted, although some shops may only accept cash.

Accessible Travel Most public areas and services are suitable for wheelchair users and less able individuals. Transport is well-equipped.

Travelling with Children Many cities have museums and other attractions that run activity days and programs for children. Entrance fees for many attractions are reduced for those under 12.

EU Travel Belgium is an EU member state and located within the Schengen Area.

LEZ Low Emissions Zones in major cities. Registration required for entry.

●●●●○ **Accessibility Score**
View our digital e-guide & find out more at
alanrogers.com/open-to-all

Tourism website visitbelgium.com

Public Holidays 1 Jan New Year's Day · Mar/Apr Easter Monday · 1 May Labour Day · May Ascension · May/Jun Whit Monday · 21 Jul National Day · 15 Aug Assumption · 1 Nov All Saints · 11 Nov Armistice Day · 25 Dec Christmas Day

Driving in Belgium Motorways are toll-free for all vehicles except those over 3.5t. Drink-driving and using your mobile whilst driving are illegal. Trams always have priority. If you are stationary, you should switch off the engine. Blue Zone parking areas exist in most major cities. Parking discs can be obtained from police stations, garages and some shops. Discs should not be used inside Blue Zone areas unless the parking meter is out of use.

Belgium

View all campsites in Belgium
alanrogers.com/belgium

See campsite map page 473

Climate

Temperate, similar to Britain. Cool, damp winters and mild summers.

	Jan	Feb	Mar	Apr	May	Jun	Jul	Aug	Sep	Oct	Nov	Dec
High	6	7	11	14	18	21	23	23	19	15	10	7
Low	1	1	3	5	9	11	14	13	11	8	4	2

A small country divided into three regions, Flanders in the north, Wallonia in the south and Brussels the capital. Belgium is rich in scenic countryside, culture and history, notably the great forest of Ardennes, the historical cities of Bruges and Ghent, and the western coastline with its long sandy beaches.

Brussels is at the very heart of Europe. It is a must-see destination with its heady mix of shops, bars, exhibitions and festivals – a multicultural and multilingual city that is a focal point of art, fashion and culture.

In the French-speaking region of Wallonia lies the mountainous Ardennes, home to picturesque villages rich in tradition and folklore.

It is a favourite of nature-lovers and walkers who enjoy exploring its many castles and forts. The safe, sandy beaches on the west coast run for forty miles. The cosmopolitan resort of Ostend, with its yacht basin and harbour, offers year-round attractions, including a carnival weekend and a Christmas market, and the myriad seafood restaurants will suit every taste. Bruges is Europe's best-preserved medieval city, crisscrossed by willow-lined canals, where tiny cobbled streets open onto pretty squares. After visiting the many museums and art galleries, why not sample some of the delicious chocolate for which the city is famous.

Alan Rogers Code: BE0574
148 accommodations
130 pitches
GPS: 51.24970, 2.96834
Post Code: B-8450

West Flanders, Flanders

www.alanrogers.com/be0574
info@camping-astrid.be
Tel: +32 59 32 12 47
www.camping-astrid.be

Open (Touring Pitches):
All year.

Camping Astrid

Camping Astrid is located on the Belgian coast and is owned and managed by the De Coster family. The site is ideal for families, with all the facilities you would expect to help you enjoy a relaxed holiday. There are around 130 pitches, with full facilities for both the summer and winter holidays, though many of these are given over to mobile accommodation or seasonal units. There are also a number of mobile homes available to rent.

Facilities include a modern game and sports facility, so visitors have plenty of options to keep them entertained. The beach is just 100 metres away. Bredene is a tidy tourist town, which has a range of bars and restaurants where you can take time out to enjoy a drink or a meal. The town is also the home of Belgium's only naturist beach, which is quite a walk from the site. The grass touring pitches have an electricity supply of 10amp.

Toilet blocks with showers, washbasins and wc's. Baby changing area. Facility for guests who are disabled. Laundry with washing machines and dryers. Motorhome service point. Tents allowed. Boules pitch. Children's playground. Sports pitches, tennis, basketball, football, skating ramp. Wi-Fi charged. Table tennis. Air hockey table. Mini football table. Baker, supermarket and restaurant within walking distance. Pets allowed.

Key Features

 Open All Year

 Pets Accepted

 Disabled Facilities

 Beach Access

 Play Area

Scan me for more information.

Alan Rogers Code: BE0543
40 pitches
GPS: 51.07645, 2.58671
Post Code: B-8660

West Flanders, Flanders

www.alanrogers.com/be0543
info@kindervreugde.be
Tel: +32 50 81 14 40
www.kindervreugde.be

Open (Touring Pitches):
Start April - End September.

Camping Kindervreugde

Kindervreugde is a small, simple site, just 500 m. from the Plopsaland theme park, and 2 km. from the beach at De Panne. Being close to the French border, it is also convenient for the ferry ports at Calais and Dunkirk. The three-hectare site has 40 large (100sqm) level grass pitches with water, drainage and 6A electricity, with a choice of shade or open aspect.

Most visitors will stay here for easy access to Plopsaland, however, a few hundred metres away is the Westhoek Nature Reserve where you can take a walk in the dunes and wander along the coast to spot Koniks (Polish primitive horse) or some Scottish Highland cattle. Beyond the dunes is the beach, which is a magnet for activities of all kinds.

The many beach and yacht clubs offer both beginners and advanced sportsmen everything needed to sail, windsurf, kitesurf, surf kayak or wave surf. Adventurers who would rather stay with their feet on shore can try speed sailing, sand sailing or kite buggying.

Basic but well maintained sanitary block. Facilities for disabled visitors. Washing machine and dryer. Baby room. Play area. Multisports field. Bicycle hire. Free WiFi over site. Small children's play area.

Key Features

 Disabled Facilities

 Beach Access

 Play Area

Scan me for more information.

Alan Rogers Code: BE0750
2 accommodations
95 pitches
GPS: 51.23439, 4.39297
Post Code: B-2050

Antwerp, Flanders

www.alanrogers.com/be0750
welcome@citycampingantwerp.be
Tel: +32 32 19 81 79
citycampingantwerp.be

Open (Touring Pitches):
All year.

City Camping Antwerp

Formerly known as Camping de Molen, City Camping Antwerp is a convenient, former municipal site located on the bank of the River Schelde, opposite the city centre. It is possible to walk into the heart of this ancient and interesting city (the historic 'Sint-Anna Voetgangerstunnel' is just under 2 km. from the campsite, and is about 500 m. long), although cycling may be a better option. The free ferry also crosses the river regularly.

The site is fairly level with tarmac roads, and has 95 pitches, 45 for touring units, 34 for campervans all with access to 10A electricity hook-ups. You will need the adapter cable (deposit payable) as the electric hook-ups are not like any you have seen before, and some long leads may be necessary. The nearby Grote Markt, Kathedraal and Groenplaats are all worth a visit. The site is located within Antwerp's Low Emission Zone, so vehicles using this site should be registered for the LEZ scheme in advance of travel.

Toilet facilities, clean when visited, could be hard-pressed at times, especially when everyone returns from a hard day of sightseeing. Basic facilities for disabled campers. WiFi over site (first 30 minutes free). Overall the facilities are quite acceptable given the relatively modest campsite fees for a city-centre site. Twin-axle caravans are not admitted; American style motorhomes may be accepted if you phone first. Swimming pool next door to the site, a separate fee payable.

Key Features

 Open All Year

 Pets Accepted

 Disabled Facilities

 Swimming Pool

 Bike Hire

Scan me for more information.

Alan Rogers Code: BE0793
146 accommodations
34 pitches
GPS: 51.03216, 5.41595
Post Code: B-3530

Limburg, Flanders

www.alanrogers.com/be0793
info@debinnenvaart.be
Tel: +32 11 52 67 20
www.debinnenvaart.be

Open (Touring Pitches):
All year.

Camping De Binnenvaart

De Binnenvaart is a well-equipped family site north of Hasselt, open all year. This is a very well equipped holiday centre with a good range of leisure amenities. The site has been developed alongside a small lake, with its own sandy beach, and is surrounded by woodland. Of the 180 pitches, 34 are for touring, all are of a good size and equipped with electricity (16A Europlug). Many pitches here are reserved all year. The site is part of the same group as BE0792 (Camping Zavelbos) and BE0780 (Camping Wilhelm Tell) both of which are nearby, and guests are able to use amenities at these sites too.

There are some excellent walking and cycle tracks through the surrounding woods. The nearby town of Hasselt is the capital of the Belgian province of Limburg. The small city dates back to the 7th century and boasts a fine cathedral (Saint Quentin) as well as an attractive pedestrianised centre.

Two sanitary blocks, one being upgraded, have facilities for disabled visitors. Motorhome services. Cafeteria and bar. Lake (swimming, fishing and windsurfing) with sandy beach. Tennis. Sports field. Minigolf. Play area. Animal park. Activity and entertainment programme. Free WiFi over site. No charcoal barbecues.

Key Features

 Open All Year

 Pets Accepted

 Disabled Facilities

 Play Area

 Bar/Restaurant

 Fishing

 Sailing

Scan me for more information.

Belgium

Alan Rogers Code: BE0796
30 accommodations
64 pitches
GPS: 51.16092, 5.31433
Post Code: B-3941

Limburg, Flanders

www.alanrogers.com/be0796
gonnie.appel@delagekempen.be
Tel: +32 11 40 22 43
www.delagekempen.be

Open (Touring Pitches):
Easter - End October.

De Lage Kempen

This is a small, good quality site of which the owners are rightly proud. There are about 100 pitches with 64 available for touring units. The pitches are large, all with 6/10A electricity, and are laid out in rows. A pleasant swimming pool complex has three heated pools, two for children and one with a large slide, and they are supervised in high season.

There is a modern bar and restaurant and a shop is open in high season. Entertainment is provided daily in the high season. This is a friendly and welcoming site with a good atmosphere. The owners have found the right balance of entertainment and time for relaxation.

Single, high quality toilet block providing very good facilities including free hot showers, washbasins in cabins and good facilities for babies and disabled visitors. Laundry facilities. Motorhome services. Small shop with fresh bread (high season). Bar/restaurant and takeaway (all season). Outdoor heated pool complex (May-Sept). Large adventure playground. Magical minigolf. Bicycle hire. WiFi over most of site (charged). Max. 1 dog.

Key Features

 Pets Accepted

 Disabled Facilities

 Swimming Pool

 Play Area

 Bar/Restaurant

 Bike Hire

Scan me for more information.

Alan Rogers Code: BE0630
90 pitches
GPS: 50.93486, 4.38257
Post Code: B-1850

Brabant, Flanders

Camping Grimbergen

www.alanrogers.com/be0630
camping.grimbergen@telenet.be
Tel: +32 479 76 03 78
camping-grimbergen.webs.com

Open (Touring Pitches):
Start April - Late September.

Well placed for visiting Brussels, this is a popular little site with a friendly atmosphere. Camping Grimbergen has 90 pitches on fairly level grass, of which around 50 have 10A electricity. Some pitches are on the small side and the site is not suitable for larger units, although some hardstandings for motorhomes have been added.

The municipal sports facilities are adjacent. The bus station is by the traffic lights at the junction of N202 and N211 and buses run into the city centre every hour, 200 m. from the site, excluding Sunday mornings.

There are limited facilities on the site, but there is a selection of restaurants available in the town. In Grimbergen itself visit Norbertine Abbey, Saint Servaas church, and the Sunday morning market. Also worth a visit are the nearby towns of Lier and Mechelen, and the botanical gardens at Meise.

Immaculate modern sanitary facilities are heated in colder months. Separate facilities for disabled visitors. Baby room. Washing machine & dryers. Motorhome services. Bar (July/Aug). Pets allowed (1 on a lead)

Key Features

 Pets Accepted

 Disabled Facilities

 Bar/Restaurant

 Scan me for more information.

Alan Rogers Code: BE0615
25 accommodations
45 pitches
GPS: 51.05367, 3.97982
Post Code: B-9240

East Flanders, Flanders

www.alanrogers.com/be0615
groenpark@scarlet.be
Tel: +32 93 67 90 71
campinggroenpark.be

Open (Touring Pitches):
Early April - Late September

Camping Groenpark

Camping Groenpark is a popular wooded campsite in the heart of the Scheldt region of eastern Flanders. Between Antwerp and Ghent, it is only 10 minutes walk from a lake and close to the Donkmeer, the second largest lake in Flanders.

There are 70 pitches, of which 45 good sized, level, grass pitches are for touring and access is good for large units. The pitches are naturally laid out in glades between the trees, some shady, some sunny and all have 16A electricity. There is an area especially for motorhomes and a large, quiet open camping meadow. The site has large shower rooms, popular with families and a giant central barbecue area.

There is no on-site entertainment, but this is an ideal area for cycling and walking, with many picturesque villages close by. You can relax on-site around the central barbecue point or stroll to the nearby bars and restaurants. The small village of Donk, only 500 m, has a weekly market and restaurants and outdoor cafés.

One large, toilet block at entrance and a smaller block on-site with cabins containing toilet, shower and washbasin. Family shower room. Washing machine and dryer. Motorhome services. No shop, bar or meals but the town is only 500 m. TV room. Play area. WiFi on part of site (charged).

Key Features

 Pets Accepted

 Play Area

Scan me for more information.

Alan Rogers Code: BE0713
60 accommodations
27 pitches
GPS: 49.94493, 5.01100
Post Code: B-5555

Namur, Wallonia

www.alanrogers.com/be0713
info@3sources.be
Tel: +32 61 73 00 51
www.3sources.be

Open (Touring Pitches):
All year.

Camping les 3 Sources

Les 3 Sources can be found between the pilgrimage village of Beauraing and Bouillon. The campsite has been owned by a Dutch family since 2004, with Belgian managers and bar staff. It is well located for exploring the Belgian Ardennes. The site boasts a number of springs, three of which feed some large ponds, which are well stocked with carp and other coarse fish. Fishing is possible for a small fee, but you are asked to return your catch to the water. The site extends over 2.5 hectares and has around 100 pitches; an increasing number of these are occupied by seasonal units, or by mobile homes and chalets.

The popular bar/restaurant provides breakfast and meals throughout the day (as well as takeaway food and local beers). This is the focal point of the site, and evening entertainment is organised here in peak season. This includes barbecues, dances and themed meals. There are over 1500 km. of marked walks through the surrounding hills, and the staff will be pleased to recommend suitable routes.

The sanitary building was built in 2008 and is beginning to look a little dated, but is still perfectly functional with modern fittings, heating and air conditioning. Play area. Three fishing ponds (small charge). Bar (selling snacks). Activity and entertainment programme. Accommodation to rent.

Key Features

 Open All Year

 Pets Accepted

 Play Area

 Bar/Restaurant

 Fishing

Scan me for more information.

Alan Rogers Code: BE0683
50 accommodations
93 pitches
GPS: 50.48528, 5.88383
Post Code: B-4900

Liège, Wallonia

Camping Parc des Sources

www.alanrogers.com/be0683
info@campingspa.be
Tel: +32 87 77 23 11
www.campingspa.be

Open (Touring Pitches):
Early April - End October.

Parc des Sources is a small, quietly situated site, close to the town of Spa (The Pearl of the Ardennes). It is on the outskirts of a large nature reserve and close to the starting point of the famous Promenade des Artistes and many other interesting walks. There are 155 grassy pitches (60-70 sq.m), of which around 90 are for touring; 70 of these have electricity (6A) and there are 12 hardstandings.

The site does not have a wide range of amenities, but there is a small shop and a bar, restaurant and takeaway available daily in high season. The nearby resort town of Spa has shops, bars and restaurants, parks and museums, as well as the Thermes de Spa, where a wide range of treatments are offered. Parc des Sources is conveniently situated for the famous Spa-Francorchamps racing circuit.

One heated toilet block is clean and well maintained, with hot showers (on payment), open style washbasins and baby changing facilities. Facilities for disabled visitors (key access). Washing machine. Motorhome services. Small shop, bar, restaurant and takeaway (open daily July/Aug). Fresh bread can be ordered (July/Aug). Outdoor swimming pool (July/Aug). Playground (under 5s). Bicycle hire. Torches useful. Free WiFi throughout.

Key Features

 Pets Accepted

 Swimming Pool

 Play Area

 Bar/Restaurant

 Bike Hire

Scan me for more information.

Alan Rogers Code: BE0705
565 accommodations
300 pitches
GPS: 50.56758, 5.11718
Post Code: B-4210

Liège, Wallonia

www.alanrogers.com/be0705
info@lhirondelle.be
Tel: +32 85 71 11 31
www.lhirondelle.be

Open (Touring Pitches):
Early April - Late October.

Camping l'Hirondelle

Part of the Capfun group, this site is set in 20 hectares of woodland, in the grounds of a castle that dates back to the 14th century. From the entrance, one gets a glimpse of the restaurant in part of the castle. There are 865 pitches with 300 for touring units, all with 10A electricity. The pitches are arranged around a huge playground, a basketball court and a building housing a games room, a supermarket and a bar.

In the high season, the site is bustling and lively, offering a full programme of entertainment with sports tournaments, discos and contests. This site has a lot to offer for families with children and teenagers. The large open-air pool with numerous flumes has something for all ages. Activity programmes are promoted on screens in all the facilities.

The two toilet blocks for touring units provide some washbasins in cabins, showers on payment, children's toilets and washbasins and a unisex baby room. Washing machine and dryer. Good provision for disabled visitors. These facilities will be very pressed to cope in high season. Shop. Bar. Restaurant. Swimming pool (15x25 m, 1/6-10/9). Huge adventure type playground. Boules. Playing field. Entertainment (High season). Games room. WiFi (free).

Key Features

 Disabled Facilities

 Swimming Pool

 Play Area

 Bar/Restaurant

 Fishing

Scan me for more information.

Alan Rogers Code: BE0720
10 accommodations
75 pitches
GPS: 50.02657, 5.51283
Post Code: B-6680

Luxembourg, Wallonia

Camping Tonny

www.alanrogers.com/be0720
info@campingtonny.be
Tel: +32 61 68 82 85
www.campingtonny.be

Open (Touring Pitches):
Late March - Early November.

With a friendly atmosphere, Camping Tonny is an attractive, small campsite in a pleasant valley by the River Ourthe. A family site, there are 75 grass touring pitches, with wooden chalet buildings giving a Tirolean feel. The pitches (80-100 sq.m) are separated by small shrubs and fir trees, 4/6A electricity is available. Cars are parked away from the units and there is a separate meadow for tents.

Surrounded by natural woodland, Camping Tonny is an ideal base for outdoor activities. In bad weather, the homely bar acts as a meeting place. There is a freestanding fireplace and a shady terrace for relaxing outside. The bar is open all season. Nearby Saint Hubert has a Basilica, the Bastogne War Museum (recommended) and a wildlife park, with wild boar, deer and other native species – all worth a visit.

Key Features

 Pets Accepted

 Play Area

 Bar/Restaurant

 Bike Hire

 Fishing

A sanitary unit (heated in cool weather) includes free showers. Baby area and laundry. Freezer for campers' use. TV lounge and library. Sports field. Boules. Games room. Playgrounds. Fishing. Bicycle hire. Cross-country skiing. WiFi (free by reception).

Scan me for more information.

Alan Rogers Code: BE0716
60 accommodations
44 pitches
GPS: 49.80884, 5.16482
Post Code: B-6880

Luxembourg, Wallonia

www.alanrogers.com/be0716
info@campingmaka.be
Tel: +32 61 41 11 48
www.campingmaka.be

Open (Touring Pitches):
Early April - Mid September.

Camping Maka

Camping Maka is a delightful, rural site on the banks of the River Semois, reputedly Belgium's cleanest river. Forty-four touring pitches, with 10A electricity and water, are sited close to the water, allowing everyone access to the river, and its banks and there is space for 30 tents. Fifty-five private mobile homes are hidden on two higher terraces. A small number of fully-equipped wooden cabins and tents are to rent.

The river is popular for swimming, fishing and canoeing. Canadian canoes, mountain bikes, barbecues and outdoor cooking equipment are available for hire. Facilities include a bar with a terrace overlooking the water and a shop. Not suitable for large units (over 8 m. long).

Adjacent to this is a good play area, a boules court and a pulley slide over the river which offers hours of fun for older children. Fly fishing is also popular (permit required).

A modern, heated toilet block includes facilities for babies and for disabled campers (key access). Pub/café/takeaway with terrace, shop (all season). Play area. Fishing. Games area. Direct river access. Campfire area. Canoe and mountain bike hire. Occasional activities and entertainment. Tents and cabins to rent. WiFi over site (charged). No electric barbecues.

Key Features

 Pets Accepted

 Disabled Facilities

 Play Area

 Bar/Restaurant

 Bike Hire

 Fishing

Scan me for
more information.

Capital Zagreb
Currency Kuna (Kn)
Language Croatian
Time Zone CET (GMT+1)
Telephone Code +385

Shops 8am to 8pm weekdays, until 2pm or 3pm on Sat and closed on Sun. Some shops shorten their hours or shut down in the summer months.

Money ATMs are widespread, accessible 24hrs a day, and some have multilingual instructions. Smaller restaurants and shops often only accept cash. Amex isn't as widely accepted as Visa and Mastercard.

Accessible Travel Largely unequipped for less able travellers but improving. Public transport in larger cities is generally good.

Travelling with Children Beaches are safe. Many museums and historical attractions run activity trails. Child fees are applicable for under 9s. The dining scene is relaxed, and many restaurants will offer a kids menu.

EU Travel Croatia is an EU member state.

There are no Low Emissions Zones currently in place.

●●○○○ **Accessibility Score**
View our digital e-guide & find out more at
alanrogers.com/open-to-all

Tourism website | croatia.hr

Public Holidays 1 Jan New Year's Day · 6 Jan Epiphany · Mar/Apr Easter Monday · 1 May Labour Day · 30 May Statehood Day · May/Jun Corpus Christi · 22 Jun Anti-Fascist Struggle Day · 5 Aug Victory Day · 15 Aug Assumption · 1 Nov All Saints · 18 Nov Remembrance Day · 25 Dec Christmas Day · 26 Dec Boxing Day

Driving in Croatia Tolls are present on some roads. Euros are sometimes accepted as payment. Roads along the coast can become congested in summer and queues are possible at border crossings. Children under 12 cannot sit in the front of a vehicle. Parking is illegal on or near a bend, intersection, brow of a hill or bus/tram or taxi stop. Drink-driving and using your mobile whilst driving are illegal.

Croatia

View all campsites in Croatia
alanrogers.com/croatia

See campsite map page 474

Climate

Warm, dry and short summers and wet and long winters. Warmer along the coast.

	Jan	Feb	Mar	Apr	May	Jun	Jul	Aug	Sep	Oct	Nov	Dec
High	12	12	15	18	22	26	29	30	25	21	17	13
Low	5	5	7	10	14	18	20	20	17	13	9	6

Croatia has developed into a lively and friendly tourist destination while retaining its coastal ports' unspoilt beauty and character, traditional towns and tiny islands with their secluded coves. Its rich history is reflected in its Baroque architecture, traditional festivals and two UNESCO World Heritage sites.

The most developed tourist regions in Croatia include the peninsula of Istria, where you will find the preserved Roman amphitheatre in Pula, the beautiful town of Rovinj with cobbled streets and wooded hills, and the resort of Umag, with a busy marina, charming old town and an international tennis centre. The coast is dotted with islands, making it a mecca for watersports enthusiasts, and there is an abundance of campsites in the area.

Further south, in the province of Dalmatia, Split is Croatia's second-largest city and lies on the Adriatic coast. It is home to the impressive Diocletian's Palace and a starting point for ferry trips to the islands of Brac, Hvar, Vis and Korcula, with their lively fishing villages and pristine beaches. The old walled city of Dubrovnik is 150 km. south. A favourite of George Bernard Shaw, who described it as 'the pearl of the Adriatic', it has a lively summer festival, numerous historical sights and a newly restored cable car to the top of Mount Srd.

41

Alan Rogers Code: CR6712
184 accommodations
284 pitches
GPS: 45.45042, 13.52220
Post Code: HR-52470

Umag, Istria

www.alanrogers.com/cr6712
stella.maris@istracamping.com
Tel: +385 052 710 900
www.istracamping.com

Open (Touring Pitches):
Mid April - Late September.

Stella Maris Umag

CampingIN Stella Maris Umag is an extremely large, sprawling site of 4.5 hectares is split by the Umag/Savudrija road. The camping site and reception are to the east of the road and the amazing Sol Stella Maris leisure complex, where the Croatian open tennis tournament is held (amongst other competitions), is to the west and borders the sea.

Located some 2 km. from the centre of Umag, the site comprises around 500 pitches including a number of which are seasonal or for tour operators. They are arranged in rows on gently sloping ground, some are shaded. The pitches all have 10A electricity. The site's real strength is its attachment to the leisure complex, with numerous facilities available to campers.

Three sanitary blocks of a very high standard. Hot water throughout. Excellent facilities for disabled visitors. Laundry facilities. Large supermarket. Huge range of restaurants, bars and snack bars. International tennis centre with pools and beach area. Watersports. Fishing (permit required from Umag). Entertainment programme and clubs for children of all ages. Communal barbecue areas. Excursions organised.

Key Features

 Book Online

 Pets Accepted

 Disabled Facilities

 Beach Access

 Swimming Pool

 Play Area

 Bar/Restaurant

 Bike Hire

Scan me for more information.

Alan Rogers Code: CR6724
877 accommodations
1519 pitches
GPS: 45.19149, 13.59686
Post Code: HR-52440

Porec, Istria

www.alanrogers.com/cr6724
bijela.uvala@istracamping.com
Tel: +385 052 410 551
www.istracamping.com

Open (Touring Pitches):
Mid April - Late September.

Camping Bijela Uvala

Bijela Uvala is a large friendly campsite with an attractive waterside location and an extensive range of facilities. The direct sea access makes the site very popular in the high season. The 2,300 pitches, 1,500 for touring, are compact and due to the terrain some have excellent sea views and breezes, however as usual these are the most sought after, so book early. They range from 60-120 sq.m. and all have electricity and water connections.

Some are formal with hedging, some are terraced and most have good shade from established trees or wooded areas. There are also very informal areas where unmarked pitches are on generally uneven ground. The topography of the site is undulating and the gravel or grass pitches are divided into zones that vary considerably.

Eight sanitary blocks are clean and well equipped with mainly British style WCs. Free hot showers. Washing machines. Facilities for disabled visitors. Motorhome services. Gas. Fridge boxes. Three restaurants/fast-food cafés, two bars and a bakery. Large well-equipped supermarket and a shop. Two swimming pool complexes, one with a medium-size pool and the other larger, lagoon-style with fountains. Tennis. Playground. Amusements. TV room. Entertainment centre for active children. WiFi (charged).

Key Features

 Pets Accepted

 Disabled Facilities

 Beach Access

 Swimming Pool

 Play Area

 Bar/Restaurant

 Bike Hire

 Fishing

Scan me for more information.

Alan Rogers Code: CR6730
537 accommodations
650 pitches
GPS: 45.10876, 13.61988
Post Code: HR-52210

Rovinj, Istria

www.alanrogers.com/cr6730
info@maistra.hr
Tel: +385 052 800 200
maistracamping.com/campsite-amarin-rovinj

Open (Touring Pitches):
Mid April - Late September.

Camping Amarin

Situated 4 km. from the centre of the lovely old port town of Rovinj, this site has much to offer. The complex is part of the Maistra group. It has 12.6 hectares of land and is adjacent to the Amarin bungalow complex.

Campers can take advantage of the facilities afforded by both areas. There are 650 pitches for touring units on various types of ground, all between 70-100 sq.m. Most are separated by foliage and 10A electricity is available.

A rocky beach backed by a grassy sunbathing area is very popular, but the site has its own superb, supervised round pool with a corkscrew slide plus a splash pool for children.

Thirteen respectable toilet blocks have a mixture of British and Turkish style toilets. Half the washbasins have hot water. Some showers have hot water, the rest have cold and are outside. Some blocks have a unit for disabled visitors. Fridge box hire. Laundry service. Security boxes. Motorhome services. Supermarket. Small market. Two restaurants, taverna, pizzeria and terrace grill. Swimming pool. Flume and splash pool. Watersports. Bicycle hire. Fishing (permit). Daily entertainment. Hairdresser. Massage. Barbecues are not permitted. Dogs are not allowed on the beach. WiFi throughout (free).

Key Features

 Book Online

 Pets Accepted

 Disabled Facilities

 Beach Access

 Swimming Pool

 Play Area

 Bar/Restaurant

 Bike Hire

Scan me for more information.

Alan Rogers Code: CR6735
380 accommodations
850 pitches
GPS: 44.80540, 13.95550
Post Code: HR-52203

Medulin, Istria

www.alanrogers.com/cr6735
arenakazela@arenacampsites.com
Tel: +385 052 577 277
www.arenacampsites.com

Open (Touring Pitches):
Mid April - Early October.

Camping Kazela

Camp Kazela is partly naturist and is situated close to Medulin, formerly a fishing port and now a busy tourist town. The site has around 850 touring units with electricity connections (12A) and 100 pitches with electricity, water and drainage. The remaining pitches are used for chalets, seasonal guests and tour operators.

The site is open with young trees and some pitches have pleasant views over the sea. Some clusters of mature trees provide a little shade, but generally, this site is something of a sun trap. The beach which borders part of the site is mainly of sharp rocks and therefore not suitable for paddling.

Six toilet blocks have British and Turkish style toilets, open washbasins with cold water only and controllable hot showers. Motorhome service point. Shopping centre with supermarket and restaurants. Two aqua parks (one FKK). Sailing and diving schools. Water-skiing. Parasailing. Trampolines. Entertainment team. Games hall. Disco. Live music. WiFi throughout. Communal barbecue area.

Key Features

 Book Online

 Naturist Site

 Pets Accepted

 Disabled Facilities

 Beach Access

 Swimming Pool

 Play Area

 Bar/Restaurant

 Scan me for more information.

45

Alan Rogers Code: CR6756
60 accommodations
330 pitches
GPS: 44.99107, 14.63065
Post Code: HR-51521

Punat, Kvarner

www.alanrogers.com/cr6756
camp.konobe@falkensteiner.com
Tel: +385 051 854 036
campingpunat.com/en/naturist-camping-konobe

Open (Touring Pitches):
Mid April - End September.

Camping Konobe

Naturist Camping Konobe is situated south of the historic fishing port of Punat on the island of Krk in a remote and quiet location. Access is down a long, tarmac road that leads to a landscaped terrain, with terraces built from natural stone.

The 330 slightly sloping pitches are in two areas, part open, part wooded, with some shade from mature trees and some have beautiful views over the Adriatic. Unmarked pitches for tents are on small terraces, with numbered pitches for caravans and motorhomes of 50-80 sq.m. on sandy grass off tarmac access roads.

The remote location makes this site ideal for quiet camping among the wild charm of a rocky and still green environment. The bustling seaside resort of Punat is only 4 km. away.

Three modern, comfortable toilet blocks with toilets, open washbasins and preset showers. Child size washbasins. Facilities for disabled visitors. Campers' kitchen with connections (no rings). Gas. Supermarket. Bar/restaurant with open-air terrace. Tennis. Minigolf. Fishing. Pebble beach. Boat launching. Evening entertainment programme for children. Croatian language lessons. Only gas and electric barbecues are permitted. ATM. WiFi on part of the site.

Key Features

 Naturist Site

 Pets Accepted

 Disabled Facilities

 Beach Access

 Play Area

 Bar/Restaurant

 Bike Hire

 Fishing

Scan me for more information.

Alan Rogers Code: CR6770
106 accommodations
344 pitches
GPS: 44.61687, 14.50808
Post Code: HR-51554

Nerezine, Kvarner

www.alanrogers.com/cr6770
info@camp-baldarin.com
Tel: +385 051 235 680
www.camp-baldarin.com

Open (Touring Pitches):
Late April - Start October.

Camping Baldarin

As one of the most secluded campsites in Cres and Losinj, Camping Baldarin enjoys a tranquil setting between dense Mediterranean forest and crystal clear sea. Most of the sites 450 pitches have access to electricity and the dedicated touring pitches benefit from up to 100m2 in space.

Whilst not all of the site is naturist, there are dedicated pitches and numerous isolated beaches that are ideal for that extra bit of privacy. The drive to the campsite is along an extremely narrow road and care is required.

The reception hosts a bar and small restaurant, whilst at the other end of the site, there is another restaurant specialising in local seafood. The beaches also house two bars and buffets along the shore.

The four toilet buildings are modern and bright, with facilities for disabled visitors and children. Shop. Beach. Bicycle hire. Fishing. Boats for hire, boat launching and trailer parking. Tennis. Gas and electric barbecues only. WiFi (charged).

Key Features

 Naturist Site

 Pets Accepted

 Disabled Facilities

 Beach Access

 Play Area

 Bar/Restaurant

 Bike Hire

 Fishing

Scan me for more information.

Alan Rogers Code: CR6769
142 accommodations
336 pitches
GPS: 44.75272, 14.77417
Post Code: HR-51280

Banjol, Kvarner

Padova Camping Resort

www.alanrogers.com/cr6769
camping@valamar.com
Tel: +385 52 465 010
camping-adriatic.com/padova-camp-rab

Open (Touring Pitches):
Mid April - Mid October.

Previously known as 'Autocamp Padova 3' Padova Camping Resort is located on the shore of Padova 3 Bay in Banjol, twenty minutes' walk from the town of Rab. The 6.5-hectare site has over 500 pitches (16A electricity), either on a flat area near the shore, or on a small, pine-clad hill, which has a remarkable view of the Old Town.

Please note that the pitches on this campsite are very close together, particularly those adjacent to the beach. There is an abundance of services and entertainment facilities, including paragliding, and quad bike and boat rental. If the shade of the pines and olive trees in the campsite does not provide sufficient protection from the summer heat, you could cool down at the adjacent sandy/pebbly beach.

Four toilet blocks (heated) equipped with British and Turkish style WCs, washbasins and showers in cubicles. Facilities for disabled visitors. Laundry. Dog shower. Shop, newsagent, bureau de change. Market selling fruit and vegetables. Bar Grill and pizza restaurants. Aqua park. Hairdresser. Fitness suite. Parasailing. Children's entertainment (July/Aug). Communal barbecue. Accommodation for hire. WiFi throughout (free).

Key Features

 Pets Accepted

 Disabled Facilities

 Beach Access

 Play Area

 Bar/Restaurant

 Bike Hire

Scan me for more information.

Alan Rogers Code: CR6915
53 accommodations
94 pitches
GPS: 44.97357, 15.64799
Post Code: HR-47245

Rakovica, Karlovac

www.alanrogers.com/cr6915
info@plitvice.com
Tel: +385 047 784 192
www.plitvice.com

Open (Touring Pitches):
Start April - End October.

Plitvice Holiday Resort

Plitvice Holiday Resort is on the Zagreb - Split road, 125 km. South of Zagreb. It is well situated for visiting the beautiful Plitvice National Park. The site is surrounded by meadows, forests, mountains, lakes and waterfalls. There are 94 pitches for touring and a number of teepees for rent. Some of the average size pitches are on grass or hard ground, with many slightly sloping (levelling blocks useful). Some have part or full shade and all have 16A electricity.

There is an excellent restaurant offering local and Croatian dishes along with an international menu. In high season, the site often gets full so early arrival is recommended. The site has recently invested heavily in glamping style accommodation including some impressive treehouses, lake houses and mobile homes.

Two modern toilet blocks with mainly open washbasins, could be stretched at times. Washing machine and dryer. Motorhome services. Small shop with fresh bread. Bar/restaurant. Small swimming pool (1/5-1/10). Play areas. Evening entertainment twice a week. Tennis. WiFi (free). The site also has a wide selection of accommodation for rent including tipis, bungalows and apartments.

Key Features

 Pets Accepted

 Disabled Facilities

 Swimming Pool

 Play Area

 Bar/Restaurant

Scan me for more information.

Alan Rogers Code: CR6845
69 accommodations
443 pitches
GPS: 43.60652, 15.92095
Post Code: HR-22202

Primosten, Dalmatia

www.alanrogers.com/cr6845
kamp-adriatik@adriatik-kamp.com
Tel: +385 022 571 223
www.adriatik-kamp.com

Open (Touring Pitches):
Mid March - End October.

Camp Adriatic

As we drove south down the Dalmatian coast road, we looked across a clear turquoise bay and saw a few tents, caravans and motorhomes camped under some trees. A short distance later we were at the entrance of Camp Adriatic.

With around 500 pitches that slope down to the sea, the site is deceptive and enjoys a one-kilometre beach frontage which is ideal for snorkelling and diving. Most pitches are level and have shade from pine trees. There are 212 numbered pitches and 288 unnumbered, all with 10/16A electricity. Close to the delightful town of Primosten, (with a taxi boat service in high season) the site boasts good modern amenities and a fantastic location.

Modern and well maintained sanitary blocks provide clean toilets, hot showers and washbasins. Facilities for disabled visitors. Bathroom for children. Washing machine and dryer. Kitchen facilities. Small supermarket (seasonal). Restaurant, bar and takeaway (all season). Sports centre. Miniclub. Beach. Diving school. Sailing school and boat hire. Entertainment programme in July/Aug. WiFi in the reception area (charged).

Key Features

 Pets Accepted

 Disabled Facilities

 Beach Access

 Play Area

 Bar/Restaurant

 Bike Hire

 Fishing

 Sailing

Scan me for
more information.

Alan Rogers Code: CR6876
50 pitches
GPS: 43.02698, 17.03180
Post Code: HR-20269

Loviste, Dalmatia

www.alanrogers.com/cr6876
marija@camplupis.tcloud.hr
Tel: +385 958 302 990
www.peljesac-lupis.com

Open (Touring Pitches):
All year.

Camping Lupis

Camping Lupis can be found at the very tip of the unspoiled Peljesac peninsula, in the small fishing village of Lovište. This site has direct access to the sea and there are fine panoramic views over the bay of Loviste. This is a small site with 50 well-shaded terraced pitches, all with 16A electricity connections. The campsite is part of a holiday complex with a number of apartments and rooms to rent. Anchorage facilities are available for small boats. The village centre is just 100 m. away and has shops, bars and restaurants.

The principal activities here are still fishing and vineyard cultivation. Tourism is very much a secondary activity and there are happily no traces of mass tourism. A number of beaches can be reached on foot and are never crowded. Given its location at the tip of a long peninsula, there is also very little motor traffic here. The nearest town of any size is Orebic, and it is possible to take a ferry from here to the adjacent island of Korcula.

Key Features

 Open All Year

 Pets Accepted

 Disabled Facilities

 Beach Access

 Play Area

 Fishing

Sanitary block with hot showers and facilities for children and disabled visitors. Washing machine and dryer. Direct beach access. Play area. Room and apartment rental. Fishing. Boat launching. WiFi (free).

Scan me for more information.

Capital Prague
Currency Czech Koruna (CZK)
Language Czech
Time Zone CET (GMT+1)
Telephone Code +420

Shops Hours can vary but generally shops are open 9am to 6pm weekdays, 9am to 1pm Sat and closed Sun. Shopping centres and tourist areas operate longer hours.

Money ATMs are widespread, accessible 24hrs a day and have multilingual instructions. Credit/debit cards are accepted in most restaurants.

Accessible Travel Behind when it comes to accessibility. Older buildings, including museums, are not well equipped. Transport in cities is improving.

Travelling with Children The country is becoming more child-friendly however, baby facilities remain rare. More often than not, restaurants will cater for children. Historical sights and attractions are partly geared towards kids. Child rates apply up to the age of 18.

EU Travel Czech Republic is an EU member state and located within the Schengen Area.

There are no Low Emissions Zones currently in place.

●●○○○ **Accessibility Score**
View our digital e-guide & find out more at
alanrogers.com/open-to-all

Tourism website visitczechrepublic.com

Public Holidays 1 Jan New Year's Day • Mar/Apr Good Friday • Mar/Apr Easter Monday • 1 May May Day • 8 May Liberation Day • 5 Jul St Cyril & St Methodius Day • 6 Jul Jan Hus Day • 28 Sep Statehood Day • 28 Oct Independence Day • 17 Nov Freedom & Democracy Day • 24 Dec Christmas Eve • 25 Dec Christmas Day • 26 Dec Boxing Day

Driving in Czech Republic The road network is well-signposted throughout the country. To use motorways, you will need a vignette which can be purchased at border points, post offices and some petrol stations. Drink-driving and using your mobile whilst driving are illegal. Dipped headlights should be used at all times. Winter tyres are compulsory between November and April. Give way to trams and buses.

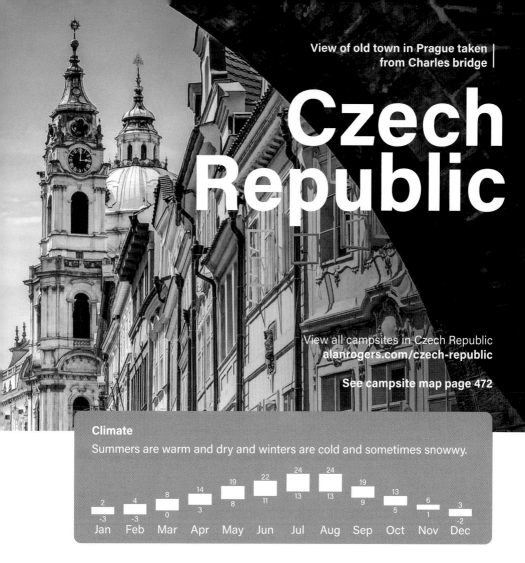

View of old town in Prague taken from Charles bridge

Czech Republic

View all campsites in Czech Republic
alanrogers.com/czech-republic

See campsite map page 472

Climate

Summers are warm and dry and winters are cold and sometimes snowwy.

Jan	Feb	Mar	Apr	May	Jun	Jul	Aug	Sep	Oct	Nov	Dec
2 / -3	4 / -3	8 / 0	14 / 3	19 / 8	22 / 11	24 / 13	24 / 13	19 / 9	13 / 5	6 / 1	3 / -2

Once known as Bohemia, the Czech Republic is a land of fascinating castles, romantic lakes and valleys, picturesque medieval squares, and famous spas. It is divided into two main regions, Bohemia to the west and Moravia in the east.

Although small, the Czech Republic has a wealth of attractive places to explore. The historic city of Prague is the hub of tourist activity and a treasure trove of museums, historic architecture, art galleries and theatres, and the annual 17-day beer festival!

The beautiful region of Bohemia, known for its Giant Mountains, is popular for hiking, skiing and other sports. West Bohemia is home to three renowned spas: Karlovy Vary, Mariánské Lázne and Františkovy Lázne, which have developed around the hundreds of mineral springs which rise in this area and offer a wide variety of restorative treatments.

Brno is the capital of Moravia in the east, lying midway between Prague, Vienna and Budapest. Visitors will admire its beautiful architecture, notably Mies van der Rohe's Villa Tugendhat. North of Brno is the Moravian Karst. The underground Punkya River has carved out a network of caves, some open to the public and connecting with boat trips along the river.

Alan Rogers Code: CZ4658
54 accommodations
80 pitches
GPS: 49.77719, 13.39012
Post Code: CZ-32300

Plzen/Maly Bolevec, West
Bohemia

www.alanrogers.com/cz4658
recepce@bolevak.eu
Tel: +420 739 604 603
wwww.bolevak.eu

Open (Touring Pitches):
Start May - End September.

Camp Ostende Bolevák

Autocamp Ostende lies on the edge of Plzeň, on the banks of Velký bolevecký rybník, surrounded by forests. The site offers around100 pitches for touring with 10A electricity hook-ups, as well as pitches for tents.

If you are looking for rental accommodation, they also have approximately 50 cabins and bungalows. On-site there is a sandy beach surrounding Lake Bolevec which offers gradual entry into the water. Here you can enjoy a pleasant swim or some gentle windsurfing or kayaking. The trees surrounding the beach offer plenty of shade - a welcome respite from the summer rays.

If you are looking to get out and about, there are some good cycle and walking routes you can take directly from the site, and if you wish to explore the local area of Plzeň, you'll find a zoo, botanical gardens, a synagogue, the cathedral of St. Bartholomew, an aircraft and military museum and an observatory and planetarium.

Washbasin and shower facilities (hot and cold). Toilets. Washing machine. Iron. Kitchen. Lounge/common room. Children's room. Restaurant. Shop (limited groceries). Lake swim. Windsurfing. Boat rental. Volleyball court, Multi-sports field. Children's playground. Games room. WiFi.

Key Features

 Pets Accepted

 Play Area

 Fishing

 Sailing

Scan me for
more information.

Alan Rogers Code: CZ4785
14 accommodations
70 pitches
GPS: 50.04408, 14.28422
Post Code: CZ-15500

Prague, Central Bohemia

www.alanrogers.com/cz4785
drusus@drusus.com
Tel: +420 608 527 229
www.drusus.com

Open (Touring Pitches):
Start April - Mid October.

Camp Drusus

Camp Drusus is a friendly, family site on the western edge of Prague. It provides a good base from which to explore this beautiful city, with the metro station only a 15 minute walk away. The site has about 70 level pitches (for touring units), with 16A electricity and varying in size (60-90 sq.m), with access off a circular, grass and gravel road.

There is no shop here but basics can be ordered at reception and one of the biggest shopping areas in Prague is only 2 km. away. You could enjoy a real Czech breakfast in the restaurant which also opens for dinner and serves as a bar. A small, fenced pond bordered with flowers is attractive. This is a pleasant, well kept and quiet site with good connections to the Czech capital.

Modern sanitary facilities. Laundry. Kitchen. Motorhome services. No shop, but basics to order at reception. Bar/restaurant. Small fitness centre. Playground. Games room with billiards. WiFi throughout (free).

Key Features

 Pets Accepted

 Disabled Facilities

 Play Area

 Bar/Restaurant

Scan me for more information.

Alan Rogers Code: CZ4855
40 pitches
GPS: 50.09194, 14.47305
Post Code: CZ-13000

Prague, Central Bohemia

Prague Central Camp

www.alanrogers.com/cz4855
praguecentralcamp@gmail.com
Tel: +420 776 308 770
www.praguecentralcamp.com

Open (Touring Pitches):
All year.

Previously known as Camping Zizkov, Central Camp is a small site close to the centre of Prague, within the grounds of a 'pension'. It has 40 touring pitches on level grass in a circular area and all have 6A electricity. Pitches are rather small, as is the entrance, but the site does take large units. There is a nice ambience here and it is close to the river where you can take a stroll. Adjacent is a large sports centre with an open-air pool, tennis courts and basketball. All necessary amenities are available on-site, including a bar in high season, but one should be aware that the pension in high season is mostly populated with youngsters.

Central Camp is a good base to visit the Czech capital for a few days and access to the centre of Prague by public transport is good (tram 200 m). In August the site could become crowded with Italian guests.

Toilet block in the pension with communal showers. Washing machine. Motorhome services. Basic kitchen. Open-air bar with terrace. Play area. Trampoline. Basketball. Beach volleyball. WiFi.

Key Features

 Open All Year

 Pets Accepted

 Play Area

 Bar/Restaurant

Scan me for more information.

Alan Rogers Code: CZ4690
30 accommodations
50 pitches
GPS: 50.72130, 14.40298
Post Code: CZ-47107

Severocesky, North Bohemia

www.alanrogers.com/cz4690
zandov@sicco.cz
Tel: +420 775 155 933
www.zandov.eu

Open (Touring Pitches):
Mid April - Mid October

Camping Slunce Žandov

Away from larger towns, near the border with former East Germany, this is pleasant countryside with a wealth of Gothic and Renaissance castles. Žandov has nothing of particular interest but Camping Slunce is a popular campsite with local Czech people.

There is room for about 50 touring units with 35 electrical connections (12A) on the level, circular camping area which has a hard road running round. Outside this circle are wooden bungalows and tall trees. The general building at the entrance houses all the facilities including reception. This is a fairly basic site but is good value for money.

The modern toilet block is good by Czech standards. Kitchen with electric rings, full gas cooker and fridges. Restaurant (all year) but under separate management has live music during high season. Kiosk for basics (May-Sept). Tennis. Swimming pool. Mountain bike hire. Playground. Large club room for games and TV. Barbecues are not permitted. Dogs are not accepted.

Key Features

 Pets Accepted

 Disabled Facilities

 Swimming Pool

 Play Area

 Bike Hire

Scan me for more information.

Alan Rogers Code: CZ4870
43 accommodations
100 pitches
GPS: 49.78328, 16.90952
Post Code: CZ-78985

Severomoravsky, North Moravia

www.alanrogers.com/cz4870
info@moravacamp.cz
Tel: +420 583 430 129
www.moravacamp.cz

Open (Touring Pitches):
Mid May - Mid October.

Autocamping Morava

This is an interesting area of contrasts – heavy industry, fertile plains and soaring mountains. Mohelnice is a small industrial town but the campsite is in a peaceful setting surrounded by trees on the northern edge. The amenities on offer, particularly for children, may tempt one to stay longer.

The site is roughly in two halves with the camping area on a flat, open meadow with a hard access road. The 100 touring pitches are not numbered or marked so pitching could be a little haphazard. There are 80 electricity connections (10A). There is little shade but the perimeter trees screen out most of the road noise.

The other part of the site is given over to a two-storey motel and bungalows with a good quality restaurant between the two sections. Good English is spoken at reception and it is a very pleasant, well-organised site.

Key Features

 Pets Accepted

 Swimming Pool

 Play Area

 Bar/Restaurant

The toilet block is satisfactory. Electric cooking rings. Restaurant (May-Oct). Kiosk/snack bar. Small shop (May-Oct). Live music (high season). Swimming pool (May-Oct). Tennis. Minigolf. Bicycle hire. Road track – driving and cycling learning area with tarmac roads, road signs, traffic lights and road markings well set up to give youngsters a practice area without the hazard of normal traffic. Playground. TV room.

Scan me for more information.

Alan Rogers Code: CZ4896
11 accommodations
50 pitches
GPS: 48.91920, 16.02560
Post Code: CZ-67152

Jihomoravsky, South Moravia

www.alanrogers.com/cz4896
camping-country@cbox.cz
Tel: +420 515 255 249
www.camp-country.cz

Open (Touring Pitches):
Start May - End October.

Camping Country

Camping Country is a well cared for and attractively landscaped site close to the historical town of Znojmo. It is a rural location, in a wine-growing region close to a national park, and with its small wine cellar, wine tasting evenings, small stables and riding school, barbecue and campfire areas, is an ideal site for a longer stay. Visitors will enjoy the cycling routes which have been set out in the national park. Camping Country has 50 pitches (all for touring units), 30 with 16A electricity, on two fields – one behind the main house taking six or eight units, the other one larger with a gravel access road.

The fields are connected by two wooden bridges (one is only fenced on one side). Varieties of low hedges and firs partly separate the pitches. To the front of the site is a paddock with two horses and facilities for minigolf, volleyball, basketball and tennis. In the garden of the main house is a small paddling pool. Colourful flowers and trees give the site a pleasant atmosphere.

Modern and comfortable toilet facilities provide British style toilets, open washbasins (cold water only) and free, controllable hot showers. Campers' kitchen. Bar/restaurant with one meal served daily. Play area. Tennis. Minigolf. Riding. Some live music nights in high season. Internet and WiFi (charged). Only gas and electric barbecues are allowed on pitches. Tours to Vienna, Brno and wine cellars organised. Torch useful.

Key Features

 Pets Accepted

 Disabled Facilities

 Swimming Pool

 Play Area

 Bar/Restaurant

 Bike Hire

 Horse Riding

Scan me for more information.

Alan Rogers Code: CZ4765
146 accommodations
150 pitches
GPS: 48.99268, 14.76748
Post Code: CZ-37901

Jihocesky, South Bohemia

www.alanrogers.com/cz4765
info@autocamp-trebon.cz
Tel: +420 384 722 586
www.autocamp-trebon.cz

Open (Touring Pitches):
Mid April - Late September.

Autocamp Trebon

Autocamp Trebon offers a happy Czech atmosphere especially around the bar/restaurant and is located on a lake where swimming, surfing and boating (the site rents out canoes) are possible.

It is close to the interesting fortifications of Trebon and not far from the historic cities of Cesky Krumlov and Ceské Budejovice, which are certainly worth a visit. Being next to a large forest, it also makes a great location for walking and cycling. The site has around 150 pitches for touring units with 7A electricity, plus a number of cabins for rent. Pitching is off tarmac access roads in two areas and there are some hardstandings for motorhomes.

An older toilet building has some old and some new facilities, including British style toilets, open washbasins and controllable hot communal showers (token from reception, cleaning variable). Washing machine. Kiosk for bread and drinks. Bar with terrace. Self-service restaurant with open-air and covered terrace. Play area. Basketball. Fishing. Canoe rental. Boat launching. Beach.

Key Features

 Pets Accepted

 Play Area

 Fishing

Scan me for
more information.

Alan Rogers Code: CZ4775
31 accommodations
50 pitches
GPS: 49.23030, 14.71900
Post Code: CZ-39201

Jihocesky, South Bohemia

www.alanrogers.com/cz4775
info@karvanky-kemp.cz
Tel: +420 603 242 157
www.karvanky-kemp.cz

Open (Touring Pitches):
Mid May - End September.

Autocamping Karvánky

This good site is owned by the local auto club and managed by enthusiastic volunteers. It surrounds a lake and is near a small river on the southern outskirts of Sobeslav. The 50 touring pitches are marked and there are 48 Europlug electricity connections spread around the lakeside.

The site gets very busy in July and August and it is clearly well used by local tourists. Being close to the busy E55 road, there is inevitably some background traffic noise.

Fishing in the lake is permitted but you will need a licence from reception. The site is next to a river so there may be a small risk of flooding.

Adequate toilet blocks provide toilets, showers (token required) and washbasins. Washing machine. Restaurant and bar with terrace. Internet point in reception (English spoken). Mountain bike and boat hire. Volleyball. Lake for fishing and boating. Small wooden cabins to rent (sleeping 4).

Key Features

 Pets Accepted

 Play Area

 Fishing

Scan me for
more information.

Capital Copenhagen
Currency Danish Krone (DKK)
Language Danish
Time Zone CET (GMT+1)
Telephone Code +45

Shops 10am to 6pm weekdays, until 4pm on Sat. Larger stores may be open Sun. Supermarkets open from 8am to 9pm. Bakeries (including in-store supermarket bakeries) may open earlier.

Money ATMs are widespread and are accessible 24hrs a day, some have multilingual instructions. Visa/Mastercard accepted widely. Amex less so.

Accessible Travel Access to buildings, transport and rural areas is improving but some areas are certainly not universally accessible yet.

Travelling with Children Very child-friendly with many attractions from theme parks and zoos to family-friendly beaches. Entry to most museums is free. Many campsites have special programs for children during peak season.

EU Travel Denmark is an EU member state and located within the Schengen Area.

There are no Low Emissions Zones currently in place.

●●●●○ **Accessibility Score**
View our digital e-guide & find out more at
alanrogers.com/open-to-all

Tourism website visitdenmark.com

Public Holidays 1 Jan New Year's Day · Mar/Apr Maundy Thursday · Mar/Apr Good Friday · Mar/Apr Easter Sunday · Mar/Apr Easter Monday · Apr/May Prayer Day · May Ascension · May/Jun Whit Sunday · May/Jun Whit Monday · 25 Dec Christmas Day · 26 Dec Boxing Day

Driving in Denmark Driving is much easier than at home as roads are much quieter. There are no tolls in Denmark except the Oresund Bridge that links the country with Sweden. Dipped headlights are compulsory at all times. There are no emergency phones on motorways, so make sure you have a mobile phone. Drink-driving and using your mobile whilst driving are illegal.

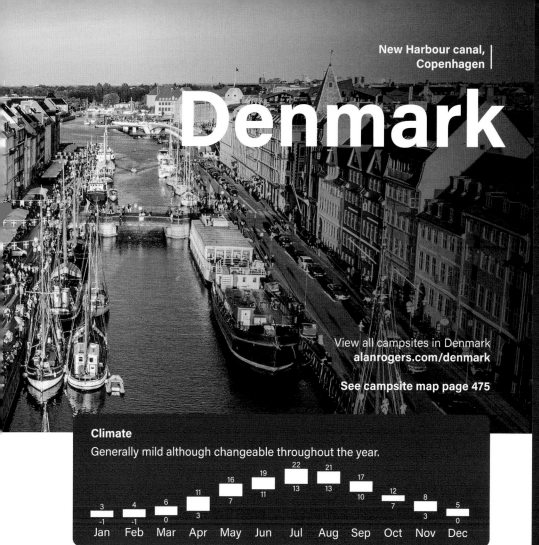

Denmark

View all campsites in Denmark
alanrogers.com/denmark

See campsite map page 475

Climate

Generally mild although changeable throughout the year.

	Jan	Feb	Mar	Apr	May	Jun	Jul	Aug	Sep	Oct	Nov	Dec
High	3	4	6	11	16	19	22	21	17	12	8	5
Low	-1	-1	0	3	7	11	13	13	10	7	3	0

Denmark offers a diverse landscape, all within a relatively short distance. The countryside is green and varied with flat plains, rolling hills, fertile farmland, many lakes and fjords, wild moors and long beaches, interspersed with pretty villages and towns.

It is the easiest of the Scandinavian countries to visit, and distances are short, so it is easy to combine the faster pace of the city with the tranquillity of the countryside and the beaches. It comprises the peninsula of Jutland and the larger islands of Zeeland and Funen, and hundreds of smaller islands, many uninhabited.

Zeeland is home to the climate-friendly capital city, Copenhagen, with its relaxing waterside cafés, vibrant nightlife, Michelin star restaurants and the stunning Frederiksborg castle. Funen is Denmark's second-largest island, linked to Zeeland by the Great Belt Bridge.

Known as the Garden of Denmark, its gentle landscape is dotted with orchards and pretty thatched, half-timbered houses. It also has plenty of safe, sandy beaches. Jutland's flat terrain makes it ideal for cycling, and its long beaches are popular with windsurfers.

63

Denmark

Alan Rogers Code: DK2378
150 accommodations
550 pitches
GPS: 57.64420, 10.46157
Post Code: DK-9982

Nordjylland, Jutland

www.alanrogers.com/dk2378
info@skagensydstrand.dk
Tel: +45 98 48 71 80
skagensydstrandcamping.dk

Open (Touring Pitches):
Late March - Late September.

Bunken Strand Camping

Ideal for families, Bunken Strand is located in natural surroundings between forest and sand dunes, by the safe, gently shelving sea. Most of the 700 pitches are arranged in tree-lined avenues and bordered on three sides by mature hedges and trees, providing peace and privacy for each unit.

Closer to the dunes and the beach, an open area is just the place for those who wish to enjoy more of the sunshine on this coast, which experiences the very best of Denmark's climate. Conveniently located close to the ports of Fredrickshavn and Hirtshals, it would make a good stopover or short stay, but has everything necessary for a longer summer stay by the sea.

Four sanitary units with family and baby rooms, kitchens and dishwashing. Modern central unit with large laundry. En-suite unit for disabled campers (key access). Motorhome services. Well stocked shop (all season). Snack bar and takeaway. Good play areas for all ages with inflatable trampolines. Games room. Minigolf. Pedal cars. Football/games field. Organised activities in the high season. Bicycle hire. Free WiFi throughout. Fishing. Good tourist information at reception. Accommodation to rent.

Key Features

 Pets Accepted

 Disabled Facilities

 Beach Access

 Play Area

 Bike Hire

 Fishing

 Sailing

Scan me for more information.

Denmark

Alan Rogers Code: DK2080
120 accommodations
220 pitches
GPS: 56.07607, 9.76549
Post Code: DK-8680

Århus, Jutland

www.alanrogers.com/dk2080
info@holmenscamping.dk
Tel: +45 86 89 17 62
holmenscamping.dk

Open (Touring Pitches):
Early April - Late September.

Holmens Camping

A warm welcome awaits you at Holmens Camping, which lies between Silkeborg and Skanderborg in a very beautiful part of Denmark. There is direct access to the Gudensø and Rye Møllesø lakes, with a slipway for guests with boats. There are canoes for hire and fishing is a speciality here (it has its own small catch and release lake). Walking and cycling are also popular activities.

Holmens has around 200 grass touring pitches, partly terraced and divided by trees and shrubs and the site is surrounded by mature trees. Almost all the pitches have 6A electricity and vary in size between 70-100 sq.m. The lake is suitable for swimming but the site also has an attractive pool complex (charged).

Sanitary blocks have washbasins in cabins and controllable hot showers (on payment). En-suite facilities with toilet, basin, shower. Baby room. Facilities for disabled visitors. Laundry. Campers' kitchen. Small shop. Snack bar and takeaway. Covered pool with jet stream and paddling pool. Pool bar. Games room. Playground. Pétanque. Pony rides. Minigolf. Fishing. Bicycle hire. Boat rental. Some activities incur a charge. WiFi (charged).

Key Features

 Pets Accepted

 Disabled Facilities

 Beach Access

 Swimming Pool

 Play Area

 Bar/Restaurant

 Bike Hire

 Fishing

Scan me for more information.

Alan Rogers Code: DK2046
100 accommodations
375 pitches
GPS: 55.62489, 9.83333
Post Code: DK-7000

Vejle, Jutland

www.alanrogers.com/dk2046
trelde@dancamps.dk
Tel: +45 75 95 71 83
www.dancamps.dk/trelde-naes

Open (Touring Pitches):
Start April - End December.

Camping Trelde Næs

Trelde Næs is a busy and lively site next to a beach accessed via 70 steep, wooden steps. It is one of Denmark's larger sites with over 500 level and numbered pitches. The 375 touring pitches all have 10A electricity and there are 37 fully serviced pitches with electricity, water, drainage and Internet access. Seasonal units take up the remaining pitches. Pitches are mainly in rows off tarmac access roads on well kept, grassy fields with some shade from bushes at the rear.

At the front of the site is a heated, open-air, fun pool with a large slide, jacuzzi and play island (seasonal) The site is right next to the beach, but also close to the nature reserve of Trelde Næs which has been part of the Royal estates since the 14th century.

Traditional toilet blocks have washbasins in cabins and controllable hot showers (card operated). Child size toilets and washbasins. Family shower room. Baby room. Laundry. Fun pool (seasonal) with island, large slide, Turkish bath, solarium and sauna. Well stocked shop. Takeaway. Several playgrounds. Minigolf. Fishing. Bicycle hire. Watersports. Full entertainment programme for children (high season). TV room. WiFi (charged). Cabins and rooms to rent.

Key Features

 Pets Accepted

 Disabled Facilities

 Beach Access

 Swimming Pool

 Play Area

 Bar/Restaurant

 Bike Hire

 Fishing

Scan me for more information.

Alan Rogers Code: DK2034
132 accommodations
145 pitches
GPS: 55.42047, 9.58440
Post Code: DK-6091

Sønderjylland, Jutland

www.alanrogers.com/dk2034
info@stensagercamping.dk
Tel: +45 75 57 22 31
stensagercamping.dk

Open (Touring Pitches):
Start April - Mid September.

Stensager Camping

For children, the main attraction of this site is sure to be the giant, 48 m. water slide. It ends in a separate pool, from which one can slip into the main fun pool and next to that is a paddling pool with a slide for toddlers.

Stensager Camping has large pitches on well kept, grassy fields. Although Stensager is only a couple of hundred metres from the sea, none of the pitches has a sea view. The rows of pitches are separated by high bushes and many different sorts of trees decorate the site. It is on sloping ground, but the pitches are level and all have 6/10A electricity.

According to the owners, most campers come here to relax on the site or the beach and to visit the historic town of Kolding with its castle, which once belonged to the Danish royal family. This is also a good site for those who like fishing, walking and cycling.

Two modern blocks provide washbasins in cabins and controllable hot showers. Children's section. Family shower rooms. Baby room. En-suite facilities for disabled people. Laundry. Motorhome services. Shop. Swimming pool (seasonal) with a giant slide, paddling pool and sauna. Playground. Minigolf. Watersports and boat launching. Daily entertainment programme for children in high season. TV room. WiFi (charged). English is spoken.

Key Features

 Pets Accepted

 Disabled Facilities

 Swimming Pool

 Play Area

Scan me for more information.

Alan Rogers Code: DK2036
89 accommodations
200 pitches
GPS: 54.88545, 9.72876
Post Code: DK-6310

Sønderjylland, Jutland

www.alanrogers.com/dk2036
info@gammelmark.dk
Tel: +45 74 44 17 42
www.gammelmark.dk

Open (Touring Pitches):
Start April - Early October.

Gammelmark Strand Camp

Gammelmark is a modern campsite with 289 terraced, level, grass pitches (200 for tourers), all with 10-13A electricity. Situated directly at the bay of Vemmingbund, in a hilly landscape, many of the pitches have great views of the Baltic sea. Fifty deluxe pitches are extra large and fully serviced.

This site combines Danish hospitality with historical interest and various family activities are available, many involving nature and the history of the area when war was waged over the Bay of Sønderborg. There are several playgrounds, a child-friendly swimming pool and pets to make friends with. It is useful as a stopover on your way north but is also a good choice for active campers.

Two modern, heated sanitary blocks include toilets, washbasins in cabins, controllable showers and excellent rooms for children and disabled visitors. Baby room. Private facilities to rent. Laundry. Campers' kitchen. Motorhome services. Shop (bread to order). Snacks (high season). Heated swimming pool. Play area. Children's farm. Fishing. Riding. Sailing and boat launching. Diving. Beach. Daily activity programme (high season). TV room. WiFi (free). Torches advised. English spoken.

Key Features

 Pets Accepted

 Disabled Facilities

 Beach Access

 Swimming Pool

 Play Area

 Fishing

 Horse Riding

Scan me for more information.

Alan Rogers Code: DK2220
7 accommodations
160 pitches
GPS: 55.13254, 10.03622
Post Code: DK-5631

Fyn, Islands

www.alanrogers.com/dk2220
info@helnaes-camping.dk
Tel: +45 64 77 13 39
helnaes-camping.dk

Open (Touring Pitches):
Mid March - Start September.

Helnæs Camping

Helnæs Camping is on the remote Helnæs peninsula to the southeast of Fyn, connected to the mainland by a small road. The site is adjacent to a nature reserve, making it ideal for walkers, cyclists and birdwatchers and for those who enjoy sea fishing (this is a great location for sea trout).

The road to the site takes you through a breathtaking environment with colourful flowerbeds on the Bobakkerne Wall to the north and large outer marches in the south. Helnæs Camping has 160 pitches, some terraced, on grassy fields sloping down towards the sea.

Almost all the pitches have beautiful views of Helnæs Bugt and the site is only 300 m. from the beach. Low rock walls and different types of young trees and low shrubs separate pitches. All have 6A electricity.

Two toilet blocks include washbasins in cabins and controllable showers. Baby room (heated). Family shower rooms. Facilities for disabled visitors. Laundry with washing machines and dryers. Campers' kitchen. Shop. Takeaway. Playground. Minigolf. Bicycle and canoe hire. Watersports. In high season small circus for children. TV lounge. Internet access. Covered barbecue area.

Key Features

 Pets Accepted

 Disabled Facilities

 Beach Access

 Play Area

 Bike Hire

 Fishing

 Sailing

Scan me for more information.

Alan Rogers Code: DK2215
13 accommodations
225 pitches
GPS: 55.36970, 10.39290
Post Code: DK-5260

Fyn, Islands

www.alanrogers.com/dk2215
odense@dcu.dk
Tel: +45 66 11 47 02
www.dcu.dk/odense

Open (Touring Pitches):
All year.

DCU Odense City Camp

Although within the confines of the city, this site is hidden away amongst mature trees and is therefore fairly quiet and an ideal base from which to explore the fairytale city of Odense.

The 225 pitches, of which 200 have electricity (10A), are on level grass with small hedges and shrubs dividing the area into bays. There are a number of seasonal units on site, together with 13 cabins. A good network of cycle paths leads into the city.

The Odense Adventure Pass (available at the site) allows unrestricted free travel on public transport within the city limits. It also offers free admission to the swimming pool and a free daily newspaper, with varying discounts on other attractions. Overnight pitches and minigolf are available.

Large sanitary unit provides modern facilities including washbasins in cubicles, family bathrooms, baby room and excellent suite for disabled visitors. Well equipped kitchen with gas hobs. Laundry with washing machines and dryer. Motorhome services. Shop. Small swimming and paddling pools. Games marquee. TV room. Large playground. Minigolf. WiFi over site (charged).

Key Features

 Open All Year

 Pets Accepted

 Disabled Facilities

 Swimming Pool

 Play Area

Scan me for more information.

Alan Rogers Code: DK2257
120 accommodations
180 pitches
GPS: 55.74170, 11.30900
Post Code: DK-4591

Sjælland, Islands

www.alanrogers.com/dk2257
info@vesterlyng-camping.dk
Tel: +45 59 20 00 66
www.vesterlyng-camping.dk

Open (Touring Pitches):
Start April - Mid October.

Vesterlyng Camping

Vesterlyng is a pleasant, quiet site close to Føllenslev and Havnsø on Sjælland. The ground slopes towards the sea and there are views from some pitches. It is an open site but some mature trees provide shade.

Vesterlyng has 180 mostly level touring pitches, 150 with 6/13A electricity. A further 100 or so pitches are used by mostly elderly, seasonal units. The pitches are on long, grassy meadows each taking 16-20 units, off tarmac access roads. Facilities on this site are basic but clean. The local beaches are ideal for swimming and a relaxing beach holiday.

Two traditional style toilet blocks (maintenance can be variable) include washbasins (open style and in cabins) and controllable hot showers. Family shower rooms. Basic facilities for disabled visitors. Washing machine and dryer. Small shop. Bar/restaurant. Swimming pool complex (charged). Minigolf. Riding. Bicycle hire. Games room with air hockey. Watersports. WiFi over site (charged). Boules. Animal enclosure. Live music nights.

Key Features

 Pets Accepted

 Disabled Facilities

 Beach Access

 Swimming Pool

 Play Area

 Bar/Restaurant

 Bike Hire

 Horse Riding

Scan me for more information.

Capital Paris
Currency Euro (€)
Language French
Time Zone CET (GMT+1)
Telephone Code +33

Shops Hours vary throughout the year, often opening for shorter hours during low and shoulder seasons. In high season shops are open 10am to noon and 2pm-7pm weekdays and Sat. Longer hours, including Sun for shops in tourist zones.

Money ATMs are widespread, accessible 24hrs a day and have multilingual instructions. Credit/debit cards are widely accepted, but don't assume every shop or cafe accepts them. Take cash for emergencies.

Accessible Travel Efforts to improve accessibility are being made but the Paris metro is unusable for wheelchair users.

Travelling with Children One of the most child-friendly countries in Europe, France has a good mix of cultural sights, historical monuments and other attractions. Each region has something different to offer. Most museums are free for under 18s.

EU Travel France is an EU member state and located within the Schengen Area.

LEZ Low Emissions Zones in most major cities. Registration required.

●●●○○ **Accessibility Score**
View our digital e-guide & find out more at

alanrogers.com/open-to-all

Tourism website france.fr/en

Public Holidays 1 Jan New Year's Day • Mar/Apr Easter Monday • 1 May Labour Day • 8 May Victory Day • May Ascension • May/Jun Whit Sunday • May/Jun Whit Monday • 14 Jul Bastille Day • 15 Aug Assumption • 1 Nov All Saints • 11 Nov Armistice Day • 25 Dec Christmas Day. Good Friday and Boxing Day are only observed in Alsace and Moselle.

Driving in France There is a comprehensive road system of Autoroutes, N roads, D roads and local C roads. Vehicles made before 2011 are banned in Paris as part of the LEZ. If you plan to drive in or through major cities, you will need a Crit'Air sticker. Drink-driving, using your mobile or earphones whilst driving or sat navs that warn of speed cameras are illegal.

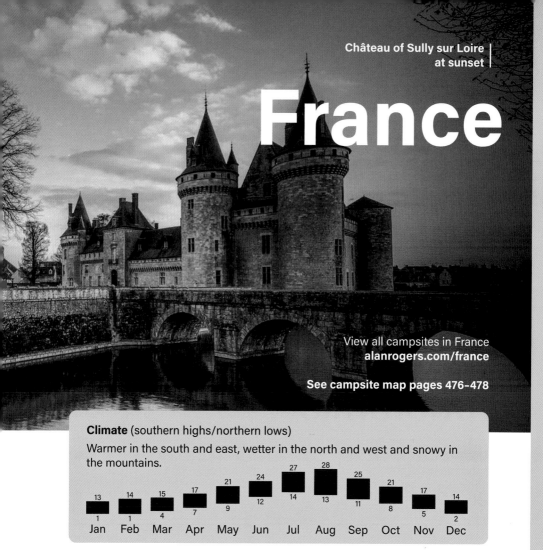

France

View all campsites in France
alanrogers.com/france

See campsite map pages 476–478

Climate (southern highs/northern lows)

Warmer in the south and east, wetter in the north and west and snowy in the mountains.

Jan	Feb	Mar	Apr	May	Jun	Jul	Aug	Sep	Oct	Nov	Dec
13	14	15	17	21	24	27	28	25	21	17	14
1	1	4	7	9	12	14	13	11	8	5	2

From the hot sunny climate of the Mediterranean to the more northerly and cooler regions of Normandy and Brittany, with the Châteaux of the Loire and the lush valleys of the Dordogne, and the mountain ranges of the Alps, France offers holidaymakers a huge choice of destinations to suit all tastes.

France boasts every type of landscape, from the wooded valleys of the Dordogne to the volcanic uplands of the Massif Central, the rocky coast of Brittany to the lavender-covered hills of Provence and snow-capped peaks of the Alps. The diversity of these regions is reflected in the local customs, cuisine, architecture and dialect.

France has a rich cultural heritage with a wealth of festivals, churches, châteaux, museums and historical monuments to visit. Many rural villages hold festivals to celebrate the local saints. You can also find museums devoted to the rural arts and crafts of the regions. The varied landscape and climate ensure many opportunities for outdoor pursuits from hiking and cycling, wind- and sand-surfing on the coast and rock climbing and skiing in the mountains. And no trip to France is complete without sampling the local food and wine.

Alan Rogers Code: FR29080
43 accommodations
127 pitches
GPS: 48.22409, -4.37186
Post Code: F-29560

Finistère, Brittany

Camping le Panoramic

www.alanrogers.com/fr29080
info@camping-panoramic.com
Tel: +33 2 98 27 78 41
www.camping-panoramic.com

Open (Touring Pitches):
Start May - Mid September.

Sites et Paysages le Panoramic is a medium-sized, traditional site, situated on quite a steep, ten-acre hillside with fine views. The 170 pitches are arranged on flat, shaded terraces, in small groups with hedges and flowering shrubs, and 20 pitches have services for motorhomes. Divided into two parts, the main upper site is where most of the facilities are located, with the swimming pool, its terrace and a playground located with the lower pitches across the road.

Some up-and-down walking is therefore necessary, but this is a small price to pay for such pleasant and comfortable surroundings. This area provides lovely coastal footpaths. The sandy beach and a sailing school at Trez-Bellec-Plage are a 700 m. walk.

The main site has two well-kept toilet blocks with another very good block opened for the main season across the road. All three include showers, washbasins in cubicles, facilities for disabled visitors, baby baths, plus laundry facilities. Motorhome services. Small shop (July/Aug). Refurbished bar/restaurant with takeaway. Barbecue area. Heated pool, paddling pool and jacuzzi (from Mid May). Playground. Games and TV rooms. Tennis. Bicycle hire. Free WiFi.

Key Features

 Book Online

 Pets Accepted

 Disabled Facilities

 Beach Access

 Swimming Pool

 Play Area

 Bar/Restaurant

 Bike Hire

Scan me for more information.

Alan Rogers Code: FR29000
406 accommodations
68 pitches
GPS: 48.65807, -3.92833
Post Code: F-29660

Finistère, Brittany

www.alanrogers.com/fr29000
contact@les-mouettes.com
Tel: +33 2 98 67 02 46
www.yellohvillage.co.uk/camping/
les_mouettes

Open (Touring Pitches):
Early April - Early September.

Camping Les Mouettes

Yelloh! Village Camping Les Mouettes is a sheltered site on the edge of an attractive bay, with access to the sea at the front of the site. In a wooded setting with many attractive trees and shrubs, the 474 pitches include 68 for touring units, all with electricity, water and drainage. The remainder are taken by tour operators and by 406 mobile homes and chalets to rent.

At the centre of the 'village' are shops, a bar, a restaurant, an entertainment stage, sports facilities and an impressive heated pool complex with swimming, paddling and water slide pools, plus a 'Tropical river', jacuzzi and sauna. There is also an excellent indoor swimming pool.

A clean sanitary block with controllable showers and washbasins in cabins. There are showers with washbasins and delightful rooms for children and babies. Facilities for disabled visitors. Laundry. Shop (limited hours outside the main season). Takeaway. Bar with TV. Restaurant/pizzeria/grill. Heated pool complex indoor (all season) and outdoor. Beauty salon. Games rooms (special one for under 5s). Play area. Multisports ground. Minigolf. Bicycle hire. Entertainment all season. Large units should phone first. Free WiFi throughout .

Key Features

 Book Online

 Pets Accepted

 Disabled Facilities

 Beach Access

 Swimming Pool

 Play Area

 Bar/Restaurant

 Bike Hire

Scan me for
more information.

Alan Rogers Code: FR29350
219 accommodations
120 pitches
GPS: 47.85656, -4.02066
Post Code: F-29170

Finistère, Brittany

Camping Fouesnant

www.alanrogers.com/fr29350
information@latlantique.fr
Tel: +33 2 98 56 14 44
www.camping-bretagne-atlantique.com

Open (Touring Pitches):
Late April - Early September.

Yelloh! Village Camping Fouesnant (previously known as L'Atlantique) is quietly situated just outside Beg-Meil. Approximately 440 pitches are predominantly used by tour operators with about 120 for touring visitors. Pitches are level and grassy, all with electricity, separated by low shrubs. Apple orchards used for cider production are also on the site.

All the facilities are grouped together in the centre including an innovative play area and pool complex with both indoor and outdoor pools, water slides and a paddling pool. The sandy beach faces the Glénan Islands and is a pleasant 400 m. walk away through a nature reserve. Coastal paths await exploration and Concarneau, Pont-Aven and La Pointe du Raz are all nearby.

Fully equipped toilet blocks (cleaned three times a day) include facilities for disabled visitors. Restaurant (July/Aug). Shop, bar, snack bar with takeaway meals and pizza (all season). Heated outdoor and indoor pools, water complex with slides (all season). Tennis. TV room. Billiards. Minigolf. Sports ground. Play area. Children's club (4-12 yrs) and evening entertainment in July/Aug. Play room for children 0-4 yrs. Bicycle hire. WiFi throughout (charged). Dogs are not accepted.

Key Features

 Book Online

 Disabled Facilities

 Beach Access

 Swimming Pool

 Play Area

 Bar/Restaurant

 Bike Hire

Scan me for more information.

Alan Rogers Code: FR22160
21 accommodations
65 pitches
GPS: 48.71372, -2.96704
Post Code: F-22580

Côtes d`Armor, Brittany

www.alanrogers.com/fr22160
contact@leneptune.com
Tel: +33 2 96 22 33 35
www.leneptune.com

Open (Touring Pitches):
Start April - Mid October.

Camping le Neptune

Situated on the Côte de Goëlo at Lanloup, le Neptune offers a peaceful, rural retreat for families. The friendly owners, François and Marie Jo Camard, keep the site neat and tidy and there is a regular programme of renovation.

There are 84 level, grass pitches (65 for touring units) separated by trimmed hedges providing privacy and all with electricity (10A). There are around 20 mobile homes to rent. Within walking distance is the local village, with a restaurant and a shop, and sandy beaches are only a short drive away.

This is a very attractive stretch of coastline and the GR34 coastal path is great for enthusiastic walkers who can happily keep going, knowing they can then hop on the Tibus, a little blue and green bus that provides a regular service along the coast road.

The modern, heated, toilet block is of a good standard, clean and well maintained and provides washbasins in cubicles and pushbutton showers. Facilities for disabled visitors. Laundry room. Motorhome services. No restaurant but good takeaway (all season). Small, well-stocked shop for basic needs. Bar with indoor and outdoor seating. Heated swimming pool with a retractable roof. Pétanque. Play area. Entertainment and children's activities in high season. WiFi over site (charged).

Key Features

 Book Online

 Pets Accepted

 Disabled Facilities

 Beach Access

 Swimming Pool

 Play Area

 Bar/Restaurant

 Bike Hire

Scan me for more information.

Alan Rogers Code: FR22460
35 accommodations
45 pitches
GPS: 48.19769, -2.41608
Post Code: F-22230

Côtes d`Armor, Brittany

www.alanrogers.com/fr22460
contact@valdelandrouet.com
Tel: +33 2 96 28 47 98
www.valdelandrouet.com

Open (Touring Pitches):
Start June - Late September.

Camping Val de Landrouët

Le Val de Landrouët is part of a large outdoor leisure complex, owned by the town of Merdrignac in central Brittany. The 45 touring pitches, set in beautifully landscaped parkland, are large, grassy and level and all have 5A electricity. There are also five mobile homes and 30 chalets available to rent. During high season, the site provides more than 20 outdoor sporting activities plus fishing, swimming and tennis, some of which require additional fees. Its position makes it a very good stop-over on the way to the west coast of Brittany.

Regular Breton folk evenings (with dancing), Breton cuisine evenings, barbecues and other entertainment is organised in the high season. Off-site, there is a great deal to see, including the pretty Breton towns of Moncontour and Jugon-les-Lacs. A visit to Rennes is a possibility.

Toilet block includes modern facilities with preset showers, washbasins in cabins, baby changing and provision for disabled visitors. Swimming pool complex. Fishing. Tennis. Play area. Bicycle hire. Entertainment and activity programme and bar, all in the main building.

Key Features

 Book Online

 Pets Accepted

 Disabled Facilities

 Beach Access

 Swimming Pool

 Play Area

 Bar/Restaurant

 Bike Hire

Scan me for more information.

Alan Rogers Code: FR56040
61 accommodations
117 pitches
GPS: 47.62206, -2.80070
Post Code: F-56610

Morbihan, Brittany

www.alanrogers.com/fr56040
camping.penboch@wanadoo.fr
Tel: +33 2 97 44 71 29
www.camping-penboch.fr

Open (Touring Pitches):
Early April - Late September.

Camping de Penboch

Sites et Paysages de Penboch is 200 metres by footpath from the shores of the Golfe du Morbihan with its many islands, with plenty to do, including watersports, fishing and boat trips.

The site, in a peaceful, rural area, is divided into two – the main part, on open ground with hedges and young trees, the other across a minor road in woodland with lots of shade.

Penboch offers 192 pitches on flat grass, 117 are for touring and they are mostly divided into groups. Electricity (10A) is available on all pitches and most also have water and drainage.

Three sanitary blocks, two on the main part (one heated) and one in the annex include washbasins in cabins. Washing facilities include private family cabins (extra charge). Laundry facilities. Motorhome services. Shop, bar and takeaway (all seasonal). Heated outdoor pool with slide and paddling pool (seasonal). Indoor pool (all season) with relaxation area, jacuzzi and massage tables. Good playground. Games room. Bicycle hire arranged. Caravan storage. American-style motorhomes are accepted in the low season. WiFi (charged).

Key Features

 Book Online

 Pets Accepted

 Disabled Facilities

 Beach Access

 Swimming Pool

 Play Area

 Bar/Restaurant

Scan me for more information.

Alan Rogers Code: FR56120
107 accommodations
186 pitches
GPS: 47.44543, -2.48396
Post Code: F-56760

Morbihan, Brittany

www.alanrogers.com/fr56120
info@chadotel.com
Tel: +33 2 99 90 30 24
chadotel.com/en/campsite-les-iles-penestin

Open (Touring Pitches):
Early April - Early November.

Camping les Iles

You will receive a warm welcome at this Chadotel campsite. The friendly receptionist encourages everyone to make the most of this beautiful region. Of the 186 pitches, 79 are for touring. Most are flat, hedged and of a reasonable size, all have 10A electricity (Europlug). Larger caravans and American-style motorhomes are advised to book. 13 pitches have sea views and overlook the beach, supplement is charged for the sea view.

There is an indoor baby playroom and a small spa on site. There is direct access to cliff-top walks and local beaches, you can even walk to small off-shore islands at low tide. The attractive heated swimming pool complex provides a focal point for all ages.

The large central toilet block is spotlessly clean with washbasins in cabins and showers. Laundry facilities. Facilities for disabled visitors. Baby room. Shop. Bar. Restaurant. Takeaway. Heated outdoor pool complex (all open all season). Bicycle hire. Riding. Activities and entertainment in July/Aug. Motorhome services across the road in Parc des Iles (mobile home section of site): Motorhome services. TV room. Multisports pitch. Tennis court. No electric barbecues. WiFi over site (charged).

Key Features

 Book Online

 Pets Accepted

 Disabled Facilities

 Beach Access

 Swimming Pool

 Play Area

 Bar/Restaurant

 Bike Hire

Scan me for
more information.

Alan Rogers Code: FR50030
60 accommodations
134 pitches
GPS: 48.79778, -1.52498
Post Code: F-50380

Manche, Normandy

www.alanrogers.com/fr50030
bonjour@lez-eaux.com
Tel: +33 2 33 51 66 09
www.lez-eaux.com

Open (Touring Pitches):
Start April - Mid September.

Château de Lez Eaux

Set in the grounds of a château, Castel Camping le Château de Lez Eaux lies in a rural situation just off the main route south, under two hours from Cherbourg. Of the 134 touring pitches all with electricity (10A, Europlug) and 90 with water and drainage. Most of the pitches are of a very good size, partly separated by trees and shrubs on flat or slightly sloping, grassy ground overlooking Normandy farmland and a small fishing lake.

The campsite offers several kinds of camping accommodation and pitch depending on your desires and needs - from treehouse to mobile-home with Jacuzzi, and chalet to camping pitches for tents, caravans and mobile homes. Activities include an indoor tropical-themed water park complete with water slides and childrens' aqua splash fun area. paddling pool, swimming pools; games area, bouncy castles, fishing lake, tennis court and bike rental.

Three sanitary blocks (1 heated) are equipped with showers, private washing cubicles and facilities for babies. Washing machines and dryers. Shop. Bar. Takeaway. Fresh bakery in the morning. Covered water park (pool, slides, paddling pool) 1 outdoor pool. Games areas and bouncy castles. Fishing lake. Football. Volleyball grounds. TV room and games room. Bicycle hire. Tennis court hire. Kids club during the summer. Summer activities: 2 concerts per week, local market, daily aqua aerobics in the indoor pool.

Key Features

 Book Online

 Pets Accepted

 Disabled Facilities

 Beach Access

 Swimming Pool

 Play Area

 Bar/Restaurant

 Bike Hire

Scan me for more information.

Alan Rogers Code: FR50250
41 accommodations
106 pitches
GPS: 49.36224, -1.74649
Post Code: F-50270

Manche, Normandy

www.alanrogers.com/fr50250
contact@camping-du-golf.fr
Tel: +33 2 33 04 78 90
www.camping-du-golf.fr

Open (Touring Pitches):
Start April - Start November.

Camping du Golf

Camping du Golf is a friendly, family campsite on the western side of the Cotentin peninsula on the Côte des Isles (the Channel Islands). Day excursions are possible to Jersey. The site is only ten minutes from the nearest sandy beach, and an hour and forty-five minutes north of Mont Saint Michel. On-site amenities include a covered, heated swimming pool, a bar and a shop, and in high season a programme of activities and entertainment is organised.

There are 106 pitches for touring units, all with 6A electricity, water and drainage and 110-180 sq.m. in size. There are plenty of holiday activities available at Camping du Golf for all the family. Children are provided with open grass and sandy areas for play and an indoor games area with table tennis tables and electronic games.

Modern toilet block and further small block by the pool. Family shower rooms. Facilities for disabled visitors. Laundry facilities. Shop. Bar. Snack bar/takeaway. Swimming pool with waterslides (from April). Play area. Basketball, football and volleyball pitch. TV room. Entertainment and activities in July/Aug. Bicycle hire. Bouncy castle. WiFi over site (charged). Mobile homes for hire.

Key Features

 Book Online

 Pets Accepted

 Disabled Facilities

 Beach Access

 Swimming Pool

 Play Area

 Bar/Restaurant

 Bike Hire

Scan me for more information.

Alan Rogers Code: FR50210
21 accommodations
89 pitches
GPS: 49.57960, -1.30760
Post Code: F-50630

Manche, Normandy

www.alanrogers.com/fr50210
camping.lerivage@wanadoo.fr
Tel: +33 2 33 54 13 76
www.camping-lerivage.com

Open (Touring Pitches):
Start April - End September.

Camping le Rivage

Camping Le Rivage is located on the Cotentin coast, around 4 km. from the harbour at Saint Vaast la Hougue. The site is just 400 m. from a sandy beach. There are 110 pitches, many of which are occupied by mobile homes and chalets (some available to rent). The touring pitches are grassy and generally sunny, most with 6A electricity connections.

On-site amenities include a swimming pool, children's pool, bar and snack bar. In high season, various activities are organised including discos and karaoke evenings. Places of interest nearby include the island of Tatihou, Sainte Mere Eglise and the D-day beaches, and Cherbourg.

The Cité de la Mer in Cherbourg is well worth a visit. Located in the massive art deco transatlantic departure buildings, this is now a major centre devoted to the theme of man's exploration of the seas, with many interactive exhibits.

Sanitary block with hot showers. Washing machine. Shop. Fresh bread. Bar, snack bar and takeaway. Swimming and paddling pools. Games room. Play area. Activity and entertainment programme. Mobile homes to rent.

Key Features

 Book Online

 Pets Accepted

 Disabled Facilities

 Beach Access

 Bar/Restaurant

Scan me for more information.

Alan Rogers Code: FR14150
103 accommodations
197 pitches
GPS: 49.34630, -0.77320
Post Code: F-14520

Calvados, Normandy

www.alanrogers.com/fr14150
info@camping-portland.fr
Tel: +33 2 31 51 07 06
www.camping-portland.com

Open (Touring Pitches):
Early April - Start November.

Camping Port'land

Camping Port'land, now a mature site, lies on the western edge of the delightful little resort of Port-en-Bessin, one of Normandy's busiest fishing ports. The 197 pitches are large and grassy with 151 for touring units, all with electricity (mainly 16A), water and wastewater, and 46 with hardstandings. There are 103 mobile homes for rent.

The camping area has been imaginatively landscaped, many pitches overlooking small fishing ponds. An attractive modern building houses the refurbished reception and a smart bar/restaurant with an interesting menu. A coastal path leads to the little town, which has a number of shops and waterfront bars and restaurants.

Main sanitary block is well maintain with controllable showers, washbasins in cubicles and an attractive baby room. En-suite unit for disabled campers. A second, more basic, block is open in high season. Heated swimming pool with paddling pool and retractable roof. Open-air pool with slides (July/Aug). Shop, bar, restaurant with takeaway (all open all season). Wood-fired pizza oven (July/Aug). Large TV and games room (1st floor with lift). Multisports pitch. Fishing. Play area. Free WiFi in main building.

Key Features

 Book Online

 Pets Accepted

 Disabled Facilities

 Beach Access

 Swimming Pool

 Play Area

 Bar/Restaurant

 Fishing

Scan me for
more information.

Alan Rogers Code: FR14070
195 accommodations
170 pitches
GPS: 49.29400, -0.06830
Post Code: F-14510

Calvados, Normandy

www.alanrogers.com/fr14070
camping.lavallee@wanadoo.fr
Tel: +33 2 31 24 40 69
www.campinglavallee.com

Open (Touring Pitches):
Start April - Start November.

Camping de la Vallée

Camping de la Vallée is an attractive site with good, well-maintained facilities, situated on the rolling hillside above Houlgate. The original farmhouse building has been converted to house a bar/brasserie and a comfortable TV lounge and billiards room overlooking the aqua park.

The site has 365 pitches with 170 for touring units (including 12 hardstandings). Open and separated by hedges, all the average sized pitches have 6/10A electricity and some also have water and drainage. Most of the site is sloping, some level, with gravel or tarmac roads. Shade is provided by a variety of well-kept trees and shrubs. The town and its beach are only a 900 m. walk. This is a popular site which is busy in high season with entertainment provided. It is used by tour operators and there are 72 attractive chalets to rent.

Three good toilet blocks include washbasins in cabins, facilities for disabled visitors, and baby rooms. Laundry facilities. Motorhome services. Shop. Bar. Restaurant and takeaway. Aqua park with covered pool and heated outdoor pool (May-Sept). Games room. Playground. Bicycle hire. Volleyball. Football. Tennis. Pétanque. Entertainment in July/Aug. WiFi (charged).

Key Features

 Pets Accepted

 Disabled Facilities

 Beach Access

 Swimming Pool

 Play Area

 Bar/Restaurant

 Bike Hire

 Scan me for more information.

Alan Rogers Code: FR14180
24 accommodations
200 pitches
GPS: 49.39735, 0.20849
Post Code: F-14600

Calvados, Normandy

www.alanrogers.com/fr14180
info@campinglabriquerie.com
Tel: +33 2 31 89 28 32
www.campinglabriquerie.com

Open (Touring Pitches):
Start April - End September.

Camping la Briquerie

La Briquerie is a large, busy site on the outskirts of the attractive and popular harbour town of Honfleur. Very well cared for and efficiently run by a family team, the site has 445 pitches, many of which are let on a seasonal basis. There are also 200 medium to large, hedged touring pitches. All have electricity (6/10A), water and drainage.

Among the main attractions here are the splendid swimming complex with indoor and outdoor pools, and its close proximity to Honfleur. The site is just half an hour from the ferry terminal at Le Havre. The large Intermarché supermarket 300 m. away has a cash machine. The bus stops here on its journey from Caen to Le Havre, calling at many villages along the coast.

Modern, clean sanitary blocks with good facilities for children and disabled visitors. Laundry room with washing machines and dryers. Grocery and crêperie (July/Aug). Large restaurant, bar and takeaway. Large pool complex with two flumes. Covered pool (April-Sept). Outdoor pool and slides (July/Aug). Sauna. Jacuzzi. Well equipped fitness room. Boules. Minigolf. Astroturf multisports court. TV. WiFi over site (free).

Key Features

 Pets Accepted

 Disabled Facilities

 Beach Access

 Swimming Pool

 Play Area

 Bar/Restaurant

Scan me for more information.

Alan Rogers Code: FR27030
52 accommodations
67 pitches
GPS: 49.23477, 0.72532
Post Code: F-27800

Eure, Normandy

www.alanrogers.com/fr27030
campingstnicolas@orange.fr
Tel: +33 2 32 44 83 55
www.campingsaintnicolas.fr

Open (Touring Pitches):
Mid March - Mid October.

Camping Saint Nicolas

This lovely site, operated by the municipal authority is located on a forested hillside above the interesting and attractive small town of Le Bec-Hellouin. The town is quite photogenic, has the usual tourist shops, several bars and restaurants and horse-drawn carriage rides. There are about 120 marked grassy pitches, 44 used for seasonal units, leaving about 70 for touring units, all with 10A hookups and some with water taps. There is limited shade from a few mature trees.

A steep footpath leads down to the town and the imposing Abbey of Bec. This is still a working monastery, which was founded in 1034, at the time of William the Conqueror, and has links to the archbishops of Canterbury. The surrounding area is very popular with artists and photographers and there is a wealth of interesting historical and cultural places to visit.

A modern heated unit has good showers, British style WCs, open and in cubicles washbasins. Extra facilities in the unit by reception, where you will find the laundry. Reception keeps snacks, soft drinks and ices. The baker calls each morning. Covered outdoor swimming pool. Playground. Playing field and tennis courts. Free WiFi over the site.

Key Features

 Pets Accepted

 Disabled Facilities

 Play Area

 Bar/Restaurant

Scan me for more information.

Alan Rogers Code: FR76130
23 accommodations
78 pitches
GPS: 49.43487, 0.82897
Post Code: F-76480

Seine-Maritime, Normandy

www.alanrogers.com/fr76130
info@campinglaforet.com
Tel: +33 2 35 37 93 43
www.campinglaforet.com

Open (Touring Pitches):
Start April - End October.

Camping de la Forêt

This is a pleasant family site with a friendly, relaxed atmosphere, owned by the Commare family who have made a number of improvements in recent years, by adding a cover to the pool and rebuilding the main toilet block. The 90 grassy pitches (78 for tourers, all with 10A electricity) are attractively located in woodland. Most pitches have some shade at different times of the day.

The nearby village of Jumièges, a short walk away, is surrounded on three sides by one of the huge bends of the River Seine - it is located in the Parc Naturel Régional des Boucles de la Seine. The great abbey at Jumièges was founded in 654 by Saint Philibert, rebuilt by the Normans and consecrated in the presence of William the Conqueror – well worth a visit!

The central toilet block is fitted out to a high standard with washbasins in cubicles, and preset showers. A second, smaller block has toilets and open-style washbasins, baby room, facilities for disabled visitors and laundry facilities. Motorhome services. Shop (bread to order). Small swimming pool with retractable roof and paddling pool (both heated high season). Playground. Boules. Games room with TV. Outdoor fitness equipment. Bicycle hire. WiFi over site (charged). Chalets, mobile homes and two tents to rent.

Key Features

 Book Online

 Pets Accepted

 Disabled Facilities

 Swimming Pool

 Play Area

 Bike Hire

Scan me for more information.

Alan Rogers Code: FR76030
39 accommodations
44 pitches
GPS: 49.90063, 1.07470
Post Code: F-76550

Seine-Maritime, Normandy

www.alanrogers.com/fr76030
camping.vitamin@wanadoo.fr
Tel: +33 2 35 82 11 11
www.camping-vitamin.com

Open (Touring Pitches):
Start April - Mid October.

Camping Vitamin

Although the address is Saint Aubin, this compact site is actually on the outskirts of Dieppe and is only a couple of kilometres from the seafront and the shops. Those arriving or leaving by ferry could find it useful for a stopover as it is just off the main N27 to Rouen. It has a very French atmosphere, with 106 privately owned mobile homes and 39 for hire.

The 44 touring pitches (all with 10A electricity) are attractively laid out on level grass, and some are positioned between the mobile homes. The Morelle family work hard to ensure that everything is as it should be, but they speak little English, so be prepared to practise your French.

Two excellent and well maintained unisex toilet blocks provide free showers and washbasins in cubicles. Facilities for disabled visitors. Baby bath. Washing machines and dryers. Motorhome services. Bar serving snacks (seasonal) and entertainment (July/Aug). Heated swimming pools, outdoor (seasonal), indoor (seasonal). Adventure playground and field for games. Multisports court. Games barn. Large pétanque pitch. Sports tournaments in high season. WiFi over site (charged).

Key Features

 Book Online

 Pets Accepted

 Disabled Facilities

 Beach Access

 Swimming Pool

 Play Area

 Bar/Restaurant

Scan me for more information.

Alan Rogers Code: FR80230
12 accommodations
80 pitches
GPS: 49.99362, 1.54381
Post Code: F-80220

Somme, Picardy

www.alanrogers.com/fr80230
domainelesmarguerites@orange.fr
Tel: +33 3 22 30 89 51
www.camping-les-marguerites.com

Open (Touring Pitches):
Late March - Start November.

Camping les Marguerites

Between Dieppe and the Baie de Somme, the beautiful Bresle Valley is a landscape of steep wooded hills, a patchwork of lakes, and the clean River Bresle that teems with salmon and sea trout. Flower Camping Les Marguerites can be found just outside the town of Gamaches and close to a watersports centre. It has 80 level touring pitches (100 sq.m), around half with 6A electricity.

This is a peaceful site where the emphasis is on the countryside and the adjacent lake, but there is a snack bar on-site and some sports tournaments and evening events in the high season. The small town of Gamaches, with a supermarket and a small selection of shops, is just a couple of minutes away by car.

Sanitary block with hot showers and facilities for children and disabled visitors. Washing machine. Motorhome services. Bar (seasonal). Covered swimming pool. Games room. Playground. Fishing. Boat launching. Activities and themed evenings (July/Aug). Bicycle hire. WiFi over site (charged).

Key Features

 Book Online

 Pets Accepted

 Beach Access

 Swimming Pool

 Play Area

 Bar/Restaurant

 Bike Hire

Scan me for more information.

Alan Rogers Code: FR80210
18 accommodations
95 pitches
GPS: 50.08676, 1.71515
Post Code: F-80132

Somme, Picardy

www.alanrogers.com/fr80210
raphael@camping-lecloscacheleux.fr
Tel: +33 3 22 19 17 47
www.camping-lecloscacheleux.fr

Open (Touring Pitches):
Start April - Mid October.

Le Clos Cacheleux

Le Clos Cacheleux is a well-situated campsite of eight hectares bordering woodland in the park of the Château Bouillancourt, which dates from the 18th century. The site is 11 km. from the Bay of the Somme, regarded as being amongst the most beautiful bays in France.

There are 95 very large, grassy pitches (230-250 sq.m) and all have electricity (10A, Europlug), five also have water and wastewater. The aim of the owners is to make your stay as enjoyable as possible by providing a high-quality site, and improvements are being made each year.

There is no shop or bar, but all visitors have access to the swimming pool, shop, bar and children's club of the sister site – le Val de Trie, 500 m. away along a steep road. A number of tents, tree houses and chalets area available for hire.

Two modern, heated sanitary blocks are clean and well maintained with a baby room and facilities for disabled visitors. Laundry room with washing machine and dryer. Motorhome service point. Fridge hire. Adult fitness area. Fishing pond. Free WiFi. Torch essential. At the sister site: shop (all season), bar with terrace. Restaurant and takeaway (seasonal). Covered pool (seasonal). Wellness centre. Library and TV room. Play area. Bouncy castle. Boules. Picnic tables. Freezer for ice packs. Finnish grill cabin. WiFi (free).

Key Features

 Book Online

 Pets Accepted

 Disabled Facilities

 Swimming Pool

 Play Area

 Bar/Restaurant

 Bike Hire

 Fishing

 Scan me for more information.

Alan Rogers Code: FR60020
5 accommodations
70 pitches
GPS: 49.56688, 2.70841
Post Code: F-60490

Oise, Picardy

www.alanrogers.com/fr60020
contact@aestiva.fr
Tel: +33 3 44 85 02 74
www.aestiva.fr

Open (Touring Pitches):
Start February - Mid December.

Aestiva Camping de Sorel

Aestiva Camping de Sorel is located north of Compiègne, close to the A1 motorway and is ideal as an overnight stop. The site has 120 large grassy pitches, of which 70 are available for touring, all with electrical connections (three with water and wastewater).

The original farm buildings have been carefully converted to house the site's main amenities including a bar, restaurant and toilet facilities. The site is open for a long season but most amenities are only open from April to September. The site is, however, close to the village of Sorel with its shops and restaurants. There are five mobile homes to rent.

Compiègne lies 15 km. to the south and its château and several interesting museums are well worth a visit. There is also an important golf course in the town. Closer to the site, the GR123 long-distance footpath runs through Sorel, and offers the opportunity to explore the surrounding countryside on foot.

Toilet block with facilities for children and disabled visitors. Laundry facilities. Motorhome services. Shop (seasonal). Bar, restaurant, snack bar (all season) and takeaway (seasonal). Play area. Boules. Hairdressing service. Multigym and sauna. WiFi throughout (charged).

Key Features

 Book Online

 Pets Accepted

 Disabled Facilities

 Play Area

 Bar/Restaurant

 Scan me for more information.

Alan Rogers Code: FR62200
4 accommodations
41 pitches
GPS: 50.91229, 1.72047
Post Code: F-62179

Pas-de-Calais, Nord/Pas-de-Calais

www.alanrogers.com/fr62200
contact@camping-les-erables.fr
Tel: +33 3 21 85 25 36
www.camping-les-erables.fr

Open (Touring Pitches):
Late March – Mid November.

Camping les Erables

This small site on the Côte d'Opale is very convenient for the Calais ferries and Eurotunnel as well as being just a few minutes from the A16. The 41 pitches are terraced and set on open ground separated by low privet hedging. There is some shade around the perimeter and all pitches have electricity (6/10A Europlug). Just two kilometres from the beach, the pitches at the top of the site have spectacular views over the coast towards the Channel, Cap Blanc-Nez and the English coastline. Most pitches have hardcore wheel tracks.

With no facilities or activities for children, this site is ideal for those who appreciate peace and quiet. The village of Escalles, an easy walk downhill towards the sea, is located on the D940 coast road between Calais and Boulogne; it has a pleasant hotel, several restaurants and an épicerie (on another campsite but open to the public).

One small, unisex toilet block, heated in low season, is fairly basic. British style toilets, washbasins (some in cubicles) and pushbutton showers (charged). Facilities for disabled visitors. Washing machine and dryer. Motorhome services (charged). Bread available to order. Caravan storage. Ice packs frozen. WiFi to some areas (free). Water points are rather scarce. Security barrier closed till 8am. If you leave early ask for code at reception. American motorhomes, twin axel caravans and pets accepted.

Key Features

 Pets Accepted

 Disabled Facilities

 Beach Access

Scan me for more information.

Alan Rogers Code: FR77030
15 accommodations
139 pitches
GPS: 48.91378, 2.73451
Post Code: F-77450

Seine-et-Marne, Paris/Ile de
France

www.alanrogers.com/fr77030
welcome@camping-jablines.com
Tel: +33 1 60 26 09 37
www.camping-jablines.com

Open (Touring Pitches):
Late March - End October.

International de Jablines

Jablines is a modern site which, with the leisure facilities of the adjacent Espace Loisirs, offers an interesting alternative to other sites in the region. Man-made lakes provide opportunities for many water-based activities. The Grand Lac is said to have the largest beach on the Ile-de-France.

The site itself has 154 pitches, of which 139 are for touring units. Most are of a good size (100-120 sq.m), often slightly sloping, with gravel hardstanding and grass, accessed by tarmac roads and marked by young trees. All have 10A electrical connections; 60 are fully serviced. There are about a dozen wooden chalets to rent.

The whole complex close to the Marne has been developed around old gravel workings. Whilst staying on the campsite admission to the Base de Loisirs is free.

Two toilet blocks, heated in cool weather, include pushbutton showers, some washbasins in cubicles. Facilities for disabled visitors. Laundry facilities. Motorhome services (charged). Shop (all season). Play area. Boules. Public telephone. WiFi throughout (free). Ticket sales for Disneyland and Parc Astérix. Mobile homes to rent.

Key Features

 Pets Accepted

 Disabled Facilities

 Play Area

Scan me for more information.

Alan Rogers Code: FR10040
180 accommodations
82 pitches
GPS: 48.51824, 3.65739
Post Code: F-10100

Aube, Champagne-Ardenne

www.alanrogers.com/fr10040
contact@lanouedesrois.com
Tel: +33 3 25 24 41 60
www.lanouedesrois.com

Open (Touring Pitches):
All year.

La Noue des Rois

This is a large, family-run site situated between Paris and Troyes. Primarily a site for the seasonal caravans and chalets belonging to Parisian weekenders, there are also 30 chalets to rent and usually about 30 pitches for touring units. A few of these are in small groups by the side of the smaller lakes but many are on unoccupied seasonal plots scattered around the site.

A small bar overlooks the small heated swimming pool (with retractable roof) and leisure pool with slides. Some sizeable carp have been caught in the main lake.

There is a main sanitary block (partially heated when necessary) in each half of the site, one on a mound therefore inaccessible to those with mobility problems. Controllable showers, washbasins in cubicles, dishwashing and laundry sinks, washing machines and a dryer. Water has to be collected from sinks in blocks. A smaller block has rooms with toilets and showers for disabled visitors, but there were touring pitches nearby when we visited. Chemical disposal at motorhome service point outside entrance. Small shop. Crêperie with bar (all year, Thu-Sun in low season). Small pool complex (seasonal). Minigolf. Tennis. Boules. Fishing. Some entertainment (high season).

Key Features

 Open All Year

 Pets Accepted

 Disabled Facilities

 Swimming Pool

 Play Area

 Bar/Restaurant

 Fishing

Scan me for more information.

Alan Rogers Code: FR10060
18 accommodations
156 pitches
GPS: 48.30276, 4.33747
Post Code: F-10220

Aube, Champagne-Ardenne

Les Rives du Lac

www.alanrogers.com/fr10060
camping.lepineauxmoines@orange.fr
Tel: +33 3 25 41 24 36
www.campinglesrivesdulac.com

Open (Touring Pitches):
All year.

This is a friendly, relaxed 6 ha. site in the heart of the Parc Naturel de la Forêt d'Orient and a very short stroll from the Lac d'Orient with swimming and fishing, and opportunities for sailing and boating (with your own equipment). There are around 200 pitches on level or gently sloping ground separated by hedges or bushes and with a choice of sunny or shady spots. All have 6A electricity and water nearby; just a dozen or so are occupied by caravans to rent.

There are excellent walking and mountain biking routes in the nearby forest or you could just stroll to the nearby bar and restaurant! The Forêt d'Orient Regional Park is a massive expanse with the village of Geraudot at its centre. To the west, the city of Troyes escaped significant war damage and merits a visit.

Two toilet blocks, one heated when necessary, the other open only in high season. Hot showers, some washbasins in cabins. Dishwashing and laundry under cover. Facilities for disabled visitors. Filling point for motorhomes. Bread etc. can be ordered. Small shop. Play area (2-6 yrs).

Key Features

 Open All Year

 Pets Accepted

 Disabled Facilities

 Play Area

 Bike Hire

 Fishing

Scan me for more information.

Alan Rogers Code: FR52050
90 accommodations
55 pitches
GPS: 48.57213, 4.84891
Post Code: F-52290

Haute-Marne, Champagne-Ardenne

www.alanrogers.com/fr52050
info@yellohvillage-en-champagne.com
Tel: +33 3 25 06 34 24
www.yellohvillage-en-champagne.com

Open (Touring Pitches):
Early May - Late November.

Camping en Champagne

Also known as Les Sources du Lac, this Yelloh! Village site is located close to the village of Eclaron and has direct access to the Lac du Der. This is a very large lake with 77 km. of shoreline and is home to over 270 species of birds.

Part of the lake is an ornithological reserve but a wide range of water-based activities are on offer in other areas. These include fishing, windsurfing and sailing, and a separate area is reserved for motorboats. There are just 55 touring pitches here and around 90 mobile homes and chalets to rent.

The reception provides information on a great variety of possible activities and destinations and also has a small shop selling basic provisions. Cycling and walking are popular activities here, with a 37 km. trail around the lake starting from the campsite.

Two toilet blocks include facilities for babies. The facilities may be under pressure at busy times. Shop for basics. Bar. Restaurant. Takeaway. Swimming pool. Paddling pool. Direct access to the lake and beach. Play area. Bicycle hire. Fishing. Ornithological activities. Activity and entertainment programme.

Key Features

 Pets Accepted

 Disabled Facilities

 Swimming Pool

 Play Area

 Bar/Restaurant

 Bike Hire

 Fishing

 Scan me for more information.

Alan Rogers Code: FR54020
7 accommodations
94 pitches
GPS: 48.96593, 5.88534
Post Code: F-54470

Meurthe-et-Moselle, Lorraine

www.alanrogers.com/fr54020
campingdelapelouse@orange.fr
Tel: +33 3 83 81 91 67
www.campingdelapelouse.com

Open (Touring Pitches):
Start April - End September.

Camping de la Pelouse

La Pelouse can be found at the heart of the Lorraine countryside, in the Meurthe-et-Moselle, and is open for a long season. Around 100 grassy touring pitches are shaded and vary in size. Most have 6A electricity connections. There are also a number of chalets available to rent all year (including models with disability access).

The site lies on the banks of the river le Rupt, which is said to have good fishing. On-site amenities here include a heated swimming pool and restaurant (with takeaway food). Evening entertainment is organised in peak season, including occasional dance evenings. Some train noise can be expected.

The nearby village of Jaulny is best known for its ruined château. This dates back to the 12th century and has links with Joan of Arc.

One central toilet block provides all necessary facilities including those for disabled visitors. Bar/restaurant. Small shop. Bread to order at reception. Motorhome services. Swimming pool. Games room. Boules. Basketball. Play area. Fishing. Some entertainment in high season. Chalets to rent.

Key Features

 Pets Accepted

 Disabled Facilities

 Swimming Pool

 Play Area

 Bar/Restaurant

 Fishing

Scan me for more information.

Alan Rogers Code: FR88290
11 accommodations
104 pitches
GPS: 48.19900, 5.84481
Post Code: F-88140

Vosges, Lorraine

www.alanrogers.com/fr88290
contact@camping-portedesvosges.com
Tel: +33 3 29 09 12 00
camping-portedesvosges.com

Open (Touring Pitches):
Start April - End October.

Camping Porte des Vosges

At Camping Porte des Vosges you are assured of a very warm welcome from the owner, Sylvie Drode. This spacious, clean and very well cared for site is situated in Lorraine, on the outskirts of the historic town of Bulgnéville and is just off the E21/A31 making it an ideal stopover as well as for longer holidays. The sloping site has trees and bushes which shade around 100 spacious touring pitches (70-150 sq.m) that are on gravel or grass and there are two equipped tents and a vintage caravan to rent. All the pitches have access to electricity (6A, Europlug) and water points are distributed throughout the site.

Bulgnéville is an attractive historic town with a thirteenth-century church and is less than three hours from Paris. Nearby attractions include the 'trail of three lakes' consisting of marked paths leading through extensive flora, fauna, forest and water environments, whilst the elegant spa towns of Vittel and Contrexéville are also accessible.

One sanitary block with showers, toilets and basins all in cubicles. Facilities for disabled visitors. Snack bar with TV and free WiFi, takeaway (all season). Fresh bread and pastries can be ordered (seasonal). Small playground. Communal barbecue.

Key Features

 Book Online

 Pets Accepted

 Disabled Facilities

 Play Area

 Bar/Restaurant

Scan me for more information.

Alan Rogers Code: FR88170
14 accommodations
125 pitches
GPS: 48.18998, 6.77563
Post Code: F-88600

Vosges, Lorraine

www.alanrogers.com/fr88170
pinasses@dial.oleane.com
Tel: +33 3 29 58 51 10
www.camping-les-pinasses.fr

Open (Touring Pitches):
Mid April - Mid September.

Camping les Pinasses

Les Pinasses is an orderly, well run family site with a small outdoor swimming pool. Traditional in style, the site is long and narrow with pitches on two levels. However the site is fronted by a fairly busy road and a railway track runs immediately behind it, and this is quite close to some pitches.

There are around 125 grassy, individual, hedged pitches of varying sizes, all with 4/6A electricity under trees plus 14 units to rent. There are also a number of seasonal units on site. The site organises a little low key animation in July and August. Due to the narrow entrance road and entry to the pitches, it is only suitable for medium and smaller units.

Four blocks of varying styles, upgraded at different times, include a mix of seated and Turkish style toilets, some washbasins in cubicles are small and narrow. Facilities for disabled campers at one block only (ramped entrance). Laundry facilities. Small shop, bar and restaurant (all July/Aug). Swimming and paddling pools (seasonal). Playground. TV room. Boules. Minigolf. Tennis. Fishing pond. American RVs are not accepted.

Key Features

 Book Online

 Disabled Facilities

 Swimming Pool

 Play Area

 Bar/Restaurant

 Fishing

Scan me for
more information.

Alan Rogers Code: FR88120
25 accommodations
64 pitches
GPS: 48.16826, 6.89025
Post Code: F-88430

Vosges, Lorraine

www.alanrogers.com/fr88120
info@camping-closdelachaume.com
Tel: +33 3 29 50 76 76
www.camping-closdelachaume.co.uk

Open (Touring Pitches):
Mid April - Mid September.

Au Clos de la Chaume

Sites et Paysages Camping Au Clos de la Chaume is a pleasant site is within walking distance of the town, on level ground with a small stream. The friendly family owners, who are British and French, live on site and do their best to ensure campers have an enjoyable relaxing stay. The grassy pitches are level, of varying sizes and with varying amounts of sun and shade. All touring pitches have electricity hook-ups (6/10A) and some are divided by shrubs and trees.

The site carries the LPO (League for Bird Protection) label with over 30 species present. There is an attractive, well fenced, modern swimming pool and an excellent small adventure-style playground. Wine tasting evenings are held in July and August.

Two modern sanitary blocks provide all the necessary facilities for families and disabled visitors. Children's sanitary facilities. Laundry with washing machines and dryers. Motorhome services. Reception keeps basic supplies (June-Aug). Modern covered swimming pool (seasonal). Play area. Games room with pool table, table football and library. Boules. Volleyball. Ping-pong tables. WIFI throughout (charged) and also a FREE WiFi limited zone.

Key Features

 Book Online

 Pets Accepted

 Disabled Facilities

 Swimming Pool

 Play Area

Scan me for more information.

Alan Rogers Code: FR57160
10 accommodations
99 pitches
GPS: 48.78447, 7.24906
Post Code: F-57370

Moselle, Lorraine

www.alanrogers.com/fr57160
info@campinglesbouleaux.fr
Tel: +33 3 87 24 18 72
www.campinglesbouleaux

Open (Touring Pitches):
Early April - Mid October.

Camping les Bouleaux

Camping Les Bouleaux is situated on the border of Lorraine and Alsace. From the site, you can take trips to enjoy the largest boat lift in Europe 'Route du Plan incliné', or a marvellous view from a magnificent height or visit the beautiful cities of Strasbourg, Nancy or Metz. If you like centuries-old castles or forts from the First World War you have many to choose from. For children, the Sainte-Croix animal park with more than 1500 European animal species is easily accessible distance from the site.

Remco and Sandy will welcome you to their child-friendly site, which is beautifully located, surrounded by natural beauty and historic sites. The site has 99 spacious pitches of at least 100m2, with plenty of sun and/or shade, for tent, caravan or motor home. There are also two Mobile Homes, Wooden Chalet and a Coco Sweet tent. Glamping enthusiasts could try one of the 6 safari tents.

Key Features

 Book Online

 Disabled Facilities

 Play Area

 Bar/Restaurant

2 Toilet blocks have showers, washbasins 7 wc's. Facility for guests who are disabled. Laundry. Baby room. Chemical toilet. Bread to order. Boules area. Children's play area. Ball games area. Terrace bar and restaurant. Snack bar. Pets allowed. Adult and children's outdoor swimming pools. Electric scooter hire. Wi-Fi free. Information area.

Scan me for more information.

Alan Rogers Code: FR67150
9 accommodations
63 pitches
GPS: 48.38796, 7.71264
Post Code: F-67150

Bas-Rhin, Alsace

www.alanrogers.com/fr67150
info@clairruisseau.com
Tel: +33 3 88 98 30 04
clairruisseau.com

Open (Touring Pitches):
Early April - End October.

Camp Au Clair Ruisseau

Situated 30 km from Strasbourg and the 'Route des Vins d'Alsace', Camping Au Clair Ruisseau combines the attractions of big city life, the beauty of the wine-growing area of Alsace and a peaceful, natural setting. Once inside the gates of the campsite, you will be transported into a green, leafy setting with a lake within the site itself, and shaded by mature birch and chestnut trees. Its 63 spacious touring pitches, all with electricity, and 34 of which are fully serviced are tastefully interspersed with pods and chalets for rent.

Children will love to spend time at the mini-farm or ride horses who live in a field that forms part of the site. The lake, in which campers may swim, fish or take a rowing boat has a safe, shallow swimming area marked out. There is no bar or restaurant on site but on Saturdays, the local Alsace speciality 'Flammenkuchen', a dough base topped with cream, cheese and ham, prepared by the owners in the traditional way, is available to take away or eat in.

Two toilet blocks including facilities for disabled campers and motorhome service point. Laundry facilities. Small shop with basic necessities, ice cream and refrigerator with chilled drinks. Lake swimming (shallow area marked out) and lake beach. Horse riding. Fishing. Boating. Wi-Fi (free on terrace, chargeable rest of site).

Key Features

 Book Online

 Pets Accepted

 Play Area

 Fishing

 Horse Riding

Scan me for more information.

Alan Rogers Code: FR68050
208 pitches
GPS: 48.19482, 7.33654
Post Code: F-68150

Haut-Rhin, Alsace

www.alanrogers.com/fr68050
camping.ribeauville@wanadoo.fr
Tel: +33 3 89 73 66 71
camping-alsace.com/camping-
pierre-coubertin-ribeauville

Open (Touring Pitches):
Mid March - Mid November.

Camping Pierre de Coubertin

The fascinating Medieval town of Ribeauvillé on the Alsace Route des Vins is within walking distance of this attractive, quietly located site. Popular and well run, it has 208 touring pitches, all with 16A electricity and some separated by shrubs or railings. There are tarmac and gravel access roads. This is a site solely for touring units – there are no mobile homes or seasonal units here. The small shop is open daily for most of the season (hours vary) providing bread, basic supplies and some wines. Only breathable groundsheets are permitted.

Worth a visit in the local area is Ferme l'Hirondelle at Ribeauvillé Gare which makes its own cheese, farm shop for milk, cheese, butter, yoghurt and regional products, and the children can visit the animals whilst you relax on the shady terrace of the bar/restaurant.

Large, heated block provides modern facilities with washbasins in cubicles. Baby facilities. Large laundry room. A smaller unit at the far end of the site is opened for July/Aug. Very good facilities for disabled campers at both units. Shop (Easter-Oct). Excellent adventure style play area with rubber base. Tennis. Boules. TV room. Free WiFi over site.

Key Features

 Pets Accepted

 Disabled Facilities

 Play Area

Scan me for more information.

Alan Rogers Code: FR68040
12 accommodations
121 pitches
GPS: 48.04255, 7.29989
Post Code: F-68420

Haut-Rhin, Alsace

Camping des Trois Châteaux

www.alanrogers.com/fr68040
camping.eguisheim@orange.fr
Tel: +33 3 89 23 19 39
www.camping-eguisheim.fr

Open (Touring Pitches):
Late March - Late October & Late
November - Mid December.

The village of Eguisheim, 'cradle of the Alsace vineyards', lies on the Alsace Route des Vins to the west of Colmar. The three châteaux from which the site gets its name are clearly visible on the hill behind the site. Being close to the village, Les Trois Châteaux is always busy. Flowers, shrubs and trees, and well-tended grass areas make this a very pleasant place.

The 121 pitches, 115 with electricity (6/10A), are either on a slight slope or a terrace and are marked and numbered, most with good shade. Around 80% of pitches have some gravel hardstandings, most of irregular shape and size. We see this site as being suitable primarily for adults rather than families.

The facilities of the fascinating village of Eguisheim are close and the site is well located for exploring this delightful part of Alsace.

The single heated sanitary block in the centre of the site has hot showers and warm water only to washbasins. Some washbasins in cubicles and facilities for disabled visitors. Motorhome services. Playground. WiFi (free). Chalets to rent.

Key Features

 Pets Accepted

 Disabled Facilities

 Play Area

 Bike Hire

Scan me for
more information.

Alan Rogers Code: FR72250
5 accommodations
86 pitches
GPS: 47.92117, 0.15677
Post Code: F-72700

Sarthe, Pays de la Loire

www.alanrogers.com/fr72250
camping-houssay@ville-spay.fr
Tel: +33 2 43 21 16 58
www.domaine-du-houssay.com

Open (Touring Pitches):
Mid April - End September.

Domaine du Houssay

This campsite is located within the leisure centre of Houssay, close to the River Sarthe. Set in 40 hectares, it is also the closest campsite to the 24-hour race circuit at Le Mans, some 6 km. away. There are 86 pitches arranged in a horseshoe shape around a lake. Pitches are of a good size and all have electricity (10A). This is a green and open site with varying degrees of shade.

The leisure centre offers a range of activities and it is a short walk into the local village of Spay for any daily needs. The campsite will be very busy when the 24-hour circuit is in use, but there is an overspill area for additional camping.

The centrally located toilet block provides toilets, showers and dishwashing and laundry sinks. Facilities for children, babies and disabled visitors. Washing machine and dryer. Motorhome services. Communal room with TV area. Bicycle, canoe and pedalo hire. Caravans and chalets to rent. Lake swimming (beach showers). Free WiFi over part of site. Waymarked trails from campsite.

Key Features

 Pets Accepted

 Disabled Facilities

 Play Area

 Fishing

 Horse Riding

Scan me for more information.

Alan Rogers Code: FR72100
20 accommodations
65 pitches
GPS: 47.70253, 0.07365
Post Code: F-72800

Sarthe, Pays de la Loire

www.alanrogers.com/fr72100
contact@lachabotiere.com
Tel: +33 2 43 45 10 00
www.lachabotiere.com

Open (Touring Pitches):
Start April - Mid October.

Camping la Chabotière

This is a delightful little municipal site on the River Loir, just a few steps from the main square of an interesting village classed as a Petite Cité de Caractère. There are 85 pitches, 65 for touring and all with access to electricity and the remainder used for wooden chalets and canvas bungalows to rent.

The main part of the site down by the river is kept vehicle free in July and August, ensuring a safer and quieter environment. A child-proof gate leads out onto the river bank and footpath. There are many opportunities for walking, cycling and sightseeing in the area.

The Château du Lude is just 9 km. away, whilst the famous Châteaux de la Loire and the historic towns of Tours, Angers and Saumur are all in striking distance, as is Le Mans with its famous motor-racing circuit.

The traditional toilet block is well maintained and kept clean; it has pushbutton showers and some washbasins in cubicles. Baby room and washbasins for children. Facilities for disabled visitors. Washing machines and dryer. Motorhome services. Quiet room with tables for playing cards and games plus free Internet access (adults only). Adventure play area. Large sports field. Bicycle hire. Fishing. Activities for children and in the evening. Free WiFi over site. Chalets to rent. No electric barbecues.

Key Features

 Book Online

 Pets Accepted

 Disabled Facilities

 Swimming Pool

 Play Area

 Bike Hire

 Fishing

Scan me for more information.

Alan Rogers Code: FR44090
58 accommodations
103 pitches
GPS: 47.44106, -2.15981
Post Code: F-44160

Loire-Atlantique, Pays de la Loire

www.alanrogers.com/fr44090
info@camping-le-deffay.com
Tel: +33 2 40 88 00 57
www.camping-le-deffay.com

Open (Touring Pitches):
Start May - End September.

Camping le Deffay

A family managed site, Camping le Deffay is a refreshing departure from the usual formula in that it is not over organised or supervised and has no tour operator units. The about 170 good sized, fairly level pitches (103 for touring) have pleasant views and are either on open grass, on shallow terraces divided by hedges or informally arranged in a central, slightly sloping wooded area. All have 10A electricity.

The bar, restaurant and covered pool are located within the old courtyard area of the smaller château that dates from before 1400. A significant attraction of the site is the large, unfenced lake which is well stocked for fishermen and even has free pedalos for children.

The main toilet block is well maintained, if a little dated, and is well equipped including washbasins in cabins, provision for disabled visitors and a baby bathroom. Laundry facilities. Shop. Bar and small restaurant with takeaway. Heated swimming pool with sliding cover and paddling pool (all season). Play area. TV. Entertainment in season including miniclub. Fishing and pedaloes on the lake. Torches useful. WiFi throughout (charged).

Key Features

 Book Online

 Pets Accepted

 Disabled Facilities

 Beach Access

 Swimming Pool

 Play Area

 Bar/Restaurant

 Bike Hire

Scan me for more information.

Alan Rogers Code: FR44360
149 accommodations
122 pitches
GPS: 47.27880, -2.49130
Post Code: F-44740

Loire-Atlantique, Pays de la Loire

www.alanrogers.com/fr44360
paludiers@flowercampings.com
Tel: +33 2 40 60 17 28
www.camping-paludiers.com

Open (Touring Pitches):
Late March - Early October.

Camping les Paludiers

Flower Camping les Paludiers is pleasantly situated at Batz-sur-Mer, a typical Breton town between La Baule and the fortified town of Guérande. The site has about 270 pitches, with 122 used for touring units on grass and sandy ground, marked and divided by shrubs. There are 70 comfort pitches with 10A electricity.

The remainder of the pitches are occupied by mobile homes, chalets and six tented lodges on stilts. At the rear of the modern reception building there is a bar and games room. Outside, a patio area overlooks a small heated swimming and paddling pool and a large play area.

Three modern sanitary blocks, each with good facilities for disabled visitors and a baby room. Laundry facilities. Motorhome services. Shop with essentials. Bar and snacks. Heated swimming and paddling pools. Play area. Games room with stage. Activities and entertainment. Communal barbecue. Bicycle hire. Free WiFi throughout.

Key Features

 Book Online

 Pets Accepted

 Disabled Facilities

 Beach Access

 Swimming Pool

 Play Area

 Bar/Restaurant

 Bike Hire

Scan me for more information.

Alan Rogers Code: FR44500
55 accommodations
63 pitches
GPS: 47.15263, -2.20820
Post Code: F-44770

Loire-Atlantique, Pays de la Loire

www.alanrogers.com/fr44500
contact@camping-laguichardiere.net
Tel: +33 2 40 21 55 09
camping-laguichardiere.net

Open (Touring Pitches):
Mid April - Late September.

La Guichardière

An easy stroll from the sea and the fishing and yachting port of la Gravette, Flower Camping la Guichardière is situated in the Loire-Atlantique between La Baule and Noirmoutier.

In a green and flowery setting, there are 210 pitches, of which 63 are for tourers. They are mainly in an area close to the facilities and are separated by hedges. Fifty-five have electricity connections (6A).

There are 25 mobile homes and chalets for hire. The welcome from the English-speaking staff is warm. The amenities of La Plaine-sur-Mer and Préfailles are within easy reach.

Traditional, well maintained sanitary block with controllable showers and some washbasins in cubicles. Baby bath. Facilities for disabled visitors. Laundry facilities. Motorhome services. Bar with a small shop, snack bar and takeaway (July/Aug and busy weekends). Heated pool and paddling pools (seasonal). Activities and entertainment for children and families (July/Aug weekdays). Tennis. Pétanque. Playground. Games area. Bicycle hire. Free WiFi in the bar area. Mooring for boats.

Key Features

 Book Online

 Pets Accepted

 Disabled Facilities

 Beach Access

 Swimming Pool

 Play Area

 Bar/Restaurant

 Bike Hire

Scan me for more information.

Alan Rogers Code: FR44350
29 accommodations
70 pitches
GPS: 47.24944, -1.37134
Post Code: F-44450

Loire-Atlantique, Pays de la Loire

www.alanrogers.com/fr44350
contact@campingduchene.fr
Tel: +33 2 40 54 12 00
www.campingduchene.fr

Open (Touring Pitches):
Start April - Mid October.

Camping du Chêne

Situated just east of the Nantes ring road, Camping du Chêne would make an ideal night halt. However, it would be a pity to push on as a very pleasant few days could be spent here. With the Loire river to the north and the Loire valley wine route to the south, there is no shortage of places to visit.

The owners, Magali and Bruno, are keen to attract more British and Dutch visitors and are working hard to make improvements to their site. There are about 100 level, grassy pitches, around 70 for touring and tents, 55 with 10A electricity. The remainder are used for the mobile homes (available all year) and four canvas bungalows.

Camping du Chêne is part of an immaculate public park, with a lake that some pitches overlook. There are many sports facilities within the park including fishing, sailing, pedalo hire and tennis courts.

Two toilet blocks are unheated with a mix of British and Turkish style toilets, pushbutton showers and some washbasins in cubicles. Bathroom for disabled visitors. Laundry. Motorhome services. Covered swimming pool. Small playground for young children. Two weeks of activities for children in high season. WiFi (free).

Key Features

 Book Online

 Pets Accepted

 Disabled Facilities

 Beach Access

 Play Area

 Bar/Restaurant

 Fishing

 Sailing

Scan me for more information.

Alan Rogers Code: FR49160
26 accommodations
88 pitches
GPS: 47.67127, -0.23599
Post Code: F-49340

Maine-et-Loire, Pays de la Loire

www.alanrogers.com/fr49160
contact-camping@lesportesdelanjou.com
Tel: +33 2 41 76 31 80
www.lesportesdelanjou.com

Open (Touring Pitches):
Early April - Late October.

Les Portes de l'Anjou

Les Portes de l'Anjou stretches alongside the River Loir, within walking distance of the small market town of Durtal, 30 km. north of Angers. There are 116 reasonably level, grassy pitches, with 88 for touring. All have 10A electricity, but long leads are necessary. They are separated by shrubs and some hedging and a variety of trees give some shade. A number of mobile homes are available to rent.

The town centre, dominated by its imposing château, has a small range of shops and restaurants can be found there. The site enjoys direct access to the River Loir and fishing is said to be good here.

Three sanitary blocks have British style toilets, washbasins in cubicles, preset showers and separate facilities for disabled visitors. Bar/snack bar. Swimming pool (July/Aug). Fishing. Games room. Canoe hire. Bicycle hire. Play area. Entertainment and activity programme. Direct river access (no swimming). Free WiFi in the reception area. Mobile homes to rent.

Key Features

 Book Online

 Pets Accepted

 Disabled Facilities

 Swimming Pool

 Play Area

 Bar/Restaurant

 Bike Hire

 Fishing

Scan me for more information.

Alan Rogers Code: FR49070
5 accommodations
85 pitches
GPS: 47.17431, -0.34730
Post Code: F-49700

Maine-et-Loire, Pays de la Loire

www.alanrogers.com/fr49070
info@campingvdv.com
Tel: +33 2 41 59 86 35
www.camping-vdv.com

Open (Touring Pitches):
Start April - End September.

La Vallée des Vignes

The enthusiasm of the English owners here comes across instantly in the warm welcome received by their guests. Bordering the Layon river, around 80 good sized grass pitches (50 for tourers) are reasonably level and fully serviced (10A electricity, water tap and drain) but have little shade. Five pitches have a hardstanding for cars.

Attractions include an enclosed bar and restaurant overlooking a generously sized sun terrace surrounding the pool. In high season there are activities for children and adults. This is an ideal base for visiting the châteaux of the Loire and the many local caves and vineyards.

The toilet block includes washbasins in cabins and dishwashing facilities. Baby room. Facilities for disabled visitors. Washing machine. Shop (seasonal). Bar meals/takeaway, swimming and paddling pools (all season). Playground, games area and football pitch. Minigolf. Bicycle hire. Volleyball. Basketball. Internet access and WiFi over part of the site. Caravan storage.

Key Features

 Book Online

 Pets Accepted

 Disabled Facilities

 Swimming Pool

 Play Area

 Bar/Restaurant

 Bike Hire

Scan me for more information.

Alan Rogers Code: FR37120
197 accommodations
189 pitches
GPS: 47.14870, 0.65480
Post Code: F-37800

Indre-et-Loire, Val de Loire

www.alanrogers.com/fr37120
contact@fierbois.com
Tel: +33 2 47 65 43 35
www.fierbois.com

Open (Touring Pitches):
Mid April - Late August.

Camping Parc de Fierbois

Castel Camping Parc de Fierbois has a wide variety of accommodation to rent if you're not bringing your own caravan or tent. There's a range of Mobile homes, Chalets, Gîtes and Treehouses. The campsite provides plenty of opportunities for a restful family holiday, but there are many activities for everyone if you prefer to be more active.

As well as a covered heated pool, you'll also find a water-park complex with toboggans, a children's club, an adventure park, including archery and a skate park, and a good restaurant and bar. The region also has a rich heritage for you to discover including chateauxVillandry, Azay-le-Rideau and Chenonceau, as well as many famous vineyards.

Two sanitary blocks are equipped with showers, private washing cubicles and facilities for babies. Washing machines and dryers. Well stocked shop. Bar. Restaurant and takeaway. Heated indoor pool. Outdoor pool with waterslides. Activity and entertainment programmes (in July and August). Bicycle hire. Fishing. Adventure park in the trees. Internet access and WiFi (charged).

Key Features

 Book Online

 Pets Accepted

 Disabled Facilities

 Swimming Pool

 Play Area

 Bar/Restaurant

 Bike Hire

 Fishing

Scan me for more information.

Alan Rogers Code: FR37010
38 accommodations
130 pitches
GPS: 47.35509, 0.63408
Post Code: F-37510

Indre-et-Loire, Val de Loire

www.alanrogers.com/fr37010
info@mignardiere.com
Tel: +33 2 47 73 31 00
www.mignardiere.com

Open (Touring Pitches):
Early April - Mid September.

Camping la Mignardière

Southwest of the city of Tours, this site is within easy reach of several of the Loire châteaux, notably Azay-le-Rideau. There are also many varied sports amenities on the site or very close by. The site has 168 numbered pitches of which 130 are for touring units, all with electricity (10A) and 37 with drainage and water. Pitches are of a good size (60-130 sq.m) on rather uneven grass, accessed by tarmac roads. The barrier gates (coded access) are closed 22.30-07.30 hrs. Reservation is essential for most of July/August.

The site's facilities are supplemented by a small 'parc de loisirs' just across the road which provides a bar and refreshments, pony rides, minigolf, small cars, playground and other amusements. There is also a watersports complex within 300 m. of the site.

Three very clean toilet blocks include washbasins in private cabins, good facilities for disabled campers, baby room and laundry facilities. Motorhome services. The well-stocked shop sells snacks (all season). Takeaway. Indoor heated swimming pools and outdoor heated pool (all season). Paddling pool. Tennis. Bicycle hire. WiFi over site (charged). Torch useful.

Key Features

 Book Online

 Pets Accepted

 Disabled Facilities

 Swimming Pool

 Play Area

 Bike Hire

Scan me for more information.

Alan Rogers Code: FR18010
28 accommodations
115 pitches
GPS: 47.48435, 2.45703
Post Code: F-18700

Cher, Val de Loire

www.alanrogers.com/fr18010
camping.aubigny@orange.fr
Tel: +33 2 48 58 02 37
www.paris-campsite.com

Open (Touring Pitches):
Start April - End September.

Camping les Etangs

Les Etangs is a site of just over 100 pitches, close to the Sancerre vineyards and the lakes of the Sologne. A member of the Flower group, this site extends over two hectares and borders a small lake (suitable for fishing). Pitches are large and grassy (most have electrical connections). There are chalets available to rent.

The town of Aubigny-sur-Nère is very close (1 km) and has a close attachment with Scotland, thanks to the 'Auld Alliance'. The town is the only one in France to celebrate French-Scottish friendship on Bastille Day. Bring your bicycle as there are many tracks running through the surrounding forests.

A covered municipal swimming pool is 50 m. from the site (a charge is made). Various activities are organised on-site during the high season, including special events for children.

Two heated toilet blocks are a good provision and are well located. Bar (high season). Swimming pool complex. Play area. Fishing (permit required). Activity and entertainment programme. WiFi over site (free). Communal barbecue areas. Chalets and tents to rent.

Key Features

 Book Online

 Pets Accepted

 Disabled Facilities

 Play Area

 Bar/Restaurant

 Fishing

Scan me for more information.

Alan Rogers Code: FR85940
120 accommodations
25 pitches
GPS: 46.78139, -2.01806
Post Code: F-85160

Saint Jean-de-Monts, Vendée

www.alanrogers.com/fr85940
zagarella@zagarella.fr
Tel: +33 2 51 58 19 82
www.zagarella.fr

Open (Touring Pitches):
Mid April - Mid September.

Camping Zagarella

Camping Zagarella is an ideal site for happy family holidays, with many facilities for children of all ages. A family run site, the management and staff are very friendly and do all they can to ensure everyone has a good time. There are 301 pitches with just 25 used for touring units, all with electricity (10A), water and wastewater. These vary in size and shape but are mainly level and grassy and divided by shrubs.

Some areas of the site are heavily wooded but there are more open parts for sun lovers. There are three tour operators here which leads to a nice mix of nationalities.

The site has both indoor and outdoor heated swimming pools with a water chute and slides and the play areas provided for younger children are very well equipped. Children's clubs and family entertainment are organised in the high season.

Two modern, unheated toilet blocks are clean and well maintained. Both contain good facilities for disabled visitors and baby baths. An additional block is rather dated. Laundry. Bar, snack bar and takeaway (seasonal). Small shop. Heated indoor pool (all season). Heated outdoor pool (seasonal). Play area. Bouncy castle. Games room. Club for children (high season). Tennis. Multisports court. Bicycle hire. Only gas barbecues are permitted. Free WiFi in bar.

Key Features

 Book Online

 Pets Accepted

 Disabled Facilities

 Beach Access

 Swimming Pool

 Play Area

 Bar/Restaurant

 Bike Hire

Scan me for more information.

Alan Rogers Code: FR85310
45 accommodations
200 pitches
GPS: 46.63632, -1.85844
Post Code: F-85470

Brétignolles-sur-Mer, Vendée

Camping la Trévillière

www.alanrogers.com/fr85310
info@chadotel.com
Tel: +33 2 51 90 09 65
chadotel.com/en/campsite-la-trevilliere-bretignolles-sur-mer

Open (Touring Pitches):
Early April - Mid September.

In a pleasant rural setting, la Trévillière is on the edge of the little resort town of Brétignolles. There are 200 pitches, 105 for touring, all with 10A electricity (Europlug, long leads required on some). Some are level, some sloping; all are separated by hedges or low bushes either with shade or more open.

Although just 2 km. from the nearest beach and less than 5 km. from the Plage des Dunes (one of southern Vendée's best beaches), la Trévillière has a more laid back feel than many other sites in the area, particularly in low season. There are heated and covered swimming pools with a water slide, a small paddling pool and a large sunbathing terrace with plenty of loungers.

Three traditional unheated sanitary blocks, a little tired in parts, include showers and washbasins in cubicles, a unit for disabled visitors and a baby room with bath, shower and toilet. Laundry facilities. Bar, small shop and snack bar with takeaway (10/6-15/9). Heated indoor and outdoor pools, slide and paddling pool. Play area. Games room. Multisports court. Basketball. Minigolf. Max. 1 dog. Charcoal barbecues allowed (no electric barbecues). Bicycle hire. WiFi throughout (charged).

Key Features

 Book Online

 Pets Accepted

 Disabled Facilities

 Beach Access

 Swimming Pool

 Play Area

 Bar/Restaurant

 Bike Hire

Scan me for more information.

Alan Rogers Code: FR85890
34 accommodations
93 pitches
GPS: 46.95781, -0.90309
Post Code: F-85290

Saint Laurent-sur-Sèvre, Vendée

www.alanrogers.com/fr85890
campinglerougegorge@wanadoo.fr
Tel: +33 2 51 67 86 39
camping-lerougegorge-vendee.com

Open (Touring Pitches):
Start April - Start October.

Camping le Rouge Gorge

A family run site, le Rouge Gorge has 93 grassy touring pitches, plus some units for rent (2-8 people) and privately owned caravans and chalets. Slightly sloping and undulating pitches are on grass in a garden-like setting and a small wildlife pond (fenced) is in the centre of the site.

Being the starting point for many hikes, this site is perfect for walkers and cyclists alike with easy access to Barbin viaduct along the Sèvre Nantaise. If that sounds too energetic, simply enjoy the covered, heated swimming pool with a paddling pool and jacuzzi.

There is also a playground with a bouncy castle and trampoline available for children in July and August, as well as a children's club and organized evening entertainment.

Two sanitary blocks are equipped with showers, private washing cubicles and facilities for babies. Washing machine and dryer. Bar. Snack and takeaway. Heated covered pool with jacuzzi and paddling pool. Activity and entertainment programmes (during school holidays). Playground including zip line and bouncy castle. Many shops in centre (800m). Canoe trips. Fishing. Internet access and WiFi at the snack bar (free).

Key Features

 Book Online

 Pets Accepted

 Disabled Facilities

 Swimming Pool

 Play Area

 Bar/Restaurant

 Scan me for more information.

Alan Rogers Code: FR17470
100 accommodations
60 pitches
GPS: 45.96747, -1.31926
Post Code: F-17190

Charente-Maritime, Poitou-Charentes

www.alanrogers.com/fr17470
info@chadotel.com
Tel: +33 5 46 76 54 97
chadotel.com/en/campsite-le-domaine-doleron-saint-georges-doleron

Open (Touring Pitches):
Early April - Late September.

Le Domaine d'Oléron

Camping le Domaine d'Oléron is a neat, well presented and well-managed site where you will receive a warm and friendly welcome from Anneke and Freddy who speak excellent English. The site is set in a peaceful rural location between Saint Pierre and Saint Georges and is part of the Chadotel group.

There are around 170 pitches of which 60 are for touring units. The pitches are generously sized (100-150 sq.m) and are mostly sunny, level and easily accessible, all with 10A electricity. The site is just 3 km. from the beach and the Forest of Saumonards. The local port, shops and restaurants are also nearby.

Two modern sanitary blocks include facilities for disabled visitors and babies. Laundry facilities. Motorhome services. Snack bar and takeaway, bar with TV (all seasonal). Bread is delivered daily. Swimming pool with slides (seasonal). Adventure-style play area. Six pétanque lanes. Bicycle hire. Organised entertainment two or three times a week in July/Aug. Gas barbecues only on pitches, communal areas for charcoal. WiFi over site (charged). Max. 1 dog per pitch.

Key Features

 Book Online

 Pets Accepted

 Disabled Facilities

 Beach Access

 Swimming Pool

 Play Area

 Bar/Restaurant

 Bike Hire

Scan me for more information.

Alan Rogers Code: FR17190
21 accommodations
294 pitches
GPS: 45.67448, -1.09623
Post Code: F-17570

Charente-Maritime, Poitou-Charentes

www.alanrogers.com/fr17190
info@logis-du-breuil.com
Tel: +33 5 46 23 23 45
www.logis-du-breuil.com

Open (Touring Pitches):
Early May - End September.

Le Logis du Breuil

The first impression on arrival at this impressive campsite is one of space. The site covers a 30-hectare expanse of farm pasture where (on different areas) cattle graze and children play. The nine-hectare camping areas are set among rows of mature and shady trees giving a dappled effect to the grassy touring pitches. All have 6/10A electricity and are very large with direct access to wide, unpaved alleys which lead on to the few tarmac roads around the site. Some serviced pitches are available.

The amenities are centred around the reception, restaurant and bar with its wooden terrace overlooking the fantastic heated indoor and outdoor pool complex complete with waterslides. The area around the site is very pleasant agricultural land and the beaches of the Atlantic coast are nearby.

Four well-maintained toilet blocks are spaced around the camping area. Laundry facilities. Motorhome services. Excellent shop, bar, restaurant and takeaway (seasonal). Swimming pools (seasonal). No evening entertainment. Play area. Indoor games area. TV room. Multisports pitch. Boules. Bicycle hire. Tennis. Archery (July/Aug). Excursions organised. WiFi on part of the site (charged). Gîtes, mobile homes and chalets to rent.

Key Features

 Book Online

 Pets Accepted

 Disabled Facilities

 Beach Access

 Swimming Pool

 Play Area

 Bar/Restaurant

 Bike Hire

Scan me for more information.

Alan Rogers Code: FR17010
120 accommodations
251 pitches
GPS: 45.58358, -0.98653
Post Code: F-17110

Charente-Maritime, Poitou-Charentes

www.alanrogers.com/fr17010
info@bois-soleil.com
Tel: +33 5 46 05 05 94
www.bois-soleil.com

Open (Touring Pitches):
Early April - Early October.

Camping Bois Soleil

Close to the sea, Bois Soleil is a large site in three parts, with serviced pitches for touring units and a few for tents. All the touring pitches are hedged and have electricity (10A), with water and drainage between two. The main part, Les Pins, is attractive with trees and shrubs providing shade. Opposite is La Mer with direct access to the beach, some areas with less shade and an area for tents. The third part, La Forêt, is for caravan holiday homes.

It is best to book your preferred area as it can be full from mid-June to late August. Excellent private sanitary facilities are available to rent, either on your pitch or at a block (subject to availability).

Each area has one large and one small toilet block. Heated block near reception. Cleaned twice daily, they include facilities for disabled visitors and babies. Launderette. Supermarket, bakery, beach shop (all seasonal). Restaurant, bar and takeaway (all seasonal). Swimming pool (heated seasonaly). Steam room. Fitness room. Tennis. Play area. TV room and library. Internet terminal (free). Wi-Fi throughout (charged). Charcoal and electric barbecues are not permitted. Dogs are not accepted in the high season.

Key Features

 Book Online

 Pets Accepted

 Disabled Facilities

 Beach Access

 Swimming Pool

 Play Area

 Bar/Restaurant

 Bike Hire

Scan me for more information.

Alan Rogers Code: FR86120
86 accommodations
14 pitches
GPS: 46.44503, 0.55929
Post Code: F-86410

Vienne, Poitou-Charentes

www.alanrogers.com/fr86120
info@domaine-de-dienne.fr
Tel: +33 5 49 45 87 63
www.defiplanet.com

Open (Touring Pitches):
Mid February - End December.

DéfiPlanet de Dienné

Previously known as Domaine de Dienné, this is, without doubt, a wonderful site and unique in what it offers. It concentrates on your well being and provides all the facilities you could wish for in achieving that aim.

The whole site extends over 47 hectares but there are just 14 pitches for touring units and these are on generous plots of 250 sq.m. All have their own water supply, drainage and 16A electricity (Europlug) and access for even the largest of units will not cause a problem.

The accommodation to rent includes Romany-style caravans, treehouses, yurts, a gîte and cottages, which are all of superb quality and again on large plots. This site cannot fail to impress from the moment you arrive.

Toilet block with washbasins and showers. Facilities for disabled visitors. Shop, bar, restaurant and takeaway. Heated indoor swimming pool (all season) and outdoor pool (July/Aug). Hairdressing salon. Riding centre. Mountain biking. Bicycle hire. Adventure park. Climbing tower. Children's games. Walking trails. Free WiFi over site. Barbecues are not permitted on pitches, communal area provided.

Key Features

 Book Online

 Pets Accepted

 Disabled Facilities

 Swimming Pool

 Play Area

 Bar/Restaurant

 Bike Hire

 Horse Riding

Scan me for more information.

Alan Rogers Code: FR58070
12 accommodations
78 pitches
GPS: 46.83499, 3.45557
Post Code: F-58300

Nièvre, Burgundy

www.alanrogers.com/fr58070
camping.decize@aquadis-loisirs.com
Tel: +33 3 86 25 14 05
aquadis-loisirs.com/camping-de-decize

Open (Touring Pitches):
Start April - Late October.

Camping de Decize

Previously known as Camping les Halles, this is a very friendly site with 78 touring pitches in an area of 1.8 hectares. Fishing enthusiasts can enjoy their passion from a waterside pitch. 12 fully-equipped mobile homes are also available for hire. You can enjoy a pleasant stay in the heart of nature, while still close to the town centre. The site lies on the banks of the River Loire in the town of Decize. It is located between the Aquatic Sports Centre and the leisure park, which has a large play area, electric boat hire, a mini-golf course and the municipal swimming pool.

The nearby Nivernais Canal and Loire Lateral Canal (following the EuroVelo 6 cycling route) are also an invitation to investigate the area. The site is also very popular with cyclists as the 'Promenade des Halles', a tree-lined avenue that starts out from the site; it is specially designed for cyclists and meets up with Nivernais Canal.

Key Features

 Book Online

 Pets Accepted

 Disabled Facilities

 Play Area

 Fishing

Three toilet blocks with showers, washbasins and WC's. Facility for visitors who are disabled. Laundry. Motorhome service point. Small shop at the reception. Bread to order. Sheltered equipped room for cyclists and hikers (microwave, freezer, dishes, table, sofa, TV). Wi-Fi all site (chargeable). Table tennis. Children's play area. Boules area. Volleyball. TV room. Games room. Minigolf course adjacent. Bike & Canoe hire adjacent. Pets welcome. Supermarket 1 mile. Earliest arrival time is 14.00.

Scan me for more information.

Alan Rogers Code: FR58060
16 accommodations
100 pitches
GPS: 46.81692, 4.05636
Post Code: F-58170

Nièvre, Burgundy

www.alanrogers.com/fr58060
info@la-gagere.com
Tel: +33 3 86 30 48 11
www.la-gagere.com

Open (Touring Pitches):
Start April - End September.

Domaine de la Gagère

At this secluded and attractive naturist campsite, you will receive a warm welcome from the enthusiastic owners, Floor and Tim. The site is spacious and well equipped with good sized, level, grassy touring pitches, some shaded and some open. Many are arranged in groups around three sides of a rectangle, between hedges. Electricity (4-10A) is supplied to all pitches, four of which are fully serviced. There are plenty of water points.

In the high season, there are organised activities, barbecues and entertainment. A children's club meets twice a week. The site lies near the southern end of the Morvan Regional Natural Park, surrounded by wooded hills, but within easy reach of all the park has to offer, plus the less well-known attractions such as the Museum of Celtic History and the welcoming Kagyu Ling, one of the largest Buddhist temples in Europe.

Three modern unisex toilet blocks, one heated, contain British style WCs, washbasins and preset communal showers. Facilities for disabled visitors. Baby room. Motorhome services. Laundry. Shop (seasonal). Bar (all season). Restaurant with snack bar and takeaway (seasonal). Satellite TV. Two heated swimming pools (one all season, the other high season). Sauna and wellness suite (seasonal). Playgrounds. Boules. Bicycle hire. Only gas and electric barbecues are permitted. WiFi over site (free).

Key Features

 Naturist Site

 Pets Accepted

 Disabled Facilities

 Swimming Pool

 Play Area

 Bar/Restaurant

 Bike Hire

Scan me for more information.

Alan Rogers Code: FR71150
32 accommodations
38 pitches
GPS: 46.62059, 3.76458
Post Code: F-71140

Saône-et-Loire, Burgundy

www.alanrogers.com/fr71150
camping.bourbonlancy@aquadis-loisirs.com
Tel: +33 3 85 89 20 98
aquadis-loisirs.com/camping-de-bourbon-lancy

Open (Touring Pitches):
Early March - Early November.

Camping de Bourbon-Lancy

Key Features

 Book Online

 Pets Accepted

 Disabled Facilities

 Bike Hire

Camping de Bourbon-Lancy is located on the edge of a waterfront and just 2 km from Therme and the Bourbon-Lancy Spa, this site has about 70 spacious and demarcated pitches on a semi-shaded 2-hectare lot. The site has 38 touring pitches and 32 mobile homes, comfortable chalets or equipped tents in a peaceful and green setting. Relaxation and well-being will punctuate your days. Bourbon-Lancy is a favourite destination for walking or cycling getaways.

Many marked tours invite you to travel (Eurovélo 6, Tour de Bourgogne, GTMC, Route de Santiago de Compostela-GR13). This medieval city is also known for the quality of its waters and its spa. Take time to stop at the site to recharge your batteries and continue your journey through Charolais woods where pastures and rivers mingle.

Two heated blocks provide showers, washbasins and wc's. Adapted for visitors who are disabled. Laundry. Baby room. Wi-Fi throughout (charged). Shop with local products. Fresh bread and pastries to order. Motorhome service area. Boules. Volleyball. Trampoline. TV room with games. Swimming pool and Children's (June/September). Bike rental (July/August). Trampoline. Table tennis. Kids' Club (July-August). Takeaway. Barbecue loan.

Scan me for more information.

Alan Rogers Code: FR71020
30 accommodations
76 pitches
GPS: 46.36369, 4.47460
Post Code: F-71520

Saône-et-Loire, Burgundy

Village des Meuniers

www.alanrogers.com/fr71020
contact@villagedesmeuniers.com
Tel: +33 3 85 50 36 60
www.villagedesmeuniers.com

Open (Touring Pitches):
Early April - Late October.

Sites et Paysages Village des Meuniers is in a tranquil setting with panoramic views. The large and welcoming reception building sets the tone for the rest of this superb site. It is set on the gentle slopes of a hilltop that has been tastefully landscaped. There is a feeling of spaciousness throughout with modern and well-kept facilities.

The 76 terraced, grassy touring pitches range from 100 to 250 sq.m. They are fairly level and all have electricity (10A) and ample water points, and 25 also have wastewater outlets. All pitches enjoy stunning views.

Key Features

 Pets Accepted

 Disabled Facilities

 Swimming Pool

 Play Area

 Bar/Restaurant

The heated sanitary facilities, mainly in a central, purpose-designed hexagonal block, with good quality modern fittings. Excellent facilities for disabled visitors. Smaller unit (also heated) in the lower area of the site, plus further toilets in the main reception building. Motorhome services. Shop, bar, restaurant and takeaway (all seasonal). Swimming pool complex with three heated pools and toboggan run (seasonal). Play area. Activities for children (high season). 18-hole minigolf. WiFi in bar and reception (free). Rental accommodation includes chalets and lodge tents with their own shower and WC.

Scan me for more information.

Alan Rogers Code: FR71190
90 pitches
GPS: 46.57372, 4.90935
Post Code: F-71700

Saône-et-Loire, Burgundy

Camping de Tournus

www.alanrogers.com/fr71190
camping-tournus@orange.fr
Tel: +33 3 85 51 16 58
www.camping-tournus.com

Open (Touring Pitches):
Start April - End September.

This very well maintained, pleasant site is just 1.5 km. from exit 27 of the A6 'Autoroute du Soleil'. It is, therefore, an ideal stop en route to and from the south of France, and reservation may be necessary for the high season. The site is 200 metres from the River Saône and 1 km. from the centre of the interesting old market town of Tournus.

All the 90 pitches are for touring and are equipped with 10A electricity and 27 have hardstanding. A few trees give some pitches varying amounts of shade. Access is very easy for large units. A municipal outdoor swimming pool is adjacent to the site and open for the high season. The surrounding area is well worth exploring with its beautiful scenery and many picturesque old towns and villages.

Two clean toilet blocks near the entrance provide all necessary facilities, including those for disabled visitors. Motorhome services. Small bar and shop in the reception area where bread can be ordered daily and light snacks purchased. Small play area. Bicycle hire. WiFi near the bar (free).

Key Features

 Book Online

 Pets Accepted

 Disabled Facilities

 Play Area

 Bar/Restaurant

 Bike Hire

 Scan me for more information.

Alan Rogers Code: FR21040
57 accommodations
152 pitches
GPS: 47.13411, 4.49840
Post Code: F-21230

Côte d`Or, Burgundy

www.alanrogers.com/fr21040
info@campingfouche.com
Tel: +33 3 80 90 02 23
www.europe.huttopia.com/site/
etang-de-fouche

Open (Touring Pitches):
Mid April - Early October.

l'Etang de Fouché

This quite large but peaceful, lakeside site with its modern bar/restaurant and swimming pool complex, is useful as a stopover, or indeed for longer stays to explore the region. It can be very busy during the school holidays, but is quiet and relaxing outside the main season.

There are over 200 good sized pitches, on fairly level grass, 152 for touring and all with 10A electricity, water and wastewater. Many are hedged and offer a choice of shade or a more open aspect. There is direct access to the adjacent lake and beach facilities. A 2 km. stroll around the lake can be pleasant. Part of the Huttopia group.

Three shower blocks provide all the necessary modern facilities (male and female are separate). Facilities for disabled visitors. Baby room. Laundry area. Shop and takeaway (seasonal). Bar and restaurant (high season plus w/e low season). Small heated outdoor swimming pool. Boules. TV/games room. Playground. Fishing. Activities and entertainment (July/Aug). Bicycle hire. Only gas barbecues are permitted. WiFi (free).

Key Features

 Pets Accepted

 Disabled Facilities

 Swimming Pool

 Play Area

 Bar/Restaurant

 Bike Hire

 Fishing

Scan me for more information.

Alan Rogers Code: FR21030
88 pitches
GPS: 47.06900, 4.80300
Post Code: F-21420

Côte d`Or, Burgundy

www.alanrogers.com/fr21030
contact@camping-savigny-les-beaune.fr
Tel: +33 3 80 24 51 02
camping-savigny-les-beaune.com

Open (Touring Pitches):
Mid March - Mid October.

Camping les Premier Prés

This popular site is ideally located for visiting the Burgundy vineyards, for use as a transit site or for spending time in the town of Beaune. During the high season, it is busy most evenings, so it is best to arrive by 4 pm. The 88 level pitches are marked and numbered, with 6A electric hook-ups and room for an awning. A former municipal site, now privately owned, it is quiet and peacefully situated alongside a small river. A 1 km. walk along the riverbank brings you to the village, which has a château and a weekly market.

Whilst the famed wine region alone attracts many visitors, Beaune, its capital, is unrivalled in its richness of art from times gone by. Narrow streets and squares are garlanded with flowers in high season and the pavement cafés are crammed with tourists. At the centre stands the stunning 15th-century Hôtel Dieu, which should not be missed.

Somewhat dated sanitary facilities are housed in a building behind reception. Additional WCs and water points are conveniently placed towards the middle of the site. Motorhome services. Ice available to purchase. Torch useful. Fishing. Bicycle hire. WiFi.

Key Features

 Pets Accepted

 Disabled Facilities

 Play Area

 Bike Hire

 Fishing

Scan me for more information.

Alan Rogers Code: FR39150
22 accommodations
90 pitches
GPS: 47.01192, 5.63050
Post Code: F-39380

Jura, Franche-Comté

Camping les Trois Ours

www.alanrogers.com/fr39150
contact@camping-les3ours-jura.com
Tel: +33 3 84 81 50 45
camping-les3ours-jura.com

Open (Touring Pitches):
Early April - Late September.

This pretty and well cared for site is in a pleasant location at the edge of the Forêt de Chaux. The adjacent River Loué will be an attraction for fishermen and river bathing is also possible. There are about 20 mobile homes and chalets to rent, and 90 shady level grassy touring pitches all with 6-10A electricity, 17 of which are premium riverside pitches.

During peak season, various activities are organised including canoeing trips and themed evenings. The restaurant, with its riverside terrace, is attractively decorated and offers a varied menu. The friendly owners can recommend numerous footpaths and cycle routes through the forest.

The royal saltworks (Salines Royales) at Arc-et-Senans were added to UNESCO's World Heritage List in 2009. Built by Ledoux in the late 18th century, this stunning ensemble is one of the finest examples of an early Enlightenment project.

One modern sanitary block provides all the usual facilities. Facilities for disabled visitors and children. Washing machine. Good restaurant and bar with TV. Outdoor pool (seasonal). Trampoline. Small adventure-style playground. Boules. Volleyball court. Table tennis. Small lake for fishing (free), river fishing (permit required). WiFi in bar area.

Key Features

 Book Online

 Pets Accepted

 Disabled Facilities

 Swimming Pool

 Play Area

 Bar/Restaurant

 Fishing

Scan me for more information.

Alan Rogers Code: FR39110
111 accommodations
106 pitches
GPS: 46.58712, 5.70105
Post Code: F-39130

Jura, Franche-Comté

www.alanrogers.com/fr39110
contact@camping-moulin.com
Tel: +33 3 84 48 31 21
www.camping-moulin.com

Open (Touring Pitches):
Late April - Mid September.

Camping le Moulin

Patornay is a pleasant village just by the River Ain where it starts to widen on its way to the Lac de Vouglans. This well equipped five-hectare campsite lies right on the riverbank, with direct access for boating, canoeing and fishing. There are around 220 slightly uneven and sloping pitches with around 110 for touring units. All have electricity (6A Europlug). Many have heavy shade and of these, 40 are in a more natural area where there is no electricity, and water taps are a bit further apart.

In July/August the site arranges activities and events for young and old. There is plenty to occupy campers on the site, but the countryside, its villages and other attractions are also well worth exploring on foot, by bicycle or by car.

Two modern toilet blocks are adequate. Facilities for disabled visitors. Baby room. Motorhome services. Washing machines and dryers. Basic shop. Fresh bread daily. Weekly mini-market. Bar, snack bar, takeaway and terrace (seasonal). Satellite TV. Games room. Swimming pool with slides and flume, paddling pool (seasonal, no Bermuda shorts). Playground. Activities for children include mini discos, parties and weekly shows. Sports field. Boules. Fishing (licence from reception). Internet and WiFi.

Key Features

 Book Online

 Disabled Facilities

 Swimming Pool

 Bar/Restaurant

 Fishing

Scan me for more information.

133

Alan Rogers Code: FR25150
40 accommodations
75 pitches
GPS: 47.10273, 6.15960
Post Code: F-25290

Doubs, Franche-Comté

www.alanrogers.com/fr25150
contact@larochedully.com
Tel: +33 3 81 57 17 79
www.camping-ornans.com

Open (Touring Pitches):
Early April - Mid October.

La Roche d'Ully

Situated in the heart of the Jura mountains and close to historic Ornan, La Roche d'Ully is a spacious, attractive and modern site, surrounded by views of wooded hills and rocky outcrops. There are 115 large pitches, 75 of which are for tourers, most have electricity (10A) and all have access to water. Divided by a variety of bushes and young trees, there is not a great deal of shade.

A feature here is the adjacent aquatic centre with two pools and many other facilities, with free entry to campers. The restaurant and bar are open all season and, being open to the public, both are busy at weekends.

The region offers many activities including cycling, hiking, canoeing and fishing. The historic town of Ornan has a museum of the painter, Gustave Courbet. Alternatively, you can relax and explore the surrounding countryside and villages at a slower pace.

One modern and clean sanitary block with massage showers. Baby room. Facilities for disabled visitors. Laundry facilities. Motorhome services. Small shop. Bar/restaurant with terrace and takeaway (from 1/5). Games room and TV in bar. Play area. Bicycle hire. Ping pong tables. Pétanque. WiFi on part of the site.

Key Features

 Book Online

 Pets Accepted

 Disabled Facilities

 Swimming Pool

 Play Area

 Bar/Restaurant

 Bike Hire

Scan me for more information.

134

Alan Rogers Code: FR25160
9 accommodations
99 pitches
GPS: 47.26588, 6.07151
Post Code: F-25220

Doubs, Franche-Comté

www.alanrogers.com/fr25160
contact@campingdebesancon.com
Tel: +33 3 81 88 04 26
www.campingdebesancon.com

Open (Touring Pitches):
Mid March - End October.

Camping de Besançon

You'll find no noisy entertainment at Camping de Besançon La Plage, so the site is perfect for those looking for peace. That said, children will enjoy the sprawling lawns, sports field, the large swimming pool and playground, and the adults will love the location on the River Doubs.

The pitches are of a good size, and all have electricity (16A), water and drainage. Choose from shaded, partially shaded or no shade pitches, on hard ground or grass. There are also bungalows and tents for rental. Within a short walk from the site is a large supermarket, and nearby is a tram stop from where you can get to the town centre. Cycling, walking and fishing are prevalent in the area, and travelling eastward for approximately an hour will have you at the Swiss border.

Clean sanitary facilities with unisex private sinks and showers. Baby room. Washing machines. Dryers. Washing up sinks. Snack bar. Fresh bread daily. Large swimming pool with diving boards. Playground. Crazy golf. Multi-sports field. Table tennis. Boules. WiFi.

Key Features

 Pets Accepted

 Swimming Pool

 Play Area

Scan me for more information.

135

Alan Rogers Code: FR39180
50 accommodations
110 pitches
GPS: 46.72324, 5.80165
Post Code: F-39300

Jura, Franche-Comté

www.alanrogers.com/fr39180
camping.sousdoriat@wanadoo.fr
Tel: +33 3 84 51 21 43
www.vacances-camping-jura-location.com

Open (Touring Pitches):
Start May - End September.

Camping Sous Doriat

Camping Sous Doriat is a delightful small family run campsite on the outskirts of the village of Monnet-la-Ville. It is surrounded by meadows and hills and has views over the village. There are 120 good sized, level grass pitches separated by trees and shrubs with varying degrees of shade. There are 110 for touring and 80 have electricity (10A). Lac de Chalain, only 4 km. away offers a beach, lake swimming and watersports.

This excellent value site is a more peaceful alternative to the larger and livelier sites close to the Lake. There are many marked walks and cycle routes in the area.

Although the site only has a bar, there is a restaurant about 100 m. from the entrance. A well-stocked supermarket in the village is an easy five-minute stroll away. Further afield are several other lakes, waterfalls and cave, well worth exploring and Switzerland is only 55 km.

Two well-appointed toilet blocks with all necessary facilities. Facilities for disabled visitors. Baby room. Small swimming pool (heated high sesaon). Bar/takeaway (seasonal). Play area. Boules. WiFi (free).

Key Features

 Book Online

 Pets Accepted

 Swimming Pool

 Play Area

 Bar/Restaurant

Scan me for more information.

Alan Rogers Code: FR19280
60 accommodations
80 pitches
GPS: 45.26904, 2.00898
Post Code: F-19320

Corrèze, Limousin

Camping du Lac

www.alanrogers.com/fr19280
camping.marcillac@aquadis-loisirs.com
Tel: +33 5 55 27 81 38
aquadis-loisirs.com/en/camping-du-lac

Open (Touring Pitches):
Early April - Late October.

On the shore of an extensive lake in the heart of the Corrèze countryside, this could be an ideal holiday base for walkers, cyclists, anglers and lovers of watersports. The site offers 140 pitches of which 60 are for touring units, the remainder being occupied by mobile homes and chalets to rent. Trees provide shade in places, and 6A electricity connections are available (some pitches may require longer cables). Water points are rather sparse.

Nearby Marcillac-la-Croisille has a weekly market (Tues) and a few shops, including a baker's and a grocery. The nearest sizeable town with a choice of shops, bars and restaurants is Tulle, attractively located on the Corrèze river. There are numerous marked footpaths and cycle tracks easily accessible and for those who enjoy treasure hunts, there is a well organised Geocaching scheme.

Key Features

 Book Online

 Pets Accepted

 Disabled Facilities

 Play Area

 Fishing

One building provides basic facilities. One modern adapted for disabled visitors. Laundry area. No shop but essentials from reception. Tourist information. TV room with library and free WiFi. Playground. Children's club twice a week (July/Aug). Table tennis, basketball and pétanque. Tennis (charged). Goat farm visits with cheese making and free tastings (July/Aug). Fishing. Direct access to lake and beach.

Scan me for more information.

Alan Rogers Code: FR19030
52 accommodations
94 pitches
GPS: 45.55960, 1.81340
Post Code: F-19260

Corrèze, Limousin

www.alanrogers.com/fr19030
camping.laplage@flowercampings.com
Tel: +33 5 55 98 08 54
www.camping-correze.com

Open (Touring Pitches):
Early April - Start October.

Camping la Plage

La Plage is situated 3 km. from Treignac across the road from Lac des Bariousses. There are 146 large grassy pitches, 94 for touring most with 6A electricity. The site is well shaded and the flat pitches are terraced down the slope. All have easy access and many have views across the lake. Swimming and fishing are possible from the sandy beach. In high season there is a lifeguard on duty and all of the site's activities are centred on the beach and lake.

There is a tunnel under the road from the site to the beach. When we visited, some of the pitches were rather cramped and the facilities were under considerable pressure at a busy time. This former municipal site is run by Flower Camping and makes a good base from which to explore the many old villages and towns.

Two clean, spacious, basic toilet blocks with all necessary facilities including those for campers with disabilities. Heated indoor swimming pool (all season). Washing machine. Small basic shop selling wine and some local specialities. Motorhome services. Snack bar on the beach (July/Aug). Fishing, canoes and pedalos. Small games room. Library with English books. Organised activities on the beach (high season). WiFi throughout. Torches recommended.

Key Features

 Book Online

 Pets Accepted

 Disabled Facilities

 Swimming Pool

 Play Area

Scan me for more information.

Alan Rogers Code: FR87100
10 accommodations
58 pitches
GPS: 45.82470, 0.99657
Post Code: F-87310

Haute-Vienne, Limousin

www.alanrogers.com/fr87100
info@camping-des-alouettes.com
Tel: +33 5 55 03 26 93
www.camping-des-alouettes.com

Open (Touring Pitches):
Start April - End September.

Camping des Alouettes

Camping des Alouettes, located in the Perigord Limousin Nature Park, 25 kilometres west of Limoges, is run by a Dutch couple who will do all they can to ensure your stay is enjoyable. The site has 68 large, level, grass pitches, mostly open, all with 10A electricity. Almost all pitches enjoy panoramic views of the area.

There is a mixture of mature and young trees providing some shade and pitches are separated by shrubs or hedging. Six mobile homes and three safari tents are to rent. On arrival, you are given a guided tour and an explanation of what is available both on and off-site, supplemented by extensive tourist information at reception.

Well kept, modern sanitary block includes facilities for disabled visitors, children and a family shower room. Washing machine. Bread can be ordered daily and delivered to your pitch. Bar (open all season). Restaurant (Mon. and Fri. with table d'hôte menu). Takeaway spit roast chicken (Wednesday). Heated swimming pool (seasonal). Football, volleyball, badminton, pétanque and table tennis. Small play area and trampoline. Small library. No charcoal barbecues. Internet access at the bar. WiFi on most pitches (charged).

Key Features

 Book Online

 Pets Accepted

 Disabled Facilities

 Swimming Pool

 Play Area

 Bar/Restaurant

Scan me for more information.

Alan Rogers Code: FR63130
34 accommodations
57 pitches
GPS: 45.57373, 2.95708
Post Code: F-63790

Puy-de-Dôme, Auvergne

www.alanrogers.com/fr63130
reposbaladin@free.fr
Tel: +33 4 73 88 61 93
www.camping-auvergne-france.com

Open (Touring Pitches):
Late April - Mid September.

Le Repos du Baladin

A lovely, small and friendly campsite that offers an excellent alternative to the larger sites in this area. The owners are aiming for a quiet, relaxing site, attracting nature lovers who want to spend time walking, cycling or touring in this beautiful region.

Attractively and well laid out, there are about 90 good sized pitches, some with superb views of the château, 60 for touring (all with 5/10A electricity, 19 also with water and drainage), and many with good privacy. They are separated by neat conifer hedges with mature trees offering varying amounts of shade. Murol and its ancient 12th-century château are half an hour's walk away.

Attractive Lac Chambon with three small supermarkets, fishing, bathing in the lake, bicycle and boat hire is 2 km. Super Besse (a winter ski resort), and bustling Le Mont Dore with a cable car to Puy de Sancy, the highest mountain in the region are 20 km. away.

An excellent, very clean and central, heated toilet block provides all the necessary amenities, including those for babies and people with mobility issues. Bar with TV. Restaurant with full menu, snacks and takeaway (seasonal). Two heated pools (one covered) and solarium (seasonal). Large playground. Boules. Free WiFi near the reception.

Key Features

 Book Online

 Pets Accepted

 Disabled Facilities

 Swimming Pool

 Play Area

 Bar/Restaurant

Scan me for more information.

Alan Rogers Code: FR63080
40 accommodations
59 pitches
GPS: 45.54317, 2.54275
Post Code: F-63690

Puy-de-Dôme, Auvergne

www.alanrogers.com/fr63080
moulindeserre@orange.fr
Tel: +33 4 73 21 16 06
www.moulindeserre.com

Open (Touring Pitches):
Early April - Mid September.

Camping le Moulin de Serre

A pleasant scenic drive brings you to this spacious and well-maintained site. It is set in a wooded valley beside a pretty river where, we are told, the locals still pan for gold. You will find a warm welcome and a relaxing atmosphere here in this lesser-known area of the Auvergne.

The 99 large pitches (59 for touring) are separated by a variety of trees and hedges giving good shade. Some pitches have hardstanding and all have electricity (5-10A), long leads may be necessary. Fresh bread and croissants are baked daily on-site, as are snacks and pizzas to order.

This tranquil site is an ideal base for walkers and cyclists, route maps for all degrees of difficulty are available from reception. It is possible to visit markets in local villages on five days of the week.

Two clean and well equipped central toilet blocks, one heated, have good facilities for babies and disabled visitors. Washing machine, dryer. Motorhome services. Takeaway, bar/snack bar, restaurant. Bread to order. Heated swimming pool (seasonal). Large play area. Tennis. Trampolines. Fishing. Canoe hire in high season. Organised activities (July/Aug). Bicycle hire. Communal barbecues. WiFi throughout. Mobile homes to rent, one adapted for disabled visitors.

Key Features

 Book Online

 Pets Accepted

 Disabled Facilities

 Swimming Pool

 Play Area

 Bar/Restaurant

 Bike Hire

 Fishing

Scan me for more information.

Alan Rogers Code: FR15040
11 accommodations
39 pitches
GPS: 44.68137, 2.26036
Post Code: F-15600

Cantal, Auvergne

Camping Moulin de Chaules

www.alanrogers.com/fr15040
camping@moulin-de-chaules.com
Tel: +33 4 71 49 11 02
www.moulin-de-chaules.com

Open (Touring Pitches):
End April - Mid October.

This is a small, peaceful and rustic site run by an enthusiastic French family, situated in a secluded wooded valley between the Cantal and the River Lot. The wide variety of trees and shrubs offer varying amounts of shade and privacy. The 50 grassy, slightly sloping, terraced pitches (39 for touring) are naturally set out on the hillside.

The 25 lower pitches on the flatter part of the site are easily accessible and have 4/10A electricity. The steep site road to the upper levels make this site unsuitable for those with walking difficulties and the narrow approach road makes it unsuitable for large outfits.

These upper pitches are only suitable for tents and trailer tents. The attractive small bar, restaurant with takeaway food and small shop are near the reception and toilet block. A solar-heated swimming pool (seasonal) accessible by steps, games/TV room, very small sports area and play area are close by.

Key Features

 Book Online

 Pets Accepted

 Swimming Pool

 Play Area

 Bar/Restaurant

 Fishing

The main toilet block is old but clean and has been partly upgraded but access is not easy for disabled visitors. Washbasins with only cold water in curtained cabins, plus baby bath. Addition small toilet block at the top of the site. Washing machine. Small bar/restaurant with takeaway. Fresh bread daily. Small swimming pool and tiny sunbathing area. Fishing in small stream passing site. Outdoor chess. Table football. WiFi in bar area.

Scan me for more information.

Alan Rogers Code: FR07630
264 accommodations
70 pitches
GPS: 44.44470, 4.36630
Post Code: F-07120

Ardèche, Rhône Alpes

www.alanrogers.com/fr07630
contact@alunavacances.fr
Tel: +33 4 75 93 93 15
www.alunavacances.fr

Open (Touring Pitches):
Early April - Late September.

Aluna Vacances

Nestled on the doorstep of the Ardèche Gorges, surrounded by nature and outdoor pursuits of all varieties; energetic ones such as rafting, cycling and swimming, and relaxing ones like walking, picnicking and exploring nature, camping at Sunêlia Aluna Vacances has something for all the family. This leafy site prides itself on its large 'closer to nature' pitches set on grass, some with hardstanding, measuring 100 to 120 sq.m. Electricity (10A) is available and there are four sanitary blocks throughout the site.

There is rental accommodation on-site as well as a modern water park, both indoor and outdoor pools with many slides, a large restaurant with a terrace and bar, a kid's club, a grocery store and a spa. Many sports are available during the high season; football, tennis, volleyball, badminton, basketball, table tennis, jeu-de-boules, aquagym and dance, plus an outdoor fitness area.

Key Features

 Book Online

 Pets Accepted

 Disabled Facilities

 Swimming Pool

 Play Area

 Bar/Restaurant

Four sanitary blocks are equipped with showers, private washing cubicles and facilities for babies and disabled guests. Washing machines and dryers. Well stocked shop. Bar with TV. Restaurant and takeaway. Waterpark with heated outdoor pools, indoor pool and slides. Sports and kid's club (seasonal). Tennis & Volleyball court. Table tennis. Boules. Multisports field. Playground. Entertainment programmes. Some off site activities bookable on site (cycling, horse riding, canoeing). WiFi (extra charge).

Scan me for
more information.

Alan Rogers Code: FR07050
307 accommodations
50 pitches
GPS: 44.41410, 4.27290
Post Code: F-07120

Ardèche, Rhône Alpes

Le Ranc Davaine

www.alanrogers.com/fr07050
contact@rancdavaine.fr
Tel: +33 4 75 39 60 55
www.camping-ranc-davaine.fr

Open (Touring Pitches):
Mid April - Mid September.

Sunêlia Le Ranc Davaine is a large, busy, family-oriented site with direct access to the River Chassezac. There are approximately 500 pitches with 50 for touring, all with electricity (10/16A) for which very long leads are required (some may cross roads).

Most pitches are scattered between static caravan and tour operator pitches on fairly flat, stony ground under a variety of trees, some of which are quite low giving much-needed shade.

The site can get very busy for much of the season. A lively entertainment programme is aimed at young children and teenagers with an enclosed disco three nights a week until 03.00.

Sunbathing areas surround the pool complex, overlooked by the terrace of the restaurant, providing very pleasant surroundings, especially attractive with evening floodlighting.

Key Features

 Book Online

 Pets Accepted

 Disabled Facilities

 Swimming Pool

 Play Area

 Bar/Restaurant

Three fully equipped sanitary blocks, very clean and modern include facilities for people with reduced mobility. Washing machines and dryers. Large shop. Internet access. Bar/restaurant, pizzeria, takeaway. Indoor swimming pool (heated), pools for relaxation and swimming, water slide and water park (all facilities all season, no shorts allowed). Large playground. Tennis. Fishing nearby. Extensive entertainment programme (Jul/Aug). Discos. Fitness area. Free WiFi on part of the site.

Scan me for
more information.

Alan Rogers Code: FR07660
56 accommodations
GPS: 44.43415, 4.41099
Post Code: F-07150

Ardèche, Rhône Alpes

www.alanrogers.com/fr07660
contact@domaine-sevenier.fr
Tel: +33 4 75 88 29 44
www.domaine-sevenier.fr

Open (Touring Pitches):
Mid March - Start November.

Domaine de Sévenier

Le Domaine de Sévenier is a modern, high-quality chalet complex enjoying a hilltop location with fine panoramic views over the surrounding garrigue, a unique mix of oak trees, juniper, rosemary and thyme. Located 4 km. from Vallon-Pont-d'Arc and 800 m. from the pretty village of Lagorce, the domaine is an old winery that has been sensitively converted and offers accommodation in well-appointed wooden chalets serving the needs of families, both large and small.

Rest and relaxation is the theme here and the restaurant has a good reputation. On-site amenities include a swimming pool and a separate children's pool. The site has links to Nature Parc Camping de l'Ardèche and guests are welcome to enjoy the camping site's evening entertainment. The site's restaurant specialises in local cuisine using local organic produce as far as possible and features a number of fine local wines. There are no touring pitches at this site.

The sanitary block Includes hot showers and provision has been made for disabled visitors. Washing machines and a dryer. Bar/restaurant. Wine cellar. Wellness centre. Outdoor heated swimming pool. Paddling pool. Activities in July/August. Playground areas. Bicycle hire on site. Fully equipped chalets for rent.

Key Features

 Pets Accepted

 Disabled Facilities

 Swimming Pool

 Play Area

 Bar/Restaurant

 Bike Hire

Scan me for more information.

Alan Rogers Code: FR07120
24 accommodations
225 pitches
GPS: 44.39804, 4.39878
Post Code: F-07150

Ardèche, Rhône Alpes

www.alanrogers.com/fr07120
info@ardechois-camping.com
Tel: +33 4 75 88 06 63
www.ardechois-camping.com

Open (Touring Pitches):
Early April - Mid October.

Nature Parc l'Ardéchois

Camping Nature Parc l'Ardéchois is a very high quality, family-run site within walking distance of Vallon-Pont-d'Arc. It borders the River Ardèche and canoe trips are run, professionally, direct from the site. This campsite is ideal for families with younger children seeking an active holiday.

The facilities are comprehensive and the central toilet unit is of an extremely high standard. Of the 250 pitches, there are 225 for touring units, separated by trees and individual shrubs. All have electrical connections (6/10A) and with an additional charge, 125 larger pitches have full services (22 include a fridge, patio furniture, hammock and free WiFi). Forming a focal point are the bar and restaurant (excellent menus) with an attractive terrace and a takeaway service. A member of Leading Campings group.

Two very well equipped toilet blocks, one superb with everything working automatically. Facilities are of the highest standard, very clean and include good facilities for babies, children and disabled visitors. Laundry facilities. Four private bathrooms to hire. Well stocked shop. Excellent restaurant, bar and takeaway. Heated swimming pool and paddling pool (no Bermuda shorts). Wellness area with sauna, hammam, jacuzzi and 4 seasons-shower. Different types of massage and treatments. Yoga. Gym. Tennis. Very good play area. Organised activities, canoe trips. Bicycle hire. Only gas barbecues are permitted. Communal barbecue area. WiFi throughout (charged).

Key Features

 Pets Accepted

 Disabled Facilities

 Swimming Pool

 Play Area

 Bar/Restaurant

 Bike Hire

 Fishing

Scan me for more information.

Alan Rogers Code: FR69020
29 accommodations
60 pitches
GPS: 46.18790, 4.69916
Post Code: F-69820

Rhône, Rhône Alpes

www.alanrogers.com/fr69020
info@beaujolais-camping.com
Tel: +33 4 74 69 80 07
www.beaujolais-camping.com

Open (Touring Pitches):
Mid April - Early October.

La Grappe Fleurie

With easy access from both the A6 autoroute and the N6, this attractive and welcoming site is situated in the heart of Beaujolais. It is perfect for overnight stops and equally inviting for longer stays to explore the vineyards and historic attractions of the region. Virtually surrounded by vineyards, but within walking distance (within 1 km) of the pretty village of Fleurie.

This popular site has 60 generous, grassy and fairly level touring pitches with individual access to water, drainage and electricity connections (10A). Wine tasting on site is arranged twice weekly in the high season. Restaurant and shopping facilities are available in the village. Skillfully terraced so that you would hardly notice, the site is very well looked after by its friendly English-speaking owners.

Two modern sanitary blocks provide more than ample facilities. Facilities for disabled visitors. Washing machine and dryer. Fridge. Bread to order. Snack bar with homemade pizza (May-Sept). Covered and heated swimming pool (15x7 m). Playground. Tennis court. Large TV/games room. Pétanque. Free Wine tasting (Tue. & Fri). Only gas barbecues are allowed. Accommodation to rent. Free WiFi.

Key Features

 Book Online

 Pets Accepted

 Disabled Facilities

 Swimming Pool

 Play Area

Scan me for more information.

Alan Rogers Code: FR26500
29 accommodations
31 pitches
GPS: 45.27130, 5.10156
Post Code: F-26530

Drôme, Rhône Alpes

www.alanrogers.com/fr26500
contact@campingdrome.fr
Tel: +33 4 75 68 86 14
www.campingdrome.net

Open (Touring Pitches):
Mid April – Late September.

Camping du Grand Cerf

Le Grand Cerf is a small, rural, former municipal site situated in the Rhone valley between the Ardeche and the Isere. It was purchased by the present owners, Cécile and Laurent, who both speak good English and provide a warm welcome.

Of the 60 terraced pitches, 31 are available for tourers, some with electricity (6/10A). A handful are fully serviced. Most pitches are hedged and shaded by mature trees and a little uneven. Many are sloping, so levelling is necessary. There are six flat open pitches without electricity. The bar/restaurant is welcoming, with a wood-burning fire and comfortable seating in addition to the eating area.

There is much to explore in the region; a ten-minute drive will take you to Hauterives, which has shops, restaurants and a weekly market.

The sanitary block has roomy preset showers and some washbasins in cubicles. One washing machine and three sinks (cold water). Shop. Bar/restaurant and takeaway (all season). Heated outdoor pool and paddling pool (seasonal). Tennis. Basketball. Mini football. Pétanque. Play area. Bicycle hire. WiFi.

Key Features

 Book Online

 Pets Accepted

 Disabled Facilities

 Swimming Pool

 Play Area

 Bar/Restaurant

 Bike Hire

Scan me for more information.

Alan Rogers Code: FR38250
23 accommodations
74 pitches
GPS: 45.10320, 5.29263
Post Code: F-38160

Isère, Rhône Alpes

www.alanrogers.com/fr38250
contact@camping-lac-marandan.
com
Tel: +33 4 76 64 41 77
www.camping-lac-vercors.com

Open (Touring Pitches):
End April - Mid September.

Camping Lac du Marandan

Flower Camping Lac du Marandan is ideally situated at the foot of the regional park of the Vercors. It has direct access to an inviting lake which has a temperature of 28 degrees at its shallowest point and is surrounded by a fine sandy beach. The resident manager will make sure you enjoy your stay.

The site has 100 pitches (74 for touring, all with 10A electricity) from 100-200 sq.m. in size and located in a wooded area where old oaks will provide shade. Many activities are possible around the lake and the area itself also offers a rich variety of sporting activities and sightseeing.

The village of Saint Romans boasts a fine heritage with a chapel, a castle and a farm, all dating from the 18th century.

One modern sanitary block has hot showers and excellent facilities for disabled visitors and children. Washing machine. Shop. Bar/restaurant (all season). Tennis courts. Boules court. Playground. Canoe hire. Fishing. Accommodation to rent. WiFi (charged).

Key Features

 Book Online

 Pets Accepted

 Disabled Facilities

 Play Area

 Bar/Restaurant

 Fishing

Scan me for more information.

Alan Rogers Code:
252 accommodations
618 pitches
GPS: 45.22372, -1.16318
Post Code: F-33990

Gironde, Aquitaine

www.alanrogers.com/fr33110
info@cca33.com
Tel: +33 5 56 09 10 25
www.cca33.com

Open (Touring Pitches):
Mid May - Mid September.

La Côte d'Argent

Camping de la Côte d'Argent is a large, well-equipped site for leisurely family holidays. It makes an ideal base for walkers and cyclists with over 100 km. of cycle lanes in the area. Hourtin-Plage is a pleasant invigorating resort on the Atlantic coast and a popular location for watersports enthusiasts.

The site's top attraction is its pool complex, where wooden bridges connect the pools and islands and there are sunbathing and play areas plus an indoor heated pool. The site has 618 touring pitches (all with 10A electricity), not always clearly defined, arranged under trees with some on sand. High-quality entertainment takes place at the impressive bar/restaurant near the entrance.

Spread over 20 hectares of undulating sand-based terrain and in the midst of a pine forest, the site is well organised and ideal for children.

Key Features

 Pets Accepted

 Disabled Facilities

 Beach Access

 Swimming Pool

 Play Area

 Bar/Restaurant

 Bike Hire

Very clean sanitary blocks include provision for disabled visitors. Washing machines. Motorhome services. Grocery store, restaurant, takeaway, pizzeria and bar. Four outdoor pools with slides and flumes (seasonal). Indoor pool (all season). Fitness room. Massage (Institut de Beauté). Tennis. Multisport area. Beach volleyball. Pétanque. Play areas. Miniclub, fitness and organised entertainment in high season. Bicycle hire (adults only). WiFi partial site (charged). Charcoal barbecues are not permitted (gaz barbecue rental on-site). Hotel (12 rooms).

Scan me for
more information.

Camping — Côte d'Argent
★★★★★

HOURTIN PLAGE

...uated 300 m from the beach
...d 4 km from the largest natural lake in France.
...out 5000m² of water park, fully heated.
...er 100km of bike paths from the campsite.

...3990 HOURTIN-PLAGE - **Tél : +33 (0)5 56 09 10 25** - info@cca33.com

www.camping-cote-dargent.com

Airotel camping

Alan Rogers Code: FR33420
54 accommodations
40 pitches
GPS: 44.77792, -1.14280
Post Code: F-33740

Gironde, Aquitaine

www.alanrogers.com/fr33420
info@lacanadienne.com
Tel: +33 5 56 60 24 91
www.lacanadienne.com

Open (Touring Pitches):
Start March - Mid November.

Camping la Canadienne

Flower Camping La Canadienne, situated between Arcachon and Lège-Cap-Ferret, just 7 km. from the beach and 1 km. from the centre of Arès, is a pleasant little resort. There is direct access to 150 km. of cycle tracks. The campsite has 37 mobile homes for rent and 40 touring pitches, all with 15A electricity.

Good shade is provided by tall oak trees. Swimming and paddling pools are centrally located, along with a shop, bar, restaurant and snack bar. In July and August, dancing, musical and paella evenings are organised, together with children's clubs (3-10 yrs) and sports tournaments. Large units may have difficulty manoeuvring onto some pitches.

La Canadienne's pool is in the shape of a boat and is pleasantly surrounded by wooden decking and straw parasols. The village centre is 1 km. away.

Modern, well designed sanitary building. Shop, bar, restaurant, snack bar and takeaway (July/Aug). Heated outdoor swimming pool (seasonal). Play area. Bicycle hire. TV room. Activity and entertainment programme. Mobile homes and equipped tents for rent. Solarium. Only gas or electric barbecues permitted on pitches. Communal barbecue area. WiFi near bar (free).

Key Features

 Book Online

 Pets Accepted

 Disabled Facilities

 Beach Access

 Swimming Pool

 Play Area

 Bar/Restaurant

 Bike Hire

Scan me for more information.

Alan Rogers Code: FR24340
38 accommodations
62 pitches
GPS: 44.90651, 0.97433
Post Code: F-24260

Dordogne, Aquitaine

www.alanrogers.com/fr24340
contact@levaldelamarquise.com
Tel: +33 5 53 54 74 10
camping-dordogne-marquise.com

Open (Touring Pitches):
Mid April - End September.

Camping le Val de la Marquise

This well kept little campsite, between Le Bugue and Les Eyzies, is an ideal base to explore the châteaux and prehistoric sites of the Périgord region. Around 100 pitches (62 for touring, all with 15A electricity) are flat, grassy and all of a good size.

The pitches are divided by shrubs and some have shade from mature trees, whilst others are more open. Reception stocks a range of basic groceries including bread and croissants made freshly on site every morning. The site retains a relaxed peaceful air and is an ideal retreat after a busy day of sightseeing in the area.

Food and wine tastings take place in the high season where local producers bring their products for tasting and to sell. The proximity of the main road to the site should not cause a problem as it is not a major route.

Clean toilet block provides first-rate facilities. Baby bath. Smaller block near reception houses good facilities for disabled visitors. Washing and drying machines. Shop, good bar, takeaway (July/Aug). Swimming pool (heated seasonal), sun terrace, paddling pool. WiFi (charged high season). Small fishing lake. Bicycle and go-kart hire. Communal barbecue.

Key Features

 Book Online

 Pets Accepted

 Disabled Facilities

 Swimming Pool

 Play Area

 Bar/Restaurant

 Bike Hire

 Fishing

Scan me for more information.

Alan Rogers Code: FR24810
56 accommodations
37 pitches
GPS: 44.82298, 0.86040
Post Code: F-24480

Dordogne, Aquitaine

www.alanrogers.com/fr24810
fromengal@domaine-fromengal.com
Tel: +33 5 53 63 11 55
www.domaine-fromengal.com

Open (Touring Pitches):
Mid April - End September.

Domaine de Fromengal

Fromengal is a good quality site in the Périgord Noir. Set in over 22 acres, it was formerly an ancient farm and now offers a relaxed family atmosphere amid a calm, tranquil and natural setting. There is abundant vegetation. The pitches are of a good size, separated by shrubs and hedging with a mixture of sunshine and shade.

There are 93 pitches, 37 for touring units, all with 6A Europlug (ten also with water and drainage). The remaining pitches are used for chalets and mobile homes to rent.

There is a good range of modern amenities, notably a fine heated swimming pool and a restaurant built in the local style and serving food from the area. During the peak season there is an entertainment and activity programme.

The single heated sanitary block includes washbasins in cabins, baby room and facilities for disabled visitors. Washing machine and dryer. Bar, takeaway and shop (July-Aug), restaurant (June-Sept). Swimming pools (one heated) and slides (seaonal). Pétanque. BMX circuit. Play area. Entertainment programme. Children's club. Library. Bicycle hire. Tennis, archery and quad bikes for children (charged). WiFi throughout (charged). Only charcoal and gas barbecues are permitted.

Key Features

 Book Online

 Pets Accepted

 Disabled Facilities

 Swimming Pool

 Play Area

 Bar/Restaurant

 Bike Hire

Scan me for more information.

Alan Rogers Code: FR40060
129 accommodations
356 pitches
GPS: 43.95166, -1.35212
Post Code: F-40560

Landes, Aquitaine

www.alanrogers.com/fr40060
contact@camping-eurosol.com
Tel: +33 5 58 47 90 14
www.camping-eurosol.com

Open (Touring Pitches):
Mid May - Mid September.

Camping Club Eurosol

Privately owned, Camping Club International Eurosol is an attractive, friendly and well-maintained site extending over 15 hectares of undulating ground, amongst mature pine trees giving good shade. Of the 356 touring pitches, 232 have electricity (10A) with 120 fully serviced. A wide range of mobile homes and chalets are available for rent.

This is very much a family site with multi-lingual entertainers. Many games and tournaments are organised and a beach volleyball competition is held regularly in front of the bar. The adjacent boules terrain is floodlit. An excellent sandy beach 700 metres from the site has supervised bathing in the high season and is ideal for surfing. The landscaped swimming pool complex is impressive with three large pools, one of which is covered and heated, and a large children's paddling pool.

Four main toilet blocks and two smaller blocks are comfortable and clean with facilities for babies and disabled visitors. Motorhome services. Fridge rental. Well stocked shop and bar (all season). Restaurant, takeaway (seasonal). Stage for live shows arranged in July/Aug. Outdoor swimming pool, paddling pool (all season) and heated, covered pool (May-July). Tennis. Multisports court. Bicycle hire. WiFi (charged). Charcoal barbecues are not permitted.

Key Features

 Pets Accepted

 Disabled Facilities

 Beach Access

 Swimming Pool

 Play Area

 Bar/Restaurant

 Bike Hire

Scan me for more information.

Alan Rogers Code: FR40200
380 accommodations
234 pitches
GPS: 43.59570, -1.45638
Post Code: F-40530

Landes, Aquitaine

Yelloh! Village le Sylvamar

www.alanrogers.com/fr40200
info@yellohvillage-sylvamar.com
Tel: +33 5 59 45 75 16
www.camping-sylvamar.com

Open (Touring Pitches):
Early April - Late October.

Yelloh! Village le Sylvamar is less than a kilometre from a long sandy beach, this campsite has a good mix of tidy, well-maintained chalets, mobile homes, a treehouse and touring pitches. The 234 touring pitches (614 in total) are level, numbered and mostly separated by low hedges. All have electricity (16A), water and drainage, some new pitches have private sanitary facilities and premium pitches with a pergola are available.

Pitches are set around a superb pool complex with pools of various sizes (one heated, one not) with a large one for paddling, a wild water river, toboggans and slides and a spectacular volcano. In a sunny setting, all are surrounded by ample sunbathing terraces and overlooked by the excellent bar/restaurant. An 800 seat amphitheatre hosts entertainment. A member of the Leading Campings group.

Key Features

 Pets Accepted

 Disabled Facilities

 Beach Access

 Swimming Pool

 Play Area

 Bar/Restaurant

 Bike Hire

Four modern toilet blocks have washbasins in cabins. Excellent facilities for babies and disabled visitors. Laundry. Fridge hire. Shop, bar/restaurant and takeaway. Swimming pool complex. Play area. Games room. Cinema, TV and video room. Fitness centre. Wellness amenities. Tennis. Football pitch. Bicycle hire. Library. Extensive entertainment programme for all ages. WiFi over site (charged). No charcoal barbecues.

Scan me for more information.

Alan Rogers Code: FR65010
26 accommodations
83 pitches
GPS: 43.26466, 0.52119
Post Code: F-65230

Hautes-Pyrénées, Midi-Pyrénées

www.alanrogers.com/fr65010
info@leglantiere.com
Tel: +33 5 62 39 88 00
www.leglantiere.com

Open (Touring Pitches):
Early April - Mid October.

Domaine l'Eglantière

A delightful naturist site with an air of calm and repose, l'Eglantière is set within 50 hectares of organic farmland and woodland for walking and is a nature lovers' paradise. The fast-flowing River Gers runs through the site, bringing opportunities for watersports and fishing.

Pitches are large and naturally shaped, most have electricity (16A, long leads). Many are separated by wildflowers, grasses and trees, ensuring shade and privacy. There is a separate wild area for tents. The clubhouse bar, restaurant and terrace have an extremely pleasing ambience overlooking the attractive swimming pool area where nudity is compulsory. The owners are welcoming and keen to promote visitors' enjoyment of the area.

Recently renovated sanitary blocks, providing covered, open plan facilities. All blocks have individual cubicles. Motorhome services. Organic produce shop (June-Aug). Clubhouse, bar (all season). Restaurant (seasonal). Takeaway food (all season). Heated swimming pool (all season). Soundproofed activities/disco area, playroom for younger children. Play area. Children's entertainment (in season). Volleyball. Badminton. Pétanque. Archery. River activities. Canoe, mountain bike hire. Trekking. Barbecues allowed. WiFi in bar and reception areas.

Key Features

 Book Online

 Naturist Site

 Pets Accepted

 Disabled Facilities

 Swimming Pool

 Play Area

 Bar/Restaurant

 Bike Hire

Scan me for more information.

Alan Rogers Code: FR32220
6 accommodations
34 pitches
GPS: 43.57720, 0.29110
Post Code: F-32320

Gers, Midi-Pyrénées

www.alanrogers.com/fr32220
campinglesileo.gers@gmail.com
Tel: +33 5 62 63 06 96
www.camping-anjou.com

Open (Touring Pitches):
Start April - End September.

Camping Le Siléo

Previously known as Camping l'Anjou, Camping Le Siléo is a very small, quiet, rural site set in a lesser-known area of the Midi Pyrénées to the west of Auch, halfway between the small villages of Montesquiou and Bassoues. You will receive a warm welcome from the friendly owner. The site has rural views over the surrounding countryside and is open from May to September.

There are 40 small to medium size, level grass pitches with 34 for touring and electricity (6A) is available. The shrubs and trees around the pitches offer some privacy and varying amounts of shade. In July and August, there is a small modernised bar with a shaded terrace, a snack bar and fresh bread is available to order.

This site has little in the way of organised entertainment and is ideal for those seeking a relaxing and stress-free holiday. There is a small garden with a play area for children to enjoy. Access on-site may be difficult for large outfits. Gas and charcoal barbecues are permitted.

Excellent toilet blocks with all necessary facilities including room for babies and campers with disabilities. Washing machine/dryer. Bar with terrace, snack bar and bread to order (seasonal). Small outdoor swimming pool with sunbathing terrace (July/Aug). Shaded garden with play area. Communal barbecue. Small farm. Boules. WiFi in one area (free).

Key Features

 Book Online

 Pets Accepted

 Disabled Facilities

Scan me for more information.

Alan Rogers Code: FR12430
20 accommodations
90 pitches
GPS: 44.19789, 3.19404
Post Code: F-12720

Aveyron, Midi-Pyrénées

www.alanrogers.com/fr12430
lesbordsdutarn@orange.fr
Tel: +33 5 65 62 62 94
www.campinglesbordsdutarn.com

Open (Touring Pitches):
Mid June - Early September.

Camping les Bords du Tarn

As its name suggests, this site is located deep within the spectacular Tarn gorges, close to the pretty village of Mostuéjouls. There are 110 spacious and shady pitches here, some of which enjoy river frontage. Most of the 90 touring pitches have 10A electrical connections.

Site facilities include a swimming pool and children's play area, as well as a private river beach. The Tarn gorges are always a popular choice for adventure sports and the site is a good base for canoeing, walking, rock climbing and canyoning. Canoe trips can be booked on-site.

Mostuéjouls is a delightful village lying at the confluence of the Tarn and the Jonte. There are a number of restaurants and cafés along its narrow streets. There is a great deal to see in the area.

The sanitary block is equipped with modern facilities including provision for disabled visitors. Small laundry. Motorhome services. Shop and bar (all season). Snacks and restaurant (July/Aug). Games room. Heated, outdoor swimming pool. Small play area. Volleyball. Boules. Fishing. Boat launching. Canoe hire. Activity and entertainment programme. Direct access to river. Mobile homes and caravans to rent. Electric barbecues are not permitted. Free WiFi throughout.

Key Features

 Book Online

 Disabled Facilities

 Swimming Pool

 Play Area

 Bar/Restaurant

 Fishing

 Scan me for more information.

Alan Rogers Code: FR12410
28 accommodations
105 pitches
GPS: 44.09984, 3.11167
Post Code: F-12100

Aveyron, Midi-Pyrénées

www.alanrogers.com/fr12410
contact@campingsaintlambert.fr
Tel: +33 5 65 60 00 48
www.camping-millau-riviere.fr

Open (Touring Pitches):
Late April - Mid September.

Camping Saint-Lambert

Camping Saint-Lambert is located at the entrance of the Gorges du Tarn, between the Grands Causses and the Cévennes, and 2.5 km. from the centre of Millau. The site has a private beach on the shady banks of the river Dourbie. The river is not fenced and was fast flowing when we visited. There are 133 pitches here, 105 of which are for touring, generally of a good size and generally well shaded. Most have electrical connections.

A number of pitches are occupied by mobile homes, bungalow style tents and caravans, available to rent. Leisure amenities include a swimming pool and children's play area. There is a small bar/snack bar and also a well stocked shop.

The Tarn Gorges are well known for the great wealth of adventure sports on offer. These include canoeing, canyoning, rock climbing and potholing.

Sanitary block with showers. Facilities for disabled visitors and easy access to bar, terrace and pool. Motorhome services. Small laundry. Shop. Bar/snack bar, takeaway (July/Aug). Swimming pool. Minigolf. Games room. Play area. Bicycle hire. Activities and entertainment. Direct river access. Fishing. Mobile homes and equipped tents to rent. Electric barbecues are not permitted. WiFi (free on part of site).

Key Features

 Book Online

 Pets Accepted

 Disabled Facilities

 Swimming Pool

 Play Area

 Bar/Restaurant

 Bike Hire

 Fishing

Scan me for
more information.

Alan Rogers Code: FR46150
22 accommodations
83 pitches
GPS: 44.44855, 1.67455
Post Code: F-46330

Lot, Midi-Pyrénées

www.alanrogers.com/fr46150
contact@camping-truffiere.com
Tel: +33 5 65 30 20 22
camping-truffiere.com

Open (Touring Pitches):
Early April - End September.

Camping la Truffière

This site is set in four hectares of mature oak woodland within the Parc Naturel Régional des Causses de Quercy with stunning natural scenery and only 2.5 km. from the clifftop village of Saint Cirq-Lapopie. La Truffière is well suited to those seeking a peaceful countryside holiday and it is a superb area for hiking.

Around 80 slightly sloping, terraced pitches are of varying sizes and on a mixture of grass and gravel. All have 6A electricity (long leads may be needed) and most have shade from mature trees. Access is good for large outfits but advanced booking is recommended.

In high season the campsite owners organise a range of activities including guided walks, château visits, sports tournaments and daily children's entertainment (not always in English). There are various walks and mountain bike trails in the area.

Two well-appointed, clean, modern toilet blocks (one heated) include facilities for disabled visitors. Motorhome services. Fridge hire. Small shop (open all season). Bar/restaurant (seasonal), terrace overlooking pool and playing field. Takeaway (seasonal). Swimming pool, paddling pool, sun terrace (seasonal). Playing field, volleyball, basketball, football. Adventure-style play area. Trampolines. Boules. English spoken. Gas and electric barbecues only on pitches (3 communal areas). WiFi near the bar.

Key Features

 Book Online

 Pets Accepted

 Disabled Facilities

 Swimming Pool

 Play Area

 Bar/Restaurant

 Scan me for more information.

Alan Rogers Code: FR46190
37 accommodations
54 pitches
GPS: 44.69197, 1.53461
Post Code: F-46240

Lot, Midi-Pyrénées

www.alanrogers.com/fr46190
contact@camping-lafaurie.com
Tel: +33 5 65 21 14 36
www.camping-lafaurie.com

Open (Touring Pitches):
Early April - Late September.

Domaine de la Faurie

A stunning array of tended shrubs and thoughtful flower planting is spread throughout this very pretty seven-hectare site, which is located on a hilltop with wide-open views of the surrounding hills and valleys. Although hidden away, it is an excellent base for exploring the Lot and Dordogne regions.

The site is separated into two distinct areas, an open, lightly shaded front section and a much more densely shaded area with tall pine trees all around the pitches.

The 54 touring pitches, with 6/10A electricity, are large and most are at least 100 sq.m. A small number also have water and drainage. There are also 37 mobile homes, chalets and tents for hire. The friendly French owners, Clotilde and Christophe will tell you that they consider the site their personal garden.

The two sanitary blocks are clean and well maintained. Facilities for children and disabled visitors. Washing machine. Motorhome services. Excellent gift shop selling regional and local produce (bread available), bar, restaurant and takeaway, swimming pool and paddling pool (all open all season). TV and games rooms. Boules. Play area. Small library. Weekly soirées in high season. Charcoal barbecues are not permitted. Free WiFi over part of site. Max. 2 small dogs.

Key Features

 Book Online

 Pets Accepted

 Disabled Facilities

 Swimming Pool

 Play Area

 Bar/Restaurant

Scan me for more information.

163

Alan Rogers Code: FR82020
10 accommodations
34 pitches
GPS: 44.18271, 1.60510
Post Code: F-82240

Tarn-et-Garonne, Midi-Pyrénées

www.alanrogers.com/fr82020
info@campingdeboisredon.com
Tel: +33 5 63 64 92 49
www.campingdeboisredon.com

Open (Touring Pitches):
All year.

Camping de Bois Redon

Charlotte and Hans de Bruin welcome their guests at Bois Redon, which is situated away from the hustle and bustle of everyday life. The 34 touring pitches are level and grassy, each with electricity (10A), and most are shaded. On-site activities include boules, basketball, volleyball and badminton, and close by you can go fishing, canoeing, climbing or caving.

Snacks and fresh drinks are available on-site - or in any of the charming local villages. In spring, orchids are mostly in bloom. Just 6 km. away is the artisan town of Saint Antonin-Noble-Val which dates back to the eighth century.

You can enjoy the relaxed nature of the site, take a stroll in the immediate area, cool off in the pool, or just read a book while the children play safely in the playground.

Centrally located heated sanitary block with showers and basic facilities for disabled visitors. Snack bar/takeaway (June-end Aug). Bread to order. Outdoor swimming pool (mid June-15/9). Play area. Sports pitch. Basketball. Volleyball. Badminton. Communal barbecue. Free WiFi. Tents and bungalows for hire. Guided walks and boules evenings.

Key Features

 Open All Year

 Pets Accepted

 Disabled Facilities

 Swimming Pool

 Play Area

 Bar/Restaurant

Scan me for more information.

Alan Rogers Code: FR09170
21 accommodations
46 pitches
GPS: 42.99762, 1.87201
Post Code: F-09600

Ariège, Midi-Pyrénées

www.alanrogers.com/fr09170
contact@camping-la-serre.com
Tel: +33 5 61 03 06 16
www.camping-la-serre.com

Open (Touring Pitches):
Mid March - Late October.

Camping la Serre

A beautiful site set in ten hectares of gentle hillside and run by Corinne and Patrick, a hardworking and very friendly French couple. There are 67 spacious pitches, 46 for touring, all with electricity (5/10A). Most are on well drained grass with shade and privacy, some are on hardstanding and there is additional hardstanding for motorhomes in wet weather.

There is a small, friendly bar and the site takes pride in not having a disco or karaoke, but preferring to enjoy and respect nature – there are superb views towards the Pyrenees. A range of well-specified chalets are available for hire. There is a marked nature trail passing through a classified nature reserve with birds, butterflies and fields of orchids.

Two main modern sanitary blocks and one small block. Good facilities for disabled campers. Child sized toilets, Baby room. Family shower rooms. Washing machines and dryers. Motorhome services. Bar, takeaway and outdoor swimming pool (July/Aug). Tennis. Volleyball. Pétanque. Mountain bike track. Extensive play area. Observation telescope. Small film theatre. Farming museum. Bicycle hire. Free WiFi over part of site. Telephone kiosk. Nature trail. Orchid and butterfly fields.

Key Features

 Book Online

 Pets Accepted

 Disabled Facilities

 Swimming Pool

 Play Area

 Bar/Restaurant

 Scan me for more information.

Alan Rogers Code: FR30030
102 accommodations
47 pitches
GPS: 43.52250, 4.14910
Post Code: F-30240

Gard, Languedoc-Roussillon

www.alanrogers.com/fr30030
contact@abridecamargue.fr
Tel: +33 4 66 51 54 83
www.abridecamargue.fr

Open (Touring Pitches):
Early April - End September.

Camping Abri de Camargue

Abri de Camargue is a well-established family site within easy reach of beaches and the town of Le Grau-du-Roi. The welcoming pool area is overlooked by the bar with a pleasant sheltered terrace, and the larger outdoor pool has surrounds for sunbathing. The smaller indoor pool is heated.

With 277 level and hedged pitches, there are 47 for touring units (mainly of 100 sq.m), 102 mobile homes or chalets to rent and the remainder are privately owned. Electricity (6A) and water are available on most, and the pitches are well maintained and shaded, with trees and flowering shrubs, quite luxuriant in parts. An air-conditioned cinema shows french films, there is also an excellent play area and a multisports court.

Three toilet blocks are modern and bright. Facilities for disabled visitors. Washing machines. Motorhome services. Shop. Bar with TV. Restaurant and takeaway. Heated indoor pool, outdoor pool and paddling pool. New multisports court. Outdoor fitness room. Cinema (air-conditioned). High-quality play area. Bicycle hire. Entertainment programme and children's club (high season). Pétanque. Music room for young visitors in high season. WiFi throughout (charged) and free at the restaurant. Site access card (deposit € 15).

Key Features

 Book Online

 Pets Accepted

 Disabled Facilities

 Beach Access

 Swimming Pool

 Play Area

 Bar/Restaurant

 Bike Hire

Scan me for more information.

Alan Rogers Code: FR30290
82 accommodations
120 pitches
GPS: 43.76579, 4.09743
Post Code: F-30250

Gard, Languedoc-Roussillon

www.alanrogers.com/fr30290
camping@massereau.com
Tel: +33 4 66 53 11 20
www.massereau.com

Open (Touring Pitches):
Mid April - Early October.

Domaine de Massereau

Two brothers, one a wine producer and one an hotelier, opened Domaine de Massereau in August 2006. It is set within a 50-hectare vineyard dating back to 1804, and the idea was to promote their wine, so tours are arranged and they now produce their own olive oil as well.

There are 202 pitches, with 120 available for touring units, all with electricity (86 with 16A electricity, water and drainage). Pitch sizes range from 90-300 sq.m. and some are equipped with a premium option including a fridge, a plancha, a wooden storage box, deckchairs, a picnic table and unlimited wifi access. The area is lightly wooded and most pitches are hedged with flowering shrubs. The other pitches are used for chalets, cottages, cabins and mobile homes to rent.

Two modern toilet block incorporates excellent facilities for children and disabled visitors. Laundry area. Motorhome services. Grocery. Restaurant, bar, snacks and pizzeria. Aquatic Park with heated swimming pool with removable dome and slide. Balneotherapy Pool, Aquatic Playground, Solarium, Jacuzzi, Sauna, Steam Bath and massage. Play area with trampoline, mini golf, tennis court, Multisport field, pétanque. Bicycle hire. Gas barbecue and fridge hire. Free WiFi (partial site)

Key Features

 Pets Accepted

 Disabled Facilities

 Beach Access

 Swimming Pool

 Play Area

 Bar/Restaurant

 Bike Hire

 Horse Riding

Scan me for more information.

Alan Rogers Code: FR34070
591 accommodations
1025 pitches
GPS: 43.26340, 3.32000
Post Code: F-34410

Hérault, Languedoc-Roussillon

www.alanrogers.com/fr34070
info@leserignanplage.com
Tel: +33 4 67 32 35 33
www.leserignanplage.com

Open (Touring Pitches):
Mid May - Late September.

Le Sérignan-Plage

Yelloh! Village le Sérignan-Plage is a lively and vibrant site with direct access onto a superb 600 m. sandy beach (including a naturist section), plus two swimming pool complexes and an indoor pool - this is a must for a Mediterranean holiday. It is a busy, friendly, family orientated site with a very comprehensive range of amenities and activities for children.

There are over 1,000 pitches for touring units, which are fairly level, on sandy soil and all have 10A electricity. The collection of spa pools (balnéo) built in Romanesque style with colourful terracing and columns is overlooked by a very smart restaurant, Le Villa, available to use in the afternoons (used by the adjacent naturist site in the mornings).

Seven modern individually designed sanitary blocks with good amenities including showers with WC and washbasins. Facilities for people with reduced mobility. Baby bathroom. Automatic laundromat. Motorhome services. Supermarket, bakery and newsagent. Other shops (2/6-14/9). ATM. Restaurants, bars and takeaway. Hairdresser. Balnéo spa (afternoons). Gym. Indoor heated pool. Outdoor pools, water playground and waterslides (all season). Tennis court. Multisport courts. Playgrounds. Trampolines. Children's clubs. Evening entertainment. Sporting activities. Bike rental. Bus to Sérignan village (Jul/Aug). Beach (lifeguards high season). WiFi on-site (charged). gas barbecues only.

Key Features

 Book Online

 Pets Accepted

 Disabled Facilities

 Beach Access

 Swimming Pool

 Play Area

 Bar/Restaurant

 Bike Hire

Scan me for more information.

Alan Rogers Code: FR11130
300 accommodations
400 pitches
GPS: 43.14368, 3.14471
Post Code: F-11100

Aude, Languedoc-Roussillon

www.alanrogers.com/fr11130
cote-des-roses@campeole.com
Tel: +33 4 68 49 83 65
ms-vacances.com/camping-campeole/camping-la-cote-des-roses/decouvrir-le-camping

Open (Touring Pitches):
End March - End September.

La Côte des Roses

This large site, located between Gruisson and Narbonne Plage, on the edge of a vast sandy beach, is now owned by the Campéole group. There are over 700 pitches with 90 safari style tents and over 300 mobile homes and chalets that vary in style. The 400 touring pitches are well spaced out amongst the sort of trees and shrubs which grow near the beach, providing varying degrees of shade. Pitches are on sandy grass with 6A electricity.

A shop, bar and snack bar provide pizzas and other snacks in the main season, and there are some musical evenings in July and August. A pool complex has been added to the site which includes a special area for children.

The colourful renovated toilet blocks are fully equipped with some en-suite showers and washbasins. Attractive provision for children and babies and facilities for disabled visitors. Washing machines. Motorhome services. Shop, bar, restaurant (high season). Swimming pool complex (seasonal). Multisports court. Play area. Communal barbecue. WiFi around reception (charged).

Key Features

 Book Online

 Pets Accepted

 Disabled Facilities

 Beach Access

 Swimming Pool

 Play Area

 Bar/Restaurant

Scan me for more information.

Alan Rogers Code: FR66060
356 accommodations
62 pitches
GPS: 42.58066, 3.03324
Post Code: F-66700

Pyrénées-Orientales,
Languedoc-Roussillon

www.alanrogers.com/fr66060
littoral@sandaya.fr
Tel: +33 2 51 22 04 64
www.campinglelittoral.com

Open (Touring Pitches):
Early April - Late September.

Camping Le Littoral

Camping Sandaya Le Littoral is only 800 metres from a fine, sandy beach via a footpath. The site offers plenty of accommodation in mobile homes as well as about 60 good sized, level touring pitches with shade and 6A electricity. An attractive pool area is open all season. Argelès is a very popular holiday resort with good sandy beaches. A free shuttle bus runs to the beach and town centre in July and August. The border with Spain is only 30 km. away.

The site has been taken over by Sandaya and is looking smart with a new reception and tarmac roadways. The site is well looked after and the pool area is particularly impressive, with indoor and outdoor pools, waterslides and paddling pools.

Large modern toilet block, fully equipped and with some washbasins in cabins. Baby bath. Some facilities for disabled visitors. Washing machines. Shop, bar, restaurants and takeaway. Outdoor and covered heated swimming pools with slides (from 15/5). Solarium. Entertainment for all in high season. Only gas barbecues permitted. Play area. Fitness room. Bicycle hire. WiFi throughout (charged). Path to beach. Max. 1 dog per pitch. Free shuttle to beach and city centre (July-Aug).

Key Features

 Book Online

 Pets Accepted

 Disabled Facilities

 Beach Access

 Swimming Pool

 Play Area

 Bar/Restaurant

 Bike Hire

Scan me for more information.

Alan Rogers Code: FR66070
262 accommodations
699 pitches
GPS: 42.70830, 3.03552
Post Code: F-66141

Pyrénées-Orientales,
Languedoc-Roussillon

www.alanrogers.com/fr66070
info@lebrasilia.fr
Tel: +33 4 68 80 23 82
www.brasilia.fr

Open (Touring Pitches):
Mid April - Early October

Yelloh! Village Le Brasilia

Situated across the yacht harbour from the resort of Canet-Plage, le Brasilia is an impressive, well-managed family site directly beside the beach. The state-of-the-art reception incorporates an information centre. Although large, it is pretty, neat and well kept with an amazingly wide range of facilities – indeed, it is camping at its best.

The 699 touring pitches are neatly hedged, most with electricity (6-10A) and 408 with water and drainage. They vary in size from 80 to 120 sq.m. and some of the longer pitches are suitable for two families together. There is a variety of shade from pines and flowering shrubs, with less on pitches near the beach. A member of Yelloh! Village and Leading Campings groups.

Nine modern sanitary blocks are very well equipped and maintained, with British style WCs and washbasins in cabins. Good facilities for children and for disabled campers. Laundry room. Motorhome services. Range of shops. Gas supplies. Bars and restaurant. Renovated pool complex (heated). New wellness centre including jacuzzi, massage and beauty rooms. Play areas. Sports field. Tennis. Sporting activities. Library, games and video room. Hairdresser. Internet café and WiFi. Daily entertainment programme. Bicycle hire. Fishing. Post office. Weather forecasts. No charcoal barbecues. Free WiFi in bar.

Key Features

 Book Online

 Pets Accepted

 Disabled Facilities

 Beach Access

 Swimming Pool

 Play Area

 Bar/Restaurant

 Bike Hire

Scan me for
more information.

Alan Rogers Code: FR04220
50 accommodations
50 pitches
GPS: 43.89778, 5.80638
Post Code: F-04300

Alpes-de-Haute-Provence,
Provence

www.alanrogers.com/fr04220
camping-lariviere@orange.fr
Tel: +33 4 92 79 54 66
www.camping-lariviere.com

Open (Touring Pitches):
Early April - Mid September.

Camping la Rivière

La Rivière is a member of the Flower group and is located on the edge of the Luberon national park, bordering the river Largue. There are 100 pitches here. These are well shaded, of a good size and mostly with electrical connections (10A). A number of pitches are occupied by mobile homes and fully equipped tents, to rent.

On-site amenities include a swimming pool, fishing lake and bar/restaurant (with takeaway food). The site becomes livelier in July and August with various activities including giant board games, dance evenings and various sports competitions.

During peak season, the campsite owner organises accompanied walks to the surrounding countryside. There is over 200 km. of waymarked paths throughout the national park and riding is also popular.

Sanitary block with facilities for babies and disabled visitors. Washing machine and dryer. Small shop. Snack bar/restaurant. Takeaway (including home made pizzas). Swimming pool. Paddling pool. Massage, yoga, archery (all charged). Fishing lake. TV room. Volleyball. Football. Boules pitch. Play area. Activity and entertainment programme (July/Aug). Mobile homes and tents to rent. WiFi (charged).

Key Features

 Book Online

 Pets Accepted

 Disabled Facilities

 Beach Access

 Swimming Pool

 Play Area

 Bar/Restaurant

 Fishing

Scan me for more information.

Alan Rogers Code: FR13220
122 accommodations
50 pitches
GPS: 43.22034, 5.62878
Post Code: F-13600

Bouches du Rhône, Provence

www.alanrogers.com/fr13220
contact@campingceyreste.com
Tel: +33 4 42 83 07 68
www.campingceyreste.com

Open (Touring Pitches):
Start April - End September.

Camping de Ceyreste

Flower Camping de Ceyreste is located on the edge of an extensive pine forest in the heart of Provence, a five minute drive from the beach of La Ciotat and its beautiful bay, Le Golfe d'Amour. There are about 170 shady pitches, most terraced, of which about 50 are for touring units, all with electricity connections (6/10A), sink and water supply. The remainder are occupied by seasonal caravans and a range of mobile homes to rent.

You can head off on foot or by mountain bike into the pine-covered slopes behind the site, or by car to explore the countryside of the Bouches-du-Rhône and the varied coastline of the Mediterranean between Marseille and Toulon.

Key Features

 Book Online

 Pets Accepted

 Disabled Facilities

 Beach Access

 Swimming Pool

 Bar/Restaurant

Two sanitary blocks have hot showers, baby baths, family rooms and facilities for disabled visitors. Dog shower. Washing machine and dryer. Motorhome services. Grocery. Bar/snack bar (July/Aug). Water park (April-Sept) with heated, landscaped pool, children's pool, water slide and solarium. Boules. Minigolf. Daytime activities and evening entertainment for children and families (July-Aug). Play area. WiFi (charged). No charcoal barbecues.

Scan me for more information.

Alan Rogers Code: FR05090
15 accommodations
85 pitches
GPS: 44.65731, 6.63306
Post Code: F-05600

Hautes-Alpes, Provence

www.alanrogers.com/fr05090
camping@lesaintjames.com
Tel: +33 4 92 45 08 24
www.lesaintjames.com

Open (Touring Pitches):
All year.

Camping Saint James-les-Pins

Les Pins enjoys a natural, peaceful setting amongst tall pine trees, with views of the surrounding mountains. The 100 grass/gravel pitches (85 for touring) enjoy good shade, and all have electricity connections (6/10A). Rock pegs are advised.

Along one side of the site is a fast-flowing small river, so children will need supervising. During high season, daily sports competitions are organised and the owners are happy to arrange walking and climbing guides.

On the opposite side of the road is a multisports complex and communal barbecue. The local village, 2 km. away, has all the usual facilities including a supermarket, ATM and railway station.

Three toilet blocks with some facilities for disabled campers. Laundry and dishwashing with cold water. Small shop, takeaway (July/Aug). Games room/TV. Play area. Multisports court. Fishing. WiFi. No personal barbecues allowed.

Key Features

 Book Online

 Open All Year

 Pets Accepted

 Play Area

Scan me for
more information.

Alan Rogers Code: FR84200
24 accommodations
114 pitches
GPS: 44.38256, 4.93049
Post Code: F-84600

Vaucluse, Provence

Camping le Garrigon

www.alanrogers.com/fr84200
contact@camping-garrigon.com
Tel: +33 4 90 28 72 94
www.camping-garrigon.com

Open (Touring Pitches):
Start February - End November.

Camping le Garrigon is a maturing site, first opened in 2010. It can be found in the pleasant Provençal countryside at Grillon, one of the historical and cultural centres of the Vaucluse. There are 114 pitches here of varying sizes and surrounded by pine, mulberry and lime-blossom trees. All pitches have electricity and water.

There are 24 air-conditioned, chalet-style mobile homes available to rent with a minimum stay requirement of just two nights. On-site amenities include a large swimming pool, a twin-track water slide and a convivial bar (with TV for sports events). There are superb views all around the site across the surrounding vineyards to Mont Ventoux and the Montagnes de la Lance.

Grillon makes up a part of the Enclave des Papes, one of four towns bought by the Avignon popes in the 14th century (probably because they liked the wine so much!).

Central sanitary block is heated and has excellent, modern facilities, including those for disabled visitors. Family shower rooms. Small shop. Bar/snack bar (May-Sept). Takeaway (July/Aug). Swimming pool. Slides. Paddling pool. Play area. TV room. Mobile homes and chalets to rent. WiFi.

Key Features

 Book Online

 Pets Accepted

 Disabled Facilities

 Beach Access

 Swimming Pool

 Play Area

 Bar/Restaurant

Scan me for more information.

Alan Rogers Code: FR84080
6 accommodations
80 pitches
GPS: 44.29680, 4.78740
Post Code: F-84500

Vaucluse, Provence

www.alanrogers.com/fr84080
camping@la-simioune.fr
Tel: +33 4 90 63 17 91
www.la-simioune.fr

Open (Touring Pitches):
1 March - 30 October

La Simioune en Provence

A warm welcome awaits you at this rural site. It is a peaceful and inexpensive base, especially for those who love horses and ponies, with the small stables adjacent. Off the beaten track, it is situated amongst tall pines on sandy, undulating ground, bordered by woods.

The 80 touring pitches are of varying size and shape, most with electricity (10A). An area of woodland is set aside for those with tents. The family owners also keep some small animals with the horses; a few goats, rabbits and chickens are a delight for young visitors. The access road may be difficult for very large units.

Perfect for outdoor activities such as mountain biking, hiking and canoeing, the small welcoming bar/restaurant provides a comfortable place to relax at the end of the day.

One clean, modern sanitary block has facilities for children and a room for disabled visitors, although the site may be difficult for wheelchairs and those with mobility problems. Washing machine. Small bar, simple meals (May-Aug). Takeaway. Small unheated swimming and paddling pools. Play area. Central barbecue area. Chalets to rent. WiFi throughout (free).

Key Features

 Book Online

 Pets Accepted

 Disabled Facilities

 Swimming Pool

 Play Area

 Bar/Restaurant

 Horse Riding

Scan me for more information.

Alan Rogers Code: FR83400
190 accommodations
40 pitches
GPS: 43.26978, 6.57311
Post Code: F-83310

Var, Côte d'Azur

www.alanrogers.com/fr83400
info@holiday-marina.com
Tel: +33 4 94 56 08 43
www.holiday-marina.com

Open (Touring Pitches):
Start March - End October.

Holiday Marina Resort

Owned and operated by an English family, this site is an established favourite with British families. It is located in the busy holiday area of the Gulf of Saint Tropez. The site has a large and well-kept pool area and its own adjacent moorings for boats up to 10 meters.

Smaller than many campsites in this area, there are 230 good sized pitches of which 40 are for touring units comprising of 20 Prestige and 20 Majestic pitches. Each of these has its own spacious bathroom with a good shower, washbasin, WC and outdoor kitchen with sink and fridge. All have a hard standing area for a caravan or motorhome plus a synthetic grassed area ensuring green grass throughout the year!

Individual private bathrooms include washbasin, shower and WC, heated towel rail, hairdryer, outside kitchen sink, outside fridge, exterior power source, plus outside dishwasher (on Majestic pitches only). Facilities for disabled visitors include one fully adapted mobile home. Laundry. Shop. The main building houses a bar, restaurant, games and TV room. The restaurant has a varied and full menu, snacks and takeaway. Heated swimming and paddling pools and jacuzzi (seasonal). New salon and spa. Miniclub and evening entertainment in the main season. Adventure playground. Sports field with football, volleyball and basketball pitches. Fishing in the adjacent river. Holiday homes and Lodges for hire. Airport shuttle. WiFi. Boat mooring and school. Vehicle wash station.

Key Features

 Book Online

 Pets Accepted

 Disabled Facilities

 Beach Access

 Swimming Pool

 Play Area

 Bar/Restaurant

 Bike Hire

Scan me for
more information.

177

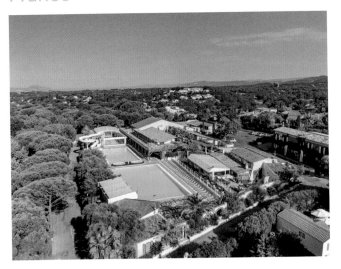

Alan Rogers Code: FR83250
350 accommodations
88 pitches
GPS: 43.44727, 6.80600
Post Code: F-83700

Var, Côte d'Azur

Douce Quiétude

www.alanrogers.com/fr83250
vacances@sandaya.fr
Tel: +33 4 94 44 30 00
www.sandaya.co.uk

Open (Touring Pitches):
Early June - Mid September

Sandaya Douce Quiétude is just a 10-minute drive from the sandy beaches at Saint Raphaël and Agay (with campsite shuttle transport) but is quietly situated at the foot of the Estérel Massif. There are around 440 pitches, 90 for touring units and 260 for fully equipped mobile homes for rent, some with air-conditioning, dishwasher and jacuzzi.

The touring pitches are set in either pleasant pine woodland or in sunny and shaded green areas. They are of a comfortable size, separated by bushes and trees with 16A electricity (Europlug), water, drainage and telephone/TV points provided. Eight have private sanitary facilities. This mature site offers a wide range of services and facilities complete with a pool complex. It can be busy in the main season yet is relaxed and spacious.

Fully equipped modern heated toilet blocks, facilities for babies and disabled visitors. Launderette. Shop, bar, restaurant and takeaway. Three swimming pools (two heated), water slide, jacuzzi. Play area. Children's club, activities for teenagers (all July/Aug). Sports area. Games room. Tennis. Minigolf. Archery. Fitness centre, sauna. Beauty salon, hairdresser and barber. Evening entertainment, shows, karaoke, discos (July/Aug). Mountain bike hire. Only gas barbecues. Shuttle bus service. WiFi throughout (charged).

Key Features

 Book Online

 Pets Accepted

 Disabled Facilities

 Beach Access

 Swimming Pool

 Play Area

 Bar/Restaurant

 Bike Hire

Scan me for more information.

Alan Rogers Code: FR83600
600 accommodations
20 pitches
GPS: 43.48563, 6.71745
Post Code: F-83600

Var, Côte d'Azur

www.alanrogers.com/fr83600
info@holidaygreen.com
Tel: +33 4 94 19 88 30
www.holidaygreen.com

Open (Touring Pitches):
Start April - End September.

Camping Holiday Green

Holiday Green is seven kilometres inland from Fréjus. It is a large, modern campsite with a fantastic view of the red massif of Esterel – very impressive as you arrive. The site has been developed on a hillside, and from the reception at the top of the hill, you look down over the large outdoor swimming pool complex, as well as a covered and heated swimming pool and water slide.

The rest of the site is terraced into the hillside and almost completely hidden in the 15 hectares of pine woods which absorb around 600 mobile homes, some 20 touring pitches and occasional sculptures. Sloping in parts, there is plenty of shade and 6/13A electricity available.

Modern, heated toilet facilities include good hot showers. Laundry. Shopping centre. Bar, restaurant, fast food. Swimming pool. Three tennis courts. Archery. Pétanque. Soundproofed disco. All open all season. Excursions on foot, on horseback and on mountain bikes (for hire) to explore the countryside. Entertainment programme of dances, concerts and festivals. Playground. Children's club (July/Aug). WiFi throughout (free). No charcoal barbecues.

Key Features

 Book Online

 Pets Accepted

 Disabled Facilities

 Beach Access

 Swimming Pool

 Play Area

 Bar/Restaurant

 Bike Hire

Scan me for more information.

Capital Berlin
Currency Euro (€)
Language German
Time Zone CET (GMT+1)
Telephone Code +49

Shops 9.30am to 8pm weekdays and Sat. All stores including supermarkets close on Sun.

Money ATMs are widespread in towns and cities and usually accessible 24 hours a day. Some have multilingual instructions. Germany is still largely cash-based, don't expect everywhere to accept cards. Amex less widely accepted.

Accessible Travel Access and assistance for wheelchair users and those who are less able is widespread.

Travelling with Children Very children-friendly with a variety of attractions. Public transport is usually half price for children. Most attractions will let under 18s in for free. Many restaurants offer a kids menu, but children are also expected to behave.

EU Travel Germany is an EU member state and located within the Schengen Area.

LEZ Low Emissions Zones in most major cities. Registration required.

●●●●● **Accessibility Score**
View our digital e-guide & find out more at
alanrogers.com/open-to-all

Tourism website | germany.travel

Public Holidays 1 Jan New Year's Day · Mar/Apr Good Friday · Mar/Apr Easter Monday · 1 May Labour Day · May Ascension · May/Jun Whit Monday · 3 Oct Day of German Unity · 25 Dec Christmas Day · 26 Dec Boxing Day · Other public holidays may be observed at a regional level. Aways check before travelling.

Driving in Germany The country's network of toll-free and well-maintained autobahns is among the best in the world. Drink-driving, using your mobile whilst driving and sat navs that warn you of speed cameras are illegal. You should overtake trams on the right unless there is not sufficient space.

Germany

View all campsites in Germany
alanrogers.com/germany

See campsite map page 479

Climate

Winters are a little colder and summers a little warmer than in the UK.

	Jan	Feb	Mar	Apr	May	Jun	Jul	Aug	Sep	Oct	Nov	Dec
High	3	5	9	14	19	22	24	24	19	14	7	4
Low	-2	-1	1	4	8	11	14	13	10	6	2	-1

With its wealth of scenic, historical and cultural interests, Germany is a land of contrasts. From the flatlands of the north to the wooded mountains in the south, with forests in the east and west, regional characteristics are a strong feature of German life and present a rich variety of folklore and customs.

Each region in Germany has its own unique identity. Home of lederhosen, beer and sausages is Bavaria in the south, with small towns, medieval castles and Baroque churches. It is also home to the fairytale 19th-century Romanesque Revival castle of Neuschwanstein. In the southwest, Baden Württemberg is famous for its ancient Black Forest and its spas and boasts the most hours of sunshine.

Further west is the stunningly beautiful Rhine Valley, where the river winds through steep hills dotted with castles, ruins and vineyards.

Eastern Germany is studded with lakes and rivers and undulating lowlands that give way to mountains. The north has busy cities such as Bremen and Hamburg as well as traditional North Sea family resorts. The capital city of Berlin, situated in the northeast of the country and once divided by the Berlin Wall, is an increasingly popular tourist destination, with its blend of old and modern architecture, zoos and aquariums, museums, art galleries, green spaces and lively nightlife.

181

Alan Rogers Code: DE25440
140 accommodations
330 pitches
GPS: 54.13880, 8.84347
Post Code: D-25761

Büsum, Schleswig-Holstein

www.alanrogers.com/de25440
info@camping-nordsee.de
Tel: +49 4834 2515
www.camping-nordsee.de

Open (Touring Pitches):
Early April - Mid October.

Campingplatz Nordsee Busum

Campingplatz Nordsee Busum campsite is in the village of Westerdeichstrich which has three districts of Butendörp, Westerdeichstrich and Stinteck. This site is great for families wanting plenty of free space. Situated in a national park and just a few steps from the green beach in Stinteck / Westerdeichstrich and the Wadden Island family lagoon of Perlebucht, Büsum. Dog walkers area on Stinteck beach. Nudists have their own beach section in the direction of Eidersperrwerk. Spacious pitches onsite, with electric, water and sewerage.

Beautiful cycling trails lead directly past the campsite to the flat Koog landscapes or along the North Sea Cycle route directly by the sea. At low tide, experience the mudflats with a guided tour arranged by the campsite. Westerdeichstrich's landmark is the historic windmill "Anna", which houses a good restaurant.

Two sanitary blocks. Disabled bathroom. Baby changing room. Easybe Dishwasher. CamperClean disposal station. E-bike rentals. Dog run and shower. Children's playground. Volleyball. Football Field. Table tennis. Bakery and shop nearby. Restaurant. WiFi, chargeable.

Key Features

 Pets Accepted

 Beach Access

 Bike Hire

Scan me for more information.

Alan Rogers Code: DE30190
160 accommodations
100 pitches
GPS: 54.50886, 9.97149
Post Code: D-24369

Waabs, Schleswig-Holstein

Ostseecamp Lehmberg

www.alanrogers.com/de30190
info@ostseecamp-lehmberg.de
Tel: +49 4358 989 3230
www.ostseecamp-lehmberg.de

Open (Touring Pitches):
Late March - Late October.

Ostseecamp Lehmberg is located in the heart of the idyllic Schwansen peninsula with stunning green landscapes and healthy Baltic Sea air. Pitches here are offered in two different sizes all with electric hook-up, there is an opportunity to pre-book a boat mooring and use of the slipway. On-site fishing lake, beach walks or a bike ride to enjoy the beautiful sunrise or sunset.

The onsite shop provides all you need, including freshly baked bread every morning. You can exchange gas bottles and purchase other camping related products. There is an onsite bistro that offers a small selection of hot and cold dishes as well as homemade cakes. Great location with various other activities to do in the area plus many small villages and towns to discover.

On site shop providing freshly baked bread, restaurant and lake fishing. Hire of paddle boards and opportunity to pre book a boat mooring. Children's play area, onsite beach, free WIFI, showers and toilet facilities with disabled access. Dogs permitted.

Key Features

 Pets Accepted

 Beach Access

 Play Area

 Fishing

Scan me for more information.

Alan Rogers Code: DE26120
20 accommodations
190 pitches
GPS: 54.14763, 10.39743
Post Code: D-24306

Plon, Schleswig-Holstein

www.alanrogers.com/de26120
info@spitzenort.de
Tel: +49 4522 2769
www.spitzenort.de

Open (Touring Pitches):
Start April - Late October.

Naturcamping Spitzen

Naturcamping Spitzen is a family run site founded in 1957. It sits on a peninsula jutting into the Great Plön Lake and provides 190 level touring pitches with 10A electricity and TV connections, many fully serviced and with panoramic views over the water.

It is only a short walk from the campsite to the centre of Plön, and to the 17th-century castle that overlooks it. The town has a railway station with regular services to Kiel and Lübeck. This is a good choice for families and people who enjoy watersports, with plenty to keep all ages occupied, both on and off the site.

Five modern, well equipped sanitary units with facilities for children and disabled visitors. Washing machines and dryers. Motorhome services. Shop with bread baked on-site. Café/restaurant and takeaway. Heated outdoor pool with slide (seasonal). Wellness and massage. Minigolf. Indoor playroom and ball pool. Playgrounds. Beach volleyball. Boat launching. Go-kart, canoe and bicycle hire. No electric barbecues. Accommodation to rent.

Key Features

 Pets Accepted

 Disabled Facilities

 Beach Access

 Swimming Pool

 Play Area

 Bike Hire

 Fishing

 Sailing

Scan me for more information.

Alan Rogers Code: DE29610
25 pitches
GPS: 53.40975, 10.59736
Post Code: D-21483

Basedow, Schleswig-Holstein

www.alanrogers.com/de29610
info@camping-lanzer-see.de
Tel: +49 4153 599171
www.camping-lanzer-see.de

Open (Touring Pitches):
Late March - Late October.

Camping Lanzer See

In the attractive countryside of Schleswig-Holstein, near the border with Lower Saxony and just 50 km. south-east of Hamburg, this pleasant rural campsite stands on the bank of the Elbe-Lübeck Canal and the shore of the lake that gives it its name.

Much of the site is devoted to holiday units, but there are 25 touring pitches on hardstanding (all with 16A Europlug, water and drainage) plus 25 tent pitches. Many occupy prime locations overlooking the canal or the lake. Anglers will be in their element here as they can sit outside their van or tent and fish, while walkers and cyclists can head off on the Alte Salzstrasse cycle path.

Nearby Lauenburg is a picturesque old town on the banks of the Elbe, with colourful half-timbered houses and the old Castle.

Two sanitary blocks (one heated) provide hot showers, washing machine and dryer and chemical disposal (eco-friendly only). Motorhome services. Kiosk with bread and newspapers (July/Aug). Gasthaus on lake-shore serving home-cooked meals. Football field and table tennis. Play area. Wooded area. Swimming and waterslide. Fishing. Canoe and rowing boat for hire. Mobile home to rent. Torches useful.

Key Features

 Pets Accepted

 Bar/Restaurant

 Bike Hire

 Fishing

Scan me for more information.

185

Alan Rogers Code: DE25001
13 accommodations
200 pitches
GPS: 53.92971, 11.27017
Post Code: D-23968

Hohenkirchen, Mecklenburg-Western Pomerania

www.alanrogers.com/de25001
info@ostsee-campingplatz.de
Tel: +49 38428 60222
www.ostsee-campingplatz.de

Open (Touring Pitches):
End April - End September.

Camping Ostseequelle

Camping Ostseequelle is located in a scenic setting, crossed by the Baltic Sea Spring stream. Close by is the 3.5km long sandy shallow beach of Wohlenberger Wiek. Youth play hut with billiards, table football and darts is located opposite the campsite.

Dining options include the restaurant Bella Italia on the campsite and Buttjes Grill&Bar (100 metres), Tamila's beach bar (400 metres) offers cocktails and music. The site has 200 touring pitches of varying sizes. Camping barrels and bungalows to rent. The local beach with wildlife, shells, stones and seaweed has a beach fee which is used to fund the removal of seaweed every 4 weeks.

Two sanitary blocks, one with individual changing rooms. Family bathroom (fee), built-in baby bath. Children's small toilet and low sink. Camping kitchen. Washing up area. EasyBe dishwashers. Playground. Table tennis. Beach volleyball court. Outdoor chess field. Children's play hut. Dogs welcome (maximum of one in high season). Electricity connection for tents (require adapter for camping plug CEE 230V). Washing machines. Tumble dryers (fee). Freezer for cooling batteries. Own fishing lakes (only with a valid fishing license). Mini shop. Restaurant, Bike Rental. WiFi free.

Key Features

 Pets Accepted

 Beach Access

 Play Area

 Bar/Restaurant

 Fishing

Scan me for more information.

Alan Rogers Code: DE37510
400 accommodations
850 pitches
GPS: 54.45444, 12.54778
Post Code: D-18375

Prerow, Mecklenburg-West
Pomerania

www.alanrogers.com/de37510
prerow@regenbogen.ag
Tel: +49 38233 331
www.regenbogen.ag

Open (Touring Pitches):
All year.

Regenbogen Prerow

Prerow is a seaside resort on the Baltic coast midway between the historic Hanseatic towns of Rostock and Stralsund. Regenbogen Camping is a large site with some 1,250 pitches and extends over two and a half kilometres along a wide, white sand beach. Pitches for caravans overlook the sea, while campers can set up their tents directly on the dunes. Rental accommodation includes tents, caravans, mobile homes and bungalows.

The nearby Darss Forest has an extensive network of footpaths and cycleways, a bridleway and tracks for horse-drawn carriages. West of the forest is West Beach – wild and romantic with rugged terrain formed by wind and waves. South of Prerow is the fascinating watery 'bodden' countryside - a birdwatchers' paradise where you can take a trip on a steam paddleboat.

The heated sanitary block has hot showers, some washbasins in cubicles, a baby room and facilities for disabled visitors. Washing machine and dryer. Motorhome services. Grocery store. Bar, snack bar and restaurant (Start May-End Oct). Thermal bath and sauna. Tennis. Playground. Minigolf. Bicycle hire. Children's entertainment. Tents, caravans, mobile homes and bungalows to rent. WiFi in some areas (charged).

Key Features

 Open All Year

 Pets Accepted

 Disabled Facilities

 Beach Access

 Play Area

 Bar/Restaurant

 Bike Hire

 Fishing

Scan me for more information.

Alan Rogers Code: DE38040
52 accommodations
500 pitches
GPS: 54.34639, 13.73444
Post Code: D-18586

Göhren, Mecklenburg-West
Pomerania

Regenbogen Göhren

www.alanrogers.com/de38040
goehren@regenbogen.ag
Tel: +49 38308 90120
www.regenbogen.ag

Open (Touring Pitches):
All year - Excl. January/February

Göhren lies alongside a sandy beach in a bay on the Baltic Sea, in one of the most beautiful areas of the island of Rügen. It is a large, modern site with 868 pitches of which 500 are for touring. Some are sheltered in the forest; others are near the beach. There is an excellent, modern 500 sq.m. wellness centre, and a bar/restaurant with a wide-ranging menu and wine list. The restaurant has a terrace overlooking a well-equipped play area.

There are many reserves including the Jasmund National Park, which has marshes, wetlands and dry grasslands, with the famous Königsstuhl chalk cliffs and beech forest. Walks, cycle routes and excursions offer a variety of ways to explore the region's beautiful woodlands. The National Park's rich flora and fauna include house martins that breed in the chalk cliffs and the rare sea eagle.

While the campsite is not specifically for naturists, there are two designated FKK areas on the nearby beach.

Key Features

 Naturist Site

 Pets Accepted

 Disabled Facilities

 Beach Access

 Swimming Pool

 Play Area

 Bar/Restaurant

 Bike Hire

Modern sanitary facilities with provision for children and disabled campers. Laundry. Supermarket and camping shop. Restaurant/bar/snack bar. Outdoor swimming pool. Fitness centre with saunas, solarium, massage programme and well equipped gym. Play area. Multisports court. Evening entertainment for adults and children. Bicycle hire. Wind surfing and sailing. WiFi (charged).

Scan me for
more information.

Alan Rogers Code: DE38160
86 accommodations
65 pitches
GPS: 53.20879, 13.07326
Post Code: D-17255

Priepert, Mecklenburg-West
Pomerania

www.alanrogers.com/de38160
info@haveltourist.de
Tel: +49 3981 24790
www.haveltourist.de

Open (Touring Pitches):
Early April - End October.

Campingplatz Am Ziernsee

Accessed along a two-kilometre long, narrow forest road, this is a very quiet and remote lakeside site that slopes gently down to the water's edge. Most of the touring area is fairly open, with a little shade, however, views of the lake are restricted by tall trees and high reed beds. Of the 150 grass pitches, around 60 are for tourers, numbered and in an open plan arrangement, all with 16A electricity. Most of the jetties leading into the lake are reserved for boat owners, but the jetty at the far end of the site allows lake access and is used by the canoeists.

The Ziernsee lies to the very south of the Mecklenburger area of lakes, and the lakes region of Brandenburg can be reached and from there, Berlin. There is no doubt that although this region has a great deal to offer holidaymakers in general, touring by canoe is understandably a most popular and healthy way of getting around, with campsites offering special rates and facilities for canoe tourers. A beginners' course in canoeing and canoe and equipment hire are available at this site's main office in Havelberge

Key Features

 Book Online

 Pets Accepted

 Play Area

 Fishing

 Sailing

Modern well maintained sanitary facilities with controllable showers (on payment card). Washing machines and dryers. Motorhome services. Small shop in reception. Fresh bread. Playground. Volleyball. Fishing. Special area for canoe touring units with a campfire and covered table. Bicycle hire. WiFi over site (charged).

Scan me for more information.

Alan Rogers Code: DE38470
58 accommodations
157 pitches
GPS: 51.36975, 12.31400
Post Code: D-04159

Leipzig, Saxony

www.alanrogers.com/de38470
info@camping-auensee.de
Tel: +49 341 4651600
www.camping-auensee.de

Open (Touring Pitches):
All year.

Campingplatz Auensee

It is unusual to find a good site in a city, but this large, neat and tidy site is one. It is far enough away from roads and the airport to be reasonably peaceful during the day and quiet overnight, and has 157 touring pitches. It is set in a mainly open area with tall trees and attractive flower beds, with some chalets and 'trekker' cabins to rent in the adjoining woodland, home to shoe-stealing foxes. The individual, numbered, flat grassy pitches are large (at least 100 sq.m), all with 16A electricity and five on hardstanding, arranged in several sections.

There is a separate area for young people with tents. Three central points supply water and barbecue areas are provided. Children of all ages are well catered for with forts and an ultra-modern climbing frame on sand, a super-swing and an enclosed court with tennis, football and basketball. A modern restaurant and a snack bar provide breakfast, lunch and supper. A popular site, it is best to arrive early.

Five central sanitary buildings with WCs, washbasins in cabins and showers. Rooms for babies and disabled visitors (key access). Kitchen and laundry rooms. Motorhome services. Restaurant and snack bar (April-Oct). Entertainment rooms. Multisports court. Play area. Barbecue area. Good English spoken.

Key Features

 Open All Year

 Pets Accepted

 Disabled Facilities

 Play Area

Scan me for more information.

Alan Rogers Code: DE38340
8 accommodations
158 pitches
GPS: 51.01452, 13.74766
Post Code: D-01217

Dresden, Saxony

www.alanrogers.com/de38340
camping-dresden@t-online.de
Tel: +49 351 4715250
www.cbm-camping.de/dresden

Open (Touring Pitches):
All year excl. Christmas to New Year.

Camping Dresden-Mockritz

Within 15 minutes of the city centre and with a bus every 20 minutes, this family-run site is ideally located for visiting one of Europe's most attractive and interesting cities. Very good English is spoken in the well-organised reception where bus tickets and plenty of tourist information are readily available.

The site has 158 touring pitches in three areas; the main short stay section has grass pitches in rows with concrete entry roads. Here the units are packed next to each other under mature trees. For longer stays there is a fairly open grass section and adjacent is a grass area for tents.

Quiet for a city site, it is easily reached from the autobahn and has a direct connection to the well organised Dresden public transport system (tickets valid all day).

Three heated sanitary blocks with controllable showers (token required) and washbasins in cabins (crowded at peak periods). Facilities for disabled visitors. Laundry room. Motorhome services. Small shop with essentials and camping goods. Bar. Restaurant with terrace. Play area. Bicycle and scooter hire. Accommodation to rent. WiFi (charged).

Key Features

 Pets Accepted

 Disabled Facilities

 Swimming Pool

 Play Area

 Bar/Restaurant

 Bike Hire

Scan me for more information.

Alan Rogers Code: DE32750
110 accommodations
300 pitches
GPS: 50.81456, 9.51779
Post Code: D-36275

Kirchheim, Hessen

www.alanrogers.com/de32750
info@campseepark.de
Tel: +49 6628 1525
www.campseepark.de

Open (Touring Pitches):
All year.

Camping Seepark

Kirchheim is just 5 km. from the A7 (50 km. south of Kassel) and also close to the Frankfurt to Dresden autobahns A5-A4 in eastern Hesse, which has the largest forested area in Germany. Pleasantly situated on the side of a valley, this is a large terraced site with some 300 level touring pitches, 50 of which are set in cul-de-sacs, and the remainder in an open area at the top of the site with views to the forest. They vary in size from 80 to 110 sq.m. but all have 16A electricity and just under half also have water and drainage.

This handy overnight stop, en-route for Berlin and Dresden, may also be used as a short break to visit Bad Hersfeld, a very pretty spa town with its old Rathaus, Ratskeller and the surrounding 16th-century houses. The area is notable for the old farm buildings and hilly landscape.

The original sanitary facilities are in the complex at the entrance with further very good facilities at the modern restaurant building higher up the site (high season and holidays). Underfloor heating and private cabins. The tent area is currently served by a portable unit. Launderette. Motorhome services. Restaurant (with breakfast) open all year.

Key Features

 Open All Year

 Pets Accepted

 Disabled Facilities

 Swimming Pool

 Play Area

 Bike Hire

Scan me for more information.

Alan Rogers Code: DE37500
13 accommodations
40 pitches
GPS: 50.37418, 11.72122
Post Code: D-95188

Issigau, Bavaria (N)

www.alanrogers.com/de37500
info@schloss-issigau.de
Tel: +49 9293 7173
www.schloss-issigau.de

Open (Touring Pitches):
Mid March - End October Excl.
Christmas to New Year.

Camping Schloss Issigau

This family-run site is small, attractive and well organised. On the left of the entrance courtyard, the small Schloss (c.1398) houses reception, a display of armour, a comfortable breakfast room and a restaurant serving regional and international dishes. Homemade cakes and drinks are served on the small terrace in front of the Schloss.

There are 40 level pitches, all with 16A electricity and five with fresh water and drainage. They are on grass with some terracing and in places, trees offer some shade. To the rear of the site, beside a pond, is a large grass sloping area for tents.

The site has easy autobahn access and is located on the edge of a quiet village 524 m. above sea level on the edge of the Frankenwald nature park where there are many interesting rambling routes.

Modern heated sanitary facilities are housed in an attractively renovated old building. Showers are controllable and free, some washbasins are in cabins. Bathroom for rent. Laundry facilities. Baby room. Kitchen. The building also houses a games room and upstairs, a sauna, solarium, fitness studio, children's play room, and a reading room. Delightful café/bar and restaurant (breakfast served). Bicycle hire. Playground. Hotel accommodation. Free WiFi over site.

Key Features

 Pets Accepted

 Bar/Restaurant

Scan me for more information.

Alan Rogers Code: DE40970
10 accommodations
125 pitches
GPS: 47.47982, 11.05389
Post Code: D-82491

Grainau, Bavaria (S)

Camping Resort Zugspitze

www.alanrogers.com/de40970
office@perfect-camping.de
Tel: +49 8821 9439115
www.perfect-camping.de

Open (Touring Pitches):
All year.

Camping Zugspitze is a top quality campsite, open all year and set in the Zugspitze region of Garmisch-Partenkirchen in the far south of Germany, close to the borders of Austria and Liechtenstein. This is one of the most beautiful tourist regions in Germany and the site has wonderful views over the surrounding countryside.

Camping Zugspitz makes an ideal base for hiking, biking and winter sports, with plenty of opportunities to discover this wonderful area. There are 125 large (80-130sq m), level pitches, many on hardstandings. They are all fully serviced (16A Europlug) with gas connections, and 50 have their own private bathrooms. Rock pegs are advised.

The Zugspitze, the highest mountain in Germany, towers over the site and a cable car journey affords stunning views over four different countries.

Modern, high quality, heated toilet block with all necessary facilities, including those for families and disabled campers. Washing machine/dryer. Winter drying room. Fifty on-pitch private bathrooms. Motorhome services. Shop. Bistro and restaurant with wine cellar. Alpine Spa. Play area. WiFi throughout.

Key Features

 Open All Year

 Pets Accepted

 Disabled Facilities

 Play Area

 Bar/Restaurant

 Skiing

 Bike Hire

Scan me for more information.

Alan Rogers Code: DE40800
9 accommodations
87 pitches
GPS: 47.66674, 9.37816
Post Code: D-88090

Immenstaad, Bavaria (S)

Schloß Helmsdorf

www.alanrogers.com/de40800
info@schloss-helmsdorf.org
Tel: +49 7545 6252
www.schlosshelmsdorf.de

Open (Touring Pitches):
Late March - Mid October.

A peaceful, relaxing campsite which is located next to Lake Constance and which ranks among one of the most beautiful holiday areas in Germany. The site has its own private marina directly on the Bodensee which is focused on water sports and moorings with some availability for campers.

There is a fine restaurant that offers regional dishes and excellent modern facilities. There are 300 pitches all providing electric hook up and access to a water point, 87 of these are available to book. Also for hire are 9 stylish, modern apartments with fabulous lake views.

The campsite is very spacious offering good size pitches and very generous toilet facilities that are not only but modern but also offer a touch of luxury.

There are drinking water fountains available everywhere, showers with hot and cold water. Generous toilet facilities with a baby changing room. Individual wash cubicles, disabled toilet. Dishwasher facilities with hot and cold water. Laundry facilities, washing machines and dryer. Sanitary waste disposal. Chest freezer for freezer packs. Well stocked supermarket with a wide range of food, sports and camping items. Sunbathing lawn right by the shore. Gas supplies: camping, butane and propane gas. Post office and phone.

Key Features

 Pets Accepted

 Disabled Facilities

 Play Area

 Bar/Restaurant

 Bike Hire

 Sailing

Scan me for more information.

Alan Rogers Code: DE34580
20 accommodations
244 pitches
GPS: 47.71237, 7.54654
Post Code: D-79415

Bad Bellingen, Baden-
Württemberg

www.alanrogers.com/de34580
info@camping-luginsland.de
Tel: +49 7635 1820
camping-luginsland.de

Open (Touring Pitches):
All year.

Campingpark Lug ins Land

If you are looking to stay in Germany, but close to the borders with France and Switzerland, this would be an excellent option. On the southern edge of the Black Forest, with its mild, dry climate and, reputedly, the most sunshine hours in Germany, Lug ins Land sits amongst vineyards with beautiful views across the Rhine Valley to the Vosges Mountains.

The site has 424 grass pitches, 244 for tourers, all with 16A electricity connections. Many visitors come to take advantage of the local mineral baths and the spa can be reached on foot through the vineyards. There is a train station nearby for trips to Basel, with its rich cultural and architectural heritage.

Clean and well maintained, heated sanitary blocks with hot showers and washbasins in cubicles. Family room. Private bathroom (WC, washbasin and shower) to rent. Facilities for disabled visitors. Washing machines and dryers. Dog shower. Motorhome services. Campers' kitchen. Small shop for essentials, snack bar and restaurant with terrace (all Start March-Mid November). Small outdoor swimming pool (Mid April-Mid October). Wellness centre. TV room. Playgrounds. Crèche. Multisports pitch. Bicycle and car hire. WiFi (charged).

Key Features

 Open All Year

 Pets Accepted

 Disabled Facilities

 Swimming Pool

 Play Area

 Bar/Restaurant

 Golf

 Horse Riding

Scan me for
more information.

Alan Rogers Code: DE34110
800 accommodations
150 pitches
GPS: 48.47765, 9.74488
Post Code: D-89150

Laichingen-Machtolsheim,
Baden-Württemberg

www.alanrogers.com/de34110
info@camping-heidehof.de
Tel: +49 7333 6408
www.camping-heidehof.de

Open (Touring Pitches):
All year.

Campingplatz Heidehof

At an altitude of 725 m. in the pleasant countryside of the Swabian Alb, this is a very large site, 90% being occupied by permanent caravans. There are about 150 pitches available to touring units. Most of these are for overnight or short stay visitors in a large field located outside the barrier, but there are a few inside the site for long term clients. All have electricity connections (16A) and the overnight section also has an area for tents.

A hotel/restaurant (open all year), although not actually on the campsite, is attached to it and directly accessible from it. The city of Ulm and Legoland are within easy reach. Being just off the A8 autobahn makes it an ideal overnight stop on the way to or from Munich, southern Bavaria or Austria.

Five good quality toilet blocks (one for the touring area) are all heated and well maintained. 25 bathrooms to rent plus three for disabled visitors. Some washbasins in cabins and free showers. Facilities for disabled visitors. Baby rooms. Laundry facilities. Motorhome services. Gas supplies. Shop with bakery. Bar and restaurant (at hotel). Swimming and paddling pools. Playgrounds. Children's club (weekends in July/Aug). Minigolf. Bicycle hire. Max. 1 dog.

Key Features

 Open All Year

 Pets Accepted

 Disabled Facilities

 Swimming Pool

 Play Area

Scan me for more information.

Alan Rogers Code: DE34150
12 accommodations
500 pitches
GPS: 48.72650, 8.08500
Post Code: D-77815

Bühl, Baden-Württemberg

www.alanrogers.com/de34150
info@campingplatz-adam.de
Tel: +49 7223 23194
campingplatz-adam.de

Open (Touring Pitches):
All year (mobile homes avail. Early
April - End September)

Camping Adam

This very convenient, family-owned lakeside site is by the
A5 Karlsruhe-Basel autobahn near Baden-Baden, easily
accessed from exit 52 Bühl (also from the French autoroute
A35 just northeast of Strasbourg). It is also a useful base for
the Black Forest. There are 180 touring pitches out of a total
of 500, most with electricity connections (10A Europlug), 100
also have water and drainage. Tents are positioned along
the outer area of the lake. At very busy times, units staying
overnight only may be placed close together on a lakeside
area of hardstanding.

The site has a well-tended look and good English is spoken.
The lake is divided into separate areas for bathing or boating
and windsurfing, with a long waterslide. The public are
admitted to this on payment and it attracts many people on
fine weekends.

Three heated sanitary buildings. Private cabins in one block, hot
showers on payment. Facilities for babies and disabled visitors.
Washing machine and dryer. Gas. Motorhome services. Shop
(Start April-End Oct). Restaurant (Start March-End October).
Takeaway (Start May-End August). Playground. Volleyball court.
Outdoor chess. Bicycle hire. Fishing. WiFi over site (charged).

Key Features

 Open All Year

 Pets Accepted

 Disabled Facilities

 Play Area

 Bar/Restaurant

 Bike Hire

 Fishing

Scan me for
more information.

Alan Rogers Code: DE32590
108 pitches
GPS: 49.27544, 7.72012
Post Code: D-67714

Waldfischbach-Burgalben,
Rhineland Palatinate

www.alanrogers.com/de32590
info@campingclausensee.de
Tel: +49 6333 5744
www.campingclausensee.de

Open (Touring Pitches):
All year.

Camping Clausensee

Clausensee is set in an attractive lakeside location in the heart of the Pfälzerwald (Palatinate Forest), a vast area of natural beauty, and one of the largest forests in Europe. The site has about 100 level, grassy pitches for tourers, some with shade and with electricity, fresh and waste water connections. A special area for large motorhomes and a quick stop facility are located at the front of the site.

Undoubtedly, the focal point of the site is the fairly large lake, which is suitable for swimming and has rowing boats and pedaloes for hire. Fishing is also permitted (permits available at reception). With its natural location, the site caters for all age groups - the large lakeside meadow is ideal for sunbathing and relaxing, and the playground will keep youngsters occupied.

One basic sanitary block has open washbasins, free controllable hot showers, baby room and facilities for disabled visitors. Laundry. Dishwashing. Motorhome services. Shop. Bar. Restaurant. Takeaway meals. Direct lake access (free to campers). Pedalos and rowing boats. Fishing. Bicycle hire. Play area. Caravans, equipped tents and chalets to rent. Free WiFi over part of site.

Key Features

 Open All Year

 Pets Accepted

 Disabled Facilities

 Play Area

 Bar/Restaurant

 Bike Hire

 Fishing

Scan me for more information.

Alan Rogers Code: DE32140
5 accommodations
41 pitches
GPS: 50.23898, 6.61467
Post Code: D-54568

Gerolstein-Müllenborn,
Rhineland Palatinate

www.alanrogers.com/de32140
camping-oosbach@t-online.de
Tel: +49 6591 7409
www.camping-oosbachtal.de

Open (Touring Pitches):
All year.

Camping Oosbachtal

In the volcanic 'Vulkaneifel' region of Germany, in a wooded valley with a waterfall and stream flowing through it, Campingplatz Oosbachtal is a haven of tranquillity for those who love nature. Its 41 touring pitches, all with electric hook-ups, 15 of which are fully serviced, can be used for tents, motorhomes or caravans. There are also five caravans for rent. Children will love to swim in the crystal clear water, (parental supervision required).

With its idyllic setting of grassy pitches backing onto a stream, set amongst mature trees, the site is an ideal base for those who like walking or cycling holidays. The owners, who live on site offer home-cooked food in the restaurant. Bring your own dish and they will provide takeaway meals, which need to be ordered in advance. The bar and communal barbecue area are popular meeting points for campers, many of whom return year after year.

Five caravans to rent. Seven flats to rent. Restaurant, bar and barbecue area on site. Takeaway meals. Sanitary block with children's facilities. Showers, WC and dishwashing facilities. Mobile greengrocer van once a week (Saturdays), bread to order daily at the bar. Children's play area and television room on site.

Key Features

 Book Online

 Open All Year

 Pets Accepted

 Disabled Facilities

 Play Area

 Bar/Restaurant

Scan me for more information.

Alan Rogers Code: DE32030
100 accommodations
200 pitches
GPS: 51.30029, 6.72514
Post Code: D-40668

Meerbusch, North Rhine-Westphalia

www.alanrogers.com/de32030
info@rheincamping.com
Tel: +49 2150 911817
www.rheincamping.com

Open (Touring Pitches):
Start April - Start October.

Rheincamping Meerbusch

Situated in the countryside, on a large, level, grassed area that stretches along the banks of the River, Rheincamping Meerbusch has 300 pitches, (200 for touring) all with 6A electricity. It is well located for visiting nearby Düsseldorf, and Cologne further south.

The site presents a relaxed atmosphere with its informal beach bar and is fairly open with shade in some areas under mature trees, and open-plan pitches. Being next to the river there is some disturbance as Rhine barges chug by, and now and then noise from Düsseldorf airport, but it is not too obtrusive.

With a central location between Cologne to the south and the Ruhr area to the north, as well as the close proximity of Belgium and Holland, the site is a good touring base. In addition, the small car ferry almost adjoining the site allows easy access to the other side of the Rhine.

Modern sanitary blocks include free controllable showers, washbasins in cabins and facilities for visitors with disabilities. Laundry room with washing machine and dryer. Small shop, bread baked on site. Beach bar and takeaway. Playing field. Play area. Boat slipway. Bicycle hire. WiFi (charged).

Key Features

 Pets Accepted

 Bar/Restaurant

 Bike Hire

 Fishing

 Scan me for more information.

201

Alan Rogers Code: DE28060
63 accommodations
98 pitches
GPS: 52.87081, 7.68717
Post Code: D-49757

Werlte, Lower Saxony

www.alanrogers.com/de28060
info@huemmlingerland.de
Tel: +49 5951 5353
www.huemmlingerland.de

Open (Touring Pitches):
All year.

Hümmlinger Land

Camping Hümmlinger Land is located on the outskirts of Werlte and close to one of the longest megalithic tombs in Germany, the so-called "Hoogen Stainer". Conveniently close to the village centre yet in the middle of nature surrounded by the beautiful Hümmling Park. The campsite has its own free 'Barefoot Path', minigolf, billiards and a sauna (extra charges). This award-winning site has around 60 touring pitches. Sleeping barrels, a shepherd's hut and a tree tent are available to rent.

For families, there's a mountain bike trail park, bowling centre, climbing hall and low ropes course nearby. Cyclists can enjoy one of the many cycle routes and walkers have access to the Hümmlinger pilgrimage route. There is a lot to discover with the Animal and Leisure Park in Thüle, the Meyer Werft shipyard in Papenburg, the wave pool in Löningen, the Fairytale Forest and the summer toboggan run in Surwold.

Ladies and gentlemen's washrooms with showers. Disabled visitor facilities. Baby changing table and bathtub. Washing Machine. Dryer. Washing Area. EasyBe Dishwasher. Shop. TV lounge. Playground. Dog Meadow. Dog Shower. WiFi.

Key Features

 Open All Year

 Pets Accepted

Scan me for
more information.

Alan Rogers Code: DE31820
5 accommodations
108 pitches
GPS: 51.98681, 9.10842
Post Code: D-32683

Barntrup, North Rhine-Westphalia

Teutoburger Wald

www.alanrogers.com/de31820
info@ferienparkteutoburgerwald.de
Tel: +49 5263 2221
www.ferienparkteutoburgerwald.eu

Open (Touring Pitches):
Early April - Mid October.

Under Dutch ownership, this site has about 110 touring pitches, all with 16A electricity. Just outside the main gate, there are nine fully serviced hardstanding pitches with charcoal grill, designed with motorhomes in mind. Although the site is sloping, the pitches are 110-250 sq.m. on mainly level grassy areas with some shade.

There are two large, fully fitted and equipped safari tents and two modern caravans to rent. Energy saving equipment has been installed in the toilet block for the production of hot water and the site is actively promoting good environmental practices. The famous fairytale town of Hameln (20 km) is worth a visit, especially on a Sunday for the Rattenfangerspiel.

Within walking distance is the attractive town of Barntrup with its castle and market. Only an hour's drive by motorway brings you to the Mohensee Dam, of the famed Dambusters story of WW2.

Key Features

 Pets Accepted

 Disabled Facilities

 Swimming Pool

 Play Area

 Bar/Restaurant

Excellent toilet block with underfloor heating and Roman baths theme inside. Roomy showers and open washbasins. Colourful children's section. Family showers. Dog shower with hairdryer. Laundry facilities. Key system for use of hot water. Motorhome services. Games room with TV. Free WiFi. Play area. Electric scooters for hire.

Scan me for more information.

Alan Rogers Code: DE30550
350 pitches
GPS: 51.78330, 10.38332
Post Code: D-38678

Clausthal-Zellerfeld, Lower
Saxony

www.alanrogers.com/de30550
camping@prahljust.de
Tel: +49 5323 1300
www.prahljust.de

Open (Touring Pitches):
All year.

Camping Prahljust

In a woodland setting, 600 metres high and well away from main roads, Camping Prahljust is a quiet site providing plenty of fresh air in an attractive location. The site slopes gently down to a lake that is used for swimming, boating, windsurfing and fishing, and in winter, ice skating.

Of the 400 pitches, 350 are reserved for touring units. These are arranged in larger, open, grass areas separated by hedges with plenty of tree cover and all have electricity connections. The Oberharz is a winter sports region and January and February are the busiest months, with cross-country skiing from the site.

During the rest of the year this attractive region has much to offer; rambling, mountain biking and rock climbing are all popular and the list of interesting places to visit is almost endless.

Three older style, heated toilet blocks (one partly refurbished) have all the usual facilities. Showers are free. Facilities for disabled visitors. Baby room. Washing machines, dryers, drying room and kitchen. Motorhome services. Shop, restaurant and bar (closed Nov). Indoor, heated swimming pool (12x9 m; no shallow end). Playground. Sauna and solarium. Clubroom. Lake trail. Beer garden. Bicycle and kayak hire. There is also a small library with books (also in English) in reception. WiFi (free).

Key Features

 Open All Year

 Pets Accepted

 Disabled Facilities

 Swimming Pool

 Play Area

 Bar/Restaurant

 Skiing

 Bike Hire

Scan me for
more information.

Alan Rogers Code: DE28260
24 accommodations
95 pitches
GPS: 51.56379, 10.15353
Post Code: D-37136

Seeburg, Lower Saxony

Camping Seeburger See

www.alanrogers.com/de28260
info@campingseeburgersee.com
Tel: +49 5502 998461
campingseeburgersee.com

Open (Touring Pitches):
Start March - Mid January.

Comfort Camping Seeburger See lies on the outskirts of the small village of Seeburg and is only a few hundred metres from the largest natural lake in Lower Saxony. The site has a long season, from the beginning of March to the end of December. The area is surrounded by the rolling hills of the Southern Hartz Mountains.

There are 120 pitches with 95 for touring, all with 16A electricity. The undelineated, level grass pitches are laid out in groups in a meadow, with the groups separated by low hedges and a few trees give shade to some pitches. There is a separate area for tents in the centre of the field where the pitches are more open. This is a quiet rural area with many marked tracks, good for birdwatching, walking and cycling.

Two older style toilet blocks with all necessary facilities with provision for babies and disabled visitors. Washing machine and dryer. Baker with a few supplies. Bar/restaurant. Play area. Tennis. Volleyball. Boules. Multisports area. Children's club (3-12 yrs), some family entertainment. Lake swimming with a grass sunbathing area, sandy beach with a separate area for small children. Small boat and pedaloes to hire. Bicycle hire. WiFi throughout (free).

Key Features

 Pets Accepted

 Disabled Facilities

 Play Area

 Bar/Restaurant

 Bike Hire

 Fishing

 Sailing

Scan me for more information.

Capital London
Currency British Pound (£)
Language English, Welsh
Time Zone GMT
Telephone Code +44

Climate Varied, hard to predict. Generally mild in the summer, more so in the south and cooler and wetter in the winter months.

Public Holidays 1 Jan New Year's Day • Mar/Apr Good Friday • Mar/Apr Easter Monday • May Early May Bank Holiday • May/June Late May Bank Holiday • Aug August Bank Holiday • 25 Dec Christmas Day • 26 Dec Boxing Day. Scotland & Northern Ireland observe regional holidays. Always check before travelling.

In June 2022, to mark the 70-year reign of Queen Elizabeth II, the UK will celebrate an additional four-day national bank holiday, with public events held.

Driving in Britain Driving is on the left, speed is measured in miles per hour and imperial measurements for road signs are used. When using motorways, never use the hard shoulder unless instructed to or if you break down (turn on your hazard lights). Tailgating, drink-driving, smoking in the car with minors present and using a mobile device whilst driving are illegal.

Low Emissions Zones in all major cities.

London has Ultra Low Emission Zones, Zero Emission Zones and congestion charges in place also. Registration is required for all foreign vehicles.

●●●●○ **Accessibility Score**
View our digital e-guide & find out more at
Visit **alanrogers.com/open-to-all**

Tourism website | visitbritain.com

Wales Boasting a diverse landscape, from lakes, mountains, rivers and valleys to beautiful coastlines and rolling wooded countryside.

Scotland From gently rolling hills and rugged coastlines to dramatic peaks punctuated with beautiful lochs, Scotland is an untamed land steeped in history.

Northern Ireland From wild coastlines to green valleys, rugged mountains and shimmering lakes to the natural phenomenon of the Giant's Causeway, Northern Ireland is crammed full of sights.

Great Britain

View all campsites in Great Britain
alanrogers.com/england
alanrogers.com/northern-ireland
alanrogers.com/scotland
alanrogers.com/wales

See campsite map page 480

Shops
Hours differ between the four nations. Generally 9am to 5pm weekdays and Sat, and 11am to 4pm on Sun. Smaller supermarkets stay open longer.

Money
ATMs are widespread (even in rural areas) and accessible 24hrs a day. Most places accept cards. Amex less widely accepted.

The United Kingdom offers a wealth of extraordinary landscapes set against the backdrop of rich and vibrant history. In terms of character and stunning scenery, it offers an unsurpassed choice of holiday activities from coast to country.

Northern England A beautiful and varied region of rolling hills and undulating moors, along with a wealth of industrial heritage and undiscovered countryside. The Yorkshire Moors, the Cumbrian lakes, the Northumbrian ancient forts and fairytale castles are all highlights not to be missed.

Southern England Rich in maritime heritage and historical attractions, the southern region comprises tranquil English countryside replete with picture-postcard villages, ancient towns, formidable castles and grand stately homes, coupled with a beautiful coastline, white-faced cliffs and lively seaside resorts.

Heart of England Spanning central England, from the ancient borders of Wales in the west across to Lincolnshire on the east coast, the Heart of England is rich in glorious rolling countryside, magnificent castles and fine stately homes.

Eastern England A perfect mix of gentle countryside and sleepy villages, it's an unspoilt region with endless skies, inland waterways and traditional beach resorts.

Western England A region of contrasts, with windswept moorlands and dramatic cliffs towering above beautiful sandy beaches.

Alan Rogers Code: UK9880
5 accommodations
50 pitches
GPS: 49.43502, -2.34859
Post Code: GY10 1SE

Sark, Channel Islands

La Valette Campsite

www.alanrogers.com/uk9880
lavalette@cwgsy.net
Tel: +44 1481 832066
www.sark.co.uk/la-valette-151

Open (Touring Pitches):
Mid March - Mid October (camping pods all year).

La Valette is one of just two options for simple camping on this wonderful island. Bring your own tent (baggage will be transported for you to and from the harbour) or rent a ready erected tent or one of four smart camping pods. With stunning sea views across to Alderney and France, the large open field slopes in places, although it should always be possible to find a level spot and there is some shelter from hedges if preferred.

There are no electrical hook-ups and the only amenity is a purpose-built toilet block. One of the joys of this car-free island is that children can experience a wonderful freedom and everyone can explore the island on foot or by bike. Mrs Adams, the owner, provides a friendly welcome and can provide a fascinating insight into Sark and the history of her beautiful granite farmhouse.

Purpose-built, small toilet block (quite a walk from the far corners of the site). Unisex facilities include two showers (fee payable), two washbasins in cabins and four WCs. Shaver points. Dishwashing sink. Torches essential. Camping pods and ready erected tents with equipment (bring sleeping bags and lighting). Luggage transportation.

Key Features

 Pets Accepted

 Beach Access

Scan me for more information.

Alan Rogers Code: UK9770
6 accommodations
150 pitches
GPS: 49.49584, -2.55433
Post Code: GY2 4TA

Saint Sampson's, Guernsey

www.alanrogers.com/uk9770
enquiries@vaugratcampsite.com
Tel: +44 1481 257468
www.vaugratcampsite.com

Open (Touring Pitches):
End April - Mid September.

Vaugrat Camping

Vaugrat Camping is a neat, well-tended site, close to the beach in the northwest of the island. Owned and well run by the Lainé family, it is centred around attractive and interesting historic granite farm buildings dating back to the 15th century, with a gravel courtyard and very pretty flower beds.

The site provides 150 pitches (with 10A electricity available) on flat, grassy meadows that are mostly surrounded by trees, banks and hedges to provide shelter. Tents and motorhomes are arranged around the edges of the fields, giving open space in the centre, and while pitches are not marked, there is sufficient room and cars may be parked next to tents. Only couples and families are accepted.

Well kept sanitary facilities are in two buildings. The first block is in the courtyard, with hot showers on payment (fee payable). Unit for disabled visitors with shower, basin and toilet (six-inch step into the building). Laundry facilities. The second block near the camping fields provides toilets, washbasins and dishwashing facilities. Shop with ice pack hire and gas (open at certain times by arrangement). Coffee barn with TV and free WiFi access. Dogs are not accepted. Torches would be useful. Fully equipped tents for hire (details from site).

Key Features

 Disabled Facilities

 Beach Access

 Play Area

Scan me for
more information.

Alan Rogers Code: UK9780
12 accommodations
100 pitches
GPS: 49.46812, -2.58843
Post Code: GY5 7QL

Castel, Guernsey

www.alanrogers.com/uk9780
info@fauxquets.co.uk
Tel: +44 1481 255460
www.fauxquets.co.uk

Open (Touring Pitches):
Start April - Start September.

Fauxquets Valley Campsite

Situated in the rural centre of the island, Fauxquets is in a pretty sheltered valley, hidden down narrow lanes away from busy roads and run by the friendly Guille family. Originally part of a dairy farm, the valley side has now been developed into an attractive campsite. Plenty of ornamental trees, bushes and flowers have been planted to separate pitches and to provide shelter around the various fields which are well terraced.

The 100 pitches are of a good size, most marked, numbered and with 6-32A electricity, offering a choice of pitches for tents and motorhomes. There is lots of open space and some friendly farm animals in surrounding enclosures. The site has fully equipped tents for hire and two comfortable log cabins.

Good toilet facilities have controllable showers, some washbasins in private cabins with a shower, baby bath and changing unit. Dishwashing facilities under cover and a tap for free hot water. Laundry room with free irons, boards and hairdryers. Heated swimming pool (13x6 m) with paddling pool (10:00-19:00). Well stocked shop with fresh produce, bread delivered daily, snacks and camping essentials. Off licence. TV and games rooms. Small play area and play field. Farm animals. Bicycle hire arranged. Torches useful. WiFi in reception (free).

Key Features

 Pets Accepted

 Beach Access

 Swimming Pool

 Play Area

 Bike Hire

Scan me for
more information.

Alan Rogers Code: UK0030
10 accommodations
90 pitches
GPS: 50.21261, -5.48928
Post Code: TR26 1EJ

Cornwall, South West

www.alanrogers.com/uk0030
recept@ayrholidaypark.co.uk
Tel: +44 1736 795855
www.ayrholidaypark.co.uk

Open (Touring Pitches):
All year.

Ayr Holiday Park

Ayr Holiday Park has an unparalleled position overlooking Saint Ives Bay and Porthmeor beach and is a popular, well cared for site. On arrival, it may seem to be all caravan holiday homes but behind them is a series of naturally sloping fields with marvellous views providing a total of 90 pitches, of which 40 are for touring caravans and motorhomes. These pitches are on grass, all with 16A electricity and several fully serviced with hardstanding.

An extra field for tents is open in July and August. A state-of-the-art toilet block provides excellent facilities in a colourful and modern design.

Saint Ives centre with restaurants, bars and supermarkets is within easy walking distance, as is the new Tate Gallery. There is direct access to the coastal footpath. Campers have use of the facilities of the hotel at the top of the site, at extra cost - indoor swimming pool, pool bar and sauna.

Key Features

 Open All Year

 Pets Accepted

 Disabled Facilities

 Beach Access

 Play Area

The excellent toilet block includes two family shower rooms and facilities for baby changing and disabled visitors. Wetsuit showers. Fully equipped laundry room. Motorhome point. Indoor swimming pool, sauna and bar in the hotel (charged). Games room with TV, hot drinks and snack machines. Adventure play area. Max. 1 dog, contact site first. Bus calls. WiFi (charged).

Scan me for
more information.

Alan Rogers Code: UK0058
146 pitches
GPS: 50.67396, -4.72664
Post Code: PL34 0BQ

Cornwall, South West

www.alanrogers.com/uk0058
UKSitesBookingService@camc.com
Tel: +44 1840 770222
www.camc.com

Open (Touring Pitches):
Mid March - Start November.

Trewethett Farm (CAMC)

Trewethett Farm Caravan and Motorhome Club site can boast some of the most dramatic views of any site in the country, overlooking Bossiney Cove and beyond to the ever-changing seascape of the Atlantic Ocean. Vans can be positioned either front or back first, ensuring your own panoramic (and occasionally wild and windy) view.

Trewethett Farm is split into four areas with 146 open pitches, 122 with 16 amp electricity, well laid out and of a good size with some on slightly sloping ground (levelling blocks may be required).

A very modern clean toilet block contains good-sized showers, washbasins in cubicles, facilities for babies (key) and disabled visitors. Two portacabin facilities adjoining the camping area are also available most of the season. Well equipped laundry room. Small shop in reception stocks basic necessities and Calor gas. Children's playground, with swings and a climbing frame. Access to water/waste and chemical disposal points are placed around the site. Motorhome service point. Wi-Fi good, charged. Pets welcome. Dog walk. Twin Axle Caravans accepted. No late night arrivals area. BBQ's allowed gas, charcoal & electricity. TV reception is good. Bus stop 300 metres. Spar 3.5 miles.

Key Features

 Book Online

 Pets Accepted

 Disabled Facilities

 Beach Access

 Play Area

Scan me for more information.

Alan Rogers Code: UK0320
7 accommodations
31 pitches
GPS: 50.37722, -4.41850
Post Code: PL13 1QS

Cornwall, South West

www.alanrogers.com/uk0320
info@looecountrypark.co.uk
Tel: +44 1503 240265
www.looecountrypark.co.uk

Open (Touring Pitches):
All year.

Looe Country Park

Looe Country Park is a lovely all year site, which will appeal to those who prefer a quiet, well kept small family site to the larger ones with many on-site activities. With good countryside views, 31 touring units can be accommodated on well-tended grass. Good sized pitches are marked with some hedging between pairs of pitches to give privacy, and most have electricity connections.

There are several hardstandings and 12 fully serviced pitches. Five mobile homes (including 2 dog-friendly) and two camping pods are available to rent. The owners, Rob and Jill, live on the park and make everyone very welcome, creating a relaxed and happy atmosphere. The nearest beach is a 15-20 minute walk from a gate in the corner of the park. This is a good area for walking with links to the coastal path through Duchy woodlands. The Monkey Sanctuary is also nearby.

Laminated teak with chrome fittings and black surfaces make an unusual but stylish and fully equipped, heated sanitary block. Family room. Laundry room. Shop (open on demand.) for gas and basics, and some camping accessories. Tourist information in reception. WiFi (free - conditions apply).

Key Features

 Open All Year

 Pets Accepted

 Beach Access

Scan me for more information.

Alan Rogers Code: UK0760
63 pitches
GPS: 50.71753, -3.78325
Post Code: EX6 6NR

Devon, South West

www.alanrogers.com/uk0760
info@barleymeadow.co.uk
Tel: +44 1647 281629
www.barleymeadow.co.uk

Open (Touring Pitches):
Mid April - Mid November.

Barley Meadow Touring Park

This peaceful little park is located on the northern edge of Dartmoor with easy access from the A30. It is sheltered from the weather by good hedging and, although not always visible from the pitches, there are open views across the moorland to the south. The 63 pitches are mostly on level grass, well-spaced, with 25 hardstandings and 38 electric hook-ups (10A). Shrubs divide some of the pitches. The site would be a suitable base for visiting Exeter, Okehampton and Plymouth, hiking over the moors or just enjoying the local area.

The Two Moors Way for walkers is only 400 yards from the site. The owners have compiled a book with over 60 things to see or do, which is very popular. The Exeter/Okehampton bus can stop outside if requested. The popular Two Moors Way is within easy walking distance of the park .

The refurbished heated toilet block is well maintained and provides all facilities including babies changing and facilities for disabled campers. Laundry and ice pack freezer. Motorhome services. Small shop for basic groceries, ice-creams, drinks, small camping items and gas. Games room with pool table. Small library and information chalet. WiFi.

Key Features

 Pets Accepted

 Disabled Facilities

 Beach Access

 Play Area

Scan me for more information.

Alan Rogers Code: UK0681
6 accommodations
91 pitches
GPS: 51.20484, -4.06417
Post Code: EX34 9SH

Devon, South West

www.alanrogers.com/uk0681
enquiries@millpark.com
Tel: +44 1271 882647
www.millpark.com

Open (Touring Pitches):
Start March - End October.

Mill Park

Mill Park is a small family run sheltered touring caravan and camping site set in an attractive wooded valley on the North Devon Coast. It has a shop, a takeaway, games room, laundry, and has many other useful facilities such as gas-changing and ice pack freezing. Several glamping options are available on-site, including three bell tents and three glamping pods.

There is also an on-site pub serving a modest menu. Mill Park is surrounded by attractive woodland and is an ideal family site as it's just a short walk to quiet beaches, both sand and pebble. Bring your Fishing tackle to Mill Park and enjoy the Lake. A stream fed 1.5-acre coarse fishing lake stocked with Carp.

Equally close by is the unspoilt and breathtaking beauty of Exmoor and the nearest village, Berrynarbor is just a five-minute walk from the site. This village dates back from the sixteenth century and earlier. There is a quaint old country pub, village stores and post office.

Key Features

 Pets Accepted

 Disabled Facilities

 Play Area

 Bar/Restaurant

 Fishing

Two Separate shower blocks - both recently refurbished and kept impeccably clean, onsite bar, well-stocked shop, fishing lake, small river flowing through the park, children's play area, games room, book swap, games library, free Internet in bar and games room. Close to beaches, secluded and quiet, very peaceful.

Scan me for more information.

Alan Rogers Code: UK1415
4 accommodations
36 pitches
GPS: 50.85779, -2.93597
Post Code: TA20 4HD

Somerset, South West

www.alanrogers.com/uk1415
stay@alpinegrovetouringpark.com
Tel: +44 1460 65079
www.alpinegrovetouringpark.com

Open (Touring Pitches):
Start April - End October.

Alpine Grove Touring Park

Situated close to both Chard and Cricket St Thomas is this peaceful woodland site is owned by Keith and Serena Wootton who go the extra mile to ensure you enjoy your stay here. Recent recipients of the Green Tourist Gold award the pitches vary in size (20 - 70 sq.m) and are on flat ground served by gravel roads giving easy access. Some informally marked pitches are tucked away in dense foliage and are very private. Electricity (10A) is supplied to 26 of the 36 touring pitches (16 hardstandings).

All the standard facilities are near reception, including a free, fenced and heated swimming pool (10x5 m). A play area is provided for children under the canopy of mature trees which shade the site.

A modest, rustic sanitary building provides all usual facilities and is kept clean and smart. There are facilities for disabled campers which double as a family bathroom. Washing machine and dryers. Reception doubles as the licensed shop selling some fresh food, milk, bread and essentials. Heated outdoor swimming pool (seasonal). Children's play area and woodland trails. Planned walks and some day activities. Bicycle hire. Four log cabins for hire. Barbecues allowed (not electric).

Key Features

 Pets Accepted

 Disabled Facilities

 Beach Access

 Swimming Pool

 Play Area

 Bike Hire

Scan me for more information.

Alan Rogers Code: UK2070
125 pitches
GPS: 50.84133, -2.19515
Post Code: DT11 9AD

Dorset, South West

www.alanrogers.com/uk2070
mail@theinsidepark.co.uk
Tel: +44 1258 453719
www.theinsidepark.co.uk

Open (Touring Pitches):
Easter - End October.

The Inside Park Touring Park

The Inside Park Touring Caravan & Camping Park is set in the grounds of an 18th-century country house that burned down in 1941. Family owned and carefully managed alongside an arable farm, this is a must for those interested in local history or arboriculture and it is a haven for wildlife and birds.

The 9-acre camping field, a little distant, lies in a sheltered, sloping dry valley containing superb tree specimens – notably cedars and walnuts. a large play area splits the field. In total there are 125 spacious pitches, 90 with 10 amp electricity and some in wooded glades.

The six acres adjoining are the old pleasure gardens of the house. The reception/toilet block and games room block are respectively the coach house and stables of the old house.

The toilet block, the original stable building provides some washbasins in cubicles, comfortably sized showers and facilities for disabled visitors and babies. Laundry room. Shop with basics, gas and camping provisions. Spacious games room. Adventure play area. Day kennelling facilities for dogs. Mountain bike course. Winter caravan storage. Free Wi-Fi around reception.

Key Features

 Pets Accepted

 Disabled Facilities

 Play Area

Scan me for
more information.

Alan Rogers Code: UK2510
230 accommodations
58 pitches
GPS: 50.67498, -1.09606
Post Code: PO35 5PL

Isle of Wight, South

www.alanrogers.com/uk2510
holiday@whitecliff-bay.com
Tel: +44 1983 872671
www.wight-holidays.com

Open (Touring Pitches):
Mid March - Start November.

Whitecliff Bay Holiday Park

Whitecliff Bay is a very large complex divided by a main road, with a holiday home and chalet park on the right-hand side (230 units), and a large area on the left-hand side also dedicated to static caravans with a decreasing area at the bottom of the hill available to touring units.

Some 58 pitches are spread over two fields, which are quite level. Most of the pitches have 16A electricity hook-ups, and there are some gravel hardstandings. It is clear that static caravan plots will increasingly reduce the number of touring pitches over the coming years.

One sanitary unit not far from reception. Showers and a suite (with shower) for disabled campers. A second suite with a hip bath/shower is at the lower block with a similar facility to serve as a baby/family room. Motorhome services. Small shop at reception. Playground. At the holiday home park: launderette, hairdresser and second larger shop. The Culver Club. Snack bars. Swimming pool (18x18 m, Whitsun-end Aug). Indoor fun pool and soft play zone (under 8s). Most facilities open Mar-Oct. Free WiFi on main site. Full programme of activities and entertainment for all ages. Fully equipped tents to rent.

Key Features

 Pets Accepted

 Disabled Facilities

 Beach Access

 Swimming Pool

 Play Area

 Bar/Restaurant

 Bike Hire

 Golf

Scan me for more information.

Alan Rogers Code: UK2887
120 pitches
GPS: 50.77498, -0.85855
Post Code: PO20 8PJ

West Sussex, South East

www.alanrogers.com/uk2887
mail@stubcroft.com
Tel: +44 1243 671469
www.stubcroft.com

Open (Touring Pitches):
Mid April - Mid October.

Stubcroft Farm Campsite

Stubcroft Farm is a six-acre family run site, set in a rural location with an emphasis on protecting the environment. The site is split into five separate areas and has 120 pitches 45 with hook up's (10 of these are hardstanding) and a further 45 non-electric pitches for tents.

The separate areas work well as families tend to be in the far field where there is plenty of space to enjoy games and activities. Whilst those requiring peace and tranquillity will find it in the other fields.

The site is well laid out with spacious pitches which has a very relaxed friendly feel about it and there is much open space to play football and various outdoor games and activities. The campsite has a really friendly family atmosphere.

There is a central Eco sanitary facilities/laundry block and a smaller additional block adjoining the camping fields. Facilities for Disabled visitors. Well stocked Shop with local meat and produce. Charging point in reception for those without hook-up and there are also four Electric Car Charging points by the reception. Camping & Calor Gas available.

Key Features

 Pets Accepted

 Beach Access

Scan me for more information.

Alan Rogers Code: UK1660
45 pitches
GPS: 51.41380, -2.12968
Post Code: SN15 2LP

Wiltshire, South West

www.alanrogers.com/uk1660
piccadillylacock@aol.com
Tel: +44 1249 730260
www.piccadillylacock.co.uk

Open (Touring Pitches):
Mid April - Mid October.

Piccadilly Caravan Park

Piccadilly Caravan Park is set in open countryside close to several attractions, notably Longleat, Bath, Salisbury Plain, Stourhead, and the picturesque village of Lacock itself. You will receive a warm welcome from the owner at this small, quiet family-owned park that has been beautifully landscaped and tended for over 30 years.

The Well kept shrubs, flowers and trees have been landscaped to provide three separate areas and create a very pleasant ambience. There are 45 well-spaced, clearly marked pitches, 12 of which have hardstanding, and 42 have electricity (10A). Two areas have been made available for tents. A bus service runs from Lacock village to Chippenham (entry to the Chippenham Museum and Heritage Centre is free of charge).

Two heated toilet blocks are well maintained and equipped. No facilities for disabled visitors. Laundry room. Ice pack service. Playground and a large, grass ball play area. Limited gas supplies. Newspapers can be ordered. WiFi (free).

Key Features

 Pets Accepted

 Play Area

Scan me for more information.

Alan Rogers Code: UK1665
36 pitches
GPS: 51.57908, -2.09732
Post Code: SN16 0EH

Wiltshire, South West

www.alanrogers.com/uk1665
ali@burtonhill.co.uk
Tel: +44 1666 826880
www.burtonhill.co.uk

Open (Touring Pitches):
Start April - End October.

Burton Hill Caravan Park

The owners of this park, Robert and Ali Simmons, tend it with pride. One field provides a flat grassy area surrounded by hedges, with open views across farmland on the outskirts of historic Malmesbury. A smaller field slopes down to the river.

The approach is through a well-tended 'village' of park homes. There are 36 pitches each with 16A electricity, with eight more for tents. There are limited amenities on-site, but you will find a choice of shops, inns and restaurants in the town, which is a short walk (10-15 minutes) across the river. Here you can also visit the Abbey House Gardens, Abbey and 15th-century marketplace.

Within easy travelling, distance are the towns of Bath, Chippenham, Tetbury, Trowbridge and Bradford-on-Avon. Also within reach are the Cotswold Water Parks, Castle Combe Racecourse and village and Westonbirt Arboretum.

Modern, well equipped and well maintained heated toilet block with free hot water. Family shower room with baby changing also provides facilities for disabled visitors. Washing machine. Motorhome services. Fishing. Max. 2 dogs.

Key Features

 Pets Accepted

 Disabled Facilities

 Fishing

 Scan me for more information.

221

Alan Rogers Code: UK2571
92 pitches
GPS: 51.83818, -1.34168
Post Code: OX20 1PT

Oxfordshire, South

www.alanrogers.com/uk2571
UKSitesBookingService@camc.com
Tel: +44 1993 812390
www.camc.com

Open (Touring Pitches):
Start March - Start November.

Bladon Chains (CAMC)

Bladon Chains Caravan and Motorhome Club site is situated on the Blenheim Estate. You will have the pleasure of seeing magnificent trees all around you, on this gently sloping site situated just outside the wall of the Palace Garden.

You can walk to the famous Bladon Church from the corner of the site to see Churchill's modest but memorable grave. You will certainly want to visit the Palace, where Churchill was born; it has also been home to the historic Dukes of Marlborough since the eighteenth century. The site has 92 grass or hardstanding pitches, most have 16 amp electricity.

A single heated toilet block provides facilities for visitors who are disabled and children. BBQs allowed: charcoal, gas, electric. Dishwashing area. Pets allowed. Dog walk. Motorhome Service Point. Chemical toilet point. Laundry. Small shop. Information Room. Wi-Fi hot spot. TV poor booster system available. Children's play area. Twin axle caravans accepted. Pets allowed. Calor Gas sales. No tents allowed. No late-night arrivals area. Defibrillator. Maximum outfit length 8 metres. Co-op 1.5 miles. Train Station (Hanborough) 4 miles. Bus stop adjacent.

Key Features

 Book Online

 Pets Accepted

 Disabled Facilities

 Play Area

Scan me for more information.

Alan Rogers Code: UK2700
12 accommodations
200 pitches
GPS: 51.54660, -0.82480
Post Code: SL6 5NE

Berkshire, South

Hurley Riverside Park

www.alanrogers.com/uk2700
info@hurleyriversidepark.co.uk
Tel: +44 1628 824493
www.hurleyriversidepark.co.uk

Open (Touring Pitches):
Start March - End October.

On the banks of the Thames, not far from Henley-on-Thames, you will find the picturesque village of Hurley where some buildings date back to 1086. Just outside the village is Hurley Riverside Park which has been family-run since 1926 and provides facilities for holiday homes, touring units, tents and moorings for boats.

The touring area is flat and separated into smaller fields. With the pitches arranged around the outside of each field and the centre left free, the park has a spacious feel, even during busy periods. There are 200 touring pitches, 146 with 10-16A Europlug, including 13 fully serviced and some on long hardstandings especially for American-style RVs. A camping field provides 62 tent pitches including some with electric hook-ups. A very popular park, there is also a large rally field.

Key Features

 Pets Accepted

 Disabled Facilities

 Play Area

 Fishing

Three wooden toilet blocks (raised on legs) include a very good unisex block with private bathrooms (shower, washbasin, toilet). The other blocks have been renovated and are well equipped. Family shower rooms in one block (shower, WC, washbasin). Separate shower and toilet facilities for disabled visitors at reception. Baby area. Launderette. Motorhome services. Well stocked shop at reception. Play area. Fishing. Electric car charging points. Temporary moorings. Nature and wildlife trail, riverside picnic grounds, slipway and fishing in season. American RVs accepted.

Scan me for
more information.

Alan Rogers Code: UK3055
150 pitches
GPS: 51.20073, 0.39333
Post Code: TN12 6PY

Kent, South East

www.alanrogers.com/uk3055
touring@thehopfarm.co.uk
Tel: +44 1622 870838
www.thehopfarm.co.uk/stay

Open (Touring Pitches):
Start March - End October.

The Hop Farm Campsite

Set in 500 acres of the Garden of England, The Hop Farm Touring & Camping Park is a popular family visitor attraction. There are plenty of activities to entertain children, including adventure play areas (indoor and outdoor), a driving school, funfair rides, the Magic Factory and the Great Goblin Hunt.

This is also the venue for many special events throughout the summer, including music festivals & shows. To one side, overlooking all this activity and the attractive cluster of oasts is the touring park which provides 150 pitches of which 75 are hardstanding on flat, open fields. Electricity (16A) and water are available. There are also 1000 pitches for tents!

Brand new state-of-the-art shower and washrooms have been added to the site to enhance guest experiences, providing a luxurious touch to their stay. Small shop (in reception) for essentials. Free entry for campers and caravanners to the Family Park with restaurant and café. Nature walks. Boat launching. Fishing. Dogs accepted but not permitted inside the visitor attraction. Activities and entertainment at the visitor attraction.

Key Features

 Pets Accepted

 Disabled Facilities

 Play Area

 Bar/Restaurant

 Fishing

Scan me for
more information.

Alan Rogers Code: UK3040
25 accommodations
110 pitches
GPS: 51.10647, 0.86809
Post Code: TN26 1NQ

Kent, South East

Broadhembury Caravan Park

www.alanrogers.com/uk3040
holidaypark@broadhembury.co.uk
Tel: +44 1233 620859
www.broadhembury.co.uk

Open (Touring Pitches):
All year.

Broadhembury Caravan & Camping Park is found in the quiet countryside just outside Ashford and within easy reach of London, Dover, Folkestone and the Kent coast There are areas for family camping with play areas and amenities designed with children in mind and separate quiet meadows just for adults with new luxury facilities.

In total, the park takes 110 touring units of any type. The well-kept pitches are on level grass and backed by tall, neat hedges; 105 with electricity connections (10/16A). In addition, six pitches are fully serviced and ten more have double hardstanding plus a grass area for an awning. The welcome is friendly at this popular park and it is often full in the main season.

Well equipped toilet block for the family areas and ecologically considered block for the couples meadows. Underfloor heating. Private cabins. High-quality facilities for disabled visitors. Well equipped laundry room. Good campers' kitchen, fully enclosed with microwaves, fridge and freezer, all free of charge. Motorhome services. Well stocked shop with local produce, wine and beer (butchers, bakery and papers to order). Internet access. Pool room, games room with video games, table football and table tennis. Two play areas (one for children under 7 yrs) one with an all-weather surface. Playing field adjacent to touring area. Campers' herb garden. WiFi over site (charged). Up to two dogs per pitch are accepted. Large units are accepted if pre-booked.

Key Features

 Adults Only

 Open All Year

 Pets Accepted

 Disabled Facilities

 Beach Access

 Play Area

Scan me for
more information.

Alan Rogers Code: UK4090
57 accommodations
80 pitches
GPS: 52.23549, -1.80265
Post Code: B95 6JP

Warwickshire, Heart of England

www.alanrogers.com/uk4090
holiday@islandmeadowcaravanpark.co.uk
Tel: +44 1789 488273
islandmeadowcaravanpark.co.uk

Open (Touring Pitches):
Start March - End October.

Island Meadow Caravan Park

Set in the beautiful rural countryside of Warwickshire, Island Meadow is a small, privately owned, family run park, surrounded by seven acres of secluded land. The park is situated on an island, formed by the River Alne with its mill race and provides a quiet and peaceful holiday setting. There is a natural mill pond and weir which are lined with mature trees, offering great coarse fishing, free of charge to all guests. All areas of the park are flat and close-mown, making the island a perfect centre for bird watching, walking, cycling or just relaxing.

The Campsite has 80 pitches in total, with 57 holiday homes (7 to rent) located around the perimeter. The 24 touring pitches are on the spacious central grassy area of the site (14 of which have "helicopter" style hard standing) all have 10 amp electric hook-ups. Only environmentally friendly groundsheets are permitted.

Two sanitary units, both heated. The original provides adequate WCs and washbasins for men, and the more modern unit has been provided for women, with a separate access shower unit for the men, and a wet room style suite for disabled visitors on one end. Laundry with washing machine, dryer and ironing facility.

Key Features

 Pets Accepted

 Disabled Facilities

 Fishing

Scan me for more information.

Alan Rogers Code: UK2755
350 accommodations
50 pitches
GPS: 52.07440, -0.84079
Post Code: MK19 7JP

Buckinghamshire, South

www.alanrogers.com/uk2755
enquiries@cosgrovepark.co.uk
Tel: +44 1908 563360
www.cosgrovepark.co.uk

Open (Touring Pitches):
Start April - Start November.

Cosgrove Park

This beautifully laid out 180-acre site encompasses no fewer than 13 (unfenced) fishing lakes and a central watersports lake too. Not far from the M1 and the A5, Cosgrove Park offers active family holidays as well as peaceful relaxation for anglers. Motorised craft are not allowed on the main lake, but oars, paddles and sails are encouraged, with tuition available if required.

Of the 400 pitches, 350 are occupied by seasonal campers, leaving just 50 for tourers. These are pleasingly sited on the top terrace and have 10A Europlugs. Early bookings are strongly advised, especially for holiday periods.

Five toilet blocks serve the touring area, two with washing machines, dryers and washing up sinks. Two blocks with facilities for disabled campers. Baby room in the restaurant. Superb shop with camping and fishing sections. Excellent restaurant and coffee bar. Takeaway and fish and chips. TV in the restaurant. Heated outdoor swimming pool with a lifeguard. Large, well-equipped playground and separate football/ball games field. Dog walking field. Fishing. Watersports. Slipways. Crazy golf. Public telephone. WiFi (charged).

Key Features

 Pets Accepted

 Disabled Facilities

 Swimming Pool

 Fishing

 Sailing

Scan me for more information.

Alan Rogers Code: UK3560
162 pitches
GPS: 52.19498, 0.03110
Post Code: CB23 7DG

Cambridgeshire, East of England

www.alanrogers.com/uk3560
enquiries@highfieldfarmtouringpark.
co.uk
Tel: +44 1223 262308
www.highfieldfarmtouringpark.co.uk

Open (Touring Pitches):
End March - End October.

Highfield Farm Touring Park

The welcome is always warm from the friendly, family owners at this delightful eight-acre park. Situated only five miles from Cambridge, yet in a wonderfully quiet touring location, it is close to major routes around the city.

The pitches are fairly level with 60 numbered pitches for caravans and motorhomes, 42 with hardstanding, and 60 for tents. All have 10A electricity. The facilities are of high quality and the grass and hedges are well cared for. Conifer hedges divide the site into five areas. There are also some shady glades for those who wish to retreat even further, and one area is reserved for those without children. A good dog walk is provided, which can be extended to a pleasant 1.5-mile walk, with seats, around the farm perimeter.

Three heated toilet blocks provide good facilities, all very clean and well maintained. No dedicated provision for disabled visitors, although one block has extra wide doors and easy access. Laundry room. Motorhome services. Shop. Gates closed 23.00-07.30.

Key Features

 Pets Accepted

Scan me for more information.

Alan Rogers Code: UK3420
81 pitches
GPS: 52.80661, 1.41708
Post Code: NR28 9NA

Norfolk, East of England

www.alanrogers.com/uk3420
enquiries@twomills.co.uk
Tel: +44 1692 405829
www.twomills.co.uk

Open (Touring Pitches):
1 March - 31 December.

Two Mills Touring Park

Two Mills is a quiet, adults-only site with a long season. Set in the bowl of a former quarry, the park is a real sun trap. It is secluded, sheltered and terraced with birdsong to be heard at all times of the day.

Neatly maintained with natural areas, varied trees, wildflowers and birds, the owners, Barbara and Ray Barnes, want to add their own touches to this popular park. Following the purchase of an adjacent field, there are now 81 average-sized, level pitches for touring units on hardstanding, including 72 serviced pitches (patio, water and wastewater drainage). All have 10/16A electricity.

This is a good centre from which to explore the north Norfolk coast, the Broads or for visiting Norwich.

Two neat, clean, central toilet blocks can be heated, and include some washbasins in cabins and en-suite facilities for disabled visitors. Washing machine, dryer and spin dryer. Motorhome services. Small shop at reception. WiFi throughout (charged on part of the site). Dogs are accepted by arrangement only. A good bus route passes close by.

Key Features

 Adults Only

 Pets Accepted

 Disabled Facilities

 Beach Access

Scan me for more information.

Alan Rogers Code: UK3510
289 accommodations
500 pitches
GPS: 52.58653, 1.65962
Post Code: NR31 9QB

Norfolk, East of England

www.alanrogers.com/uk3510
breydon.water@park-resorts.com
Tel: +44 1493 780357
www.parkdeanresorts.co.uk

Open (Touring Pitches):
Start March - End October.

Breydon Water Holiday Park

Owned by the Parkdean Resorts group, these well established holiday parks (formerly Liffens Holiday Park and Welcome Holiday Centre) are in a semi-rural area on the edge of the Norfolk Broads within easy reach of Great Yarmouth.

Breydon Water Holiday Park comprises the two parks, now named Bure Village (caravan holiday homes only) and Yare Village, which are just a short walk apart along a country lane. Visitors at each park may use the facilities at the other.

Yare Village has over 500 pitches which include 211 touring pitches (168 with 16A electricity) on a separate open, level and grassy area. The remaining pitches are used for caravan holiday homes, most privately owned, some to rent.

One toilet block offers clean, spacious, but fairly standard facilities. Unit for disabled campers. Baby room. Laundry. Shop. Entertainment complex with restaurant, two bars and takeaway. Swimming and paddling pools (seasonal). Play area and playfield.

Key Features

 Disabled Facilities

 Swimming Pool

 Play Area

 Bar/Restaurant

Scan me for more information.

Alan Rogers Code: UK4411
110 pitches
GPS: 52.74532, -2.67120
Post Code: SY4 4GB

Shropshire, Heart of England

www.alanrogers.com/uk4411
UKSitesBookingService@camc.com
Tel: +44 1743 709334
www.myccc.co.uk/eburyhill

Open (Touring Pitches):
Start April - End October.

Ebury Hill C&C Club

Ebury Hill Camping & Caravanning Club site is a basic facilities site in the Shropshire countryside. Pitch up at Ebury Hill, and you will be experiencing a little piece of history; nearly 3,000 years ago, the area was an Iron Age hill fort. Today the site provides a peaceful haven and an abundance of local wildlife, including squirrels, badgers, rabbits and birds. There is an attractive fishing lake stocked with carp, perch, roach and tench.

This is a UNESCO World Heritage Site and a monument to the Industrial Revolution in a beautiful setting. Award-winning museums bring the Victorian era to life through their many interactive exhibits and displays. There are no toilet or showers (other than a toilet for backpackers). Fishing is available with an Environment Agency rod licence. The site has 110 grass or hardstanding pitches (some seasonal). Most have an electric hook-up point.

Key Features

 Pets Accepted

 Play Area

The site does not have a toilet block. Laundry. Dishwashing area. Chemical toilet point. Motorhome service point. Information area. Backpacker facility. Telephone. Wi-Fi free. Gas sales. Ice pack freezer. Pets welcome. Dog walk. Children's play area. Caravan & motorhome storage. Earliest time of arrival 13.00

Scan me for
more information.

Alan Rogers Code: UK3775
10 accommodations
76 pitches
GPS: 52.96123, -0.66727
Post Code: NG32 2HU

Lincolnshire, Heart of England

www.alanrogers.com/uk3775
info@wagtailcountrypark.co.uk
Tel: +44 7814 481088
www.wagtailcountrypark.co.uk

Open (Touring Pitches):
All year.

Wagtail Country Park

There has been a small campsite here for many years, but the current owner has transformed the appearance of the original camping area alongside an attractive little fishing lake and has created a larger lake with additional pitches and facilities.

There are 76 touring pitches (some seasonal), all with electricity (16 amp), on gravel hardstanding and separated by grass borders, raised flower beds or timber beams. Tents are not accepted. A pleasant walkway runs along the embankment bordering the (unfenced) main lake.

The site is a member of the Caravan and Motorhome Club Affiliated Site Scheme but visitors who are not members of the club are also very welcome.

Two small heated buildings near the original pitches each provide an en-suite controllable shower, washbasin and WC. A new heated and well equipped toilet block includes a toilet for visitors who are disabled and laundry facilities. No children's facilities. Motorhome service point. Security barriers. Small shop. Gas supplies. Secure caravan storage. Fishing (£5 per person). Wi-Fi over site (charged). No late-night arrivals area. Pets allowed. Dog walk. Train station 1.5 miles.

Key Features

 Open All Year

 Pets Accepted

 Fishing

Scan me for more information.

Alan Rogers Code: UK3680
135 accommodations
227 pitches
GPS: 53.23329, -0.12243
Post Code: LN9 5PP

Lincolnshire, Heart of England

www.alanrogers.com/uk3680
ashbypark@btconnect.com
Tel: +44 1507 527966
www.ashbypark.co.uk

Open (Touring Pitches):
Start March - End November.

Ashby Park

Ashby Park is a pleasant, well-run park located in 70 acres of former gravel pits that now provide seven attractive fishing lakes. There is a series of clearings occupied by privately owned caravan holiday homes, seasonal caravans and 127 touring pitches. All have access to 16A electricity and 100 pitches also have hardstanding, water tap and drainage.

Lakeside pitches will no doubt appeal to anglers, whereas families with young children will probably prefer to be further away from the lakes, as they are unfenced. One field caters for dog owners. Nearby is the bustling market town of Horncastle, renowned for its antique shops.

Three toilet blocks are well maintained and equipped, with open style washbasins and controllable showers; all hot water is metered (payable). Good en-suite facilities for disabled visitors. Laundry room with washing machine and dryer. Limited dishwashing (a long walk from lakeside pitches). Motorhome services. Gas supplies. Fishing (day ticket from £6). WiFi.

Key Features

 Pets Accepted

 Disabled Facilities

 Beach Access

 Fishing

Scan me for
more information.

Alan Rogers Code: UK3803
28 pitches
GPS: 53.18996, -1.61644
Post Code: DE4 2EB

Derbyshire, Heart of England

www.alanrogers.com/uk3803
grouseandclaret.matlock@marstons.co.uk
Tel: +44 1629 733233
grouseandclaretcaravanpark.co.uk

Open (Touring Pitches):
All year.

Grouse & Claret Caravan Park

The Grouse and Claret Caravan Park is a very picturesque site with a riverside setting. It is located to the rear of the pub and adjacent to the River Derwent. There are 28 hardstanding pitches that are well laid out around the site although some can be a little close to each other. All pitches have a 16 amp electric hook-up. The adjoining pub serves good quality food and drinks all day every day.

The site is unable to take any tents or gazebos. It is located between Matlock and Bakewell on the main A6, in the village of Rowsley. Nearby is the Peak Shopping Village with its good selection of small retail outlets. This site is also well placed for visiting the towns of Matlock, Bakewell and Buxton, as well as Gullivers Kingdom, Haddon Hall and Chatsworth House, all a short drive from the site.

There is one recently refurbished toilet and shower block serving the site. Washing up area and chemical disposal point. Recycling facilities. There is no on-site shop, although these can be found nearby. Unfenced water adjoining the site (River Derwent). Free Wi-Fi on site accessible to all pitches. Dogs are welcome. Secure barrier at site entrance. Fire equipment on site. The site is open all year. Bus stop opposite the site to Matlock and Bakewell. Cars are parked off site in pub car park rather than on site.

Key Features

 Open All Year

 Pets Accepted

 Play Area

 Bar/Restaurant

Scan me for more information.

234

Alan Rogers Code: UK3920
59 pitches
GPS: 53.30572, -1.12882
Post Code: S80 1ER

Nottinghamshire, Heart of England

www.alanrogers.com/uk3920
riversideworkshop@hotmail.co.uk
Tel: +44 1909 474118
www.riversideworksop.co.uk

Open (Touring Pitches):
All year.

Riverside Caravan Park

A town centre touring park, adjacent to the Worksop cricket ground, this four-acre site is surprisingly peaceful. For those who cannot resist the thwack of leather on willow, this site is ideal. Access is difficult with a small bridge and sharp turn so large units will find this restrictive/impossible.

Riverside is within easy walking distance of the town centre shopping precinct, and the Chesterfield Canal runs close to its northern side offering towpath walks and fishing (children would need to be watched). Of the 59 marked level pitches, many are seasonal and the remainder are for touring, mainly on gravel hard-standing, 7 are on grass and some are separated by trees and low rails, and all have 10A electric hook-ups. There is good site lighting.

The single sanitary unit near reception can be heated and has all the usual facilities, Limited facilities for disabled visitors. No laundry. Motorhome services. Gas supplies. WiFi over site (charged).

Key Features

 Open All Year

 Pets Accepted

Scan me for more information.

Alan Rogers Code: UK5360
79 pitches
GPS: 53.58880, -3.04400
Post Code: PR8 3ST

Mersey, North West

www.alanrogers.com/uk5360
info@willowbankcp.co.uk
Tel: +44 1704 571566
www.willowbankcp.co.uk

Open (Touring Pitches):
All year - Excludes February.

Willowbank Touring Park

Well situated for the Sefton coast and Southport, Willowbank Holiday Home & Touring Park is set on the edge of sand-dunes amongst mature, -windswept trees. Entrance to the park is controlled by a barrier, with a pass-key issued at the excellent reception building which doubles as a sales office for the substantial, high-quality caravan holiday home development.

There are 79 touring pitches, 30 on gravel hardstandings, 16 on grass and a further 33 pitches, all with 10A electricity; these are on grass hardstanding using an environmentally friendly reinforcement system. Large units are accepted by prior arrangement.

The purpose-built, heated toilet block is of a high standard including an excellent bathroom for disabled visitors, although the showers are rather compact. Baby room. Laundry. Motorhome services. Play area. Field for ball games. Beauty treatments. WiFi throughout (charged).

Key Features

 Pets Accepted

 Disabled Facilities

 Beach Access

 Play Area

Scan me for more information.

Alan Rogers Code: UK4670
2 accommodations
39 pitches
GPS: 54.07267, -2.04199
Post Code: BD23 5NU

North Yorkshire, Yorkshire

www.alanrogers.com/uk4670
info@woodnook.net
Tel: +44 1756 752412
www.woodnook.net

Open (Touring Pitches):
All year - Excludes February

Wood Nook Caravan Park

Wood Nook is a family run park in the heart of Wharfedale, part of the Yorkshire Dales National Park. The site includes six acres of woodland with quite rare flora and fauna. Reception is in the farmhouse, as is the small shop. The gently sloping fields have gravel roads and provide 39 touring pitches (30 with gravel hardstanding). All have 10 amp electricity and nearby water and chemical disposal points.

There is also room for 31 tents and there are some caravan holiday homes to let. The access road is narrow for a short distance, so care should be taken. The Thompson family are very friendly, always willing to have a chat, although Wood Nook is still a working farm producing beef cattle.

Converted farm buildings provide dated but clean sanitary facilities which can be heated. Washbasins in cubicles for ladies. Roomy showers (in another building – coin-operated). Laundry facilities. Motorhome services. Licensed shop for basics and gifts (from Easter). Gas. Small play area. Internet access in reception. Wi-Fi throughout (free).

Key Features

 Pets Accepted

 Play Area

Scan me for more information.

Alan Rogers Code: UK4638
4 accommodations
28 pitches
GPS: 54.08185, -1.24105
Post Code: YO61 1RY

North Yorkshire, Yorkshire

Alders Caravan Park

www.alanrogers.com/uk4638
enquiries@homefarmalne.co.uk
Tel: +44 1347 838722
www.alderscaravanpark.co.uk

Open (Touring Pitches):
Start March - End October.

The Alders is located in the village of Alne, nine miles from the centre of York, and has been carefully developed and managed on a working farm in historic parkland. The drive from reception around the village cricket ground to the pitches gives a real feeling of space.

The extra-large pitches are arranged in small bays designed to give privacy and separate the 28 touring pitches (16 with 6/10A Europlug) from the seasonal units, storage and camping pods. Service tracks throughout allow site maintenance without compromising privacy. Woodland walks and a water meadow with wildflowers enhance the wonderful peace and tranquillity. Occasional light aircraft noise.

The first-rate toilet blocks are heated with family-sized shower rooms, one also has a bath (fee for baths). The newer block includes en-suite bathrooms with baths or showers. Laundry facilities. Provision for disabled visitors. Motorhome services. Shop (serves as local village shop). Gas is sold at reception. Only 2 dogs accepted per pitch.

Key Features

 Pets Accepted

 Disabled Facilities

 Bar/Restaurant

Scan me for
more information.

Alan Rogers Code: UK4621
3 accommodations
30 pitches
GPS: 54.25422, -0.85203
Post Code: YO62 6SS

North Yorkshire, Yorkshire

www.alanrogers.com/uk4621
enquiries@clifffarmholidays.com
Tel: +44 1751 473792
www.clifffarmholidays.com

Open (Touring Pitches):
All year.

Cliff Farm Holidays

Cliff Farm Holidays is a 30-pitch touring caravan site that has spacious, hard standing pitches with 16 amp electric hook up. Every pitch can receive free Wi-Fi along with stunning views of the surrounding countryside. Touring site guests have the use of a warm and clean toilet/shower block including disabled facilities and a laundry room. A pot wash area with hot water is also available for use.

Well behaved dogs are welcome on site but are to be always kept on a lead. There are dog walks around the farm for guests to admire the fantastic panoramic views of Ryedale. Sinnington village is only a 15-minute walk with beautiful woodland and river walks. It also hosts a welcoming pub and restaurant, The Fox and Hound.

A single, warm and clean toilet/shower block includes facility for guests who are disabled. Baby changing facility. Laundry room. Pot wash area. Wi-Fi free. Gas sales. Well behaved dogs are welcome on site but are to be always to be kept on a lead. Dog walks. TV reception good. Charge for awnings.

Key Features

 Open All Year

 Pets Accepted

 Disabled Facilities

Scan me for more information.

Alan Rogers Code: UK4550
12 accommodations
225 pitches
GPS: 54.23573, -0.37612
Post Code: YO11 3NN

North Yorkshire, Yorkshire

www.alanrogers.com/uk4550
UKSitesBookingService@camc.com
Tel: +44 1723 583171
www.camc.com

Open (Touring Pitches):
Start March - Start November.

Cayton Village (CAMC)

Cayton Village Caravan and Motorhome Club Site is just three miles from the hustle and bustle of Scarborough, it is a peaceful, attractive haven. Originally just a flat field with caravans around the perimeter, years of hard work have produced a park which is well designed and very pleasing to the eye with quality facilities.

There 225 pitches including 190 hardstanding and some serviced, all with electricity. The late arrivals area also has electrical hook-ups and a water point - this is useful as the gates are locked at night and anyone leaving early is also expected to use it, so as not to disturb others.

Four toilet blocks (key code locks) can be heated and have high-quality fixtures and fittings. Some showers are preset, others are controllable. Two family shower rooms, family bathroom and baby facilities. Large room for disabled visitors. Two laundry rooms. Reception and shop including gas and caravan spares. Adventure playground. Nature trail and dog walks. Caravan storage. Wi-Fi at The Laurels. Motorhome service point. Chemical toilet point. Pets allowed. Dog walk. 6 Glamping Pods. 6 Glamping Cabins. Tents accepted. BBQ's allowed. Defibrillator. Twin axle caravans accepted. Late-night arrivals area. Tents allowed. Bus stop adjacent. Train station 2 miles. Earliest time of arrival 12 noon. Maximum outfit length 8.5 metres.

Key Features

 Book Online

 Pets Accepted

 Disabled Facilities

 Beach Access

 Play Area

Scan me for more information.

Alan Rogers Code: UK5520
8 accommodations
97 pitches
GPS: 54.41715, -2.99528
Post Code: LA22 0HX

Ambleside, Cumbria

www.alanrogers.com/uk5520
info@skelwith.com
Tel: +44 15394 32277
www.skelwith.com

Open (Touring Pitches):
Start March - Mid November.

Skelwith Fold

Skelwith Fold has been developed in the extensive grounds of a country estate taking advantage of the wealth of mature trees and shrubs. Over 300 privately owned caravan holiday homes and 97 touring pitches are absorbed into this unspoilt natural environment, sharing it with red squirrels and other wildlife in several discrete areas branching off the central, mile-long main driveway. Touring pitches (no tents) are on gravel hardstanding and metal pegs will be necessary for awnings. Electricity hook-ups (10-16A) and basic amenities are available in all areas.

You will find endless pleasure exploring over130 acres of wild woodland and, if early risers, it is possible to see deer, foxes, etc. at the almost hidden tarn deep in the woods. There are plenty of paths to follow, leading to a wealth of discoveries, including our mystical tarn, sculptures and breath-taking views of the Langdale Pikes and surrounding fells.

Key Features

 Pets Accepted

 Disabled Facilities

 Play Area

Three toilet blocks, well situated to serve all areas, have the usual facilities including laundry, drying and ironing rooms. Facilities for disabled visitors. Motorhome services. Well stocked, licensed shop. Battery charging, gas and caravan spares and accessories. Adventure play area. Astroturf sports pitch. Library with computer. E-bicycle hire. Family recreation area with picnic tables and goal posts in the Lower Glade. WiFi. Dishwashing facilities by EasyBe

Scan me for
more information.

Alan Rogers Code: UK5711
2 accommodations
100 pitches
GPS: 54.61891, -2.06502
Post Code: DL12 0TL

Co. Durham, Northumbria

www.alanrogers.com/uk5711
leekworthcaravanpark@live.co.uk
Tel: +44 1833 640582
www.caravancampingteesdale.co.uk

Open (Touring Pitches):
Early March - End October.

Leekworth Camping Park

Leekworth Caravan & Camping Park is situated on the outskirts of the historic market village of Middleton in Teesdale, very close to Barnard Castle. The stunning natural beauty of the North Pennines surrounds the site which sits on the banks of the River Tees. The famous Teesdale Way cuts alongside the site joining onto the Pennine Way and Middleton village, with its country shops and cafes only a 10-minute walk away.

An adult only section with limited pitches is available, you must be quick to book these. The site has 100 grass or hardstanding pitches (some seasonal). There is also a stone built self catering cottage & glamping pod available for hire.

Single heated shower block (fee payable) wash basins & WC's. Hairdryer electric points. Disabled toilet and shower. Washing up area. Chemical toilet disposal. Freezer. On-site shop. Half-size football goal posts. Fire pits for hire. Pets allowed. Free fishing on the River Tees, (rod licence required). Dog walking areas. Winter storage. Store & Pitch. Wi-fi. Daily pizza delivery. BBQ's 40cm from the ground are allowed. Disposable BBQ's not allowed. Earliest arrival time 1.30pm.

Key Features

 Pets Accepted

 Disabled Facilities

 Fishing

Scan me for more information.

Alan Rogers Code: UK5785
16 pitches
GPS: 55.74740, -2.10489
Post Code: TD15 2XT

Northumberland, Northumbria

www.alanrogers.com/uk5785
stay@chainbridgecaravansite.co.uk
Tel: +44 7554 953697
www.chainbridgecaravansite.co.uk

Open (Touring Pitches):
Start March - End November.

Chainbridge Caravan Site

Chainbridge Touring Caravan Site is a beautifully laid out L-shaped park is for adults only and quietly situated down a non-classified road that leads to a chain bridge over the River Tweed, linking Scotland and England. The owners are very welcoming and many visitors return time and time again.

The park offers 16 hardstanding touring pitches off a gravel driveway. All have electricity (16A) and freshwater. With very little noise from all but the birds, this is a very tranquil site. Berwick-upon-Tweed is on the doorstep, just four miles away, and just inland you'll find Northumberland's fine sandy beaches. The park is easily accessible from both north and south of the border.

Three unisex toilets provide washbasins and showers with underfloor heating. No dedicated facilities for disabled visitors. Coin-operated washing machine and dryers. Kitchen with sink, freezer and microwave. Motorhome services. TV room and lounge. Trout fishing. Riverside walks. Cycle paths. WiFi (limited area).

Key Features

 Adults Only

 Pets Accepted

 Beach Access

 Fishing

Scan me for more information.

Alan Rogers Code: UK6061
2 accommodations
30 pitches
GPS: 51.52577, -3.04107
Post Code: CF23 8HH

Glamorgan, South Wales

www.alanrogers.com/uk6061
mariaphipps718@btinternet.com
Tel: +44 7983 615984
www.tycochleisure.com

Open (Touring Pitches):
All year.

Ty Coch Campsite

Ty Coch have been welcoming campers for over 10 years and you will quickly discover that the owners are passionate about hospitality and really enjoy sharing the beautiful 10-acre smallholding with campers who appreciate a laid back, friendly and informal campsite. Ty Coch Campsite is a wonderful adults-only oasis on the coast road within 15 minutes drive of Cardiff and Newport. This part of South East Wales has a wide choice of activities, including walking the beautiful coastal path, visits to Historic Houses & National Museums.

The site is within a short drive of some of the most wonderful market towns, the seaside and the countryside. On the doorstep are the beautiful Peterstone Lakes Golf Course, fishing lakes, a farm park, and two local pubs with good food. The site has 30 grass or hardstanding pitches all with an electric hook-up point. Shepherd's huts available to hire this quirky accommodation is sure to be an away stay you will never forget! With access to all of our on-site showers, toilets and campers kitchen.

Small toilet block with showers, washbasin, WC's and hairdryer. Dishwashing area. Gated entry. Information area. Motorhome service point. Ice pack freezer. Battery charging. Kitchen. Pets allowed. Dog walking field. Earliest arrival time 13.00. Wi-Fi charged.

Key Features

 Adults Only

 Open All Year

 Pets Accepted

 Scan me for more information.

Alan Rogers Code: UK6041
30 pitches
GPS: 51.89593, -3.28870
Post Code: LD3 7JY

Powys, Mid Wales

www.alanrogers.com/uk6041
lydjenkins@hotmail.co.uk
Tel: +44 1874 676674
www.talybontfarmcamping.co.uk

Open (Touring Pitches):
Start April - End September.

Talybont Farm Camping

Talybont Farm site is situated on a working farm in a beautiful setting on the edge of a picturesque village, six miles from Brecon in the beautiful Brecon Beacons National Park. The village has a shop/post office/off licence, four pubs with good food, all within a five-minute walk and close to the canal.

There is a lot to do in the area, bike rides, pony treks, sailing on Llangorse Lake, lovely walks to suit all ages, fishing and golf. Brecon has regular farmers markets; a theatre and leisure centre and Hay-on-Wye is a famous book town. The site has 30 pitches for tourers/motorhomes/tents and 20 electric hook-up points.

Toilets and Showers. Facility for guests who are disabled. Laundry. Chemical Disposal Point. Pets Allowed. Dog walk. Off-site facilities. Food Shop 300 yards. Bar/Pub 300 yards. Restaurant 300 yards. Indoor Heated Pool 6 miles. Fishing 100 yards. Golf Course 6 miles. Horse Riding 6 miles. Tents allowed. Wi-Fi free. TV reception poor. Charge for awnings and pets.

Key Features

 Pets Accepted

Scan me for more information.

Alan Rogers Code: UK5960
88 pitches
GPS: 51.95158, -3.90030
Post Code: SA19 9NG

Carmarthenshire, West Wales

www.alanrogers.com/uk5960
aberma@tiscali.co.uk
Tel: +44 1550 777868
www.abermarlaiscaravanpark.co.uk

Open (Touring Pitches):
Mid March - Mid November.

Abermarlais Caravan Park

Apart from the attractions of south or mid-Wales for a stay, this sheltered, family-run park could also double as a useful transit stop close to the main holiday route for those travelling to Pembrokeshire. In a natural setting, up to 88 touring units are accommodated in one fairly flat, tapering, five-acre grass field edged by mature trees and a stream. Pitches are numbered and generously spaced around the perimeter and on either side of a central, hedged spine at the wider end, with 46 electrical hook-ups (10A) and one hardstanding. Backpackers have a small, separate area.

The park is set in a sheltered valley with a range of wildlife and nine acres of woodland walks. There is also an old walled garden, with some pitches and lawns, that screens the park, both audibly and visibly, from the A40 road. However, the most sought after pitches are beside the stream a haven for wildlife. A torch would be useful.

The one small toilet block is older in style but is clean, bright, cheerful and adequate with controllable showers. Two external, covered dishwashing sinks but no laundry facilities (nearest about 5 miles). Motorhome services. Shop doubles as the reception. Gas supplies. Play area with tennis and volleyball nets and play equipment. Winter caravan storage.

Key Features

 Adults Only

 Pets Accepted

Scan me for more information.

Alan Rogers Code: UK5982
3 accommodations
60 pitches
GPS: 51.69326, -4.75340
Post Code: SA70 8RD

Pembrokeshire, West Wales

www.alanrogers.com/uk5982
info@trefalunpark.co.uk
Tel: +44 1646 651514
www.trefalunpark.co.uk

Open (Touring Pitches):
Early April - End October.

Trefalun Park

Only four miles from Tenby and the beaches of Carmarthen Bay, Trefalun Park is an open, nicely laid out campsite with a friendly atmosphere engendered by the owners. The site is very modern and well kept with all roads and pitches maintained, along with the 60 generously sized touring pitches with electric hook-up. Hardstandings have been created, some with full services. This park will suit those, particularly families, looking for a quiet holiday and also the more active who favour walking, cycling or watersports. There is a mobile home park in the adjacent field, which is owned by the site and maintained to the same high standard.

A large fenced recreational area has a variety of adventure type play equipment and a football pitch. Heatherton World of Activities and Manor wildlife park are a short walk away, Oakwood Theme Park is a 20-minute drive. Pembroke and Manorbier with their respective castles are nearby, plus many other historic monuments close by.

Key Features

 Pets Accepted

 Disabled Facilities

 Beach Access

 Play Area

Modern heated sanitary block, with showers and some washbasins in cubicles. Separate, fully equipped suite for disabled visitors and families. Separate baby room. Laundry. Motorhome services. Gas. Large children's play area. Modern reception providing local information. Wi-Fi (charged).

Scan me for more information.

Alan Rogers Code: UK6000
29 pitches
GPS: 51.98308, -4.94666
Post Code: SA65 9TA

Pembrokeshire, West Wales

www.alanrogers.com/uk6000
info@gwaunvale.co.uk
Tel: +44 1348 874698
www.gwaunvale.co.uk

Open (Touring Pitches):
Start April - End October.

Gwaun Vale Touring Park

In a superb rural setting with wonderful views across the countryside towards the sea, Gwaun Vale provides 29 pitches. On mainly level grass, with one terrace above another, connected by an oval, gravel and tarmac road, ten pitches have hardstanding and 21 have 10A electricity connections. There are plenty of water points and several picnic tables.

A useful little shop doubles as a reception with a well-presented display of tourist information and a variety of books on local walks, to buy or borrow. One can also borrow a barbecue, iron and board, or a baby bath.

The toilet block, beside reception and to one side of the site has been refurbished and is neat, clean and heated. Cheerful laundry room with a laundry sink, washing machine and dryer and two dishwashing sinks. Shop. Play area in a small sloping fenced field with adventure type equipment and a field for dogs adjoining. Entrance barrier (deposit for key) – if reception is closed, telephone for a key.

Key Features

 Pets Accepted

 Beach Access

Scan me for more information.

Alan Rogers Code: UK6005
40 pitches
GPS: 52.13001, -4.45401
Post Code: SA44 6RE

Ceredigion, West Wales

www.alanrogers.com/uk6005
info@brynaweloncp.co.uk
Tel: +44 1239 654584
www.brynawelon.co.uk

Open (Touring Pitches):
Start March - End October.

Brynawelon Camping Park

Brynawelon Touring & Camping Park is a friendly, attractive and well-appointed campsite. It is in a stunning rural location within two miles of the Ceredigion coast with its beaches, and close to the River Teifi with plenty of water-based activities.

All 40 pitches have electricity hook-ups and of these, 25 also have water and drainage and hardstanding. Ten all-weather pitches for tents have been added. The remainder are on level grass. The park has ample room for children to play, an enclosed play area, an indoor games room with TV, and a sauna next to reception. Buzzards, red kites, owls and the occasional eagle can be seen from the park.

There is also a wide variety of small birds. A wide choice of Blue Flag beaches can be found along the coast, there are dolphin trips from New Quay ten miles away and white water rafting on the Teifi at Llandysul. The Teifi is also a well-known canoeing and fishing river.

Modern toilet block with toilets, showers, washbasins in cabins, two full suites in each side and a separate room for families and disabled visitors. Laundry/kitchen with washing machine, tumble dryer, ironing board and iron, fridge/freezer, microwave, kettle and toaster. Enclosed play area. Games room with table football, electronic games, TV and library. Sauna (charged). Dog walking area. WiFi (charged).

Key Features

 Pets Accepted

 Disabled Facilities

 Beach Access

 Play Area

Scan me for more information.

Alan Rogers Code: UK6012
2 accommodations
145 pitches
GPS: 52.37858, -3.84600
Post Code: SY23 3JW

Ceredigion, West Wales

www.alanrogers.com/uk6012
enquiries@woodlandsdevilsbridge.
co.uk
Tel: +44 1970 890233
www.woodlandsdevilsbridge.co.uk

Open (Touring Pitches):
Early April - Late October.

Woodlands Caravan Park

Woodlands Caravan Park is a well-established, family-run site near Aberystwyth, set amidst some of the most beautiful scenery Mid Wales has to offer. It is situated in Devils Bridge, a small village nestling at the top of the Rheidol Valley, 12 miles inland from the coastal town of Aberystwyth. It is an ideal base for touring Mid Wales, walking, cycling, mountain biking, birdwatching, fishing or just relaxing and taking in the fresh air.

The adjacent 400-acre farm offers pleasant walks and beautiful scenery. You can expect to see a Red Kite flying over the site, and in the near distance, you will hear the heart-warming toot of the Vale of Rheidol steam train as it approaches Devils Bridge from Aberystwyth.

Toilet block, centrally heated and provides showers, washbasins, WC's & hairdryers. Facility for visitors who are disabled. Family room. Laundry room. Dish washing area. Playing area. Table tennis. Ball games area. Shop stocks groceries, newspapers and camping accessories. Gas sales. Ice pack freezer. Bike shelter. Tea room. Friday & Saturday evening takeaway menu. Earliest arrival time is at 2 pm. Wi-Fi free.

Key Features

 Pets Accepted

 Disabled Facilities

Scan me for more information.

Alan Rogers Code: UK6370
240 pitches
GPS: 52.73300, -4.06618
Post Code: LL42 1YR

Gwynedd, North Wales

www.alanrogers.com/uk6370
info@hendremynach.co.uk
Tel: +44 1341 280262
www.hendremynach.com

Open (Touring Pitches):
All year- Excludes February.

Hendre Mynach Camping Park

Hendre Mynach Touring Caravan & Camping Park is a large family park, stretching out along the beach on the outskirts of Barmouth. Colourful flowers brighten the steep entrance to this site (help is available to get out if you are worried). Of the 240 pitches, all for touring, 60 are on hardstanding with 10A electricity, and 39 are fully serviced. The beach is only 200 yards away but is separated from the park by a railway line. It can be crossed by pedestrian operated gates, which could be a worry for those with young children.

The quaint old seaside and fishing town of Barmouth is about a 30-minute walk along the prom. Here you will find 'everything'. The reception will provide leaflets with maps of local walks. Snowdonia National Park and mountain railway, the famous Ffestiniog railway, and castles and lakes everywhere provide plenty to see and do.

Two traditional toilet blocks offer adequate facilities for the whole family, including those for disabled campers (a long way from some pitches). Motorhome services. Small shop (Easter-1/11). Play area. WiFi (charged).

Key Features

 Pets Accepted

 Disabled Facilities

 Beach Access

 Play Area

Scan me for more information.

Alan Rogers Code: UK6615
61 accommodations
59 pitches
GPS: 53.09326, -3.79923
Post Code: LL24 0AL

Gwynedd, North Wales

www.alanrogers.com/uk6615
riverside@morris-leisure.co.uk
Tel: +44 1690 710310
www.morris-leisure.co.uk

Open (Touring Pitches):
All year - Excludes January.

Riverside Touring Park

This is a delightful, peaceful, eight-acre site owned and operated by the Morris Leisure Group. It is set just a few minutes' walk away from the beautiful village of Betws-y-Coed, a perfect location to visit the stunning Snowdonia National Park. Betws-y-Coed is widely acclaimed as one of the most attractive villages in Great Britain.

There are a total of 120 spacious pitches, 61 for mobile homes and 59 for tourers (all hardstanding; 20 are super pitches and there are a few grass tent pitches). All have 16 amp electricity and digital TV. The area has something for everyone – sportsmen, anglers, walkers, nature lovers and families. Listen for the owls hunting at night. The site is adjacent to the railway station, hence some train noise is inevitable.

The heated toilet block is housed in a modern, brick-built building (key access) has walk-in style shower cubicles. Separate cubicles with WCs for men and similar for women. Facilities for children and visitors who are disabled. Some of the pitches are quite a distance from the toilet block. Washing machine and dryer. Dishwashing sinks. Reception sells a few essentials and has a selection of caravan accessories including gas sales. Motorhome services. Digital TV booster system. Dog walk (max. 2 per unit). No arrivals before 13.00. Gazebos are not allowed. Tents allowed. Pets allowed. Dog walk adjacent. Wi-Fi. BBQs allowed. Earliest time of arrival 13.00. Maximum outfit length 8.5metres. Bus stop 400 metres. Train station adjacent.

Key Features

 Pets Accepted

 Disabled Facilities

Scan me for more information.

Alan Rogers Code: UK6696
5 accommodations
24 pitches
GPS: 53.23392, -3.83500
Post Code: LL32 8SY

Conwy, North Wales

www.alanrogers.com/uk6696
enquiries@wernfarmcaravanpark.co.uk
Tel: +44 1492 650257
www.wernfarmcaravanpark.co.uk

Open (Touring Pitches):
Mid March - End October.

Wern Farm Caravan Park

Wern Farm is a touring caravan park with a self-catering holiday cottage situated at the edge of the Snowdonia National Park. This is an ideal location for a holiday or short break exploring the tourist attractions, outdoor activities and natural beauty of North Wales. Wern Farm is a tranquil two-acre landscape site located within the beautiful Conwy Valley with unrivalled scenic views across the valley. The small, spacious, touring caravan park has 24 hard-standing pitches all with electric hook-up and also offers glamping pods.

The park is situated on the B5106 only 3.5 miles inland from the medieval town of Conwy and is also within easy reach of the well-known resorts of Llandudno, Colwyn Bay, Rhos-on-Sea, Betws-y-Coed and not forgetting the charming island of Anglesey.

Key Features

 Pets Accepted

A single toilet block provides showers, washbasins and toilet facilities. Laundry. Chemical toilet emptying area. Waste recycling area. Dogs are welcome, but owners are requested to always keep their pets on a lead, take them off the site for walks and always clean up after them properly. Wi-Fi charged. No tents allowed. There is a bus stop by the site entrance on the B5106. TV reception fair. Charge for awnings.

Scan me for more information.

Alan Rogers Code: UK6885
30 pitches
GPS: 54.75597, -4.58153
Post Code: DG8 9SG

Dumfries and Galloway,
Lowlands

www.alanrogers.com/uk6885
kingsgreencaravanpark@gmail.com
Tel: +44 1988 700489
www.kingsgreencaravanpark.com

Open (Touring Pitches):
Start March - End October.

Kings Green Caravan Park

Kings Green Caravan Park is owned and run by the Port William Community Association with regular warden visits. All the profits from the site go back into the village for the benefit of the residents.

Kept very natural and situated beside the sea overlooking Luce Bay and the to the Mull & Rhins of Galloway (on some days the Mountains of Mourne in Ireland are visible). To the south sits the Isle of Man. It is situated on the southern fringes of Port William, well known for its harbour and fishing community.

The all grass, open site provides 30 marked and numbered pitches for caravans, motorhomes and tents (21 with 16A electricity).

The small toilet block (key entry) is kept very clean and has vanity style washbasins, free electric showers and hair dryers. Facilities for disabled visitors include WC and washbasin (Radar key). Laundry area with dishwashing. Information room always open. Large play and ball game area adjacent. WiFi (free).

Key Features

 Pets Accepted

 Disabled Facilities

 Beach Access

 Play Area

Scan me for more information.

Alan Rogers Code: UK6940
11 accommodations
40 pitches
GPS: 55.01017, -4.05630
Post Code: DG7 3NE

Dumfries and Galloway,
Lowlands

www.alanrogers.com/uk6940
office@lochkenholidaypark.co.uk
Tel: +44 1644 470282
www.lochkenholidaypark.co.uk

Open (Touring Pitches):
Start March - Mid November.

Loch Ken Holiday Park

Loch Ken Holiday Park is a very well maintained site on the shore of the loch, opposite the RSPB bird reserve and the Galloway Forest Park – it is a peaceful haven in an Area of Outstanding Natural Beauty.

This is a family-owned park with 40 touring pitches and 34 caravan holiday homes, 11 of which are to rent. The touring pitches, all with 16A electricity, are separate and are arranged in an open plan way with loch views, on good sized hardstandings, with three on neatly mown grass. There is a separate tent field offering some pitches with electricity. Mature trees border the park and provide an area for walking dogs.

The heated toilet block has been completely refurbished to modern standards and was exceptionally clean when we visited. Separate facilities in a modern prefabricated unit are provided in the tent field. Facilities for disabled visitors. Laundry room. Gas supplies. Well stocked shop. Two play areas. Outdoor chess. Herb garden. Bicycles, canoes, kayaks, pedaloes and dinghies for hire. Boat launching (permit from reception). Fishing (permit). WiFi (free).

Key Features

 Pets Accepted

 Disabled Facilities

 Beach Access

 Play Area

 Bike Hire

 Fishing

 Sailing

Scan me for more information.

Alan Rogers Code: UK7025
43 pitches
GPS: 55.44100, -5.11397
Post Code: KA27 8SE

North Ayrshire, Lowlands

www.alanrogers.com/uk7025
enquiries@campingarran.com
Tel: +44 1770 820320
www.campingarran.com

Open (Touring Pitches):
Mid March - Mid October.

Seal Shore Camping Site

A warm welcome awaits here on the island of Arran from the resident owner, Maurice Deighton. Located on the southernmost point of the island, Seal Shore Camping & Touring Site is a quiet and peaceful park situated along its own private beach with wonderful sea views.

The open, grassy area, sloping in parts, takes caravans, motorhomes and tents with ten electricity connections (16A). The reception doubles as a shop selling basics with a TV room adjacent. There are communal picnic and barbecue areas. The Kildonan Hotel is next door serving restaurant and bar meals. Permits are available for loch fishing and charters are available from the owner, a registered fisherman. Golfers can choose from seven courses.

The good toilet block is clean and tidy and includes full facilities for disabled visitors that double as a baby room. Laundry room with washing machine, dryers and iron. Indoor dishwashing with fridge and freezer. Shop. Camping gas. Beach. Fishing. Sailing. Covered barbecue area.

Key Features

 Pets Accepted

 Disabled Facilities

 Beach Access

 Bar/Restaurant

 Fishing

Scan me for more information.

Alan Rogers Code: UK7046
2 accommodations
26 pitches
GPS: 55.95519, -3.59472
Post Code: EH49 6PL

West Lothian, Heart of Scotland

Beecraigs Camping

www.alanrogers.com/uk7046
mail@beecraigs.com
Tel: +44 1506 284516
www.beecraigs.com

Open (Touring Pitches):
All year.

Beecraigs Caravan & Camping Site is an ideal countryside retreat, with modern toilet facilities and a perfect base from which to explore Central Scotland, Trossachs, Glasgow and Edinburgh. Situated in the Bathgate Hills within Beecraigs Country Park but only 2 miles south of Linlithgow town.

The site provides a countryside setting with much to offer within the Country Park and the local area. This open all year site has 26 hardstanding pitches each with an electric hook-up. There is also a small grass area for tents. 2 Glamping lodges available to hire.

Two toilet & shower blocks, disabled provision with bath, Dishwashing facilities. Baby changing facility. Laundry with washer & dryer. Tourist information. Gas sales. BBQ sites. Chemical toilet point. Children's play area. Visitor Centre. Café. Tents allowed. Motorhome service point. Security barrier. Pets allowed. Dog walk. TV reception fair. Late-night arrivals area.

Key Features

 Open All Year

 Pets Accepted

Disabled Facilities

 Play Area

Scan me for
more information.

Alan Rogers Code: UK7075
40 accommodations
129 pitches
GPS: 55.95985, -2.46221
Post Code: EH42 1SA

East Lothian, Heart of Scotland

www.alanrogers.com/uk7075
info@thurstonmanor.co.uk
Tel: +44 1368 840643
www.verdantleisure.co.uk/thurston-manor

Open (Touring Pitches):
All year- Excludes January and February.

Thurston Manor Leisure Park

In a rural setting and nestling at the foot of the Lammermuir hills, this holiday park offers either a restful or a lively stay. It is close to historic Dunbar with its beaches, harbour and ruined castle. The 129 touring pitches are set away from the 510 holiday homes. All have 10A electricity connections. Thirty of these are super pitches with electricity, water and drainage.

The indoor heated swimming pool and leisure complex offer space to relax and work out. There are woodland walks, safe play areas for children and fishing in a well-stocked pond. With so much to do on-site, it would be tempting not to venture out, but the East Lothian coastline has much to offer. Within a short drive, there are many villages with their quaint harbours.

The clean, well equipped and fully heated sanitary block provides constant hot water for showering, dishwashing and family bathing. Shop. Restaurant and sports bar. Leisure centre with heated swimming pool (10x6 m), sauna, steam room, fitness room and solarium. Play areas. Function room with live family entertainment. WiFi.

Key Features

 Pets Accepted

 Disabled Facilities

 Beach Access

 Swimming Pool

 Play Area

 Bar/Restaurant

 Fishing

Scan me for more information.

Alan Rogers Code: UK7225
99 pitches
GPS: 56.47344, -4.32164
Post Code: FK21 8TN

Stirling, Heart of Scotland

www.alanrogers.com/uk7225
UKSitesBookingService@camc.com
Tel: +44 1567 820245
www.camc.com

Open (Touring Pitches):
Mid March - Start November.

Maragowan (CAMC)

Maragowan Caravan and Motorhome Club Site is a picturesque family holiday location nestled on the bank of the River Lochay in Scotland. It is within comfortable walking distance of the quaint little holiday town of Killin where you can idle the time away in the various shops and restaurants.

The site puts you within easy reach of a wealth of fun outdoor activities. 99 mainly hardstanding pitches all with 16 amp electricity. Some seasonal pitches. There is a 9-hole golf course and trout fishing is permitted in the river (free) without a permit. Cycling routes are in close proximity and mountain bikes can be hired in the village of Killin. Kayaking, hill walking and mountaineering can all be undertaken from the site.

A single toilet block provides facilities for visitors who are disabled and children. Laundry. Showers. Wash basins. Dish washing. Motorhome service point. Chemical toilet point. Defibrillator. Children's play area. Information room. Wi-Fi charged. BBQs allowed gas, electric & charcoal. TV reception good. Pets allowed. Dog walk. Twin axle caravans accepted. Late-night arrivals area. Telephone. Security barrier. Bus stop 400 metres. Co-op 0.5mile. Petrol station 3.2 miles. No Tents allowed.

Key Features

 Book Online

 Pets Accepted

 Disabled Facilities

 Play Area

 Fishing

Scan me for more information.

Alan Rogers Code: UK7310
40 accommodations
12 pitches
GPS: 56.37522, -4.00650
Post Code: PH6 2JY

Perth and Kinross, Heart of Scotland

www.alanrogers.com/uk7310
alowe20@aol.com
Tel: +44 1764 670411
twentyshillingwoodcaravanpark.co.uk

Open (Touring Pitches):
Mid March - End October.

Twenty Shilling Wood

Everyone gets a warm welcome from the Lowe family when they arrive at Twenty Shilling Wood. Set amongst 10.5 acres of wooded hillside, this unusual park has a few touring pitches for caravans and motorhomes (no tents), plus a number of owner-occupied caravan holiday homes.

However, with terracing and landscaping, not many of these are visible and flowering trees and shrubs help to hide them.

The lowest level is the entrance where there is a late arrivals area and visitor car park. You will be escorted to your pitch. There are just 12 level touring pitches on gravel with grass bays between them, all with 10A electricity hook-ups.

Clean and spacious toilet blocks have some washbasins in cubicles for both men and women (key access; deposit required). Dishwashing area and laundry. No shop. Gas available. Games room with pool table, table tennis (both free) and lounge area with comfortable seating and well stocked library. Fenced adventure playground for all ages. Entrance barrier (deposit for card). Only two dogs per pitch are accepted. Fenced dog walking area.

Key Features

 Pets Accepted

 Play Area

Scan me for more information.

Alan Rogers Code: UK7825
13 accommodations
90 pitches
GPS: 56.46924, -5.69828
Post Code: PA65 6AY

Argyll and Bute, Heart of Scotland

Shieling Holidays

www.alanrogers.com/uk7825
bookings@isleofmullcampsite.co.uk
Tel: +44 1680 812496
shielingholidays.co.uk

Open (Touring Pitches):
Start March - Start November.

This lovely site looks across the Sound of Mull to the mainland, and on a clear day, Ben Nevis can be seen from the tent pitches. There are 31 hardstanding pitches for tourers, all with 13A electricity hook-ups, plus 59 tent pitches. The tent pitches are on astroturf and strong pegs and a hammer are available from reception if required.

Rental accommodation is in two cottages and 13 Shielings (traditionally a Gaelic hut, but in this case, tents made of a very thick white material). Some are en-suite, carpeted and have gas and electricity. Most pitches have wonderful views.

The modern, clean toilet block can be heated and has free showers and hairdryers. Two Sheiling toilet blocks are in the tent area, along with baths and facilities for disabled visitors. Family shower room. A well equipped laundry and covered clothes lines. Motorhome services. Games room. Bicycle hire and boat launching. Free WiFi in reception and common room (open 24 hours; no mobile signal).

Key Features

 Pets Accepted

 Disabled Facilities

 Beach Access

 Play Area

 Bike Hire

 Fishing

Scan me for more information.

Alan Rogers Code: UK7782
2 accommodations
15 pitches
GPS: 57.07478, -4.82663
Post Code: PH35 4HG

Highland, Highlands and Islands

www.alanrogers.com/uk7782
enquiries@faichemard-
caravancamping.co.uk
Tel: +44 1809 501314
www.campsite.faichemard.scot

Open (Touring Pitches):
Start April - Late October.

Faichemard Farm Camping

Faichemard Farm is an adult only site, idyllically located on the outskirts of Invergarry in the Scottish Highlands. It has been run by the same family since 1935 and visitors can expect a very warm and helpful welcome. There is stunningly beautiful scenery from the 15 level touring pitches, many on hardstanding and all with 10A electricity and its own picnic table.

A few pitches look across a pond towards one of the toilet blocks, while a second block is further up the hillside. There is an abundance of wildlife here, and deer, pine martins, red squirrel and even the occasional golden eagle can be seen.

Two modern, heated and well equipped toilet blocks have very large showers, shaver points and hairdryers. One block also has an en-suite unit for disabled visitors. Close to reception is a large undercover area with a laundry and a fridge/freezer. Free WiFi over site. Dogs are welcome on a short lead.

Key Features

 Adults Only

 Pets Accepted

 Disabled Facilities

Scan me for more information.

Alan Rogers Code: UK7670
2 accommodations
125 pitches
GPS: 57.33480, -3.61862
Post Code: PH26 3JQ

Highland, Highlands and Islands

www.alanrogers.com/uk7670
warden@caravanscotland.com
Tel: +44 1479 872474
www.caravanscotland.com

Open (Touring Pitches):
All year.

Grantown-on-Spey

Granton-on-Spey Caravan Park is peacefully situated on the outskirts of the town, with views of the mountains in the distance. There are 125 well-tended gravel and grass pitches for caravans and motorhomes, all with 10/16 amp electricity and 69 offer fresh and wastewater facilities. In addition to this, a number of super pitches also offer 16 amp electricity, Wi-Fi and individual Freesat TV box.

A further 12 pitches are used for seasonal occupation and there is space for 50 or more tents. Trees and flowers are a feature of this attractive, landscaped location. The wardens escort visitors to their pitch and will help to site caravans if necessary. Caravan holiday homes are located in a separate area of the park.

Key Features

 Open All Year

 Pets Accepted

 Disabled Facilities

 Play Area

The modern toilet and shower block is complete with laundry and drying room. A further block provides good, clean toilet facilities, with washing cabins for ladies. Facilities for visitors who are disabled. Baby & toddler wash room. Laundry room. Motorhome services. Gas, ice-creams, cold drinks and camping accessories available at reception. Children's play area. Games room with table tennis and pool table. Wi-Fi over site (charged). Pets welcome. Dog walk adjacent. BBQs allowed. TV reception booster system. Tents accepted. Caravan and motorhome secure storage. Bus stop 800 metres. Earliest arrival time 12 noon.

Scan me for more information.

Alan Rogers Code: UK7560
15 accommodations
62 pitches
GPS: 57.09110, -2.23968
Post Code: AB12 5FX

Aberdeenshire, Grampian

www.alanrogers.com/uk7560
deeside@woodleisure.co.uk
Tel: +44 1250 878123
www.woodleisure.co.uk/our-parks/
deesid

Open (Touring Pitches):
All year.

Deeside Holiday Park

Deeside Holiday Park is a tranquil retreat set in the Southern valley of the River Dee, ideal for getting away from it all. Choose to spend your time exploring Royal Deeside and the Cairngorms National Park or soaking up the atmosphere in the lively city of Aberdeen.

The site has a wide choice of self-catering accommodation including lodges, safari tents, holiday homes and glamping/camping pods. The site offers 62 pitches for tourers, motorhomes and campervans as well as a spacious grassy area for camping.

Deeside has long been a favourite destination for the Royal family and for many other visitors to the North-East of Scotland. Steeped in history and tradition, the area is a must for heritage lovers with its castles and folklore, whisky distilleries and museums and of course its atmospheric stone circles history comes to life at every turn.

Key Features

 Pets Accepted

 Disabled Facilities

 Play Area

Heated toilet block provides showers, washbasins & WC's. Facility for visitors who are disabled. Family bathrooms. Laundry. Chemical toilet point. Children's play area. Shop. TV lounge. Games room. BBQ area. Pets welcome. Dog walk. Security barrier. Recycling. Wi-Fi, charged.

Scan me for more information.

Alan Rogers Code: UK7750
1 accommodations
50 pitches
GPS: 57.62202, -6.19600
Post Code: IV51 9JX

Isle of Skye, Highlands and Islands

Staffin Caravan & Camping Site

www.alanrogers.com/uk7750
staffincampsite@btinternet.com
Tel: +44 1470 562213
www.staffincampsite.co.uk

Open (Touring Pitches):
Easter - Mid October.

This site is just outside the village of Staffin on the east coast of Skye. There are 50 touring pitches, 26 with 16A electricity and hardstanding and 24 on grass without electricity. Pitches on the upper terrace enjoy lovely views of the sea. The entrance to the site from the main road is by a single track road.

A marked walk from the site across the headland leads to the seashore and slipway (good for walking dogs). Skye has many activities to offer and for the truly dedicated walker the Cuillins are the big attraction and the hills above Staffin are demanding in places!

The site provides an excellent base for hill walkers and climbers or for those of you who prefer an evening summer stroll, there are excellent walks nearby. The site is situated amongst the rural, unspoilt community of North Skye and has lots to offer for all that choose the location for a break. Dogs are welcome and nearby walks are provided.

The sanitary block includes large, controllable showers. There are some hot water dishwashing sinks and laundry. Small campers' kitchen with microwave, table and seating. Bicycle hire. WiFi throughout (charged).

Key Features

 Pets Accepted

 Beach Access

 Bike Hire

Scan me for more information.

Alan Rogers Code: UK7666
3 accommodations
75 pitches
GPS: 57.73167, -5.70223
Post Code: IV21 2BX

Highland, Highlands and Islands

www.alanrogers.com/uk7666
info@gairlochcaravanpark.com
Tel: +44 1445 712373
www.gairlochcampsite.co.uk

Open (Touring Pitches):
Start April- Start November.

Gairloch Holiday Park

Gairloch is a small site with 75 touring pitches, 35 are hardstanding, 25 have hook-up there are also 35 non-electric tent pitches. Two modern static holiday homes are for hire as well as a six-bedroom holiday cottage. All pitches and the cottage have spectacular views across Loch Gairloch to The Isle of Sky.

Gairloch Holiday Park is a family-run park that is situated beside the sea at Strath which is the main crafting township in the historical parish of Gairloch. Gairloch Holiday Park is ideally situated as a touring centre for Wester Ross. It is also located within 6 miles of the world-famous Inverewe Gardens.

The village of Gairloch is within easy walking distance from the park and features a wide array of amenities including a quality butcher, grocery and provisions. The location makes it an excellent stopover for the N500 coastal route as well as a relaxing holiday destination.

Modern toilets, showers & disabled facilities, Chemical, grey & general waste disposal, Laundry, Dishwashing, WIFI, Dog friendly

Key Features

 Pets Accepted

 Beach Access

Scan me for more information.

Alan Rogers Code: UK7730
60 pitches
GPS: 58.35142, -5.15677
Post Code: IV27 4TG

Highland, Highlands and Islands

www.alanrogers.com/uk7730
info@scouriecampsitesutherland.com
Tel: +44 1971 502060
www.scouriecampsitesutherland.com

Open (Touring Pitches):
Easter - End September.

Scourie Caravan & Camping Park

This is a family-run park, which has a number of firm terraces with 60 pitches, which gives it an attractive layout – there is nothing regimented here. Perched on the edge of the bay in an elevated position, practically everyone has a view of the sea and a short walk along the shore footpath leads to a small sandy beach.

The park has tarmac and gravel access roads, with well-drained grass and hardstanding pitches, some with 10A electricity hook-ups. A few are on an area which is unfenced from the rocks (young children would need to be supervised here).

The toilet facilities can be heated. Showers have no divider or seat. Laundry. Motorhome services. The Anchorage restaurant at the entrance to the park (used as reception at quiet times) serves meals at reasonable prices, cooked to order (seasonal). Boat launching. Fishing permits can be arranged.

Key Features

 Pets Accepted

 Disabled Facilities

 Bar/Restaurant

Scan me for
more information.

Alan Rogers Code: UK7735
2 accommodations
82 pitches
GPS: 58.56449, -4.74221
Post Code: IV27 4PZ

Highland, Highlands and Islands

www.alanrogers.com/uk7735
stay@sangosands.com
Tel: +44 1971 511726
www.sangosands.com

Open (Touring Pitches):
All year (limited facilities November
- February.)

Sango Sands Oasis Site

Sango Sands Oasis Caravan & Camping Site is a quiet, ten-acre site overlooking the beautiful Sango Bay, a Blue Flag beach. The site was established by the family in 1978 and they continue to work hard to improve the facilities each year.

There are 82 pitches for tents and touring caravans, 70 with 16A electricity. The land is well-drained and fairly level. It is possible to see whales, porpoises, dolphins and seals from the site plus a variety of sea birds that nest nearby. An ideal area for walkers, including the less adventurous, there are numerous marked paths and there is an excellent variety of angling, from rivers to the sea.

The renovated toilet and shower blocks are lit at night but a torch may be useful. Free showers with curtains (Apr-Oct). Showers and toilets are separate. With the beach so close don't be surprised to find sand in the showers. En-suite facilities for disabled visitors. Laundry with sinks, washing machines, dryers, irons and boards. Campers' kitchen with cooking rings. Café, bar and licensed restaurant. TV. Games room with pool and darts. Barbecues permitted off ground. Motorhome service point. WiFi (charged). Two caravans for hire. From Nov-March only the toilets and electric hook-ups are available, with cold water.

Key Features

 Open All Year

 Pets Accepted

 Disabled Facilities

 Beach Access

 Bar/Restaurant

Scan me for
more information.

Alan Rogers Code: UK7745
56 pitches
GPS: 58.61549, -3.34484
Post Code: KW14 8XD

Highlands, Highlands and Islands

www.alanrogers.com/uk7745
UKSitesBookingService@camc.com
Tel: +44 1847 821319
www.camc.com

Open (Touring Pitches):
End March - Start October.

Dunnet Bay (CAMC)

Dunnet Bay Caravan and Motorhome Club site is close to the village of Dunnet and next to a lovely sandy beach. Dunnet Bay is situated between the A836 and the sand dunes, looking out to Dunnet Head, the most northerly point of mainland Britain. There are 56 fairly level, grass touring pitches (two for tents), all with 16 amp electricity hook-ups.

It is an ideal location for birdwatchers (a ferry trip around the Stacks of Duncansby is possible) and anglers, who can enjoy both sea and freshwater fishing. A good choice for those who enjoy solitary tranquillity, at Dunnet Bay site you can admire the stunning views over clean washed sands to lovely Dunnet Head.

Key Features

 Book Online

 Pets Accepted

 Disabled Facilities

 Beach Access

The beautifully clean, single, modern, heated toilet block has controllable showers, hairdryers and cubicles. Well equipped en-suite unit for disabled visitors. No children's facility. Washing machine and dryer. Vegetable preparation area. Ice blocks are frozen on request. Information room. Gas sales. No children's play area. Defibrillator. Motorhome services. Essentials available in reception. Dog walk adjacent. Wi-Fi hot spot. BBQ's allowed. TV reception good. Twin axle caravans accepted. No late-night arrivals area. Tents allowed. Bus stop 800 metres. Mini Market 3 miles. Earliest time of arrival 12noon. Maximum outfit length 9.2 metres.

Scan me for more information.

Alan Rogers Code: UK8550
24 pitches
GPS: 54.48933, -6.75735
Post Code: BT71 6DY

Dungannon, Co. Tyrone

Dungannon Park

www.alanrogers.com/uk8550
parks@midulstercouncil.org
Tel: +44 28 8772 8690
www.midulstercouncil.org/
DungannonPark

Open (Touring Pitches):
Start March - End October.

This small touring park nestles in the midst of a 70-acre park with a multitude of tree varieties, brightly coloured flower beds and a charming 12-acre fishing lake. The touring pitches, some with lake views, are on hardstanding, each with dedicated water, waste and 16A electricity connections. Hedging provides some separation. There is also an unmarked grass area for tents. Run by Dungannon Council, the park, which also incorporates tennis courts, football and cricket pitches, lies about one mile south of Dungannon town.

The site has an excellent range of facilities incorporating a mixed coarse/game fishery, café and gift shop, tennis courts, football & cricket pitches, a children's play area and a barbeque site while walkers can enjoy the miles of interesting pathways that circumscribe the parkland, which from the high ground have splendid viewpoints of Dungannon Town and the surrounding countryside. The modern visitor amenity caters for an extensive range of needs with splendid sanitary (disabled included) facilities and washing/laundry amenities onsite.

Key Features

 Pets Accepted

 Disabled Facilities

 Play Area

 Fishing

Sanitary facilities are to the rear of the Amenity Centre and include showers (by token), washbasins, baby changing mat and spacious unit for disabled visitors. Laundry room with washing machine and dryer. Excellent play area. TV lounge. Tennis. Fishing. Walking. Orienteering.

Scan me for
more information.

Alan Rogers Code: UK7014
36 pitches
GPS: 54.22528, -5.88329
Post Code: BT33 0LN

Newcastle, Co. Down

www.alanrogers.com/uk7014
info@windsorholidaypark.co.uk
Tel: +44 28 4372 3367
www.windsorholidaypark.co.uk

Open (Touring Pitches):
All year.

Windsor Holiday Park

A family-run quiet holiday park, with level and spacious grass pitches. With an ideal location being only a 1-minute drive or a 5-minute walk to the centre of the seaside town of Newcastle, at the foot of the Mourne Mountains, with many cafes, restaurants and bars. There are 3 touring areas, with the furthest from the reception appearing bigger than the others. Pitches are well maintained, well-drained and all have 16A electrical hookups. There is a games room.

Some of the pitches have a view of the mountains. A limited number of touring pitches from 1 March to 31 October. Ideal for a family holiday near the sea. the site has dedicated bbq and picnic areas.

One clean and well-kept toilet block with 3 showers/washroom. Separate laundry room with washing machines (tokens available from reception). Sinks for hand and dishwashing. Chemical disposal point and custom grey waste disposal are located next to the toilet block. Children's play area, shop, WiFi, Pets Allowed.

Key Features

 Pets Accepted

 Disabled Facilities

 Play Area

Scan me for more information.

Capital Athens
Currency Euro (€)
Language Greek
Time Zone EET (GMT+2)
Telephone Code +30

Shops Hours vary throughout the year, with many shops operating on shorter hours in low and shoulder seasons. In high season 8am to 2pm Mon, Wed, Sat and 8am to 2pm and 5pm to 9pm Tues, Thurs, Fri.

Money ATMs are widespread and most are accessible 24hrs a day and have multilingual instructions. Credit/debit cards are accepted in urban areas but it's handy to have cash.

Accessible Travel Although improving, much of Greece is difficult to navigate for wheelchair users and those who are less able.

Travelling with children Greece has plenty of green spaces, historical attractions and sandy beaches. Greek culture is all about sharing so restaurants will always be accommodating towards children. Make sure to bring mosquito repellant.

EU Travel Greece is an EU member state and located within the Schengen Area.

♲ **LEZ** Low Emissions Zones in Athens. Foreign vehicles do not need to register.

●●○○○ **Accessibility Score**
View our digital e-guide & find out more at
alanrogers.com/open-to-all

Tourism website visitgreece.gr

Public Holidays 1 Jan New Year's Day • 6 Jan Epiphany • Mar Orthodox Ash Monday • 25 Mar Independence Day • Apr/May Orthodox Good Friday • Apr/May Orthodox Easter Sunday • Apr/May Orthodox Easter Monday • 1 May Labour Day • Jun Orthodox Whit Sunday • Jun Orthodox Whit Monday • 15 Aug Assumption • 28 Oct Ochi Day • 25 Dec Christmas Day • 26 Dec Boxing Day

Driving in Greece Road signs are written in Greek and in English. Some roads have tolls. In Athens, parking is prohibited within the Green Zone unless signposts state otherwise. Drink-driving, using you mobile whilst driving are illegal. Dashcams are legal but using footage for insurance purposes is prohibited.

View of Oia, situated on the island of Santorini

Greece

View all campsites in Greece
alanrogers.com/greece

See campsite map page 481

Climate

Mediterranean climate with plenty of sunshine, mild temperatures and limited amount of rainfall.

	Jan	Feb	Mar	Apr	May	Jun	Jul	Aug	Sep	Oct	Nov	Dec
High	14	14	17	21	25	30	34	34	29	23	19	15
Low	7	7	9	12	17	21	24	24	20	16	12	8

Greece is made up of clusters of islands with idyllic sheltered bays and coves, golden stretches of sand with dunes, pebbly beaches, coastal caves with steep rocks and black volcanic sand and coastal wetlands. Its rugged landscape is a monument to nature with dramatic gorges, lakes, rivers and waterfalls.

Nestling between the Aegean, Ionian and Mediterranean waters, Greece has over 13,000 km of coastline. A largely mountainous country, its backbone is formed from the Pindus range, which extends as far as Crete, the largest of Greece's 6,000 islands, themselves peaks of the now-submerged landmass of Aegeis.

Mount Olympus in the north of the country, known from Greek mythology as the abode of the gods, is the highest mountain (2,917 m).

The Greek islands have something to offer every visitor – the vibrant nightlife of Mykonos, the 'honeymoon' island of Santorini, Rhodes, where the modern city sits alongside the medieval citadel, and Corfu with its Venetian and French influences. The mainland is home to some of the most important archaeological sites, including the Acropolis, the Parthenon and Delphi.

Alan Rogers Code: GR8370
55 accommodations
30 pitches
GPS: 39.66440, 19.84430
Post Code: GR-49083

Corfu, Ionian Islands

Camping Dionysus

www.alanrogers.com/gr8370
laskari7@otenet.gr
Tel: +30 2661 091417
dionysuscamping.gr

Open (Touring Pitches):
Start April - Mid October.

The Ionian island of Corfu is known by most as a popular tourist destination but perhaps not considered by many for camping. The hourly ferry from Igoumenitsa takes 90 minutes to cross to Kerkyra. Many ferries from Italian ports now stop here en-route to either Igoumenitsa or Patras, so it is possible to break your journey to mainland Greece.

The north of the island now has some good campsites and Dionysus is amongst them, with its 107 pitches of which 30 are suitable for caravans and motorhomes.

The site, south of Dassia, slightly slopes and has been terraced in part to provide grassy pitches under old olive trees, which offer some shade. Of course, almost every sporting activity and leisure pursuit can be found on the island and the necessary bookings can be made in reception.

Two good toilet blocks include showers, WCs and washbasins. Washing machine. Small shop, bar and restaurant (seasonal). Swimming pool (seasonal). Bicycle hire. WiFi throughout (free).

Key Features

 Pets Accepted

 Beach Access

 Swimming Pool

 Bar/Restaurant

 Bike Hire

Scan me for more information.

Alan Rogers Code: GR8255
32 accommodations
100 pitches
GPS: 39.71318, 21.61528
Post Code: GR-42200

Kalambaka, Thessaly

www.alanrogers.com/gr8255
tsourvaka@yahoo.gr
Tel: +30 2432 022293
www.campingkastraki.com

Open (Touring Pitches):
All year.

Vrachos Kastraki

The region of Meteora is named after the impressive rock formations which rise out to the plain of Thessaly and which now have ancient monasteries clinging to their summits. Camping Vrachos Kastraki is ideally placed to visit this unusual landscape, as it is situated in a valley surrounded by mountains and huge, natural sculptures.

There are around 300 pitches, many quite small and suitable only for tents. 16A Electricity is said to be available for all, but in some cases cables would have to cross the roads. Individual pitches are not marked and you may pitch where you like. There is plenty of shade from mature almonds, acacias and poplars.

There is a warm welcome on arrival, which immediately helps the visitor unwind after the journey through the mountain passes. The site owners can advise on the numerous places of interest to visit. For the adventurous visitor, rock climbing, abseiling, canoeing and mountain biking can be organised from the site.

Two modern sanitary blocks provide British style WCs and open washbasins. Laundry room. Cooking facilities with picnic areas. Shop. Bar, restaurant and snack bar. Outdoor swimming pool (seasonal). Play area.

Key Features

 Open All Year

 Swimming Pool

 Play Area

 Bar/Restaurant

Scan me for more information.

Alan Rogers Code: GR8140
141 accommodations
120 pitches
GPS: 40.17062, 23.85352
Post Code: GR-63088

Nikiti, Central Macedonia

www.alanrogers.com/gr8140
info@lacaracamping.gr
Tel: +30 2375 091444
www.lacaracamping.gr

Open (Touring Pitches):
Start May - End September.

Lacara Camping

This back to basics campsite has two springs and a stream flowing into a small marsh and 10 km. of forest roads in private woodland, an idyllic location, but with a risk of mosquitos following a period of rain. On the east coast of the Sithonia peninsula, the setting is stunning.

The 120 pitches that are suitable for caravans (out of a total of 250) are small, on dry ground with little grass and set among trees leading down to a sandy beach. Pitches are marked by low wooden rails, and the buildings are of very basic construction. All the toilets are Turkish style.

The closest village of any size is Vourvourou, a small fishing village with a handful of tavernas and seafood restaurants. Boat hire is available here or if you're feeling active, you could take the trail to the top of Mt. Itamos which offers vistas of the villages and bays below.

A number of basic toilet blocks include showers, WCs (Turkish style) and washbasins. Kitchens. Laundry with washing machine. Beach bar. Small shop. Restaurant. Sandy beach. Bamboo huts and wooden bungalows to rent. Tennis.

Key Features

 Beach Access

 Bar/Restaurant

 Fishing

Scan me for
more information.

Alan Rogers Code: GR8475
14 accommodations
85 pitches
GPS: 39.01953, 23.22675
Post Code: GR-34200

Pefki, Central Greece

www.alanrogers.com/gr8475
info@campingpefki.gr
Tel: +30 2226 040469
campingpefki.gr

Open (Touring Pitches):
Start June - End August.

Camping Pefki

Evia, the second largest Greek Island, offers dramatic scenery and the north end of the island provides an opportunity to get away from the crowds of Attica. It also offers an alternative route between Athens and Thessaloniki and avoids the boring motorway route towards Lamia.

Opened in 1986, Camping Pefki is an older site, just across the road from the sea and a small beach. There are 85 small pitches and bungalows available to rent.

All the pitches are under screens and the site is covered with trees and shrubs, and serviced by a narrow, winding road. Altogether, this restricts access for large units.

However, those looking for a quiet, simple site next to the sea in a beautiful corner of the island will not be disappointed, even if the facilities are a bit older and the site lacks facilities offered by larger sites in more popular areas.

Basic toilet blocks include facilities for disabled visitors. Two kitchens include sinks, gas hobs and fridges. Laundry with washing machine. Small shop. Bungalows to rent.

Key Features

 Pets Accepted

 Disabled Facilities

 Beach Access

 Fishing

Scan me for more information.

Alan Rogers Code: GR8580
43 accommodations
12 pitches
GPS: 37.67660, 24.04820
Post Code: GR-19500

Sounio, Attica

www.alanrogers.com/gr8580
campingbacchus@hotmail.com
Tel: +30 2292 039572
campingbacchus.gr

Open (Touring Pitches):
All year.

Camping Bacchus

Camping Bacchus is a small but welcoming site in a remote area. Just a handful of its 55 pitches are available for tourers with the rest taken up by mobile homes and caravans to rent. The site is on partly sloping ground with shade provided by pine trees. It is 100 m. from a sandy beach, where there are great views out over the Aegean Sea and its islands.

The campsite shop opens all year but stock is rather limited. There is also a bar (all year) and restaurant (May to October). The temple of Poseidon is only 4.5 km. along the coastal road.

In ancient times this magical place was the last sign of civilisation for Athenian sailors as they left their home shores. Nowadays it is a popular destination for day trips from Athens and is best experienced at sunset when the sea glows fiery red.

Three old sanitary blocks with British style WCs, washbasins with cold water only, two also have controllable showers. Washing machine. Shop. Bar. Restaurant (May-Oct). Communal area for barbecues. Small play area. WiFi.

Key Features

 Open All Year

 Pets Accepted

 Beach Access

 Play Area

 Bar/Restaurant

 Fishing

Scan me for more information.

Alan Rogers Code: GR8700
16 accommodations
90 pitches
GPS: 36.95188, 21.69561
Post Code: GR-24001

Pylos, Peloponnese

www.alanrogers.com/gr8700
info@erodioss.gr
Tel: +30 2723 023269
erodioss.gr

Open (Touring Pitches):
Mid April - Late October.

Camping Erodios

Owner Efthymios Panourgias has given great thought to what is needed and has provided everything to the highest possible standard, in an environmentally friendly way. The owner is constantly on the site ensuring these standards are maintained and usually has plans for further improvements.

The 90 pitches have maturing trees to provide shade, which is most welcome given the high temperatures, even in the low season. There is direct access to a sandy beach and the glorious turquoise sea in a sheltered bay north of the busy town of Pylos. One of the best sites in Greece.

Three good toilet blocks include showers, WCs and washbasins. Facilities for disabled visitors. Two kitchens with sinks, electric hobs and fridges. Laundry. Motorhome services. Very good shop (all season). Bar/café with Internet access, self-service restaurant/takeaway (seasonal). Play area for under 5s. Car and motorbike hire. Communal barbecue. Accommodation for rent. Free WiFi throughout.

Key Features

 Pets Accepted

 Disabled Facilities

 Beach Access

 Play Area

 Bar/Restaurant

 Fishing

Scan me for more information.

Alan Rogers Code: GR8662
9 accommodations
100 pitches
GPS: 37.88579, 21.11280
Post Code: GR-27050

Ilia, Peloponnese

www.alanrogers.com/gr8662
camping_melissa@yahoo.gr
Tel: +30 2623 095213
www.campingmelissa.gr

Open (Touring Pitches):
Start April - End October.

Camping Melissa

Campsite Melissa is located on the beach in Kástro, West Greece, situated by the sea. The 100 campsite pitches are marked out and are on sloping ground and have a mixture of full, partial or no shade.

The beachside location makes this an ideal site for watersports enthusiasts, with a shallow family-friendly beach. Onsite facilities include a restaurant, which is self-service and a beach bar that offers a selection of snacks. The sanitary facilities are reasonably modern and clean.

Nearby attractions include the castle at Chlemoutsi, with the ancient city of Olympia is around two hours away. Ferries to the island of Zákynthos depart from the small port of Kyllini about 15 minutes North of the campsite.

WiFi available. Pets allowed (Max 2 dogs) BBQs permitted. Twin-Axle vehicles permitted. Laundry facilities are available. Self-service restaurant and bar. Small children's playground.

Key Features

 Beach Access

 Play Area

 Bar/Restaurant

 Fishing

Scan me for more information.

Alan Rogers Code: GR8315
8 accommodations
60 pitches
GPS: 38.15009, 21.57711
Post Code: GR-25002

Kato Alissos, Peloponnese

www.alanrogers.com/gr8315
costasde@gmail.com
Tel: +30 2693 071249
camping-kato-alissos.gr

Open (Touring Pitches):
Start April - Early November.

Camping Kato Alissos

Kato Alissos can be found 21 km. west of Patras, the capital of the Peloponnese and has direct access to a long beach. This is an attractive but basic site with lemon, orange and olive trees providing a pleasant camping environment. At the heart of the site, the bar/restaurant specialises in traditional Greek cuisine and has welcome shade from a giant olive tree, said to be over 1,000 years old.

There is another bar that has fine panoramic views across Patraikos Bay. Pitches here are well shaded and all are equipped with electrical connections. Various activities are organised throughout the season, including Greek folk music and dancing.

Patras is Greece's third-largest city and worth a visit. The city is home to Saint Andrew's church, the largest in the Balkans. Further afield, Ancient Olympia is one of the great sites of Greek antiquity and is highly recommended. Alternatively, Kalavrita is a delightful hilltop town, renowned for the monasteries of Mega Spileo and Saint Lavra, and best visited by the scenic Odontotos railway.

Key Features

 Beach Access

 Play Area

 Bar/Restaurant

 Fishing

Basic, but clean sanitary facilities include showers with free hot water. Laundry facilities. Restaurant. Bar. Takeaway. Shop. Playground. Activity and entertainment programme. Direct beach access. Free WiFi.

Scan me for more information.

Capital Dublin
Currency Euro (€)
Language English and Gaelic
Time Zone GMT
Telephone Code +353

Shops 9.30am to 6pm Mon to Sat (to 8pm Thurs in cities), noon to 6pm Sun.

Money ATMs are widespread and accessible 24hrs a day. Visa/Mastercard are widely accepted, Amex only by major retailers and Diners/JCB rarely accepted. Rural areas are often more reliant on cash.

Accessible Travel All new buildings are wheelchair-friendly. In cities, most buses have low-floor access. Trains are accessible (contact in advance).

Travelling with children Children are welcomed in Ireland, although family facilities aren't always accessible in rural spots. Most restaurants accept children although some high-end establishments may not. Children under five travel free on all public transport.

EU Travel Ireland is an EU member state with a land border with the UK.

There are no Low Emissions Zones currently in place.

●●●●○ **Accessibility Score**
View our digital e-guide & find out more at

alanrogers.com/open-to-all

Tourism website | ireland.com

Public Holidays 1 Jan New Year's Day · 17 Mar St Patrick's Day · Mar/Apr Easter Monday · Early May May Day · Early Jun June Bank Holiday · Early August Bank Holiday · Late Oct October Bank Holiday · 25 Dec Christmas Day · 26 Dec Boxing Day

Driving in Ireland Driving is on the left-hand side, and roads are generally well maintained. Tolls exist on some routes, although most toll stations don't accept cards, so make sure to carry change. Signposts are in both Gaelic and English in most areas. Drink-driving, using your mobile whilst driving and sat navs that warn you of speed cameras are illegal.

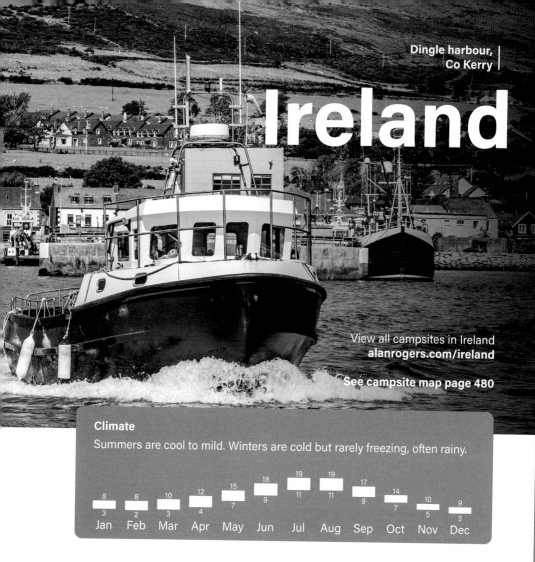

Ireland

View all campsites in Ireland
alanrogers.com/ireland

See campsite map page 480

Climate

Summers are cool to mild. Winters are cold but rarely freezing, often rainy.

	Jan	Feb	Mar	Apr	May	Jun	Jul	Aug	Sep	Oct	Nov	Dec
High	8	8	10	12	15	18	19	19	17	14	10	9
Low	3	2	3	4	7	9	11	11	9	7	5	3

Ireland is made up of four provinces: Connaught, Leinster, Munster and Ulster, comprising 32 counties, 26 of which lie in the Republic of Ireland.

Famed for its folklore, traditional music and friendly hospitality, the Republic of Ireland offers spectacular scenery within a relatively compact area. With plenty of beautiful areas to discover and a relaxed pace of life, it is an ideal place to unwind.

Ireland is the perfect place to indulge in a variety of outdoor pursuits while taking in the glorious scenery. There are plenty of waymarked footpaths which lead through woodlands, across cliffs, past historical monuments and over rolling hills. With its headlands, secluded coves and sandy beaches, the dramatic coastline is fantastic for watersports or for just simply relaxing and watching the variety of seabirds that nest on the shores.

The Cliffs of Moher, in particular, is a prime location for birdwatching and Goat Island, just offshore, is where puffins make their nesting burrows.

In the south, the beautiful Ring of Kerry is one of the most visited regions. This 110-mile route encircles the Inveragh Peninsula and is surrounded by mountains and lakes. Other sights include the Aran Islands, the Rock of Cashel and the bustling cities of Dublin, Galway and Cork.

Alan Rogers Code: IR8635
26 pitches
GPS: 55.23039, -7.79308

Co. Donegal, North West

www.alanrogers.com/ir8635
rosguillholidaypark@yahoo.ie
Tel: +353 749155766
www.rosguillholidaypark.com

Open (Touring Pitches):
Start May - End September.

Rosguill Holiday Park

Rosguill Park is a quiet, family-owned Caravan and Camping site, located on a stunning peninsula that forms part of the rugged and beautiful North West Donegal coast. The site is surrounded by six long, clean, sandy beaches, all within walking distance, plus a number of other beaches nearby all in Downings. The site is predominantly occupied by privately owned mobile homes but offers 26 touring pitches, 12 of which have concrete hardstanding, 10A electricity and water, the remainder are on grass without services. All of the touring pitches face the beautiful Mulroy Bay and enjoy amazing views.

It is little wonder that it is popular with tourists. The stunning landscape provides an excellent backdrop to a glass of wine or a tasty barbecue after a hard day relaxing on one of the many beaches, or sightseeing along the stunning 11 km. 'Wild Atlantic Way' with breathtaking vistas around every bend of this wonderful coastline.

Well-appointed en-suite sanitary block in the touring area. Facilities for disabled visitors. Family shower rooms. Campers' kitchen. Laundry facilities. Tennis. Multisports field. Pitch and putt. Bicycle hire. Play area.

Key Features

 Pets Accepted

 Disabled Facilities

 Beach Access

 Play Area

 Bike Hire

 Fishing

Scan me for more information.

Alan Rogers Code: IR9100
1 accommodations
113 pitches
GPS: 53.30445, -6.41533

Co. Dublin, Dublin

Camac Valley Camping

www.alanrogers.com/ir9100
reservations@camacvalley.com
Tel: +353 14640644
www.camacvalley.com

Open (Touring Pitches):
All year.

Opened in 1996, this campsite is not only well placed for Dublin, but also offers a welcome stopover if travelling to the more southern counties from the north of the country, or vice versa. Despite its close proximity to the city, and the constant noise from the dual carriageway, being located in the 300-acre Corkagh Park gives it a 'heart of the country' atmosphere.

There are 113 pitches on hardstanding for caravans, laid out in bays and avenues, all fully serviced (10A Europlug). Maturing trees and shrubs separate pitches and roads are of tarmac. Beyond the entrance gate and forecourt stands an attractive, timber-fronted building housing the site amenities.

After a day of sightseeing in Dublin, which can be reached by bus from the site, Camac Valley offers an evening of relaxation with woodland and river walks in the park or a number of first-class restaurants and pubs within easy driving distance.

Key Features

 Open All Year

 Pets Accepted

 Disabled Facilities

 Play Area

 Fishing

Heated sanitary facilities include good-sized showers (token). Facilities for disabled visitors. Baby room. Laundry. Shop (for basics) and coffee bar. Playground with wooden play frames and safety base. Fishing. Electronic gate-controlled from reception and 24-hour security. WiFi (free).

Scan me for more information.

Alan Rogers Code: IR9155
10 accommodations
100 pitches
GPS: 52.93869, -6.22898

Co. Wicklow, Heart

www.alanrogers.com/ir9155
hiddenvalleyholidays@gmail.com
Tel: +353 867272872
www.hiddenvalley.ie

Open (Touring Pitches):
Mid March - End September.

Hidden Valley Camping

This pleasant, level park occupies over seven hectares on both banks of the pretty Avonmore River near the small town of Rathdrum. It has 110 pitches arranged around a boating pond. The pitches are mostly concrete hardstandings with a few on grass. All have 16A Europlugs and close access to a water tap and waste drainage. Across a fine footbridge is a large, flat area for tents – most of them used by families at holiday time.

This site boasts one of the finest adventure play areas in Ireland. Archery, digital paintballing and crazy golf are all available. There are rowing boats and canoes for hire on the park's shallow lake, gentle water flumes, chutes and an impressive array of play equipment.

Well equipped and very modern toilet block finished in local slate. Facilities for visitors with disabilities. Motorhome services. Laundry. Hobs for cooking. Small shop, bar, restaurant and takeaway (all April-Sept). Fishing in the river may be arranged. Impressive play park. Canoes and boats for hire on lake. Bicycle hire. Log cabins to rent. Dogs must be kept on a lead. WiFi.

Key Features

 Pets Accepted

 Disabled Facilities

 Play Area

 Bar/Restaurant

 Bike Hire

 Fishing

 Golf

Scan me for more information.

Alan Rogers Code: IR9300
178 accommodations
140 pitches
GPS: 52.51686, -6.23785

Co. Wexford, South East

www.alanrogers.com/ir9300
info@morriscastlestrand.com
Tel: +353 539130124
www.morriscastlestrand.com

Open (Touring Pitches):
Early April - End September.

Morriscastle Strand

Whether you use this park as a stopover, to or from Rosslare Port, or choose it for a more extended stay, you will find it to be a quiet relaxing location. Situated minutes from the pretty village of Kilmuckridge it offers well maintained and clean facilities.

The 140 pitches are numbered and marked by concrete slabs, each with electricity (10A) and drainage point. Spacing can be a little tight in the high season when the park gets very busy. There are 170 privately owned caravan holiday homes on-site, but these are unobtrusive and kept separate by tall hedging. The entrance to the touring park is to the right of reception by way of a tarmac drive. This leads to the secluded, gently sloping, grass pitches that enjoy an open aspect. They overlook marshland which attracts wild geese and ducks, while the sea brings in crabs, eels and fish.

Two sanitary blocks, one opened for the high season, include showers, WCs and facilities for disabled visitors. Launderette. Motorhome services. Good night lighting. Shop, snacks and takeaway in high season. Games room (from June). Two tennis courts. Play area. Dogs are only accepted in certain areas.

Key Features

 Disabled Facilities

 Play Area

Scan me for more information.

Alan Rogers Code: IR9330
180 accommodations
103 pitches
GPS: 52.09477, -7.54617

Co. Waterford, South East

Casey's Caravan & Camping Park

www.alanrogers.com/ir9330
golf@rosapenna.ie
Tel: +353 5841919
www.caseyscaravanpark.com

Open (Touring Pitches):
Mid March - End October.

This is a very large park by Irish standards. Set on 20 acres of flat grass, edged by mature trees, this family-run park is well managed and offers 284 pitches which include 103 touring pitches, 75 with electrical hook-ups (10A Europlug) and 53 with hardstanding. There is even a large, open and flat field without services for high season overspill arrivals. The remainder are occupied by caravan holiday homes.

There is direct access from the park to a sandy, Blue Flag beach with a resident lifeguard during July and August. A highly recommended leisure centre is adjacent should the weather be inclement. The park is 5.5 km. from Dungarvan, a popular town for deep sea angling, from where charter boats can be hired and three, 18-hole golf courses are within easy driving distance.

The central toilet block (key system), has good facilities kept spotlessly clean. Showers on payment. Small laundry with washing machine and dryer. A further modern block provides an excellent campers' kitchen, laundry room and toilet for disabled visitors. Large adventure play area. Large, well-equipped games room. TV lounge. Minigolf. Gas supplies. Full-time security staff in high season. Play area for under 4s. Bicycle hire. Free WiFi throughout.

Key Features

 Pets Accepted

 Disabled Facilities

 Beach Access

 Play Area

Scan me for more information.

Alan Rogers Code: IR9370
2 accommodations
45 pitches
GPS: 52.41614, -8.21047

Co. Tipperary, Shannon

Ballinacourty House

www.alanrogers.com/ir9370
info@camping.ie
Tel: +353 6256559
www.camping.ie

Open (Touring Pitches):
Start April - End September.

Ballinacourty House and its cobble-stoned courtyard form the centrepiece of this south-facing park with views of the Galtee Mountains. Accessed by a tree-lined lane, the reception area is in part of the renovated 18th-century building, as is the adjoining restaurant.

The park is level with 38 touring pitches with 6A Europlugs, and seven grassy pitches for tents. Some areas are shaded and there are open spaces to accommodate rallies and larger groups. Self-catering cottages and B&B are also available. This tranquil site is very appealing to families with young children. It is an excellent base from which to tour the Rock of Cashel, the Mitchelstown Caves, Swiss Cottage and the towns of Tipperary, Cahir and Cashel.

Sanitary facilities provide free hot water and showers. Baby room. Laundry with ironing facilities. Campers' kitchen. Ice pack freezing. Licensed restaurant (early booking advised). Motorhome services. Gas supplies. Frisbee golf. TV and games rooms. Picnic benches. Tennis. Play area. WiFi (free).

Key Features

  Pets Accepted

  Play Area

  Bar/Restaurant

Scan me for more information.

Alan Rogers Code: IR9420
4 accommodations
26 pitches
GPS: 52.95720, -7.83937

Co. Tipperary, Shannon

www.alanrogers.com/ir9420
info@tipperarycaravanpark.com
Tel: +353 50521519
tipperarycaravanpark.com

Open (Touring Pitches):
Easter - End October (other times by
advance phone call).

Streamstown Camping

This family run site, set on a dairy farm in the centre of Ireland, has been open for over 40 years. It is conveniently situated off the M7 Dublin-Limerick road and makes a good overnight halt or for a longer stay if you are seeking a quiet, restful location with little to disturb the peace.

There are 26 touring pitches (10A Europlug), ten with hardstanding and separated by low hedges. The remainder are on grass and more suitable for units with awnings. This is a working farm and the owners, who are friendly and welcoming, have made some attractive improvements.

The sanitary facilities are very clean and housed in a modern block. Showers (free), toilets and washbasins (two washbasins are in cubicles). Facilities for disabled visitors in family shower room. Good laundry room. Motorhome services. Good campers' kitchen with fridge/freezer, electric cooker and TV. Small play area. TV, pool table and games room. Caravan storage. Accommodation to rent. A torch would be useful.

Key Features

 Pets Accepted

 Disabled Facilities

 Play Area

Scan me for
more information.

Alan Rogers Code: IR9480
40 pitches
GPS: 51.94787, -8.54622

Co. Cork, South West

www.alanrogers.com/ir9480
info@blarneycaravanpark.com
Tel: +353 214516519
www.blarneycaravanpark.com

Open (Touring Pitches):
Mid March - End October.

Blarney Camping Park

There is a heart of the country feel about this 'on the farm' site, yet the city of Cork is only an 8 km. drive. What makes this friendly, family-run park so appealing is the welcome you receive on arrival and the friendliness throughout your stay. Its secluded location and neat spacious pitches add to its appeal. The terrain on the three-acre park is elevated and gently sloping, commanding views towards Blarney Castle and the surrounding mountainous countryside.

The 80 pitches, 40 of which have hardstanding and 10A Europlug, are with caravans near the entrance with tents pitched slightly further away. There are gravel roads, well tended young shrubs and a screen of mature trees. Tidy hedging marks the park's perimeter.

Key Features

 Pets Accepted

 Disabled Facilities

 Play Area

Excellent toilet facilities are housed in converted farm buildings. Reception and small shop are now at the entrance. Good facilities for disabled visitors. Laundry room. Campers' kitchen. Motorhome services. Shop (Start June - End August). TV lounge. Playground. WiFi throughout (free). Delightful 18-hole golf and pitch and putt course.

Scan me for more information.

Alan Rogers Code: IR9500
19 pitches
GPS: 51.56693, -9.09702

Co. Cork, South West

www.alanrogers.com/ir9500
meadowcamping@eircom.net
Tel: +353 2833280
www.camping-ireland.ie/parks/cork/
meadow-camping-park

Open (Touring Pitches):
Easter - Mid September.

The Meadow Camping Park

Key Features

 Pets Accepted

 Beach Access

The picturesque stretch of coast from Cork to Skibbereen reminds British visitors of Devon before the era of mass tourism. This is rich dairy country with green meadows all around and thanks to the warm and wet Gulf Stream climate, it is also a county of gardens and keen gardeners.

The Meadow is best described not as a site but as a one-acre garden surrounded, appropriately, by lush meadows. The owners, who live on the park, have arranged accommodation for 19 pitches, 14 with 6A electric hook-ups (12 Europlugs), among the flower beds and shrubberies of their extended garden. There are 10 hardstandings. This site is not suitable for large units.

Facilities are limited but well designed and maintained with brand new solar panels. Showers on payment. Washing machine and dryer. Larger units may be accepted depending on length and available space; contact park before arrival. Football and cycling are not permitted on the park. No electric barbecues. WiFi throughout.

Scan me for more information.

Alan Rogers Code: IR9570
5 accommodations
20 pitches
GPS: 51.75562, -9.76193

Co. Kerry, South West

Creveen Lodge Camping Park

www.alanrogers.com/ir9570
info@creveenlodge.com
Tel: +353 646683131
www.creveenlodge.com

Open (Touring Pitches):
Easter - End September.

The Healy Pass is the well known scenic summit of the R574 road that crosses the Beara Peninsula, shortening the original journey from Kenmare Bay in the north to Bantry Bay in the south by nearly 70 km. As this narrow coast road starts to climb steeply, on the mountain foothills, you will arrive at Creveen Lodge, a working hill farm with a quiet, homely atmosphere.

The park provides 20 attractive pitches, 10 with 10A electricity and an area of hardstanding for motorhomes. To allow easy access, the steep farm track is divided into a simple one-way system. Creveen Lodge, commanding views across Kenmare Bay, is split between three gently sloping fields separated by trees. The park is carefully tended with neat, rustic picnic tables informally placed. Although not so famed as the Iveragh Peninsula, around which runs the Ring of Kerry, the northern Beara is a scenically striking area of County Kerry. This is walking and climbing countryside or, of interest close by, is Derreen Gardens.

Well-appointed and maintained, the small toilet block provides token-operated showers. Communal room with cooking facilities, a fridge, freezer, TV, ironing board, fireplace, tables and chairs. Reception is in the farmhouse. Play area. Accommodation (3 cottages, 2 caravans) to rent. WiFi available outside the reception area.

Key Features

 Pets Accepted

 Beach Access

 Play Area

Scan me for
more information.

Alan Rogers Code: IR9610
42 pitches
GPS: 51.94152, -10.24465

Co. Kerry, South West

www.alanrogers.com/ir9610
mortimer@campinginkerry.com
Tel: +353 669472806
www.campinginkerry.com

Open (Touring Pitches):
Easter - Mid September

Mannix Point Camping

A tranquil, beautifully located seashore park, it is no exaggeration to describe Mannix Point as a nature lovers' paradise. Situated in one of the most spectacular parts of the Ring of Kerry, overlooking the bay and Valentia Island, the rustic seven-acre park commands splendid views in all directions.

The park road meanders through the level site and offers 42 pitches of various sizes and shapes, many with shelter and seclusion and all with 10A electricity. A charming, old flower-bedecked fisherman's cottage has been converted to provide facilities including reception, excellent campers' kitchen and a cosy sitting room with turf fire.

Toilet and shower facilities were clean when we visited. Modern and well-equipped campers' kitchen and dining area. Comfortable campers' sitting room. Laundry facilities with washing machines and dryer. Motorhome services. Picnic and barbecue facilities. Fishing and boat launching from site. Playing field. WiFi throughout.

Key Features

 Pets Accepted

 Beach Access

 Play Area

 Sailing

Scan me for more information.

Alan Rogers Code: IR9590
20 accommodations
82 pitches
GPS: 52.07071, -9.58573

Co. Kerry, South West

Fossa Caravan & Camping Park

www.alanrogers.com/ir9590
fossaholidays@eircom.net
Tel: +353 646631497
www.fossacampingkillarney.com

Open (Touring Pitches):
Start April - End September.

This park is in the village of Fossa, ten minutes by car or bus (six per day) from Killarney town centre. Fossa Caravan Park has a distinctive reception building and hostel accommodation. The park is divided in two – the touring caravan area lies to the right, tucked behind the main building and to the left is an open grass area mainly for campers.

The 83 compact touring pitches, with 10/15A electricity and drainage, have hardstanding and are angled between shrubs and trees in a garden setting. To the rear at a higher level and discreetly placed are 30 caravan holiday homes, sheltered by the thick foliage of the wooded slopes which climb high behind the park.

Modern toilet facilities include showers on payment. En-suite unit for campers with disabilities. Laundry room. Campers' kitchen. TV lounge. Tennis. Play area. Picnic area. Games room. Security patrol. WiFi on part of site.

Key Features

 Pets Accepted

 Disabled Facilities

 Play Area

Scan me for more information.

Alan Rogers Code: IR9550
5 accommodations
30 pitches
GPS: 52.24393, -9.98579

Co. Kerry, South West

www.alanrogers.com/ir9550
anchorcaravanpark@eircom.net
Tel: +353 667139157
www.anchorcaravanpark.com

Open (Touring Pitches):
Easter - End September.

Anchor Caravan Park

Of County Kerry's three long, finger like peninsulas which jut into the sea, Dingle is the most northerly. Anchor Caravan Park is 20 km. west of Tralee, the main town, and under 4 km. south of Castlegregory on Tralee Bay. Its situation, just 150 m. from a fine sandy beach, provides ideal opportunities for safe bathing, boating and shore fishing.

A secluded and mature, five-acre park, it is enclosed by shrubs and trees that give excellent shelter. There are 30 pitches, most with electricity and 13 also with drainage and water points. Although there are holiday homes for hire, these are well apart from the touring pitches. The approach roads to the park are narrow and may be difficult for larger units.

Toilet facilities (entry by key) are kept very clean and provide showers on payment, two private cabins, some low level washbasins and a toilet with handrail. No facilities for disabled campers. Laundry facilities (incl. drying room, clothes lines and ironing). Campers' kitchen with fridges, freezers and seating. Motorhome services. Two play areas. Games and TV rooms. Electric barbecues are not permitted. WiFi throughout.

Key Features

 Pets Accepted

 Beach Access

Scan me for more information.

Alan Rogers Code: IR9460
25 pitches
GPS: 52.94070, -9.05893

Co. Clare, Shannon

Corofin Village Camping Park

www.alanrogers.com/ir9460
info@corofin.camping.com
Tel: +353 656837683
www.corofincamping.com

Open (Touring Pitches):
Start April - End September.

This compact green oasis in the centre of the village of Corofin occupies one acre and adjoins the family's hostel. The owners, Jude and Marie Neylon, live on the site and have a policy of always having a family member on hand at all times. They are very environmentally aware and have excellent recycling facilities.

There are 25 touring pitches, 18 with electricity and there are ample water points. The site now includes a small separate tent area which is quite private and well sheltered. A campers' kitchen, laundry room and the TV and games room are separate to the hostel facilities. This little site is neat and well maintained and makes an ideal base for sightseeing throughout Clare. Site is not suitable for large units.

The sanitary block is bright and clean with free hot showers. Separate facilities for disabled campers. Laundry room with washing machine and dryer. Campers' kitchen. TV and games room. CCTV security. Free WiFi throughout. Torches useful.

Key Features

 Pets Accepted

 Disabled Facilities

Scan me for more information.

Alan Rogers Code: IR8810
20 pitches
GPS: 53.84910, -9.31190

Co. Mayo, West

www.alanrogers.com/ir8810
info@loughlannagh.ie
Tel: +353 949027111
www.loughlannagh.ie/caravan-camping

Open (Touring Pitches):
Start April - End August.

Lough Lannagh Caravan Park

Lough Lannagh is an attractive holiday village on the lakeshore, which comprises quality accommodation, self-catering cottages and a caravan park. A lakeside path takes you into Castlebar (15-minute stroll) with its many restaurants, pubs, theatres and shops. County Mayo's main attractions are also within a short drive.

The caravan park has 20 touring pitches, well laid out in a separate dedicated corner of the village, all on hardstanding with electric connections. There is a separate grass area for tents. One reception area serves all and is situated to the right of the security barrier; check-in prior to 18:00. There are many on-site activities for all the family.

One modern heated sanitary block provides washbasins and well equipped, preset showers. En-suite unit for disabled visitors (has a bath but now shower). Laundry room with sink, washing machines and dryers near reception. Café serving breakfast (daily), snacks, lunch etc. Two play areas. Boules. Badminton. Tennis. Lakeside circular walk. Dogs accepted by prior arrangement.

Key Features

 Pets Accepted

 Disabled Facilities

 Beach Access

Scan me for more information.

Alan Rogers Code: IR8730
16 accommodations
84 pitches
GPS: 53.97535, -10.07790

Co. Mayo, West

www.alanrogers.com/ir8730
info@achillcamping.com
Tel: +353 9843211
www.achillcamping.com

Open (Touring Pitches):
Easter - Mid September.

Keel Sandybanks

This is a park offering a taste of island life and the opportunity to relax in dramatic, scenic surroundings. Achill, Ireland's largest island, is 24 km. long and 19 km. wide and is connected to the mainland by a bridge. The wide-open site is situated beside the Blue Flag beach near Keel village.

Although there are static holiday mobile homes on this site, the 84 touring pitches are kept separate. There are 50 pitches with hardstanding and some are located at the perimeter fence overlooking the beach. Although sand-based, the ground is firm and level. Roads are tarmac and there is direct access to the beach which is supervised by lifeguards.

Two modern toilet blocks serve the site, one at the entrance gate beside reception and the other in a central position. Heated facilities include WCs, washbasins and hot showers (on payment). Hairdryers. Laundry with irons and ironing boards. En-suite facilities for disabled visitors at the reception block. Campers' kitchen and dining room. Motorhome services. Play area. TV/ games room. Watersports enthusiasts can enjoy surfing, kite surfing, canoeing and board sailing on Keel Strand and Lough. Fishing trips can be arranged. WiFi throughout (charged).

Key Features

 Pets Accepted

 Disabled Facilities

 Play Area

Scan me for
more information.

Alan Rogers Code: IR8750
10 accommodations
50 pitches
GPS: 54.13450, -9.15850

Co. Mayo, West

Belleek Park Camping

www.alanrogers.com/ir8750
lenahan@belleekpark.com
Tel: +353 9671533
www.belleekpark.com

Open (Touring Pitches):
Start March - Start November, by
arrangement all year.

Belleek has a quiet woodland setting, only minutes from Ballina, a famed salmon fishing centre. With excellent pitches and toilet block, the family owners are committed to ensuring that it is immaculate at all times. From the entrance gate, the park is approached by a drive that passes reception and leads to 80 well-spaced pitches.

With a very neat overall appearance, 50 pitches have hardstanding and electricity hook-ups, and you may choose your pitch. Sports facilities within a short distance of the park include a swimming pool, tennis and bicycle hire. There is a Blue Flag beach at Ross.

Key Features

 Pets Accepted

 Disabled Facilities

 Beach Access

 Play Area

Spotlessly clean, tastefully decorated toilet block providing metered showers. Baby bath. Facilities for disabled campers. Laundry facilities. Reception includes a shop and a tea room also serving breakfast. Campers' kitchen and emergency accommodation with beds provided. TV room. Games room. Play area. Ball game area. Tennis. Barbecue area. Free WiFi over site.

Scan me for more information.

Alan Rogers Code: IR8825
52 pitches
GPS: 53.98125, -8.23517

Co. Roscommon, West

www.alanrogers.com/ir8825
info@loughkey.ie
Tel: +353 719662212
www.loughkey.ie

Open (Touring Pitches):
Start April - Mid September.

Lough Key Camping Park

This caravan and camping park is set deep in the 320 hectares of the Lough Key Forest Park. Comprising mixed woodland including giant red cedar, beech, ash and oak trees, the forest is bounded by Lough Key and incorporates several of its islands.

The rustic design of the main building on the park (which houses reception, a campers' kitchen, a lounge, and the sanitary and laundry facilities) blends well with the wooded environment. The well-landscaped, five-hectare site provides space for 52 touring units with electricity connections and ample water points, and many of the pitches are within the woodland. There is a separate area for tents.

The main toilet block includes metered hot showers. Facilities for disabled campers (key required). Campers' kitchen and sheltered eating area. Laundry. Play area in the centre of the park with adventure type play equipment in a hedged area, plus seating for parents. Forest walks and trails. Boat tours and boat hire. Security barrier closed at night. Site security patrol.

Key Features

 Pets Accepted

 Disabled Facilities

 Play Area

Scan me for more information.

Capital Rome
Currency Euro (€)
Language Italian
Time Zone CET (GMT+1)
Telephone Code +39

Shops Hours vary throughout the year, with many shops operating on shorter hours in low and shoulder seasons. In high season 9am to 1pm and 3.30pm to 7.30pm Mon to Sat. Outside of cities, most close on Sun. Some also close on Mon morning.

Money ATMs are widespread and are accessible 24hrs a day, some have multilingual instructions. Credit/debit cards are widely accepted, some smaller shops and trattorias may not take them.

Accessible Travel Not as well-equipped for wheelchair users as some of its European neighbours. Awareness is growing and museums/galleries offer reduced rates with ID.

Travelling with Children Very kid-friendly. Beaches are generally safe. State-run attractions are often free to EU citizens under 18 years of age. Few restaurants open before 7.30pm although pizzerias usually open earlier.

EU Travel Italy is an EU member state and located within the Schengen Area.

♻ **LEZ** Low Emissions Zones in some major cities. Registration required.

●●○○○ **Accessibility Score**
View our digital e-guide & find out more at
alanrogers.com/open-to-all

Tourism website | italia.it

Public Holidays 1 Jan New Year's Day · 6 Jan Epiphany · Mar/Apr Easter Sunday · Mar/Apr Easter Monday · 25 Apr Liberation Day · 1 May International Workers' Day · 2 Jun Republic Day · 15 Aug Assumption · 1 Nov All Saints · 8 Dec Immaculate Conception · 25 Dec Christmas Day · 26 Dec Boxing Day.

Driving in Italy Tolls are payable on the autostrada network. A pre-paid Via card can be used to pay, or an electronic tag called Telepass can be purchased. An overhanging load, e.g. a bicycle rack, must be indicated by a large red/white hatched warning square. An unladen weight of over 50% of the weight of the towing vehicle must have service brakes on all wheels. Blue signs signal parking. Drink-driving and using your mobile whilst driving are illegal.

Italy

View all campsites in Italy
alanrogers.com/italy

See campsite map page 482

Climate

Hot summers and mild, dry winters in the south whilst the north is cooler
with heavy snow in winter.

Jan	Feb	Mar	Apr	May	Jun	Jul	Aug	Sep	Oct	Nov	Dec
12	14	16	19	24	28	31	32	27	23	17	13
3	3	6	8	12	16	19	19	15	12	7	4

Once the capital of the Roman Empire,
Italy was unified as recently as 1861;
thus, regional customs and traditions
have not been lost. Its enviable
collections of art, literature and culture
have had worldwide influence and
continue to be a magnet for visitors
who flock to cities such as Venice,
Florence and Rome.

In the north, the vibrant city of Milan
is the fashion capital of the world and
home to the famous opera house, La
Scala, as well as Da Vinci's 'The Last
Supper. It is also a good starting-off
point for the Alps; the Italian Lake
District, incorporating Lake Garda, Lake
Como and Lake Maggiore; the canals of
Venice and the lovely town of Verona.

The hilly towns of central Italy are
especially popular, with Siena, San
Gimignano and Assisi among the most
visited. The historic capital of Rome
with its Colosseum and Vatican City is
not to be missed.

Naples is an ideal base for visiting
Pompeii and the breathtaking scenery
of the Amalfi coast. The city also has
a charm of its own – winding narrow
streets and crumbling façades inset
with shrines sit alongside boutiques,
bars and lively street markets amid
chaotic traffic and roaring scooters.

Alan Rogers Code: IT62420
15 accommodations
80 pitches
GPS: 45.80188, 8.42047
Post Code: I-28016

Orta San Giulio, Piedmont

www.alanrogers.com/it62420
info@campingorta.it
Tel: +39 0322 90267
www.campingorta.it

Open (Touring Pitches):
Start March - End December.

Camping Orta

Lake Orta is a delightful, less-visited small lake just west of Lake Maggiore. The site is on a considerable slope and most of the 80 touring pitches (all with 6A electricity) are on the top grass terrace with spectacular views across the lake to the mountains beyond. There are some superb lakeside pitches across the main road (linked by a pedestrian underpass) although there is some traffic noise here.

Amenities include a large game and entertainment room and a traditional Italian bar and restaurant serving good value family meals. Some English is spoken by the Guarnori family, who take pride in maintaining their uncomplicated site to a high standard. Book ahead to enjoy the lakeside pitches. If you are anxious about towing a large caravan to the top terraces, the owner will help out with his tractor.

Four modern sanitary blocks are clean and well maintained providing mainly British style toilets, coin operated showers and an excellent unit for disabled visitors. Laundry facilities. Motorhome services. Good quality shop, bar and restaurant with basic menu serving good value Italian family meals (also takeaway, all season). Playground. Large games/TV room. WiFi in reception/bar area (charged). Fishing. Bicycle hire. Boat launching. Lake swimming and watersports.

Key Features

 Pets Accepted

 Disabled Facilities

 Play Area

 Bar/Restaurant

 Bike Hire

 Fishing

Scan me for more information.

Alan Rogers Code: IT64045
15 accommodations
72 pitches
GPS: 44.48898, 8.34713
Post Code: I-15018

Spigno Monferrato, Piedmont

www.alanrogers.com/it64045
info@tenutasquaneto.it
Tel: +39 0144 91744
www.tenutasquaneto.it

Open (Touring Pitches):
Late April - Late September.

Camping Tenuta Squaneto

After years of experience in the camping industry, Barbara and Pieter Witschge have built their dream – Tenuta Squaneto, natural camping with brilliant facilities. Its location is deep in the countryside with no villages, shops or restaurants in the immediate area. The 72 grassy, level touring pitches (100-120 sq.m) have wonderful views and 35 have water, wastewater and TV connections. There are also 15 Lodgetents for rental.

The site is in a small valley with trees all around, there is a river to walk along, fish or simply swim and play in. A lovely lake is central to the site and the nearby swimming pool is stunning with a large whirlpool and a children's shallow play pool with wonderful frogs and turtles that spray water.

Two modern sanitary blocks offer full and luxurious facilities including those for disabled visitors. Some pitches have private facilities including cooker, fridge and luxury facilities (small extra daily charge). Fresh bread is available to order. Quality restaurant and bar. Attractive swimming pool and paddling pool. Large children's play area. Beach volleyball. Barbecues are allowed subject to local restrictions. Cooking groups in low season, weekly wine tastings. River swimming. WiFi in reception (free).

Key Features

 Pets Accepted

 Disabled Facilities

 Beach Access

 Swimming Pool

 Play Area

 Bar/Restaurant

 Bike Hire

 Horse Riding

Scan me for more information.

Alan Rogers Code: IT64060
8 accommodations
58 pitches
GPS: 44.08333, 8.21033
Post Code: I-17031

Campochiesa di Albenga, Ligúria

www.alanrogers.com/it64060
info@campingbellavista.it
Tel: +39 0329 5923683
www.campingbellavista.nl

Open (Touring Pitches):
Mid March - Mid November.

Camping Bella Vista

Owned and run by the multilingual, Dutch Kox family, this site has 58 level pitches, separated in places by hedges and trees. The pitches are in rows, loosely ringed by bungalows.

Two sizes of pitch are offered: 50 and 80 sq.m. with a sink and tap for every four pitches. Electricity (6A) is available. Large units will experience manoeuvring difficulties and must phone ahead to use an alternative entrance. This is an inexpensive and thus crowded site in the high season.

Following an uninspiring approach through plastic-covered market gardens, the Ligurian Alps make a pleasant backdrop to this closely-packed campsite.

The single modern block is clean with British style toilets. Shower water is solar heated, washbasins have cold water only. Single facility for disabled campers although the unit doubles as a baby room with a washing machine and ironing equipment. Shop (seasonal). Bar. Takeaway with restrictions (seasonal). Swimming pool and separate paddling pool. Limited entertainment in the main season. Play area. Aviary. Free WiFi throughout.

Key Features

 Book Online

 Pets Accepted

 Disabled Facilities

 Beach Access

 Swimming Pool

 Play Area

 Bar/Restaurant

Scan me for more information.

Alan Rogers Code: IT64130
104 accommodations
50 pitches
GPS: 44.26365, 9.44190
Post Code: I-16039

Sestri Levante, Ligúria

www.alanrogers.com/it64130
info@campingmaremonti.com
Tel: +39 0185 44348
www.campingmaremonti.com

Open (Touring Pitches):
Mid March - Start November.

Camping Mare Monti

Mare Monti is a neat and tidy site set high in the hills with spectacular views overlooking the small town of Sestri Levante. The owner and his staff are relaxed and very friendly. The site has around 150 pitches, 50 of which are for touring with 6A electricity, all set on terraces. The remaining pitches are taken by seasonal units, and there are also a number of mobile homes for rental.

A small shop and a bar with its impressive terrace and wonderful views overlook a neat swimming pool. Access to the site and within is difficult and the site is therefore more suitable for smaller units. The rural location, together with good facilities offers a quiet and relaxing atmosphere for your stay. We would not recommend this site for disabled visitors.

Two refurbished toilet blocks are modern, bright and spotlessly clean. British and Turkish style WCs. Hot showers. Washing machine and dryer. Small shop, bar with takeaway (April-Oct). Outdoor swimming pool with separate pool for children (June-Oct). Volleyball. Communal barbecues. Minibus to town (July/Aug). English is spoken. WiFi on part of site (free).

Key Features

 Book Online

 Pets Accepted

 Disabled Facilities

 Beach Access

 Swimming Pool

 Bar/Restaurant

Scan me for more information.

Alan Rogers Code: IT62630
492 accommodations
400 pitches
GPS: 45.44165, 10.67920
Post Code: I-37019

Peschiera del Garda, Lake Garda

www.alanrogers.com/it62630
info@camping-bellaitalia.it
Tel: +39 0456 400688
www.camping-bellaitalia.it

Open (Touring Pitches):
Early March - Late October.

Camping Bella Italia

Peschiera is a picturesque village on the southern shore of Lake Garda, and Camping Bella Italia is a very attractive, large, well organised and very busy site in the grounds of a former farm, just west of the centre of the village.

Half of the 1,200 pitches are occupied by the site's own mobile homes and chalets and by tour operators; there are some 400 touring pitches, most towards the lakeside and reasonably level on grass under trees. All have 16A electricity, water and wastewater and are separated by shrubs.

There are some fine views across the lake to the mountains beyond. A superb promenade allows direct access to the town.

Six modern toilet blocks have British style toilets, washbasins and showers. Baby rooms and facilities for disabled visitors. Washing machines. Motorhome services. Infirmary. Shops. Gelateria. Bars. Waiter service restaurant and terrace and two other restaurants (one in the old farm building). Swimming pools. Tennis. Archery. Playgrounds (small). Games room. Watersports. Fishing. Bicycle hire. Organised activities and entertainment. Mini club. WiFi over part of site (charged). ATMs. Dogs are not accepted.

Key Features

 Book Online

 Disabled Facilities

 Swimming Pool

 Play Area

 Bar/Restaurant

 Bike Hire

 Sailing

Scan me for more information.

Alan Rogers Code: IT62105
117 pitches
GPS: 46.31057, 11.63176
Post Code: I-38037

Predazzo, Trentino - Alto Adige

www.alanrogers.com/it62105
info@campingvalleverde.it
Tel: +39 0462 502394
www.campingvalleverde.it

Open (Touring Pitches):
Start May - End September.

Camping Valle Verde

Beautifully located in the Dolomites, at a height of just over 1,000 metres, Camping Valle Verde is an attractive family run site. There are 117 level pitches with mountain views, set on shallow, grassy terraces with some tree shade; all have 3A electricity.

From the site, there is plenty of walking in the forests alongside rushing mountain streams enclosed in small rocky canyons, with waterfalls and an abundance of flora and fauna. The site produces its own map of suggested rambling/cycle routes, however, a detailed map of the area is an added advantage.

The comfortable site restaurant, formally an alpine shelter, with its wood-fired pizza oven and terrace, is a very welcoming refuge after a day spent in the mountains.

Modern toilet block with all necessary facilities including those for babies and campers with disabilities. Washing machine/dryer. Motorhome services. Restaurant, snack bar, takeaway (mid May-mid Sept). Play area. Sports area. Volleyball. Football. Paddling in adjacent stream. Bicycle hire. WiFi over site (charged).

Key Features

 Pets Accepted

 Disabled Facilities

 Play Area

 Bar/Restaurant

 Bike Hire

 Fishing

Scan me for more information.

Alan Rogers Code: IT61500
39 accommodations
168 pitches
GPS: 45.96405, 11.75913
Post Code: I-32030

Rocca di Arsiè, Veneto

www.alanrogers.com/it61500
info@campinglago.com
Tel: +39 0439 58540
www.campinglago.com

Open (Touring Pitches):
Late April - Mid September.

Camping Al Lago di Arsiè

This small, quiet site with its beautiful lakeside setting, surrounded by steep, tree-clad hills is under the same ownership as Camping Lago di Levico (IT62290). It is located at the southern edge of the Dolomites and is only 110 km. from Venice and the Adriatic. This is an ideal site to spend some time just relaxing, walking or cycling in this most attractive region.

The main camping area slopes gently down to the lake and has some shade; it has 168 touring pitches, all with 4/6A electricity. There is a large area catering for both tents and caravans, plus a separate 'Sosta' area for motorhomes stopping over. We enjoyed the restaurant which is also used by locals.

Two central toilet blocks have controllable showers and a mixture of Turkish and British style toilets. Washbasins (open-style) and sinks (under cover) have only cold water, but there are taps from which to collect hot water. Washing machines and dryer. Motorhome services. Facilities for disabled visitors. Bar (with Sky TV). Restaurant/pizzeria with takeaway (all season). Play area. Games room. WiFi throughout (free).

Key Features

 Book Online

 Pets Accepted

 Disabled Facilities

 Play Area

 Bar/Restaurant

 Bike Hire

 Fishing

Scan me for more information.

Alan Rogers Code: IT60320
428 accommodations
560 pitches
GPS: 45.45666, 12.50055
Post Code: I-30013

Cavallino-Treporti, Veneto

www.alanrogers.com/it60320
info@campingcavallino.com
Tel: +39 0419 66133
www.campingcavallino.com

Open (Touring Pitches):
Late March - End October.

Camping Village Cavallino

This large, well-ordered site is part of the Baia Holiday Group. It lies beside the sea with direct access to a superb beach of fine sand, which is very safe and has lifeguards. The site is thoughtfully laid out with large touring pitches shaded by olives and pines. All pitches have 6/10A electricity, some have water and they are generally flat and enjoy shade from mature pines.

The pleasant pool, restaurant, entertainment and most other services are at the centre of the site. We enjoyed the hubbub from this area, but also the ability to find peace on the periphery. You should have a great family holiday here.

For visiting Venice, there is a bus to the ferry at Punta Sabbioni which is 20 minutes away. The charming ferry journey takes 40 minutes and drops you directly at Saint Mark's Square.

Two modern toilet blocks are well spaced and can be heated. They provide every modern requirement and include facilities for disabled campers. Dog shower. Launderette. Motorhome services. Supermarket. Bazaar. Restaurant with large terrace. Takeaway. Pizzeria. Swimming pools and whirlpool (May-Sept). Minigolf. Playground. Bicycle hire. Fishing. Entertainment programme. ATM. WiFi (charged). Dogs are accepted in certain areas. Mobile homes to rent.

Key Features

 Book Online

 Pets Accepted

 Disabled Facilities

 Beach Access

 Swimming Pool

 Play Area

 Bar/Restaurant

 Bike Hire

Scan me for more information.

Alan Rogers Code: IT66610
60 accommodations
135 pitches
GPS: 43.67611, 10.75277
Post Code: I-56020

Montopoli, Tuscany

www.alanrogers.com/it66610
info@toscanavillage.com
Tel: +39 0571 449032
www.toscanavillage.com

Open (Touring Pitches):
All year.

Camping Toscana Village

This area was once a forest surrounding the attractive medieval Tuscan village of Montopoli. Toscana Village has been thoughtfully carved out of the hillside under mature pines and it is ideal for a sightseeing holiday in this central and peaceful area.

The 135 level pitches (some large) are on shaded terraces and are carefully maintained. All pitches have 6A electricity. The amenities are centrally located close to the top of the hill in a pleasant modern building.

English is spoken by the helpful reception staff who also organise a programme of visits and events. The restaurant has a terrace where there are views of the surrounding countryside.

Two modern and clean toilet blocks have quality facilities including British style toilets, hot water at all the stylish sinks, private cabins plus two large en-suite cubicles. Facilities for disabled visitors. Washing machines and dryer. Motorhome services. Shop (bread to order), restaurant, pizzeria/barbecue (grill night on Saturdays), takeaway (all seasonal). Swimming pool (June-Sept). Play area. Bicycle hire. Organised activities and tours. Torches useful. WiFi over site (charged).

Key Features

 Book Online

 Open All Year

 Pets Accepted

 Disabled Facilities

 Swimming Pool

 Play Area

 Bar/Restaurant

 Bike Hire

Scan me for more information.

Alan Rogers Code: IT66100
30 accommodations
77 pitches
GPS: 43.80650, 11.30510
Post Code: I-50014

Fiesole, Tuscany

www.alanrogers.com/it66100
panoramico@florencevillage.com
Tel: +39 0555 99069
www.campingpanoramicofiesole.com

Open (Touring Pitches):
Start April - Start November.

Panoramico Fiesole

Camping Village Panoramico Fiesole is a mature but pleasant site in a superb hilltop situation offering wonderful views over Florence. The 120 pitches, all with 5A electricity, are on terraces and steep walks to and from the various facilities could cause problems for guests with mobility problems. There is shade in many parts of the site.

The pool is on the upper level along with the restaurant/bar, and the views are really stunning. Some evenings you can hear music from the nearby Roman amphitheatre famous for its classical entertainment in summer.

Two tastefully refurbished toilet blocks have mainly British style WCs, free hot water in washbasins and good showers. Washing machines and dryers. Fridges, freezer, microwaves, irons and little cookers for campers' use. Shop (seasonal). Bar and restaurant (seasonal). Swimming pool (seasonal). Play area. Nursery. Torches are required in some parts. English is spoken. Free shuttle service to Fiesole and back. WiFi on part of the site (charged).

Key Features

 Book Online

 Pets Accepted

 Swimming Pool

 Bar/Restaurant

Scan me for more information.

Alan Rogers Code: IT66640
4 accommodations
61 pitches
GPS: 43.58235, 11.13828
Post Code: I-50020

Marcialla (Certaldo), Tuscany

www.alanrogers.com/it66640
info@campingchianti.it
Tel: +39 0571 669334
www.campingchianti.it

Open (Touring Pitches):
Start April - Early November.

Panorama del Chianti

Formerly named Toscana Colliverdi, Camping Panorama del Chianti has undergone some development. A small country hillside site in Tuscany, it has space for 61 large units on deep terraces and two areas for tents. All the terrace pitches have 3/5A electricity. There are panoramic views of the surrounding countryside. If you are content to be self-supporting and wish to explore Tuscany with the advantage of reasonable campsite fees, then this could be for you.

A small bar with a tiny terrace offers welcoming cool drinks, excellent coffee, aperitif with local products, fresh bread and a good breakfast in the mornings. Other supplies and good restaurants are available in the village of Marcialla 700 m. away.

A small, clean toilet block is on the second terrace with British style toilets, showers and washbasins, plus dishwashing and laundry sinks, all with hot water. No facilities for disabled campers. Washing machine. Motorhome services. Small bar and terrace (basic supplies on sale). Communal barbecue. Good size above ground pool (seasonal). Play area. WiFi over part of the site.

Key Features

 Book Online

 Pets Accepted

 Beach Access

 Swimming Pool

 Play Area

 Bar/Restaurant

Scan me for more information.

Alan Rogers Code: IT66650
14 accommodations
170 pitches
GPS: 43.15520, 11.33230
Post Code: I-53016

Casciano di Murlo, Tuscany

www.alanrogers.com/it66650
camping@lesoline.it
Tel: +39 0577 817410
www.lesoline.it

Open (Touring Pitches):
All year.

Camping le Soline

Le Soline is a country hillside site with wonderful views of the beautiful Tuscan landscape from its steep slopes and a very pleasant atmosphere. Just 20 km. south of Siena and 1 km. from the village of Casciano, it has neat, numbered terraced pitches for large units and tents, all with 6A electricity and Europlugs, water and wastewater. Olive trees provide some shade.

The kind and attentive Broggini family spare no efforts in making your stay a pleasant memory and are extremely hard working to this end. The site offers a quiet location out of season and a busy family atmosphere in the summer period. A dip in one of the pools is very refreshing in the heat of the summer, followed by a cool drink on the terrace.

A high quality, heated sanitary block is on the third terrace, providing mixed British and Turkish style WCs and generous hot showers (on payment). Facilities for disabled campers and children. Family washroom. Motorhome services. Gas supplies. Laundry. Freezer. Restaurant, bar and pizzeria (open usually April to October). Well stocked shop (summer only). Swimming pools (open usually May to September included, depending on weather). 12-person whirlpool (can be covered). Playground. Excursions (June-Aug). Volleyball. Gas, electric and charcoal barbecues permitted. Communal barbecue area. WiFi over site (free). Mobile homes and bungalows to rent.

Key Features

 Book Online

 Open All Year

 Pets Accepted

 Disabled Facilities

 Swimming Pool

 Play Area

 Bar/Restaurant

Scan me for more information.

Alan Rogers Code: IT66720
35 accommodations
60 pitches
GPS: 42.91101, 10.84347
Post Code: I-58020

Scarlino, Tuscany

www.alanrogers.com/it66720
info@fontino.it
Tel: +39 0566 37029
www.fontino.it

Open (Touring Pitches):
Late April - End September.

Camping Village Il Fontino

The name means Little Fountain as springs provide all the drinking water here. The Maurizio family have worked hard to provide a most pleasant site for campers. There are 60 terraced pitches for touring units on a sloping site, all with 3/6A electricity and shade from mature olives. Once settled on the pitch, cars are parked separately.

The 25 m. pool with its separate paddling pool is the site's strength – it is stunning, safe and free. As you swim you can enjoy the views over the town of Follonica below you, whilst in turn, the village of Scarlino sits hundreds of metres above on the clifftop. A large, very attractive building in the centre of the site, restored in traditional style, houses the restaurant/pizzeria, shop and bar with a rooftop terrace.

Two sanitary blocks provide hot showers (timer). Mostly Turkish style toilets, cold water at washbasins. Single facility for disabled visitors. Washing machines and dryer. Bar/restaurant and takeaway. Shop. Swimming and paddling pools. Entertainment programme and mini-club (high season). Play area. Bicycle hire. WiFi over part of the site (charged). Free bus in high season to beach with watersports.

Key Features

 Book Online

 Pets Accepted

 Disabled Facilities

 Beach Access

 Swimming Pool

 Play Area

 Bar/Restaurant

Scan me for more information.

Alan Rogers Code: IT65060
8 accommodations
127 pitches
GPS: 43.95973, 12.80388
Post Code: I-61010

Pesaro, Marche

www.alanrogers.com/it65060
info@campingparadiso.it
Tel: +39 0721 208579
www.campingparadiso.net

Open (Touring Pitches):
Start March - End October.

Camping Paradiso

Camping Paradiso is quite close to Pesaro, home of Rossini (annual concerts held in August). The site is quite simple and is a tranquil base to avoid August's beach crowds, although with easy access to some of the region's best beaches and the nightlife in nearby Gabicce Mare. The site is located on a hilltop in San Bartolo Natural Park. There are over 100 touring pitches (65 with electrical connections 3/9A) which are of a good size and well shaded with a fine variety of different trees. The site also has a number of wooden chalets to rent.

Many excursions are possible from the site, some of the most popular being to Rimini, Urbino and Pesaro. This is also a very rich area for walking and mountain biking and the site management will be pleased to recommend possible itineraries.

The toilet block is beneath the reception building. Motorhome services. Small shop, bar (seasonal). Snack bar, takeaway and swimming pool (seasonal). Play area. Communal barbecue. WiFi over part of the site (charged).

Key Features

 Book Online

 Pets Accepted

 Disabled Facilities

 Beach Access

 Swimming Pool

 Play Area

 Bar/Restaurant

Scan me for
more information.

Alan Rogers Code: IT66520
50 accommodations
208 pitches
GPS: 43.08810, 12.15610
Post Code: I-06063

Sant Arcangelo-Magione,
Umbria

www.alanrogers.com/it66520
camping@italgest.com
Tel: +39 0758 48238
www.italgest.com

Open (Touring Pitches):
Late March - End September.

Villaggio Italgest

Camping Villaggio Italgest is a mature, pleasant site with 208 touring pitches (with 6A electricity) on level grass with plenty of shade. Cars are parked away from the pitches. The site offers a wide variety of activities with tours organised daily. The somewhat dated swimming pool complex is next to the bar/restaurant and there is a play area nearby. Directly on the shore on the south side of Lake Trasimeno, Sant Arcangelo is ideally placed for exploring Umbria and Tuscany. The deep lake is a pleasant feature but may present a hazard to unsupervised children.

There is limited entertainment for children and adults in high season, in a very Italian style. The play areas vary and some were in need of renovation. The bar/disco remains open until 01.00. This site could be used as a base for exploration or as a place to relax, but it is somewhat dated.

The two sanitary blocks have been completely refurbished. They have mainly British style WCs and free hot water in the washbasins and showers. Children's toilets. Baby room. Limited facilities for disabled visitors. Motorhome services. Washing machines and dryers. Well equipped campers' kitchen. Shop, bar, restaurant, pizzeria and takeaway (all year). Swimming pool complex with slides and paddling pool (seasonal). Tennis. Play area. TV (satellite) and games rooms. Disco. Films. Watersports, motorboat hire and lake swimming. Fishing. Charcoal barbecues not permitted. Mountain bike and scooter hire. Internet and WiFi (free in some areas). Wide range of activities, entertainment and excursions.

Key Features

 Book Online

 Pets Accepted

 Disabled Facilities

 Swimming Pool

 Play Area

 Bar/Restaurant

 Bike Hire

 Fishing

Scan me for
more information.

Alan Rogers Code: IT68140
130 accommodations
180 pitches
GPS: 41.95618, 12.48240
Post Code: I-00189

Roma, Lazio

www.alanrogers.com/it68140
info@villageflaminio.com
Tel: +39 0633 32604
www.villageflaminio.com

Open (Touring Pitches):
All Year.

Flaminio Camping Park

Flaminio Village Camping Bungalow Park is a high quality campsite near Rome, with many flowers, shrubs and trees giving some shade. Being 400 metres from the main road it is protected from traffic noise. Although it is quite a large site, there are around 180 pitches for tourers, all with 6A electricity, which are approached by brick access roads. The excellent sanitary block is close to both camping areas, as is the restaurant, bar and info point.

There is reasonable space allocated to touring units with many of these pitches in area C of average/small size so check your allocated pitch. Some pitches in area B are larger, and have water and electricity. Many large groups use the site so booking is recommended. There are about 130 well-equipped bungalows attractively arranged in a village-style setting on the slopes. BBQs are not allowed on pitches.

The sanitary facilities are of very high quality including provision for disabled visitors and a very good baby room. Motorhome services. Bar/pizzeria and restaurant. Well stocked shop. Swimming pool (hats required), pool bar and solarium (seasonal). Bicycle hire. Bus service. Torches useful. Pick-up service to and from Ciampino airport. A small electric bus runs between reception and pitches. Wi-Fi throughout.

Key Features

 Book Online

 Open All Year

 Pets Accepted

 Disabled Facilities

 Swimming Pool

 Play Area

 Bar/Restaurant

 Bike Hire

Scan me for
more information.

Alan Rogers Code: IT67920
2 accommodations
300 pitches
GPS: 41.78002, 13.86777
Post Code: I-67030

Opi, Abruzzo

www.alanrogers.com/it67920
ilvecchiomulino@tiscali.it
Tel: +39 0863 912232
www.campingvecchiomulino.it

Open (Touring Pitches):
All year.

Camping Il Vecchio Mulino

Il Vecchio Mulino enjoys a fine woodland setting on the slopes of Monte Marsicano, at the heart of the Abruzzo National Park. The site is open all year and is popular for walking and cycling in the summer and is well located for the Pescasseroli and Macchiarvana ski resorts in the winter.

The focal point of the site is the old mill and the attractively restored farm buildings housing the restaurant and bed and breakfast accommodation. The restaurant serves local Abruzzese cuisine and is open from May to September. The pitches here are spacious and level and all are equipped with an electrical connection.

This is a friendly site with traditional facilities showing signs of wear. The town of Opi is very attractive and just 1 km. away. There is a great deal to see in Abruzzo and the site is well placed for exploring the region. Look for the trout and other fish in the mill stream – these supply the restaurant.

Centrally located toilet block. Motorhome services. Small shop (local produce). Bar/restaurant. Snack bar. Sports field. Play area. Games room. Barbecue area. Fishing.

Key Features

 Open All Year

 Pets Accepted

 Disabled Facilities

 Play Area

 Bar/Restaurant

Scan me for more information.

Alan Rogers Code: IT67970
27 accommodations
110 pitches
GPS: 42.08800, 14.73667
Post Code: I-66055

Marina di Vasto, Abruzzo

Camping Il Pioppeto

www.alanrogers.com/it67970
infocampeggio@ilpioppeto.it
Tel: +39 0873 801466
www.ilpioppeto.it

Open (Touring Pitches):
Mid May - Mid September.

Camping & Residence Il Pioppeto lies to the south of Pescara and is a clean and friendly family site. It is well maintained and tidy, with 110 level pitches with 5A electricity and plenty of shade. The local food offered in the small, unassuming restaurant is superb and reasonably priced (cash only). Diners can eat inside or enjoy the atmosphere on the terrace, although there is some road noise. The delightful beach, just outside the site, is long and very wide, so there is no difficulty in escaping from the maddening crowd.

Abruzzo prides itself on being Italy's greenest region and the nearby National Park is well worth a visit and is ideal for walking or mountain biking. The friendly D'Ugo family will be pleased to recommend possible itineraries and are very keen to ensure that you enjoy your stay.

The four toilet blocks of differing sizes are of a good standard, although some washbasins have only cold water. Excellent new motorhome services. Supermarket. Bar and snack bar. Restaurant. Play area. Games room. Entertainment and children's club in peak season. Adjacent beach. Chalets for rent. Bicycle hire. WiFi over part of site.

Key Features

 Pets Accepted

 Disabled Facilities

 Beach Access

 Play Area

 Bar/Restaurant

 Bike Hire

 Fishing

 Sailing

Scan me for more information.

Alan Rogers Code: IT68420
22 accommodations
60 pitches
GPS: 40.65971, 14.41820
Post Code: I-80069

Vico Equense, Campania

www.alanrogers.com/it68420
info@campingsantantonio.it
Tel: +39 0818 028570
www.campingsantantonio.it

Open (Touring Pitches):
Mid March - End October.

Camping Sant' Antonio

A quiet place with very basic facilities, this little site is just across the road from Seiano marina and tiny beach (no views due to the high stone wall). The site would suit caravanners who like a peaceful (for Italy) location. There are only 60 pitches that are in shade offered by orange, lemon and walnut trees.

Pitches are reasonably flat and have 5A electricity and access to them is easy on the flat ground. Access to the site is challenging and unsuitable for larger units, down a long steep narrow curving road via a very sharp turn just after a tunnel and high overpass. The final entrance is through a covered opening in a stone wall.

In summer (mid-June to end-Sept.) there is a regular bus service to the Circumvesuviana railway which runs to Sorrento, Pompei, Herculaneum and Naples and it is possible to catch a boat to Capri. English is spoken by the Maresca family, who run the site.

The single sanitary block provides hot and cold showers, washbasins and British style WCs. Hot water is on payment. Small shop, bar and restaurant. Dogs are not accepted in August.

Key Features

 Pets Accepted

 Bar/Restaurant

Scan me for more information.

Alan Rogers Code: IT68650
170 accommodations
1000 pitches
GPS: 39.87475, 18.14112
Post Code: I-73059

Ugento, Puglia

Camping Riva di Ugento

www.alanrogers.com/it68650
info@rivadiugento.it
Tel: +39 0833 933600
www.rivadiugento.it

Open (Touring Pitches):
Mid May - Mid October.

There are some campsites where you can be comfortable, have all the amenities at hand and still feel you are connecting with nature. Under the pine and eucalyptus trees of the Bay of Taranto foreshore is Camping Riva di Ugento. Its 1000 pitches nestle in and around the sand dunes and the foreshore area.

They have space and trees around them and differ in size since the environment dictates the shape of many. The sea is only a short walk from most pitches and some are at the water's edge. The site buildings resemble huge wooden umbrellas and are in sympathy with the environment. We were sorry to leave the site, which was by far the best we found in the area.

Twenty toilet blocks all with WCs, showers and washbasins (check opening times before pitching). Modern bathrooms. Supermarket and boutique. Bar. Restaurant and takeaway. Swimming and paddling pools (Seasonal, charged). Tennis. Bicycle hire. Watersports incl. windsurfing school. Cinema. TV in bar. Entertainment for all ages (Seasonal). Dogs are not accepted. Modern play area. Beach volleyball. Bicycle hire. ATM. WiFi over site (charged).

Key Features

 Book Online

 Beach Access

 Swimming Pool

 Bar/Restaurant

 Bike Hire

Scan me for more information.

Alan Rogers Code: IT68830
47 accommodations
100 pitches
GPS: 38.90892, 16.80945
Post Code: I-88050

Cropani Marina, Calabria

www.alanrogers.com/it68830
info@campinglungomare.com
Tel: +39 0961 551155
www.campinglungomare.com

Open (Touring Pitches):
Start April - Mid October.

Villaggio Lungomare

Villaggio Camping Lungomare is a small, family-run site close to the town of Cropani Marina. There are 100 marked pitches that are well laid out. All have 6A electricity and water points nearby, and shade is provided on most by tall pine trees.

The site has a private sandy beach which is accessed across a small road, just 20 m. from the pitches. Just outside the site, close to the entrance/reception area, there are also a number of mobile homes/chalets available for rent.

The friendly and helpful owner is able to arrange excursions to various places of interest. An excellent base for sightseeing with a National Park and waterfalls nearby which are well worth visiting.

Two toilet blocks include showers and WCs (Turkish and British style). Facilities for disabled visitors. Washing machine. Motorhome services. Bar and restaurant/pizzeria. All weather football pitch. Play area. Entertainment in high season. Accommodation to rent. WiFi on part of site.

Key Features

 Book Online

 Pets Accepted

 Disabled Facilities

 Beach Access

 Play Area

 Bar/Restaurant

 Fishing

Scan me for more information.

Alan Rogers Code: IT69230
36 accommodations
80 pitches
GPS: 37.53232, 15.12012
Post Code: I-95126

Catania, Sicily

www.alanrogers.com/it69230
info@campingjonio.com
Tel: +39 0954 91139
www.campingjonio.com

Open (Touring Pitches):
All year.

Camping Jonio

This is a small, uncomplicated and tranquil city site with the advantage of being on top of a cliff at the water's edge. The 80 level touring pitches (40-50 sq.m) are on gravel with shade from some tall trees and artificial bamboo screens. The sanitary facilities are adequate (some private facilities for hire).

There is no pool, but the views of the water compensate and there are delightful rock pools in the sea just a few steps from the campsite. An attractive restaurant offers food in the summer high season. Camping Jonio is ideal for a short stay to unwind.

You could bask in the sun on the rocky platforms and dive into the clear waters, or take advantage of the many excursions to the local historical sites. Excellent winter rates are available for long-stay visitors. Five languages including English are spoken and access to the site is good.

Basic, but clean sanitary facilities in two blocks, one small block for men and another for women. Laundry with rooftop drying area. Shop. Bar and restaurant. Takeaway. Basic old-style playground (supervision recommended). Entertainment (high season). Diving school. Access to a small gravel beach. Excursions. WiFi over site (charged).

Key Features

 Open All Year

 Pets Accepted

 Disabled Facilities

 Beach Access

 Play Area

Bar/Restaurant

Fishing

Scan me for more information.

Alan Rogers Code: IT69175
24 accommodations
180 pitches
GPS: 37.26935, 13.58350
Post Code: I-92100

Agrigento, Sicily

www.alanrogers.com/it69175
info@campingvalledeitempli.com
Tel: +39 0922 411115
www.campingvalledeitempli.com

Open (Touring Pitches):
All year.

Camping Valle dei Templi

This site shares its name with Sicily's premier attraction, the UNESCO World Heritage listed complex of temples and old city walls of the ancient town of Akragas, although these are about 2.5 km. to the north. Built as a beacon for homecoming sailors, the five Doric temples built on a ridge are an impressive sight even at a distance. This site is therefore a good base from which to explore these ruins, together with the numerous coach loads of tourists. With 180 unmarked pitches, about half are suitable for caravans and campers. The majority have access to 8A electricity.

The site occupies a sloping, suburban location and has a good swimming pool and sun deck (in use during high season). Tents pitch informally around the site. The modern, large town of Agrigento is about 4 km. and a regular bus service operates from outside the site.

The single sanitary block in the centre of the site provides WCs, showers and washbasins. Facilities for disabled visitors. Motorhome services. Washing machine. Bar and takeaway service (seasonal). Swimming pool (1-July until end of the season). Playground. Free WiFi throughout.

Key Features

 Open All Year

 Pets Accepted

 Disabled Facilities

 Beach Access

 Swimming Pool

 Play Area

 Bar/Restaurant

 Bike Hire

Scan me for
more information.

Alan Rogers Code: IT69550
422 accommodations
450 pitches
GPS: 41.12436, 9.06759
Post Code: I-07020

Aglientu, Sardinia

Camping Baia Blu la Tortuga

www.alanrogers.com/it69550
info@campinglatortuga.com
Tel: +39 0796 02200
www.campinglatortuga.com

Open (Touring Pitches):
Late March - Mid October.

Tortuga is named after the giant turtle-like rock off the site's beautiful sandy beach and is a large, professionally run campsite. The 450 sizeable touring pitches (all with 3/10A electricity) are on grass and coarse-grained sand and mostly shaded by tall pines with banks of colourful oleanders and superb wide paved boulevards providing easy access.

This is a busy, bustling site with plenty to do, with its attractive bars and restaurants close to the beach. The excellent play areas are cleverly placed to allow parents a break whilst enjoying lunch and dinner, but there are no pools here. The site's full entertainment programme, based in a pleasant auditorium, is first class.

Four excellent, clean sanitary blocks (most with solar panels for hot water) with free hot showers, WCs, bidets and washbasins. Facilities for disabled campers. Quality private shower/washbasin cabins for rent. Washing machines and dryers. Motorhome services. Supermarket, restaurant and bars, self-service restaurant, snack bar and takeaway (open all season). Gas. Bazaar. Gym. Massage (July/Aug). Hairdresser. Doctor's surgery. Playground. Tennis. Games and TV rooms. Windsurfing, kite surfing and diving schools. Internet point and WiFi area (charged). Massage centre (July/Aug). Entertainment and sports activities (mid-May-Sept). Excursions. Barbecue area (not permitted on pitches). Specially adapted mobile homes are available for family members with disabilities.

Key Features

 Book Online

 Pets Accepted

 Disabled Facilities

 Beach Access

 Play Area

 Bar/Restaurant

 Bike Hire

 Fishing

Scan me for
more information.

Alan Rogers Code: IT69750
98 accommodations
186 pitches
GPS: 39.29230, 9.59870
Post Code: I-09043

Muravera, Sardinia

www.alanrogers.com/it69750
info@tiliguerta.com
Tel: +39 0709 91437
www.tiliguerta.com

Open (Touring Pitches):
Start May - Mid October.

Tiliguerta Camping Village

This family site situated at Capo Ferrato has been owned by the same family for a quarter of a century and improvements are made every year, all of them in sympathy with the environment. The 186 reasonably sized pitches are on sand and have 3A electricity. Some have shade and views of the superb, sandy beach and the sea beyond.

The very attractive traditional site buildings are centrally located and contain a good quality restaurant and bar. These have a charming ambience with their high arched ceilings. Shaded terraces allow comfortable viewing of the ambitious entertainment programme. Cars must be parked away from pitches.

Three renovated sanitary blocks. One has private bathrooms and facilities for children and disabled visitors. Toilets are a mixture of Turkish and British style. Laundry facilities. Motorhome services (extra charge). Shop, restaurant and snack bar/takeaway (seasonal). Play area. Live music concerts. Dog beach. Miniclub and entertainment in high season. Tennis. Water aerobics. Sailing. Sub-aqua diving. Windsurfing school. Riding. Torches essential. Bicycle hire. WiFi over site (charged). Communal barbecue areas.

Key Features

 Book Online

 Pets Accepted

 Disabled Facilities

 Beach Access

 Play Area

 Bar/Restaurant

 Bike Hire

 Fishing

Scan me for more information.

Alan Rogers Code: IT69860
20 accommodations
150 pitches
GPS: 39.00530, 8.38730
Post Code: I-09017

Sant'Antioco, Sardinia

www.alanrogers.com/it69860
tonnaracamping@tiscalinet.it
Tel: +39 0781 809058
www.campingtonnara.it

Open (Touring Pitches):
Mid April - Late October.

Camping Tonnara

A small, attractive campsite, Tonnara is situated on the west side of Sant'Antioco island in the southwest corner of Sardinia. Access to the island is via a causeway and Tonnara is in the pretty Cala Sapone inlet with its delightful private sandy beach and rocky outcrops.

The 150 sandy pitches (with 6A electricity) are terraced down to the sea with small trees and some artificial shade. Some are very close to the beach and most enjoy fabulous views of the inlet. The local seafood is good and cooked to perfection in the small restaurant where you can sit out on the terrace and watch the sunsets. The pool is very relaxing.

Two modern sanitary blocks have both Turkish and British style toilets, washbasins (cold water only) and great hot showers. Facilities for disabled campers. Superb facilities for children. Baby bathing area. Washing machine. Motorhome services. Neat little shop. Restaurant and snack bar (all season). Swimming pool (caps compulsory). Two well equipped play areas. Bicycle hire. Tennis. Bocce. Beach. Beach volleyball. Sub-aqua diving arranged. Excursions. WiFi (charged). No barbecues allowed. Torches essential.

Key Features

 Book Online

 Pets Accepted

 Disabled Facilities

 Beach Access

 Swimming Pool

 Play Area

 Bar/Restaurant

 Fishing

Scan me for more information.

Capital Luxembourg City
Currency Euro (€)
Language Letzeburgesch,
French and German
Time Zone CET (GMT+1)
Telephone Code +352

Shops 9am to 6pm Mon to Sat.
Shops are closed Sun except
on the run up to Christmas.
Supermarkets and shopping
centres often stay open for
longer hours. Some shops are
closed Mon morning.

Money ATMs are widespread
and are accessible 24hrs a day.
Credit/debit cards are widely
accepted.

Accessible Travel Although
hilly, Luxembourg is generally
wheelchair-friendly. Buses and
trams are fitted with ramps,
check before using trains.

Travelling with children A
very family-friendly country.
Some attractions will offer free
admission for young children.
Most restaurants will cater for
children. Public transport is free
to use across the country.

EU Travel Luxembourg is an
EU member state and located
within the Schengen Area.

There are no Low
Emission Zones currently
in place.

●●●●● **Accessibility Score**
View our digital e-guide & find out more at
alanrogers.com/open-to-all

Tourism website visitluxembourg.com

Public Holidays 1 Jan New Year's Day • Mar/
Apr Easter Monday • 1 May Labour Day • 9
May Europe Day • May Ascension • May/
Jun Whit Monday • 23 Jun National Day • 15
Aug Assumption • 1 Nov All Saints • 25 Dec
Christmas Day • 26 Dec Boxing Day.

Driving in Luxembourg There are no road
tolls. Many holidaymakers travel through
Luxembourg to take advantage of lower
fuel prices, thus creating traffic congestion,
especially in summer. Blue zone parking
exists in the capital, but we suggest using the
free-to-use park and ride or public transport.
Dipped headlights are recommended during
the day. Drink-driving and using your mobile
whilst driving are illegal.

Luxembourg

View all campsites in Luxembourg
alanrogers.com/luxembourg

See campsite map page 473

Climate

The summers, often extending from May to late October, are mild and winters are cold and wet.

Jan	Feb	Mar	Apr	May	Jun	Jul	Aug	Sep	Oct	Nov	Dec
4	5	10	14	18	21	23	23	18	13	8	5
-1	-1	2	5	9	11	13	13	10	7	3	0

The Grand Duchy of Luxembourg is a sovereign state lying between Belgium, France and Germany. Divided into two areas: the spectacular Ardennes region in the north and the rolling farmlands in the south, bordered on the east by the wine-growing area of the Moselle Valley.

Most attractions are within easy reach of Luxembourg's capital, Luxembourg-Ville, a fortress city, perched dramatically on its rocky promontory overlooking the Alzette and Petrusse Valleys. The verdant hills and valleys of the Ardennes are a maze of hiking trails, footpaths and cycle routes – ideal for an activity holiday.

The Moselle Valley, famous for its sweet wines, is just across the river from Germany; its charming hamlets can be discovered by bicycle or by boat. Popular wine tasting tours take place from late spring to early autumn. Echternacht is a good base for exploring the Mullerthal region, known as 'Little Switzerland.' Lying on the banks of the River Sûre, its forested landscape is dotted with curious rock formations and castle ruins, notably those at Beaufort and Larochette. The pretty Schießentümpel cascade is worth a visit.

Alan Rogers Code: LU7500
19 accommodations
95 pitches
GPS: 49.94651, 5.80102
Post Code: L-9689

Tarchamps, Diekirch

www.alanrogers.com/lu7500
umbierg@pt.lu
Tel: +316 21 26 78 28
www.umbierg.lu

Open (Touring Pitches):
Mid March – End October.

Camping Um Bierg

This small site is set on a hillside overlooking the small village of Tarchamps and although tidy, it is looking rather worn. The upper area has two terraces with around 90 generously sized, level grass pitches for tourers, all with 6A electricity. Once pitched, cars must be left at the car park by the entrance.

There is a small swimming pool and a bar/restaurant where evening meals must be ordered in advance. The friendly and helpful owners bake their own bread, which is sold on-site. The lack of dedicated facilities and steps to the toilet blocks make this site unsuitable for disabled visitors. Large units would find access challenging due to the very narrow approach roads through the village.

In the low season, this site is ideally suited to couples looking for a peaceful holiday in good walking country. It is very popular in high season with families with young children.

The toilet block in the touring area has clean showers and toilets. A second block is available adjacent to reception. Both can be heated and are accessed by steps. Laundry facilities. Heated swimming pool (July/Aug). Entertainment for children. WiFi (charged on-site, free at reception and on the terrace).

Key Features

 Pets Accepted

 Swimming Pool

 Play Area

 Bar/Restaurant

Scan me for more information.

Alan Rogers Code: LU7850
259 accommodations
222 pitches
GPS: 49.87750, 5.99283
Post Code: L-9156

Heiderscheid, Diekirch

www.alanrogers.com/lu7850
info@fuussekaul.lu
Tel: +352 26 88 88 1
fuussekaul.lu

Open (Touring Pitches):
All year.

Camping Fuussekaul

This site lies in the rolling wooded hills of central Luxembourg, not far from the lakes of the Sûre river dam. Of around 400 pitches, 220 of varying sizes are for touring units, all with a 6/16A electricity connection. There are some super pitches with private electricity and water.

The site consists of winding roads, some sloping, along which the pitches are set in shaded areas. The touring area (separate from the chalets and seasonal pitches) is well equipped with modern facilities, but with very little provision for visitors with disabilities.

Children who visit Fuussekaul (the name means fox hole) won't want to leave as there is so much for them to do. There is a fun pool, a paddling pool, exciting play areas, and an entertainment programme for all ages, including popular tractor rides.

Excellent sanitary blocks provide showers (token), washbasins (in cabins and communal) and children and baby rooms with small toilets, washbasins and showers. Laundry. Parking and service area for motorhomes. Well stocked shop. Bar. Restaurant and takeaway. Swimming pool (seasonal). Beauty salon. Playgrounds. Cross-country skiing when snow permits. Bicycle hire. Children's club. WiFi over most of site (charged).

Key Features

 Open All Year

 Pets Accepted

 Disabled Facilities

 Swimming Pool

 Play Area

 Bar/Restaurant

 Bike Hire

Scan me for more information.

Alan Rogers Code: LU7490
30 accommodations
60 pitches
GPS: 49.91389, 6.00083
Post Code: L-9181

Tadler, Diekirch

www.alanrogers.com/lu7490
info@camping-toodlermillen.lu
Tel: +352 83 91 89
camping-toodlermillen.lu

Open (Touring Pitches):
Mid April - Mid September.

Camping Toodlermillen

Camping Toodlemillen is beautifully situated in a quiet rural valley alongside the River Sûre. A network of footpaths can be accessed from the site including an international waymarked route. Pony and horse riding is available from the site. The 90 level grass pitches have 6A electricity and are generally open, with some shade by the river.

A small bistro/snack bar opens in high season and the small shop is a useful addition since the site is some distance from amenities. Play areas cater for children of different ages and a twice-weekly activity programme is organised in the high season. Nature lovers will find plenty of interest in the area, notably the otters which can occasionally be seen from the riverbank. Wildlife interpretation boards are placed on the site to encourage children to watch for wildlife.

A large, modern sanitary block is conveniently sited and has preset showers (charged), children's toilets and facilities for disabled visitors. Laundry facilities. Shop stocking essentials. Bar, restaurant and takeaway (July/Aug). Two play areas for younger and older children. Activities and entertainment weekly. Riding (July/Aug). Free WiFi.

Key Features

 Pets Accepted

 Disabled Facilities

 Play Area

 Bar/Restaurant

 Horse Riding

Scan me for more information.

Alan Rogers Code: LU7930
34 accommodations
70 pitches
GPS: 49.92542, 6.04716
Post Code: L-9164

Goebelsmühle, Diekirch

www.alanrogers.com/lu7930
info@campingdunord.lu
Tel: +313 13 20 20 80
campingdunord.lu

Open (Touring Pitches):
Start April - End October.

Camping Du Nord

Camping Du Nord is a family run campsite with friendly Dutch owners. It is located in the beautiful wooded valley of Bourscheid/Goebelsmühle. It has a long season, open from April until the end of October. There are just over 100 reasonably level, unmarked pitches, many with little shade, including about 30 long stay or accommodation pitches.

All pitches have 10A Europlug. They are laid out in a sunny, grassy meadow along the banks of the shallow River Sûre. This is an ideal place to cool off on a hot day, bathing, fishing, messing around in small boats or having a drink in the small bar/restaurant.

The site is close to the small village of Ingeldorf which has public transport to the capital. It is only 420 km. from Calais and 360 km. from Amsterdam, making it an ideal overnight or longer stay site.

There are a number of modern toilet blocks with all the necessary facilities. Washing machine and dryer. Bread delivery. Small bar, restaurant and takeaway. Club for children and some family entertainment (July/Aug). Small playground. Volleyball. Walking and hiking maps. WiFi throughout (charged).

Key Features

 Pets Accepted

 Play Area

 Bar/Restaurant

 Fishing

Scan me for more information.

Alan Rogers Code: LU7530
16 pitches
GPS: 49.93209, 6.21568
Post Code: L-9401

Vianden, Diekirch

www.alanrogers.com/lu7530
touristinfo@vianden.lu
Tel: +352 83 42 57
www.visit-vianden.lu

Open (Touring Pitches):
All year.

Camperpark Vianden

Previously known as Camping op dem Deich, this is an 'aire' style site in a most convenient location, only a short riverside walk from the medieval town of Vianden, with its fortified walls and cobbled streets. This riverside site is partly set in a former orchard where the fruit trees remain to offer shade.

The level touring pitches are numbered but not separated, and vehicles using the popular riverside pitches may need long cables to reach the 16A electricity supply. There is no shop, bar or restaurant on-site, but it is a very short walk into Vianden, where all facilities can be found.

A lovely location where fishing and kayak launching are both possible from the site. Campervans and motorhomes only, with pitch fees payable via a ticket machine.

The modern shower block can be heated in cooler periods. Excellent ramped access for disabled visitors. No washing machine and dryer available. Fishing. Gas barbecues only. WiFi throughout (charged).

Key Features

 Open All Year

 Pets Accepted

 Disabled Facilities

 Play Area

 Fishing

Scan me for more information.

Alan Rogers Code: LU7730
48 accommodations
144 pitches
GPS: 49.87286, 6.18923
Post Code: L-9359

Bleesbrück, Diekirch

Camping Bleesbrück

www.alanrogers.com/lu7730
info@camping-bleesbruck.lu
Tel: +352 80 31 34
www.camping-bleesbruck.lu

Open (Touring Pitches):
Start April - Mid October.

Camping Bleesbrück, a family run site, is centrally located in rolling countryside, ideal for exploring the Ardennes and the Eifel. The surrounding farmland and forests lie within the Our, a natural park which can be explored on foot or by bicycle. The main site is enclosed by trees and offers 144 shaded and unshaded touring pitches with electricity (10A). There is a separate 30-pitch naturist area, screened off at the far end of the main site.

The River Blees flows past and offers opportunities for the angler. An entertainment programme is available for adults and children. Both electric and standard bicycles can be hired on-site, and guided walks and cycle routes run past the site.

Key Features

 Pets Accepted

 Disabled Facilities

 Play Area

 Bar/Restaurant

 Bike Hire

 Fishing

Two sanitary units, one a separate unit for the naturist site, include washbasins in cabins, baby room and facilities with access for disabled visitors. Washing machine and dryer. Motorhome services. Bar. Terraced restaurant (seats 60). Takeaway (snacks). TV and games room. Sports field and a large playground. Outdoor table football. Fishing. Bicycles and E-bike rental. Accommodation includes huts, mobile homes, apartments and chalets. WiFi (charged).

Scan me for more information.

Alan Rogers Code: LU7610
326 accommodations
121 pitches
GPS: 49.78508, 6.21033
Post Code: L-7633

Larochette, Luxembourg District

Birkelt Village

www.alanrogers.com/lu7610
birkelt@humancompany.com
Tel: +352 87 90 40
birkelt.humancompany.com

Open (Touring Pitches):
Late April - Mid September.

This is very much a family site with a great range of facilities provided. It is well organised and well laid out, set in an elevated position in attractive, undulating countryside. A tarmac road runs around the site with around 450 large grass pitches (Appx. 120 for touring), some slightly sloping, many with a fair amount of shade, on either side of gravel access roads in straight rows and circles.

The main activities take place adjacent to the large, circular, all-weather family pool. This is an outdoor pool in the high season and is covered and heated in cooler weather. Several play areas are dotted all over the site.

Three modern heated sanitary buildings well situated around the site include mostly open washbasins (6 cabins in one block). Baby baths. Facilities (including accommodation to rent) for wheelchair users. Washing machines and dryers. Motorhome services. Shops. Coffee bar. Restaurant with terrace. Swimming pool with a sliding cupola (heated all season). Outdoor pool for toddlers. Play areas. Trampolines. Volleyball. Minigolf. Tennis. Bicycle hire. Riding. Internet points. Free WiFi.

Key Features

 Pets Accepted

 Disabled Facilities

 Swimming Pool

 Play Area

 Bar/Restaurant

 Bike Hire

 Horse Riding

Scan me for more information.

Alan Rogers Code: LU7660
3 accommodations
161 pitches
GPS: 49.57180, 6.10900
Post Code: L-1899

Luxembourg, Luxembourg
District

www.alanrogers.com/lu7660
caravani@pt.lu
Tel: +352 47 18 15
www.ccclv.lu

Open (Touring Pitches):
Week before Easter - 31 October.

Camping Kockelscheuer

Camping Kockelscheuer is a municipal site owned by the city of Luxembourg and is 4 km. from its centre. It is managed by an enthusiastic couple and is quietly situated (although there can be some aircraft noise at times). On a slight slope, there are 161 individual pitches of good size, either on flat ground at the bottom of the site or on wide flat terraces with easy access, all with 16A electricity.

There is also a special area for tents, with picnic tables and, in the reception building, a tent campers' lounge. For children, there is a large area with modern play equipment on safety tiles and next door to the site is a sports centre. There is a friendly welcome, charges are reasonable and English is spoken.

Two fully equipped, identical sanitary buildings, both very clean. Washing machines. Motorhome services. Shop (order bread the previous day). Snack bar. Restaurant in adjacent sports centre also with tennis, squash, pitch and putt and golf driving range. Restroom. No entry for vehicles (reception closed) 12.00-14.00. Free WiFi throughout.

Key Features

 Pets Accepted

 Disabled Facilities

 Play Area

Scan me for more information.

Capital Amsterdam
Currency Euro (€)
Language Dutch. French and German also widely spoken
Time Zone CET (GMT+1)
Telephone Code +31

Shops Hours vary throughout the year, with many shops operating on shorter hours in low and shoulder seasons. In high season 10am to 6pm Tues to Fri, 10am to 5pm Sat and Sun and noon to 5pm or 6pm on Mon (if at all). Supermarkets are open 8am to 8pm.

Money ATMs are widespread and are accessible 24hrs a day. Credit/debit cards accepted mostly. Cash is still widely used.

Accessible Travel Generally very good, especially in cities. Public buildings and transport are well equipped. WCs in restaurants can be difficult for wheelchair users.

Travelling with children Amsterdam is one of Europe's most child-friendly cities. We recommend you stay clear of the Red Light District. Beaches are safe. Restaurants are kid-friendly, nearly all offer children's menus and colouring crayons.

EU Travel Netherlands is an EU member state and located within the Schengen Area.

LEZ Low Emissions Zones in all major cities. Registration required.

●●●●○ **Accessibility Score**
View our digital e-guide & find out more at
alanrogers.com/open-to-all

Tourism website holland.com

Public Holidays 1 Jan New Year's Day · Mar/Apr Good Friday · Mar/Apr Easter Sunday · Mar/Apr Easter Monday · 27 Apr King's Day · 5 May Liberation Day · May Ascension Day · May/Jun Whit Sunday · May/Jun Whit Monday · 25 Dec Christmas Day · 26 Dec Boxing Day.

Driving in the Netherlands There is a comprehensive motorway system but due to the high density of population, all main roads can become very busy, particularly in the morning and evening rush hours. There are no toll roads. Trams should be overtaken on the right unless unsafe. Drink-driving, using your mobile whilst driving and sat navs that warn you of speed cameras are illegal.

Netherlands

View all campsites in Netherlands
alanrogers.com/netherlands

See campsite map page 483

Climate

Temperate with mild winters and warm summers.

Jan	Feb	Mar	Apr	May	Jun	Jul	Aug	Sep	Oct	Nov	Dec
6	7	10	14	18	20	22	22	19	15	10	7
1	1	3	5	8	11	13	13	11	8	4	2

With vast areas of the Netherlands reclaimed from the sea, nearly half of the country lies at or below sea level. The result is a flat, fertile landscape crisscrossed with rivers and canals. Famous for its windmills and bulb fields, it also boasts some of the most impressive coastal dunes in Europe.

No visit to the Netherlands would be complete without experiencing its capital city, Amsterdam, with its maze of canals, bustling cafés, museums and summer festivals.

The fields of South Holland are an explosion of colour between March and May when the world's biggest flower auction takes place at Aalsmeer.

The Vecht valley and its towns of Dalfsen, Ommen and Hardenberg are best explored by bicycle, while Giethoorn, justly dubbed the 'Venice of Holland', has to be seen from a boat. The Kinderdijk windmills on the Alblasserwaard polder are a UNESCO World Heritage Site.

The islands of Zeeland are home to beautiful old towns such as Middelburg, the provincial capital, Zierikzee, with its old harbour and the quaint old town of Veere.

Netherlands

Alan Rogers Code: NL5530
230 accommodations
75 pitches
GPS: 51.38221, 3.45819
Post Code: NL-4504 PS

Nieuwvliet, Zeeland

www.alanrogers.com/nl5530
info@campingzonneweelde.nl
Tel: +31 117 371 910
www.campingzonneweelde.nl

Open (Touring Pitches):
All year.

Camping Zonneweelde

This site is only 600 m. from kilometres of wide, sandy beaches, making it ideal for family holidays. Children will enjoy a walkway and a large slide through the dunes to reach the beach. There are around 70 touring pitches, a wide choice of luxury holiday cottages and log cabins, plus places for seasonal caravans. Electricity (10A) is available throughout.

The Natural Reserve of Het Zwin is nearby (ideal for birdwatching) and many interesting villages are in the area. The landscape is perfect for exploring on bicycles along the safe, well-signed routes. This site should appeal to children of all ages and feature a character called Professor Zouterik.

Modern, heated, well maintained sanitary buildings provide roomy adjustable showers and some washbasins in cabins. Family shower room. Children's bathroom. Laundry facilities. Supermarket. Restaurant, bar and terrace. Separate takeaway. Swimming pool (unheated) and a separate pool for children with slides and water features. Play areas and sports field. Boules. Volleyball. Children's entertainment (in holiday periods). Excursions for adults (low season). Bicycle hire. WiFi over site (charged).

Key Features

 Open All Year

 Pets Accepted

 Beach Access

 Swimming Pool

 Play Area

 Bar/Restaurant

 Bike Hire

Scan me for more information.

Netherlands

Alan Rogers Code: NL6990
46 accommodations
261 pitches
GPS: 51.55578, 3.51516
Post Code: NL-4363 RJ

Aagtekerke, Zeeland

www.alanrogers.com/nl6990
westhove@ardoer.com
Tel: +31 118 581 809
www.westhove.ardoer.com

Open (Touring Pitches):
Late March - Late October.

Camping Westhove

Camping Westhove is an ideal site for all ages and has some high-quality play facilities for children. It is situated on the island Walcheren (the garden of Zeeland). There are 360 spacious pitches of which 261 are for touring with 6A electricity.

Entertainment possibilities are endless – whether you wish to enjoy the beach, nature or the towns. There are marked tracks through the woods and dunes, and historical villages and towns with opportunities for cycling, walking and riding. The site's sanitary facilities are of a high standard, and there is an excellent modern wellness and fitness centre.

Three heated sanitary units with washbasins in cabins, showers and WCs and en-suite facilities. Baby room. Free hot water. Launderette with ironing facilities. Well stocked supermarket. Bar. Good restaurant. Snack bar. Fresh bread is available daily. Heated indoor swimming pool. Paddling pool. Excellent wellness and fitness centre. Indoor and outdoor play areas. Sports field. Boules. Bicycle and tricycle hire. Entertainment team in high season. Miniclub. Recreation area. TV. Electronic games. WiFi (charged). Dogs are not accepted in the high season.

Key Features

 Pets Accepted

 Disabled Facilities

 Beach Access

 Swimming Pool

 Play Area

 Bar/Restaurant

 Bike Hire

Scan me for more information.

Alan Rogers Code: NL5585
30 accommodations
125 pitches
GPS: 51.54936, 3.80706
Post Code: 4484 NT

Kortgene, Zeeland

www.alanrogers.com/nl5585
paardekreek@ardoer.com
Tel: +31 113 302 051
www.paardekreek.nl

Open (Touring Pitches):
Late March - Early November.

Camping De Paardekreek

Located directly on the Veerse Meer, with access to the vast lake, this superb family site has additional but not sole, appeal for watersports enthusiasts. This is a wonderful site for families with children. There are both seasonal pitches and pitches for touring units, all fully serviced including 10A electricity, television and WiFi. The pitches are pleasant and some are directly by the water's edge and with boat launching facilities, water and a sailing school on-site, many units have a boat of some sort.

There is an exciting indoor water adventure play park with a long water chute and a small beach also allows swimming and zip wire fun over the water. There are facilities as table tennis, basketball and volleyball. A varied programme of entertainment for young children and teenagers is provided during Dutch school holidays except for Christmas holidays.

Three very good toilet blocks and one smaller unit include en-suite shower rooms. Excellent facilities for disabled visitors, babies and children. Motorhome services. Pleasant bar with terrace. Restaurant. Snack bar with takeaway. Indoor heated water adventure area and water chute. Lake swimming. Adventure play areas with trampolines. Indoor play area. Mooring facilities. Storage for surf boards and boat trailers. Bicycle hire. Pedal kart hire. Dune buggy hire. Entertainment for children in high season. WiFi (charged).

Key Features

 Pets Accepted

 Disabled Facilities

 Beach Access

 Swimming Pool

 Play Area

 Bar/Restaurant

 Bike Hire

Scan me for more information.

Alan Rogers Code: NL6948
90 accommodations
218 pitches
GPS: 51.73906, 3.80237
Post Code: NL-4326 LJ

Renesse/Noordwelle, Zeeland

De Zeeuwse Kust

www.alanrogers.com/nl6948
info@strandparkdezeeuwsekust.eu
Tel: +31 111 468 282
www.strandparkdezeeuwsekust.nl

Open (Touring Pitches):
All year (limited facilities October - April)

Whether you want relaxation, something for the children, the seaside or activities, you will find all of these at De Zeeuwse Kust located just 250 m. from the sea with its beautiful sandy beach. The outstanding, hotel standard facilities contained within the centrally located building are in a class of their own, offering a haven whatever the weather. From the open plan kitchen, the oversized wooden stools, to the open fireplace, they are all first class.

This site has 218 spacious and comfortable pitches, all with electricity (16A), water, waste water and TV connections. Thirty-two pitches have private sanitary provision. The modern sanitary unit is heated and includes facilities for children and disabled visitors.

Modern, first-class sanitary building providing showers, washbasins, private cabins, family shower rooms and other facilities for children and disabled visitors. Launderette. Shop/mini-market. Fresh bread (all year). Heated swimming pool. Play areas (indoors and outdoors). Sports field. Motorhome services. Outdoor table football. Games room. Small film theatre. Recreation room. Entertainment team (special holidays, weekends and July/Aug). Sauna. Whirlpool. First aid post. Free WiFi. Dogs welcome all year – showers available near the sanitary block.

Key Features

 Open All Year

 Pets Accepted

 Disabled Facilities

 Beach Access

 Swimming Pool

 Play Area

 Bar/Restaurant

 Bike Hire

Scan me for more information.

Alan Rogers Code: NL5598
275 accommodations
80 pitches
GPS: 51.70565, 4.13606
Post Code: NL-3244 LK

Nieuwe Tonge, Zuid-Holland

www.alanrogers.com/nl5598
info@degrevelingen.nl
Tel: +31 187 651 259
www.degrevelingen.nl

Open (Touring Pitches):
Mid March - Late October.

Camping De Grevelingen

Camping de Grevelingen is ideally located on the edge of the Grevelingenmeer water sports area, on Goeree-Overflakkee, on the border of South Holland and Zeeland. From the site, the Randstad seems far away. And yet, via the Rotterdam ring road, it is only half an hour. Three-quarters of an hour to the outskirts of Breda and an hour to Antwerp.

The beautiful Grevelingenmeer, which is located behind the dike is ideal for surfers and water sports enthusiasts. Cycling and walking routes are plentiful. The site has 200 pitches. A large part of the site consists of mobile homes and chalets available for hire. The 80 touring pitches have 10 Amp electric hook-up points, water, wastewater and TV. In winter you will find Flamingos nearby, a colony of up to 60.

The heated toilet blocks provide showers, washbasins and WC's. Motorhome service point. Laundry. Snack bar. Recreation room with bar. Fresh bread on Saturday and Sunday. Library. Beach. Boat launch. Fishing pond. Children's play area. Football pitch. Charging station for electric cars. Zip wire. Boules court. Boat parking area. Newspaper sales. Tourist information. Kids' chill room. Bicycles, including electric ones available to rent. Supermarket 2 kilometres.

Key Features

 Book Online

 Pets Accepted

 Disabled Facilities

 Beach Access

 Play Area

 Bike Hire

 Fishing

 Sailing

Scan me for more information.

Alan Rogers Code: NL6840
250 pitches
GPS: 52.32007, 4.56625
Post Code: NL-2114 AP

Vogelenzang, Noord-Holland

Camping Vogelenzang

www.alanrogers.com/nl6840
camping@vogelenzang.nl
Tel: +31 235 847 014
www.vogelenzang.nl

Open (Touring Pitches):
Late March - Late September.

Camping Vogelenzang is a friendly campsite with 600 pitches, located 9 km. from the North Sea beaches. The cities of Haarlem and Amsterdam with their old streets are within reach. There are 250 level, grassy pitches for touring caravans and tents, 140 with 16A electricity connections. There is a separate area for motorhomes. Mature trees and hedges provide shade.

A small play park adjoins the high season entertainment area and the children's pool, which is fenced but with an opening. The large, outdoor pool is not heated. The well-stocked shop has fresh bread daily. Some areas of the site would benefit from attention.

Four modern and one older toilet block provide toilets, open washbasins with cold water, washbasins in cabins with hot and cold water, controllable showers, a family shower room and baby room. Motorhome services. Shop, Bar and snack bar (seasonal). Unheated outdoor swimming pool (25x12 m) with separate paddling pool. Play area. Sports field. Extensive high season recreation programme. WiFi over part of the site (charged). Dogs are not accepted.

Key Features

 Disabled Facilities

 Beach Access

 Swimming Pool

 Play Area

 Bar/Restaurant

 Bike Hire

Scan me for more information.

Alan Rogers Code: NL6705
9 accommodations
120 pitches
GPS: 52.64210, 4.72329
Post Code: NL-1817 ML

Alkmaar, Noord-Holland

www.alanrogers.com/nl6705
info@campingalkmaar.nl
Tel: +31 725 116 924
campingalkmaar.nl

Open (Touring Pitches):
All year.

Camping Alkmaar

Camping Alkmaar is a friendly, family run campsite on the outskirts of the charming town of Alkmaar and near the artisan village of Bergen. A short cycle ride will take you to the peaceful countryside of Noord-Holland with its dunes, wide sandy beaches, woods and unique polder landscape.

Alternatively, a stroll along the canals in the picturesque heart of Alkmaar with its architecture, culture and cheese market may appeal. This is a tranquil site - there is no bar or restaurant and radios are not permitted. All 120 touring pitches have 6/10A electricity; 46 have hardstanding, and 21 are comfort pitches with water and drainage. A regular bus service runs to the town centre and the train station for connections to Amsterdam.

Modern sanitary block in the touring area is clean and well maintained and has coin-operated showers and open style washbasins. Facilities for disabled visitors. Washing machine and dryer. Two motorhome service points. Play area. Fishing. Bicycle hire. WiFi over part of site (charged).

Key Features

 Open All Year

 Pets Accepted

 Disabled Facilities

 Beach Access

 Play Area

 Bike Hire

 Fishing

Scan me for more information.

Camping Stortemelk

Netherlands

Alan Rogers Code: NL6029
105 accommodations
900 pitches
GPS: 53.30440, 5.07962
Post Code: NL-8899 BX

Vlieland, Friesland

www.alanrogers.com/nl6029
info@stortemelk.nl
Tel: +31 562 451 225
www.stortemelk.nl

Open (Touring Pitches):
Start April - End September.

Camping Stortemelk is located on the West Frisian island of Vlieland, separated from a broad sandy beach by high dunes. The island is car (and caravan) free, therefore this is a traditional tent campsite. with around 900 pitches.

Pitching is haphazard, partly on the grassy dunes with some good views of the campsite. Most fields are slightly sloping and special long sand pegs are needed (these can be provided at reception). There are specific fields for youngsters and groups.

A number of attractive, traditionally-styled chalets are available to rent. On-site amenities include De Bolder, a convivial café/restaurant, which is the base for concerts, as well as the campsite's activity programme. Strict rules apply for nighttime curfew.

Five modern toilet blocks are well distributed over the site and provide open style washbasins, preset hot showers, attractive children's facilities and a baby room. Facilities for disabled campers. Supermarket. Café/restaurant. Playgrounds. Volleyball. Fishing. Some entertainment is provided. Direct beach access. Free WiFi over site.

Key Features

 Beach Access

 Play Area

Y Bar/Restaurant

 Fishing

Scan me for more information.

349

Netherlands

Alan Rogers Code: NL6030
300 accommodations
190 pitches
GPS: 53.45339, 5.80476
Post Code: NL-9164 MA

Buren, Friesland

Klein Vaarwater

www.alanrogers.com/nl6030
info@kleinvaarwater.nl
Tel: +31 519 542 156
kleinvaarwater.nl

Open (Touring Pitches):
All year.

Recreatieoord Klein Vaarwater is a bustling family holiday park on the interesting island of Ameland. The site is 1 km. from the North Sea beaches and has its own indoor pool, with bars, restaurants, supermarket and party centre. Klein Vaarwater has 187 touring pitches (all with 16A electricity), of which 130 also have water, wastewater and cable. Pitching is off hardcore access lanes, on fields taking 6-10 units on grass. The level pitches are numbered and partly separated by young trees. Some of the pitches enjoy good views over the countryside.

Touring pitches are on separate fields from the 440 mobile homes and holiday bungalows. On-site is an entertainment centre, where you can enjoy the swimming pool with waterslide and fun paddling pool, boules, bowling and minigolf, and there is a full fitness room.

Four heated toilet blocks have open style washbasins, hot showers (free of charge) and facilities for disabled visitors and families. Washing machines and dryers. Supermarket. Bar, restaurant, snack bar. Boutique. Indoor pools (25x15 m) with waterslide and fun paddling pool. Fitness centre. Playing field. Boules pitch. Bowling alley. Minigolf. Entertainment programme for young and old (seasonal). WiFi (free).

Key Features

 Open All Year

 Pets Accepted

 Disabled Facilities

 Beach Access

 Swimming Pool

 Play Area

 Bar/Restaurant

 Bike Hire

Scan me for more information.

Alan Rogers Code: NL6080
125 pitches
GPS: 53.16237, 5.41688
Post Code: NL-8862 PK

Harlingen, Friesland

Camping De Zeehoeve

www.alanrogers.com/nl6080
info@zeehoeve.nl
Tel: +31 517 413 465
www.zeehoeve.nl

Open (Touring Pitches):
Start April - Mid October.

Superbly located, directly behind the sea dyke of the Wadden Sea and just a kilometre from the harbour of Harlingen, De Zeehoeve is an attractive and spacious site. It has 300 pitches (125 for touring units), all with 16A Europlug connection and 20 with water, drainage and electricity. There are 16 hardstandings for motorhomes and larger units. Some pitches have views over the Harlingen canal where one can moor small boats.

An ideal site for rest and relaxation, for watersports or to visit the attractions of Harlingen and Friesland. After a day of activity, one can wine and dine in the site's modern restaurant or at one of the many pubs in the town.

Three sanitary blocks include open style washbasins with cold water only, washbasins in cabins with hot and cold water, controllable showers (on payment). Family showers and baby bath. Facilities for disabled visitors. Cooking hob. Launderette. Motorhome services. Bar/restaurant (July/Aug). Play area. Bicycle hire. Boat launching. Pedalo and canoe hire. Fishing. Extensive entertainment programme (July/Aug). Bed and breakfast. Hikers' cabins and boarding houses. Dog exercise area. WiFi (charged).

Key Features

 Book Online

 Pets Accepted

 Disabled Facilities

 Beach Access

 Play Area

 Bar/Restaurant

 Bike Hire

 Fishing

Scan me for more information.

Alan Rogers Code: NL6048
180 accommodations
164 pitches
GPS: 53.02973, 5.72424
Post Code: NL-8626 GG

Offingawier, Friesland

www.alanrogers.com/nl6048
potten@rcn.nl
Tel: +31 515 415 205
www.rcn.nl/en/holiday-park/holland/
friesland/rcn-de-potten

Open (Touring Pitches):
Mid March - Late October.

Camping De Potten

RCN De Potten is a good choice for lovers of watersports. This campsite is located on a peninsula on the Sneekermeer. The site has its own marina with boat launching facilities (charge applies). All manner of water transport is on offer here: motorboats, rowing boats, sailing boats, canoes, and more besides!

Sailing lessons are organised (from eight years old), and include special family sessions. About 160 touring pitches are large and grassy, have 10A electricity connections and limited shade. Many have fine views across the lake. There are 13 chalets (with wooden terraces), 50 villas and 30 bungalows to rent, many with great lake views.

Clean toilet facilities with preset showers, washbasins and cabins and toilets. Launderette. Restaurant with lake view, bar and snack bar. Bakery. Sports area. Play area with giant chess and draughts. Tennis. Minigolf. Trampolines. Boats, bicycles and go-karts for hire. Sailing school for children (from 8 years) and for adults. Boat launching and mooring facilities. WiFi (charged).

Key Features

 Book Online

 Pets Accepted

 Disabled Facilities

 Swimming Pool

 Play Area

 Bar/Restaurant

 Bike Hire

 Golf

Scan me for more information.

Alan Rogers Code: NL6126
18 accommodations
250 pitches
GPS: 53.03597, 6.73941
Post Code: NL-9463 TA

Eext, Drenthe

www.alanrogers.com/nl6126
info@hondsrug.nl
Tel: +31 592 271 292
www.hondsrug.nl

Open (Touring Pitches):
Start April - End September.

Camping de Hondsrug

This site is targeted at young families and is located at the Hondsrug (literally dog's back), an escarpment of around 70 km. rising up above the flat country below. In keeping with the canine theme, this site uses a dachshund as its motif. There are 250 grassy touring pitches here, all with 6/10A electricity, of which 110 are large serviced pitches with water and drainage and 16 are Comfort Plus with their own small toilet block.

The pitches are divided by young shrubs and bushes so there is hardly any shade. There is a large outdoor swimming pool and also a subtropical indoor pool and a children's pool. These are reserved in the morning for parents and their children (up to 6 years) and anyone older than 30.

Good heated toilet blocks including separate facilities for children and disabled guests. Family rooms. Shop. Restaurant and takeaway. Outdoor pool. Indoor pools and steam bath. Playgrounds and sports areas. Bouncy cushion. Bicycle hire. Fishing. Activity and entertainment programme.

Key Features

 Pets Accepted

 Disabled Facilities

 Swimming Pool

 Play Area

 Bike Hire

 Fishing

Scan me for more information.

Alan Rogers Code: NL6129
1 accommodations
180 pitches
GPS: 52.77899, 6.68632
Post Code: NL-7855 TA

Meppen, Drenthe

www.alanrogers.com/nl6129
info@bronzenemmer.nl
Tel: +31 591 371 543
www.de-bronzen-emmer.nl

Open (Touring Pitches):
Late March - Late October.

De Bronzen Emmer

De Bronzen Emmer is in the centre of three nature reserves, close to the German border in the southwestern part of Drenthe. The 180 level and grassy touring pitches are attractively laid out and average 100 sq.m. in size. All have 10A electricity and are shaded by mature trees. There are 60 fully serviced pitches. To the front of the site is a heated indoor pool and paddling pool with a small slide and an open-air paddling pool. Here also are a sauna, sunbeds, recreation hall, small café and a playground.

De Bronzen Emmer derives its name from excavations where a bronze bucket was found. It borders the Mepperdennen woodland nature reserve, and nearby is the Het Mantingerzand nature reserve where cattle still graze freely.

Two well placed, traditional-style toilet blocks (one heated) with toilets, washbasins (open style and in cabins) and free, preset hot showers. Laundry. Motorhome services. Small shop for basics, small restaurant with bar and open-air terrace, takeaway (seasonal). Heated indoor swimming pool (20x10 m) with paddling pool and open-air paddling pool (seasonal). Sauna and sunbeds. Bicycle hire. Playing field. Fishing. Tennis. Playground. Activity team in high season. WiFi throughout (free).

Key Features

 Book Online

 Pets Accepted

 Disabled Facilities

 Swimming Pool

 Play Area

 Bar/Restaurant

 Bike Hire

 Horse Riding

Scan me for
more information.

Alan Rogers Code: NL6158
55 accommodations
337 pitches
GPS: 52.81337, 6.37893
Post Code: NL-7991 PB

Dwingeloo, Drenthe

www.alanrogers.com/nl6158
reservation@rcn.eu
Tel: +31 850 400 700
www.rcn.nl/rcn-de-noordster

Open (Touring Pitches):
All year.

Camping De Noordster

RCN de Noordster can be found in the Dutch National Park Dwingelderveld, a beautiful expanse of moorland in the northern Netherlands. Hours of long walks through fields of purple heather and deep into ancient forests are possible here. The site offers just over 300 touring pitches, all with 10A electricity, well-shaded under large trees and surrounded by colourful shrubs.

A range of mobile homes and chalets is available to rent, including some units specially adapted for visitors with disabilities. There are several playgrounds here and other leisure amenities include an outdoor pool (with waterslide), children's and toddlers' pools and various water games.

Five clean, modern toilet blocks. Launderette. Restaurant, bar, café and takeaway. Bakery and small shop at reception. Fun paddling pool. Evening entertainment. Play area. Minigolf. Sports hall. Multisports field. Bicycle and go-kart hire. Skateboard track with half pipe. WiFi throughout (free).

Key Features

 Book Online

 Open All Year

 Pets Accepted

 Disabled Facilities

 Swimming Pool

 Play Area

 Bar/Restaurant

 Bike Hire

Scan me for more information.

Alan Rogers Code: NL6502
100 pitches
GPS: 52.65664, 6.30191
Post Code: NL-7955 PT

IJhorst, Overijssel

www.alanrogers.com/nl6502
info@devossenburcht.nl
Tel: +31 522 441 626
www.devossenburcht.nl

Open (Touring Pitches):
All year.

Camping De Vossenburcht

A pleasant, wooded family campsite in a rural location in the north of the country, Familiecamping De Vossenburcht has 370 pitches of which many are seasonal, with 100 available for tourers and some accommodation for hire. They are level, a few in the open but mainly among the trees, and with electrical connections available.

This is one of the most beautiful parts of Overijssel where you can still enjoy the beautiful forests and farmland. Nearby are moors, fens and attractive old farmhouses. The village of IJhorst has a few shops whilst the neighbouring towns of Meppel, Hoogeveen and Zwolle offer a wider choice of shops, bars and restaurants. Nearby, the recreation lake of De Zwarte Dennen also has a mountain bike trail, a jogging track and several hiking trails.

Heated sanitary block with provision for babies, children and disabled visitors. Washing machines and dryers. Motorhome service point. Bar with pool table and TV, snack bar with takeaway provision (seasonal). Heated outdoor swimming and children's pools (seasonal). Large children's playground. Children's entertainment in the high season. Table tennis and table football. WiFi throughout (charged).

Key Features

 Book Online

 Open All Year

 Pets Accepted

 Disabled Facilities

 Swimming Pool

 Play Area

 Bar/Restaurant

Scan me for more information.

Alan Rogers Code: NL6504
100 accommodations
80 pitches
GPS: 52.42528, 6.99160
Post Code: NL-7635 NH

Lattrop, Overijssel

www.alanrogers.com/nl6504
info@rammelbeek.nl
Tel: +31 541 229 368
www.rammelbeek.nl

Open (Touring Pitches):
Late March - Mid October.

Camping De Rammelbeek

Camping de Rammelbeek in Overijssel is a real family business with Henri Groeneveld as current owner together with his wife he has taken over from his father, Hennie Groeneveld. It has 220 pitches (some seasonal, some annual), 80 for touring units of which 33 have private toilet facilities.

All touring pitches are at least 100m2. Some are equipped with a 10amp electric hook-up point, waste and fresh water connection. The pitches on the lakeside have 6amp. electricity. The site also has Safari tents and Mobile homes available to hire. Get a breath of fresh air in the wooded area or take the cultural path with a visit to one of the many Twente estates or regional producers.

Three toilet blocks have showers washbasins and WC's. Facility for visitors who are disabled. Baby room. Laundry with washing machine and dryer. Dishwashing area. Chemical toilet point. Indoor heated swimming pool. Children's pool. Water slide. Lake with beach. Trampoline. Fishing pond. Snack bar. Shop. TV room. Restaurant. Takeaway. Indoor play area. Boules area. Games room. Table tennis. Multisports pitch. Wi-Fi free. Barbeques allowed. Dogs allowed low season. Dog walk.

Key Features

 Book Online

 Pets Accepted

 Disabled Facilities

 Swimming Pool

 Play Area

 Fishing

Scan me for more information.

Alan Rogers Code: NL6454
6 accommodations
80 pitches
GPS: 52.20994, 6.95189
Post Code: NL-7534 PA

Enschede, Overijssel

www.alanrogers.com/nl6454
info@twentse-es.nl
Tel: +31 534 611 372
twentse-es.nl

Open (Touring Pitches):
All year.

Camping De Twentse Es

De Twentse Es lies between Enschede and Glanerbrug in a natural setting. The site has 300 pitches of which 80 are used for touring units. All pitches are equipped with 10A electricity, water, drainage, cable and WiFi connections.

In the high season, an animation team organises activities; for example, a theatre for small children and sports activities for the older ones. Fishing is possible in the pond on the site. The German border is very close with excursions to Munster or Osnabruck very easy. Plenty of information about walking and cycling routes is available from reception. A member of the Citycamps group.

Heated sanitary building with washbasins in cabins. Laundry facilities. Shop. Bar. Café. Snack bar. Heated swimming and paddling pools. Play area. Sports pitch. TV room. Entertainment in high season. WiFi.

Key Features

 Book Online

 Open All Year

 Pets Accepted

 Swimming Pool

 Bar/Restaurant

 Fishing

Scan me for
more information.

Alan Rogers Code: NL5865
3 accommodations
65 pitches
GPS: 51.99120, 6.27960
Post Code: NL-6999 DT

Hummelo, Gelderland

Camping De Graafschap

www.alanrogers.com/nl5865
info@camping-degraafschap.nl
Tel: +31 314 343 752
www.camping-degraafschap.nl

Open (Touring Pitches):
All year.

De Graafschap is an attractive, family-friendly site located on the outskirts of the beautiful Kruisbergse forest between Doetinchem and Hummelo, a large green area perfect for hiking, mountain biking and cycling enthusiasts. Pitches here are all of a good size, on average 125-150 sq.m.

There are 65 touring and 65 permanent pitches on several well kept grassy fields, all with electricity (6A), water, drainage and cable TV connection (charged). There is a cosy canteen offering snacks and drinks and a small shop in the reception for all your daily essentials. Finnish Kotas and mobile homes are available to rent throughout the year.

Doetinchem is the shopping capital of the region. In the centre, you will find everything from established antique shops to little speciality shops down small cobbled streets. Markets are also popular here every Tuesday and Saturday. The site also offers organised cycling trips and walking trails, with details available from reception.

Two heated sanitary blocks with free hot water and baby room. Launderette. Motorhome services. Small shop. Canteen. Playground. Boules. WiFi (charged).

Key Features

 Book Online

 Open All Year

 Pets Accepted

 Play Area

 Bike Hire

Scan me for more information.

Netherlands

Alan Rogers Code: NL6336
45 accommodations
150 pitches
GPS: 52.18692, 5.62458
Post Code: NL-3781 NJ

Voorthuizen, Gelderland

www.alanrogers.com/nl6336
ackersate@ardoer.com
Tel: +31 342 471 274
www.ackersate.nl

Open (Touring Pitches):
Late March - Late October.

Camping Ackersate

This is a sophisticated, wooded site with 150 touring pitches out of a total of 490, all with 6/10A electricity. The swimming pool has a fun pool with slides, a large pool for young children, imaginatively designed, a separate pool for length swimming and even a flume. Also popular, is the cosy restaurant/bar.

There is a play club for children, a playing field and a petting farm. Other activities available include minigolf, table tennis and a pool table. Active visitors might enjoy a game of volleyball or football. A member of the Ardoer Group.

Voorthuizen is a small town close to the site, while Amersfoort, Apeldoorn, The Kröller-Müller Museum (a large collection of Van Gogh paintings), and the Hoge Veluwe National Park are all easily visited by car.

Three toilet blocks are conveniently situated around the touring areas. En-suite unit for disabled campers. Laundry. Well stocked shop. Bar with TV. Restaurant. Snack bar/takeaway. Heated indoor pool. Play area. Entertainment for younger children (high season). Bicycle hire. WiFi over site. Accommodation for hire. Max. 1 dog per pitch.

Key Features

 Pets Accepted

 Disabled Facilities

 Swimming Pool

 Bar/Restaurant

 Bike Hire

Scan me for more information.

Alan Rogers Code: NL5695
9 accommodations
22 pitches
GPS: 51.90114, 5.02646
Post Code: NL-4243 JS

Nieuwland, Zuid-Holland

www.alanrogers.com/nl5695
receptie@degrienduil.nl
Tel: +31 183 351 512
www.degrienduil.nl

Open (Touring Pitches):
All year.

Camping de Grienduil

A compact, family run site located in the area known as The Green Heart of the Netherlands. You should expect a heartwarming welcome from the enthusiastic owner at de Grienduil, which has a total of 22 touring pitches ranging in size from 100 to 120 sq. metres and with computer-controlled current (6-16A) to the electricity hook-ups. Your unit will be placed on-site by the owner, as cars are left outside the campsite.

There is a choice of rental accommodation, including a luxury Romany-style caravan. Be sure to arrive before Friday to take advantage of the 'all you can eat' pizza experience, where you roll your own dough base! This is a perfect place to experience the green agricultural heart of the Netherlands.

One central, heated sanitary block has unisex facilities, with open washbasins, coin-operated showers and hot water for dishwashing. Motorhome services. Pizza oven and terrace. Takeaway. Ice-cream, drinks and essentials. Bread to order. Breakfast service. Adventure-style playground. WiFi over site (free).

Key Features

 Book Online

 Open All Year

 Pets Accepted

 Swimming Pool

 Play Area

 Bar/Restaurant

 Bike Hire

 Fishing

Scan me for more information.

Alan Rogers Code: NL6200
229 accommodations
229 pitches
GPS: 52.27021, 5.48871
Post Code: NL-3896 LB

Zeewolde, Flevoland

Erkemederstrand

www.alanrogers.com/nl6200
info@erkemederstrand.nl
Tel: +31 365 228 421
www.erkemederstrand.nl

Open (Touring Pitches):
Mid March - Late October.

Erkemederstrand is a leisure park in Flevoland with direct access to the Nuldernauw where there is Flevolands longest sandy beach, a lake and a forest. It provides a campsite for families, a marina, an area for youngsters to camp, a camping area for groups and a recreation area for day visitors.

The campsite itself is divided into two areas: one before the dyke at the waterfront and one behind the dyke. The pitches are spacious (125-150 sq.m) and most have electricity, water and drainage. The focal point of the site and marina is the De Jutter beachside restaurant.

Six neat, clean and heated toilet blocks (access by key; exclusively for campers). Washbasins in cabins, showers and family bathrooms (some charges for hot water). Laundry facilities. Well stocked supermarket, bar, restaurant and takeaway (all open all season). Several play areas and children's farm. Watersports facilities and lake swimming. Fishing. Football pitch. Minigolf. Bicycle hire. Extended entertainment programme. WiFi (charged). Beach and shower for dogs.

Key Features

 Book Online

 Pets Accepted

 Play Area

 Bar/Restaurant

 Bike Hire

 Fishing

 Sailing

Scan me for more information.

Alan Rogers Code: NL6290
41 accommodations
265 pitches
GPS: 51.97656, 5.43013
Post Code: NL-4021 GG

Maurik, Gelderland

www.alanrogers.com/nl6290
receptie@eilandvanmaurik.nl
Tel: +31 344 691 502
www.eilandvanmaurik.nl

Open (Touring Pitches):
Start April - Start October.

Eiland van Maurik

Camping Eiland van Maurik is beside a lake in the centre of an extensive nature and recreation park in the Nederrijn area. These surroundings are ideal for all sorts of activities – swimming, windsurfing, water-skiing or para-sailing, relaxing on the beach or fishing. There is even an animal farm for the children. The site has 265 numbered, flat pitches, all fully serviced (10A electricity). You could enjoy pancakes in the Oudhollandse restaurant with its views over the water. There is direct access from the site to the lakeside beach.

In the event of bad weather, the site has the Eiland Aquatura, a sheltered outdoor swim and play facility for young children, and an indoor play palace (Avontura), where in high season games and activities are organised for children. This is a site for families.

The three toilet blocks for tourers include washbasins (open style and in cabins), controllable showers and a baby room. Launderette with iron and board. Shop. Bar/restaurant/pizzeria (all season). Play areas (one indoors). Playing field. Tennis. Minigolf. Bicycle hire. Go-karts. Water-skiing. Sailing and motorboat hire. Para-sailing. Animal farm. Entertainment in high season (incl. riding). Max. 2 dogs.

Key Features

 Book Online

 Pets Accepted

 Play Area

 Bar/Restaurant

 Bike Hire

 Fishing

 Horse Riding

 Sailing

Scan me for more information.

Netherlands

Alan Rogers Code: NL5880
337 accommodations
381 pitches
GPS: 51.70472, 5.43048
Post Code: NL-5382 JX

Vinkel, Noord-Brabant

www.alanrogers.com/nl5880
info@libema.nl
Tel: +31 735 343 536
www.dierenbos.nl

Open (Touring Pitches):
Mid March - Late October.

Camping Dierenbos

Dierenbos is a large site, with motel accommodation and a bungalow park in addition to its approximately 700 pitches. These are divided into several grassy areas, many in an attractive wooded setting. There are 381 for touring units, all with electrical connections (4-10A) and some with full services (water and TV connection).

A small, landscaped lake has sandy beaches and is overlooked by a large, modern play area. Some of the touring pitches also overlook the water. Campers are entitled to free entry to several attractions. The varied amenities are located in and around a modern, central complex. They include heated outdoor swimming pools, an indoor sub-tropical pool with slide and jet stream, and a ten-pin bowling alley.

Eight toilet blocks are well situated with a mixture of clean and simple facilities (some unisex) with some warm water for washing and some individual washbasins. Baby room. Supermarket. Bar. Modern restaurant. Snack bar/takeaway (high season). Free outdoor heated swimming pools (seasonal). Indoor pool (on payment). Ten-pin bowling. Tennis. Minigolf. Boules. Sports field. Bicycle hire. Pedaloes. Fishing. Barbecue area. Play areas on sand. Many organised activities in season. Conference facilities. Max. 1 dog per pitch.

Key Features

 Pets Accepted

 Disabled Facilities

 Swimming Pool

 Play Area

 Bar/Restaurant

 Bike Hire

 Fishing

 Scan me for more information.

Alan Rogers Code: NL6550
52 accommodations
650 pitches
GPS: 51.27411, 5.93197
Post Code: NL-6088 NT

Roggel, Limburg

Camping De Leistert

www.alanrogers.com/nl6550
info@leistert.nl
Tel: +31 475 493 030
www.leistert.nl

Open (Touring Pitches):
Early April - End September (Accom to start November).

This large, long-established site in the wooded Limburg province of south Holland provides 1,200 pitches, of which 650 are touring pitches. With its varied amenities, the site would be a good choice for families with small children and teenagers.

Most of the pitches are not separated but are arranged in hedged groups with tall, mature trees. They are serviced with electricity (4-16A), cable TV connections, water and drainage. A recreation programme is organised for all ages in the high season.

Key Features

 Book Online

 Pets Accepted

 Disabled Facilities

 Swimming Pool

 Play Area

 Bar/Restaurant

 Bike Hire

 Fishing

Five toilet blocks are fully equipped, with good facilities for children. Covered plaza with supermarket, bar, restaurant, snack bar, games and TV room and disco, indoor pool. Outdoor pool (both pools with lifeguard). Minigolf. Tennis. Adventure playground. Rowing, fishing and sandy beach. Bicycle hire with plentiful racks all over the site. Go-Kart track. Skateboarding ramps. Mini zoo. Gas refill at supermarket. Recreation programme (high season). WiFi over site (charged). Chalets to rent. Dogs welcomed in a designated area.

Scan me for more information.

Alan Rogers Code: NL5965
275 pitches
GPS: 51.31989, 5.57434
Post Code: NL-6027 RD

Soerendonk, Noord-Brabant

www.alanrogers.com/nl5965
info@slotcranendonck.nl
Tel: +31 495 591 652
www.slotcranendonck.nl

Open (Touring Pitches):
Late March - Late October.

Slot Cranendonck

Surrounded by woodland and moors, not far from Limburg and the Belgian border, this is an attractive campsite with the appearance and ambience of a park. A large pond used for fishing is in the centre of the site.

Several areas surrounded by trees and hedges accommodate tents, caravans and motorhomes with pitches arranged around the edges. Each pitch has 6A Europlug, cable TV connections, water and drainage.

The site provides many amenities and a variety of facilities for leisure. This is an excellent area for cycling and walking. In high season, large units should telephone ahead.

Three toilet buildings have the most modern facilities including family and baby bathrooms. Facilities for disabled visitors. Free hot water. Well stocked supermarket. Bar, restaurant and takeaway with reasonable prices. Indoor and outdoor (seasonal) swimming pools both with paddling pools (no lifeguards). Large playground. Volleyball. One tennis court. Football pitch. Trampoline. Fishing. Minigolf. Children's club and other entertainment (high season). Covered playground. Bicycle hire. WiFi (charged)

Key Features

 Pets Accepted

 Disabled Facilities

 Swimming Pool

 Play Area

 Bar/Restaurant

 Bike Hire

 Fishing

Scan me for more information.

Alan Rogers Code: NL5540
359 accommodations
102 pitches
GPS: 51.62901, 4.83950
Post Code: NL-4904 SG

Oosterhout, Noord-Brabant

De Katjeskelder

www.alanrogers.com/nl5540
kkinfo@katjeskelder.nl
Tel: +31 162 453 539
www.katjeskelder.nl

Open (Touring Pitches):
Start April - End October.

This site is to be found in a wooded setting in a delightful area of Noord-Brabant. It is well established and offers extensive facilities with an impressive modern reception area. Around the 25 hectare site, there are many bungalows and 102 touring pitches, all with electricity, water and wastewater. Motorhomes are accepted (on hardstandings near the entrance), as well as tents and caravans.

This tropical indoor water playground with slide is free for campers and the site also has a large, outdoor swimming pool and children's pool, both supervised. This is idyllic cycling and walking countryside and many well-known attractions such as the Efteling theme park and the Biesbosch nature park lie within a short drive.

Key Features

 Pets Accepted

 Disabled Facilities

 Beach Access

 Swimming Pool

 Play Area

 Bar/Restaurant

 Bike Hire

One heated sanitary block provides facilities including a family shower room, baby room and provision for disabled visitors. Laundry. Supermarket. Restaurant, bar, snack bar, pizzeria and takeaway. Indoor tropical pool. Outdoor swimming pools (all season, but closed when the air temperature is below 8 degrees). Playfield. Tennis. Bicycle hire. Minigolf. Several play areas for small children. Large adventure playground. Entertainment for children (all season). WiFi over site (charged).

Scan me for more information.

Capital Oslo
Currency
Norwegian Krone (NOK)
Language Norwegian
Time Zone CET (GMT+1)
Telephone Code +47

Shops Hours vary throughout the year, with many shops operating on shorter hours in low and shoulder seasons. In high season 10am to 5pm Mon to Sat and until 7pm on Thurs. Supermarkets 9am to 11pm Mon to Fri and until 10pm Sat.

Money ATMs are widespread and accessible 24hrs a day. Credit cards are universally accepted. The country is fast becoming cashless although you should always bring cash for emergencies.

Accessible Travel Generally well equipped for disabled visitors, especially in cities. Public transport and street crossings are good but planning ahead is always a smart idea.

Travelling with children A great country for children. Oslo is home to many parks and museums but not all attractions are children-friendly. Attractions are often free for under 6s and discounted for under 16s.

EU Travel Norway is not an EU member state but is located within the Schengen area.

LEZ Low Emissions Zones in most major cities. Registration required.

●●●○○ **Accessibility Score**
View our digital e-guide & find out more at
alanrogers.com/open-to-all

Tourism website visitnorway.com

Public Holidays 1 Jan New Year's Day • Mar/Apr Maundy Thursday • Mar/Apr Good Friday • Mar/Apr Easter Sunday • Mar/Apr Easter Monday • 1 May Labour Day • 2 Jun Constitution Day • May Ascension • May/Jun Whit Sunday • May/Jun Whit Monday • 25 Dec Christmas Day • 26 Dec Boxing Day.

Driving in Norway Be prepared for long tunnels and hairpin bends. Some roads are closed to caravans (check the tourist website). Vehicles must have sufficient road grip, and it may be necessary to use winter tyres with or without chains. Use dipped headlights during the day. Vehicles entering major cities must pay a toll, and other tolls are levied on certain roads. Drink-driving and using a mobile whilst driving are illegal.

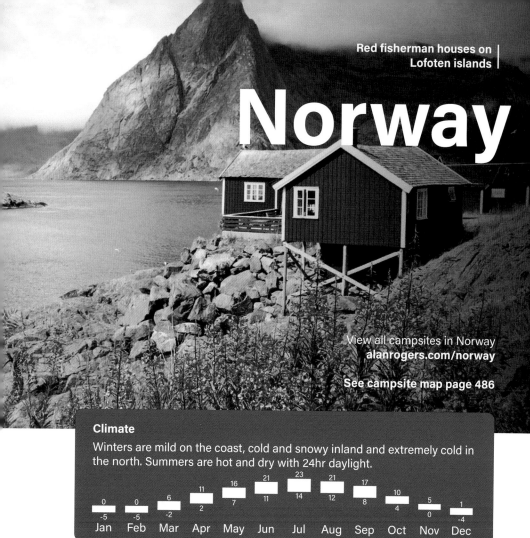

Norway

View all campsites in Norway
alanrogers.com/norway

See campsite map page 486

Climate

Winters are mild on the coast, cold and snowy inland and extremely cold in the north. Summers are hot and dry with 24hr daylight.

	Jan	Feb	Mar	Apr	May	Jun	Jul	Aug	Sep	Oct	Nov	Dec
High	0	0	6	11	16	21	23	21	17	10	5	1
Low	-5	-5	-2	2	7	11	14	12	8	4	0	-4

A land full of contrasts, from magnificent snow-capped mountains, dramatic fjords, vast plateaux with wild, untamed tracts to huge lakes and rich green countryside. With nearly one-quarter of the land above the Arctic Circle, Norway has the lowest population density in Europe.

Norway is made up of five regions. In the heart of the eastern region, Oslo has everything one would expect from a major city and is the oldest of the Scandinavian capitals. The west coast boasts some of the world's most beautiful fjords, with plunging waterfalls and mountains.

In the heart of central Norway, Trondheim is a busy university town with many attractions, notably the Nidarosdomen Cathedral. The sunniest region is the south; its rugged coastline with white wooden cottages is popular with Norwegians and ideal for swimming, sailing, scuba diving and fishing.

The north is the Land of the Midnight Sun and the Northern Lights. It is home to the Sami, the indigenous people of Norway, whose traditions include fishing, hunting and reindeer herding. The scenery varies from forested valleys and narrow fjords to icy tundra. There are several cities worth visiting, including Tromsø, with the Fjelheisen cable car, Polaria aquarium with bearded seals, and the Arctic Cathedral.

Alan Rogers Code: NO2428
30 pitches
GPS: 69.30411, 16.06641
Post Code: N-8483

Andenes, Nordland

www.alanrogers.com/no2428
camping@whalesafari.no
Tel: +47 41 34 03 88
www.whalesafari.no

Open (Touring Pitches):
Start June - End August.

Andenes Camping

Lying on the exposed west coast of Andøy, between the quiet main road and white sandy beaches, this site is an exceptional location for viewing the midnight sun. Extremely popular, often to the point of overcrowding, the site offers mountain and ocean views. It is only three kilometres from the Andenes town, the base of the popular tourist attraction, Whalesafari.

There is space for an unspecified number of touring units and you park where you like. With only 30 pitches, with 16A electricity connections, it is advisable to arrive by mid-afternoon. Late arrivals may pitch and pay later when reception opens. Level areas of grass with some hardstanding can be found on gently sloping ground.

Visitors come to Andenes for the chance to see whales at close quarters, and Whalesafari is deemed the world's largest, most successful Arctic whale watching operation for the general public.

Key Features

 Pets Accepted

 Beach Access

 Play Area

One building houses basic sanitary facilities, each providing two toilets, two showers (NOK 10) with curtains and three washbasins. In each half, one toilet is suitable for disabled visitors and includes a washbasin. The reception building houses a well-equipped kitchen, a large sitting/dining room, 2 showers, WC and washbasin. Laundry facilities. Motorhome services. Chemical disposal (charged 30 NOK). Picnic tables. Swings for children. WiFi (free).

Scan me for more information.

Alan Rogers Code: NO2455
52 accommodations
150 pitches
GPS: 68.33888, 16.85780
Post Code: N-8540

Ballangen, Nordland

www.alanrogers.com/no2455
post@ballangencamping.com
Tel: +47 76 92 76 90
www.ballangen-camping.no

Open (Touring Pitches):
Start March - End December.

PlusCamp Ballangen

Ballangen is a pleasant, lively site conveniently located on the edge of a fjord with a small sandy beach, with direct access off the main E6 road. The 150 marked touring pitches are mostly on sandy grass, with electricity (16A) available to all. There are a few hardstandings, also 52 cabins for rent. A TV room has tourist information, coffee and games machines and there is a heated outdoor pool and waterslide (charged), free fjord fishing and boat hire.

During the summer, the nearby Ballagen Museum documents the mining history of the region. Unfortunately, visitors are no longer permitted to visit the Martinstollen mine, which was one of the regions main employers. Narvik with its wartime connections and museums is just 40 km. away.

Sanitary facilities include some washbasins in cubicles, facilities for disabled visitors, sauna and solarium. Kitchen with sinks, two cookers and covered seating area. Laundry. Motorhome services. Well stocked shop. Café and takeaway (1/5-1/9). TV/games room. Swimming pool and waterslide (1/6-31/8, charged). Minigolf. Fishing. Boat and bicycle hire. Pedal car hire. Mini zoo. Playground. Covered barbecue areas.

Key Features

 Pets Accepted

Disabled Facilities

 Beach Access

 Swimming Pool

 Play Area

 Bar/Restaurant

 Bike Hire

 Fishing

Scan me for more information.

Alan Rogers Code: NO2485
26 accommodations
50 pitches
GPS: 66.46108, 15.09520
Post Code: N-8630

Storforshei, Nordland

www.alanrogers.com/no2485
post@krokstrand.as
Tel: +47 75 16 60 02
www.facebook.com/Krokstrandas

Open (Touring Pitches):
Start June - End August.

Krokstrand Camping

In a stunning location, this site is a popular resting place on the long trek to Nordkapp and is only 18 km. from the Arctic Circle and its visitor centre. There are 50 unmarked touring pitches set amongst birch trees with electricity connections (10A) and a number of cabins available to rent.

In late spring and early summer, the river alongside, headed by rapids, is impressive and there remains the possibility of the surrounding mountains being snow-capped. A reception kiosk is open 08.00-10.00 and 15.00-22.00 in high season, otherwise, campers are invited to find a pitch and pay later at the hotel complex opposite.

One modern, well maintained and clean, small sanitary unit includes four showers (on payment). Laundry with washing machine and dryer. Small kitchen with double hot plate, microwave and sink. Motorhome services. Shop. Brightly painted play area with trampoline. Minigolf. Fishing. An impressive high ropes course is available (fee payable)

Key Features

 Pets Accepted

 Play Area

 Fishing

 Scan me for more information.

Alan Rogers Code: NO2495
18 accommodations
20 pitches
GPS: 64.26590, 12.28673
Post Code: N-7760

Snasa, Nord-Trøndelag

Vegset Camping

www.alanrogers.com/no2495
vegset.camping@gmail.com
Tel: +47 93 20 67 54
vegsetcamping.no

Open (Touring Pitches):
Easter - Mid October.

Located within forested lakeside slopes, this small, pleasant site is seven kilometres south of Snåsa. Although directly accessible from the E6 road, it is set well back on the banks of Lake Snåsavatn. There are a small number site-owned cabins, a number of static units and space for about 20 touring units on slightly sloping ground.

There are 10/16A electricity connections available. For those travelling to or from Northern Norway, Vegset provides a good resting point or night halt. However, it is possible to explore Snåsa, the centre for the South Lapp people with their own boarding school, museum and information centre.

The Bergasen Nature Reservation is close to the village and is famous for its rare flora, especially orchids. The Gressamoen National Park is also near.

Key Features

 Disabled Facilities

 Play Area

 Fishing

The heated toilet block provides showers, plus a shower with a toilet suitable for disabled visitors. Another small unit has a kitchen with a small oven and double hob, washing machine and drying rack. Reception has a sitting room overlooking the lake and doubles as a TV room with a kiosk selling a small selection of groceries, drinks and confectionery (seasonal). Swimming, boat hire and fishing (licence from site). WiFi (free).

Scan me for
more information.

Alan Rogers Code: NO2490
8 accommodations
30 pitches
GPS: 63.08114, 7.59569
Post Code: N-6530

Averøy, Møre og Romsdal

www.alanrogers.com/no2490
info@skjerneset.com
Tel: +47 71 51 18 94
www.skjerneset.com

Open (Touring Pitches):
Start April - End October.

Skjerneset Bryggecamp

Uniquely centred around a working fishing quay set in an idyllic bay, Skjerneset Camping has been developed to give visitors a historical insight into this industry. It steps back in time in all but its facilities and offers boats to hire and organised trips on a working fishing boat.

Found on the tiny island of Ekkilsøya off Averøy, there is space for 30 caravans and motorhomes on gravel hardstandings landscaped into rocks and trees, each individually shaped and sized and all having electricity connections (10/16A).

There are grassy areas for tents on the upper terraces and a small number of fully equipped cabins.

Central unisex sanitary block has open washbasins and hot showers, a large well-equipped kitchen, dining area with TV, small laundry, large drying room and several lounge areas. Additional smaller separate sex sanitary blocks each have WC, shower and enclosed washbasin. Kitchen. Fish preparation and freezing areas. Motorhome services. Sauna. Satellite TV. Motorboat hire. Free bicycle hire. Free WiFi. Organised sea fishing and sightseeing trips in owner's sea-going boat. Sales of fresh fish and prepared fish dishes for guests to heat.

Key Features

 Pets Accepted

 Disabled Facilities

 Beach Access

 Bike Hire

 Fishing

Scan me for more information.

Alan Rogers Code: NO2370
38 accommodations
70 pitches
GPS: 61.03190, 5.35124
Post Code: N-5961

Brekke, Sogn og Fjordane

Botnen Camping

www.alanrogers.com/no2370
boten.camping@enivest.com
Tel: +47 57 78 54 71
www.botnencamping.com

Open (Touring Pitches):
Start May - End September.

For those travelling north on the E39 beyond Bergen, there are surprisingly few attractive sites until one reaches the southern shore of the mighty Sognefjord, close to the ferry crossing from Oppedal to Lavik. A left turn towards Brekke takes you to the family-run Botnen Camping overlooking the fjord and with wonderful views of distant mountains.

There are about 70 mostly level touring pitches, all with 10A electricity, from where you may see passing cruise ships and porpoises searching for mackerel. It has its own jetty and harbour, with motorboats and canoes for hire. Fully serviced pitches and a modern sanitary unit are well kept.

The motorboats for hire and the shoreline itself provide opportunities for fishermen. The campsite has a collection of photos of past notable catches and has a fish cleaning station and freezers that campers can freely use.

Key Features

 Pets Accepted

 Beach Access

 Play Area

 Bike Hire

 Fishing

 Sailing

Toilet block with washbasins and showers (on payment). Tidy sanitary unit with modern facilities, kitchen, laundry and reception above. Motorhome services. Small shop. Trampoline. Swimming, fishing and boating in fjord. Bicycle hire. Boats and canoes for hire. WiFi over site (charged).

Scan me for
more information.

Alan Rogers Code: NO2660
150 pitches
GPS: 58.99888, 6.09217
Post Code: N-4100

Jørpeland, Rogaland

www.alanrogers.com/no2660
info@preikestolencamping.com
Tel: +47 48 19 39 50
www.preikestolencamping.com

Open (Touring Pitches):
All year.

Preikestolen Camping

Taking its name from one of Norway's best-known attractions, the Preikestolen (Pulpit Rock) cliff formation, Preikestolen Camping is situated in the beautiful region of Rogaland, surrounded by high mountains and deep fjords. This is a site where you could easily stay a few days to explore the beautiful region.

The friendly owners are happy to help with maps and guidance. The site is laid out in a relaxed way with an open, level grass area where trees and bushes create pleasant little 'rooms' for your tent, caravan or motorhome. There are 150 pitches, 56 with electricity (10/16A), water tap and wastewater drainage.

The famous and outstanding cliff of Preikestolen was probably formed by the action of frost over 10,000 years ago. From the cliff, 604 m. above fjord level, there are magnificent views over Lysefjorden with its green glacier water. Even the most experienced tourist must find this scenery breathtaking.

The modern heated sanitary block has showers, washbasins in cubicles and facilities for disabled visitors. Room with sinks but no cookers - all with free hot water. Washing machines and dryers. Motorhome services. Freezer. Small shop and craft shop (1/5-30/9). Restaurant and takeaway (1/5-30/9). Fishing. Play area. WiFi over part of site (free).

Key Features

 Open All Year

 Pets Accepted

 Disabled Facilities

 Beach Access

 Play Area

 Fishing

Scan me for more information.

Alan Rogers Code: NO2615
7 accommodations
40 pitches
GPS: 59.68837, 11.29286
Post Code: N-1860

Trogstad, Østfold

www.alanrogers.com/no2615
olberg@jarenfri.no
Tel: +47 69 82 86 10
www.jarenfri.no

Open (Touring Pitches):
1 May - 1 October - Other times
by arrangement.

Olberg Camping

Olberg is a delightful small farm site, close to Lake Øyeren and within 70 km. of Oslo. There are around 40 large, level touring pitches all with 10-16A electricity connections, on neatly tended grassy meadows with trees and shrubs. The reception building also houses a small gallery with paintings, glasswork and other crafts.

A short drive down the adjacent lane takes you to the beach on Lake Øyeren, and there are many woodland walks in the surrounding area. Please bear in mind that this is a working farm. In high season, fresh bread is available (except Sunday) and coffee, drinks, ices and snacks are provided. The old church and museum at Trøgstad, and Båstad church are worth visiting. Forest and elk safaris are arranged.

Key Features

 Pets Accepted

 Disabled Facilities

 Beach Access

 Play Area

 Bar/Restaurant

Excellent, heated sanitary facilities are fully equipped and include a ramp for wheelchair access and one bathroom for families and disabled visitors. Laundry facilities. Washing machine. Motorhome services. Kitchenette with full size cooker and food preparation area. Kiosk. Snacks available. Craft gallery. Playground. WiFi (charged).

Scan me for more information.

Capital Lisbon
Currency Euro (€)
Language Portuguese
Time Zone GMT
Telephone Code +351

Shops Hours vary throughout the year, with many shops operating on shorter hours in low and shoulder seasons. In high season 9.30am to noon and 2pm to 7pm Mon to Fri. 10am to 1pm Sat.

Money ATMs can be found in towns and cities, are accessible 24hrs a day and most have multilingual instructions. Less common in rural areas. Not everywhere accepts credit/debit cards so take cash just in case.

Accessible Travel Access is limited but improving. Newer public buildings are required to cater for wheelchair users. Accessible parking spaces are available but are often occupied.

Travelling with children Portugal has a lot to offer children. Lisbon has a good choice of attractions. The Algarve is one of the best destinations for kids with its long sandy beaches, zoos, water parks and boat trips.

EU Travel Portugal is an EU member state and located within the Schengen area.

♻ **LEZ** Low Emissions Zone in Lisbon. Registration required.

●●○○○ **Accessibility Score**
View our digital e-guide & find out more at
alanrogers.com/open-to-all

Tourism website visitportugal.com

Public Holidays 1 Jan New Year's Day • Mar/Apr Good Friday • Mar/Apr Easter Sunday • 25 Apr Liberation Day • 1 May Labour Day • 10 Jun National Day • May/Jun Corpus Christi • 15 Aug Assumption • 5 Oct Republic Day • 1 Nov All Saints • 1 Dec Independence Restoration Day • 8 Dec Imaculate Conception • 25 Dec Christmas Day.

Driving in Portugal The standard of roads is very variable; even some of the main roads can be very uneven. Tolls are levied on some auto-estradas. An electronic tag called Via Verde can be purchased for repeat trips. Drink-driving, using a mobile whilst driving and satnavs that warn of speed cameras are illegal. Parked vehicles must face the same direction as moving traffic.

Portugal

View all campsites in Portugal
alanrogers.com/portugal

See campsite map page 484

Climate

Hot summers and mild winters with comparatively low rainfall in the south, heavy rain in the north.

Jan	Feb	Mar	Apr	May	Jun	Jul	Aug	Sep	Oct	Nov	Dec
15	16	18	19	22	26	28	28	26	22	18	15
8	9	11	12	14	17	18	19	18	15	12	9

Portugal is the westernmost country of Europe, situated on the Iberian peninsula, bordered by Spain in the north and east, with the Atlantic coast in the south and west. Despite its relatively small size, the country offers a tremendous variety, both in its way of life and its history and traditions.

Every year the Algarve is the destination for some ten million sunseekers and watersports enthusiasts who love its sheltered sandy beaches and clear Atlantic sea. In contrast, the lush hills and forests of central Portugal are home to historic buildings and monuments, particularly the capital city of Lisbon, adjacent to the estuary of the River Tagus. Lisbon's history can still be seen in the Alfama quarter, which survived the devastating earthquake of 1755; at night, the city comes alive with vibrant cafés, restaurants and discos.

The land becomes rather impoverished to the southeast of Lisbon, consisting of stretches of vast undulating plains dominated by cork plantations. Most people head for Evora, a medieval walled town and UNESCO World Heritage Site. The Minho area in the north is said to be the most beautiful part of Portugal, home to the country's only National Park and vineyards producing the famous Port wine.

Alan Rogers Code: PO8010
60 accommodations
242 pitches
GPS: 41.86635, -8.85844
Post Code: P-4910-180

Caminha, Viana do Costelo

www.alanrogers.com/po8010
infocaminha@orbitur.pt
Tel: +351 258 028 702
www.orbitur.com

Open (Touring Pitches):
All year.

Camping Caminha

In northern Portugal, close to the Spanish border, Orbitur Camping Caminha is a pleasant site, just 200 m. from the beach. It has an attractive and peaceful setting in woods alongside the river estuary that marks the border with Spain and on the edge of the little town of Caminha. Of around 300 pitches, just 25 are available for touring with electricity (5/15A Europlug), the remainder are occupied by permanent units and chalets to rent.

The site is shaded by tall pines with other small trees planted to mark large sandy pitches. The main site road is surfaced but elsewhere take care not to get trapped in soft sand. Pitching and parking can be haphazard. Static units are grouped together on one side of the site.

Water points, electrical supply and lighting are good. With a pleasant, open feel about the setting, fishing and swimming are possible in the estuary, and from the rather open, sandy beach.

The clean, well maintained toilet block is modern with British style toilets, open style washbasins and hot showers, plus beach showers. Facilities for disabled visitors and babies. Laundry facilities. Motorhome services. Supermarket, bar with satellite TV (Start Aug-End Sept. Restaurant and takeaway (Start Aug-Mid Sept). Bicycle hire. Entertainment in high season. Charcoal barbecues are permitted.

Key Features

 Open All Year

 Pets Accepted

 Beach Access

 Play Area

 Bar/Restaurant

 Bike Hire

Scan me for more information.

Alan Rogers Code: PO8391
11 accommodations
42 pitches
GPS: 41.84612, -6.86033
Post Code: P-5300 516

Bragança, Trás-os-Montes

Cepo Verde

www.alanrogers.com/po8391
info@montesinho.com
Tel: +351 273 999 371
www.montesinho.com

Open (Touring Pitches):
Start March - End October.

Parque de Campismo Cepo Verde is a quiet and family-oriented campsite, with an extraordinary landscape within the Montesinho National Park. Its beautiful surroundings make it an ideal site for keen hikers, with clearly marked walking trails nearby and maps available from reception. The site serves traditional Portuguese dishes within a cosy atmosphere. The restaurant specialises in affordable regional dishes such as wild boar, local cheeses and a tasty chestnut pudding, making it the perfect place to gather and dine with family and friends.

A bus service operates from just outside the site, taking you to nearby Bragança with its impressive medieval castle, or take a drive to the stunning Azibo lake and take a dip or soak up the sun on its beaches. Choose to rest your head at this peaceful and tranquil site and you will be treated to quiet pitches in the open woods, shaded by impressive chestnut, cherry and oak trees. The site has around 40 touring pitches with 6 amp electric hook-up.

Key Features

 Pets Accepted

 Disabled Facilities

 Swimming Pool

 Play Area

 Bar/Restaurant

Toilet block with showers and wash basins. Disabled facilities. Laundry. Late arrivals area without electric hook-up. Motorhome service point. Bar. Restaurant. Swimming pool. Children's play area. Takeaway. Wi-Fi charged. Pets welcome. BBQs not permitted on pitches. BBQ point. Supermarket 8 kilometres. Chalets available to rent.

Scan me for
more information.

381

Alan Rogers Code: PO8030
75 accommodations
620 pitches
GPS: 41.46280, -8.77361
Post Code: 4570-275

Póvoa de Varzim, Porto

www.alanrogers.com/po8030
inforioalto@orbitur.pt
Tel: +351 252 615 699
www.orbitur.com

Open (Touring Pitches):
All year.

Camping Rio Alto

Camping Rio Alto, Estela, is located close to the town of Póvoa de Varzim. It has excellent facilities, which include a mini-market, restaurant, bar, self-service, social halls, free swimming pool for users, four shower blocks with continuous hot water, nearly 600 electricity points and ten dishwashing blocks. It also has an area of plots for caravans and mobile homes.

Make the most of your stay and get to know the area and visit Ofir and Esposende. This site also makes an excellent base for visiting Porto, which is some 35 km. South of Estela. It has pitches on sandy terrain and is next to what is virtually a private beach. The beach is accessed via a novel double tunnel in two lengths of 40 m. beneath the dunes (open 09.00-19.00). The beach shelves steeply at some tidal stages (lifeguard - high season).

Four well-equipped toilet blocks have hot water. Laundry facilities. Facilities for disabled visitors. Gas supplies. Motorhome service point. Shop (high season). Restaurant (high season). Bar, snack bar (all year). Swimming pool (high season). Tennis. Playground. Games room. Surfing. TV. First-aid post. Car wash. Evening entertainment twice weekly in season. Bicycle hire can be arranged by reception. WiFi.

Key Features

 Open All Year

 Pets Accepted

 Disabled Facilities

 Beach Access

 Swimming Pool

 Play Area

 Bar/Restaurant

Scan me for more information.

Alan Rogers Code: PO8460
72 accommodations
220 pitches
GPS: 39.62028, -9.05639
Post Code: P-2450-138

Nazaré, Leiria

www.alanrogers.com/po8460
booking.nazare@ohairesorts.com
Tel: +351 262 561 800
www.ohairesorts.com/nazare/en

Open (Touring Pitches):
Mid February - End December.

Ohai Nazaré Resort

Ohai Nazare Outdoor Resort is a pleasant, well-managed site, formerly known as Vale Paraiso. Its reception and amenities buildings create a good impression and a warm welcome is offered.

Occupying eight hectares of undulating pine woods, the site has over 250 shady pitches, mainly in the valley and on terraces on either side. Many are occupied by seasonal units, but there are around 220 marked pitches of varying sizes with 6/10A electricity available.

Others pitches on sandy ground are suitable for tents and there are areas occupied by chalets, canvas bungalows and teepees for rent. Many of the pitches have electricity, water and wastewater/chemical disposal.

Four sanitary blocks are equipped with showers and private washing cubicles. Washing machines and dryers. Restaurant. Heated outdoor pool, slide swimming pool, spa, kids playground, gym and sports areas (padel court, volleyball). Activity and entertainment programmes (during school holidays). Surf lessons, bike-rent, free WiFi throughout.

Key Features

 Book Online

 Open All Year

 Pets Accepted

 Disabled Facilities

 Beach Access

 Swimming Pool

 Play Area

 Bar/Restaurant

Scan me for more information.

Alan Rogers Code: PO8400
5 accommodations
65 pitches
GPS: 39.99157, -8.78877
Post Code: P-3105-158

Outeiro do Louriçal, Leiria

www.alanrogers.com/po8400
tamanco@me.com
Tel: +351 964 639 011
www.campismo-o-tamanco.com

Open (Touring Pitches):
Start March - End October.

Campismo O Tamanco

O Tamanco is a peaceful countryside site, with a homely almost farmstead atmosphere; you will have chickens and geese wandering around and there is a farmyard including goats and pot-bellied pigs. The enthusiastic Dutch owners, Irene and Hans, are sure to give you a warm welcome at this delightful little site.

The 65 good sized pitches are separated by cordons of all manner of fruit trees, ornamental trees and flowering shrubs, some on level grassy ground, others tucked away in glades. There is 6/10A electricity to most pitches, although long leads may be needed. Five pitches are suitable for large motorhomes. There is some road noise on pitches at the front of the site.

The single toilet block provides very clean and generously sized facilities including controllable showers, washbasins in cabins. Hot water to all basins and most sinks. Suite for disabled visitors can also be used for families. As facilities are limited they may be busy in peak periods. Washing machine and dryer. Bar with TV. Restaurant (set Portuguese meals three times weekly in low season, full menu in July/Aug). Roofed patio with fireplace. Internet access. Swimming pool. Wooden chalets and yurts for hire.

Key Features

 Pets Accepted

 Disabled Facilities

 Beach Access

 Swimming Pool

 Play Area

 Bar/Restaurant

 Bike Hire

Scan me for more information.

Alan Rogers Code: PO8550
3 accommodations
30 pitches
GPS: 39.70075, -8.27820
Post Code: P-2240-333

Ferreira do Zêzere, Santarem

www.alanrogers.com/po8550
info@cerejeira.com
Tel: +351 249 361 756
www.cerejeira.com

Open (Touring Pitches):
Mid March - Start October.

Camping Quinta da Cerejeira

This is a delightful, small, family-owned venture run by Gert and Teunie Verheij. It is a converted farm (Quinta) which has been coaxed into a very special campsite. You pitch where you choose, under fruit and olive trees on gently sloping grass below the house or on terraces beyond.

There is space for 30 units with 18 electricity connections (6A). It is very peaceful with views of the surrounding green hills from the charming vine-covered patio above a small swimming pool. A visit to Tomar to explore the temple and legends of the Knights Templar is highly recommended.

Nearby Ferreira do Zêzere has shops, bars and restaurants, whilst Tomar offers a wider choice along with its numerous historical and architectural sights.

The single rustic sanitary building has British style WCs with hot showers and pairs of washbasins in cubicles (cold water only). Washing machine. Facilities for disabled campers are available. Baker calls daily. Rustic room serves as reception and lounge with library, small kitchen and self-service bar (tea, coffee, soft drinks, bottled beer, wine). Swimming pool with terrace. WiFi in upper part of site (free). Three apartments to rent.

Key Features

 Pets Accepted

 Swimming Pool

Scan me for more information.

Camping Idanha-a-Nova

This attractive and well laid out site is located in the quiet, unspoilt countryside close to a reservoir near the small town of Idanha-a-Nova. The site has spacious, unmarked pitches on wide grassy terraces and electricity (16A) is included in the price.

Amenities include tennis courts with stadium-style spectator seating and a medium-sized swimming pool with a paddling pool, together with several playgrounds. A good supermarket, restaurant, bar and terrace complex is located centrally on site but these are only open in the high season.

In low season there are few visitors on the site and cleaning and services can be variable. English was spoken when we visited.

Four large toilet blocks, built in the traditional Portuguese style, provide quality installations with some washbasins in private cabins, hot showers with dividers, foot baths and facilities for disabled visitors. Laundry. Supermarket (Start July-End Sept). Café and bar (Start June- End Sept). Restaurant (Start July-Mid Sept). Swimming pool. Tennis. TV room. Vending machines. Medical post. Car wash. Canoe hire.

Alan Rogers Code: PO8360
11 accommodations
350 pitches
GPS: 39.95049, -7.18701
Post Code: P-6060-192

Idanha-a-Nova, Castelo Branco

www.alanrogers.com/po8360
parquecampismo@cmcd.pt
Tel: +351 277 201 029
www.cmcd.pt/gestao-de-projetos/parque-de-campismo

Open (Touring Pitches):
All year.

Key Features

 Open All Year

 Pets Accepted

 Disabled Facilities

 Swimming Pool

 Bar/Restaurant

Scan me for more information.

Alan Rogers Code: PO8340
9 accommodations
238 pitches
GPS: 38.55729, -7.92586
Post Code: P-700-703

Évora, Évora

www.alanrogers.com/po8340
infoevora@orbitur.pt
Tel: +351 266 705 190
www.orbitur.com

Open (Touring Pitches):
All year.

Camping Évora

Close to the historic former provincial capital (now a UNESCO World Heritage Site), Camping Évora is well located for a short stay to explore the fascinating town and its castle.

There is space for around 238 touring units, most on level, sandy pitches separated by low hedges and with well-developed shade; larger units can pitch on undulating ground beneath tall trees. Electrical connections (6A) are available throughout, although long cables may be needed.

The surrounding area has a number of interesting megalithic monuments. Being close to the motorway from Spain to Lisbon, this could also be useful as an overnight stop.

Being on the outskirts of Évora, there are plenty of shops, bars and restaurants within easy reach, as well as supermarkets, banks and garages.

Two traditional toilet blocks provide free hot showers, open style washbasins and British style WCs. No facilities for disabled visitors. Laundry. Motorhome services. Small supermarket (Aug only). Bread to order from reception. Bar with snacks and takeaway (Mid June-Mid Sept). Swimming pool (Start April-End Sept). Tennis. Play area. WiFi throughout (free).

Key Features

 Open All Year

 Pets Accepted

 Swimming Pool

 Play Area

 Bar/Restaurant

Scan me for
more information.

Alan Rogers Code: PO8180
221 accommodations
740 pitches
GPS: 37.73190, -8.78301
Post Code: P-7645-300

Vila Nova de Milfontes, Beja

www.alanrogers.com/po8180
geral@campingmilfontes.com
Tel: +351 283 996 140
www.campingmilfontes.com

Open (Touring Pitches):
All year.

Camping Milfontes

This popular site, with good facilities, has the advantage of being open all year and is within walking distance of the town and beach. As such, it makes a perfect base for those visiting out of the main season, or for long winter stays when fees are heavily discounted.

Well lit and fenced, it has around 900 shady pitches (740 for touring units) on sandy terrain, many marked out and divided by hedges. There is an area, mainly for motorhomes, where you just park under the trees. Some pitches are small and cars may have to be parked in an internal car park. Electricity (6A) is available throughout.

The town has a good covered market as well as the usual shops, bars and restaurants. There are opportunities for watersports, fishing, canoeing and swimming from the resort beaches.

Four clean and well-maintained toilet blocks. Two have en-suite units for disabled visitors with ramped entrances. Mainly British style WCs, bidets, washbasins (some with hot water), controllable showers and limited facilities for children. Laundry. Motorhome services. Supermarket, bar, snacks and takeaway (all seasonal). Outdoor pool (High season). TV room. Playground. Car wash. Gas supplies. WiFi throughout (free).

Key Features

 Open All Year

 Pets Accepted

 Disabled Facilities

 Beach Access

 Swimming Pool

 Play Area

 Bar/Restaurant

Scan me for more information.

Alan Rogers Code: PO8230
36 accommodations
600 pitches
GPS: 37.03528, -7.82250
Post Code: P-8700

Olhão, Faro

Camping Olhão

www.alanrogers.com/po8230
parque.campismo@mais.pt
Tel: +351 289 700 300
www.sbsi.pt/atividadesindical/
Servicos/ParquedeCampismo

Open (Touring Pitches):
All year.

The large, sandy beaches in this area are on offshore islands reached by ferry and are, as a result, relatively quiet. This site, on the edge of town, has around 600 pitches, all with 6A electrical connections available. Its many mature trees provide good shade. The pitches are marked in rows divided by shrubs, although levelling will be necessary in places and the trees make access tricky on some.

There is a separate area for tents and places for very large motorhomes. Seasonal units take up one-fifth of the pitches, the touring pitches filling up quickly in July and August, so arrive early. The site has a relaxed, casual atmosphere, though there is some subdued noise in the lower area from an adjacent railway. The amenities are also very popular with the local Portuguese who have access to them in high season.

Eleven sanitary blocks are adequate, kept clean even when busy and are well sited so that any pitch is close to one. Two blocks have facilities for disabled visitors. Laundry. Excellent supermarket. Kiosk. Restaurant/bar. Café and general room with cable TV. Playgrounds. Swimming pools (all year, charged in season). Tennis courts. Bicycle hire. Internet at reception and Free WI-FI

Key Features

 Open All Year

 Pets Accepted

 Disabled Facilities

 Beach Access

 Swimming Pool

 Play Area

 Bar/Restaurant

 Bike Hire

Scan me for
more information.

389

Alan Rogers Code: PO8210
28 accommodations
1400 pitches
GPS: 37.10639, -8.25361
Post Code: P-8200-555

Albufeira, Faro

www.alanrogers.com/po8210
geral@campingalbufeira.net
Tel: +351 289 587 629
www.campingalbufeira.pt/en

Open (Touring Pitches):
All year.

Camping Albufeira

The spacious entrance to this site will accommodate the largest of units. A very pleasant, well-run site, it has space for 1400 touring units on generally flat ground with some terracing on the upper area: trees and shrubs giving reasonable shade in most parts. Pitches are not marked or numbered and you can take as much space as you wish. Electrical connections (10A) are available throughout. Winter stays are encouraged with the main facilities remaining open, including a pool.

An attractively designed complex of traditional Portuguese-style buildings on the hill houses the impressive range of restaurants and bars with the pool complex adjacent. It has large sunbathing terraces with pleasant views and is surrounded by a variety of flowers, shrubs and well-watered lawns, complete with a fountain.

Very clean and spacious toilet blocks include hot showers and open-style washbasins (hot water to some). Launderette. Motorhome services. Very large supermarket. Kiosk (English papers). Waiter and self-service restaurants. Pizzeria. Bars. The main facilities are open all year. Swimming pools. Satellite TV. Soundproofed disco. Tennis. Playground. Bicycle hire. WiFi over part of site (charged). First aid post with doctor nearby. Car wash. ATM. Car hire.

Key Features

 Open All Year

 Pets Accepted

 Disabled Facilities

 Beach Access

 Swimming Pool

 Play Area

 Bar/Restaurant

 Bike Hire

Scan me for more information.

Alan Rogers Code: PO8202
132 accommodations
240 pitches
GPS: 37.10111, -8.73278
Post Code: P-8600-109

Lagos, Faro

www.alanrogers.com/po8202
info@turiscampo.com
Tel: +351 282 789 265
www.turiscampo.com/en

Open (Touring Pitches):
All year.

Turiscampo Algarve

Yelloh! Village Turiscampo is an outstanding site that has been thoughtfully refurbished and updated since it was purchased by the friendly Coll family in 2003. The site provides 240 pitches for touring units, mainly in rows of terraces, 197 of which have 6/10A electricity, some with shade. There are 43 deluxe pitches with water and drain. The upper terraces are occupied by 132 bungalows for rent.

Just down the road is the fashionable resort of Praia de Luz with a beach, shops, bars and restaurants. Head west and the road takes you to Sagres and the western tip of the Algarve. Portugal's 'Land's End' remains unspoilt and there are numerous rocky coves and little sandy beaches to explore. A member of Leading Campings and Yelloh! Village groups.

Two heated toilet blocks provide outstanding facilities. There is a third facility beneath the pool. Spacious controllable showers, hot water throughout. Children & baby room. Facilities for disabled visitors. Dog shower. Laundry facilities. Shop. Gas supplies. Modern restaurant/bar with buffet & some theme party dinners. Pizza bar & takeaway. Swimming pools (All year) with extensive terrace & Jacuzzi. Aquagym. Wellness facility. Bicycle hire. Entertainment on the bar terrace. Miniclub. Two playgrounds. Boules. Archery. Multisports court, WiFi (Partial coverage) on payment.

Key Features

 Book Online

 Open All Year

 Pets Accepted

 Disabled Facilities

 Beach Access

 Swimming Pool

 Play Area

 Bar/Restaurant

 Scan me for more information.

Capital Ljubljana
Currency Euro (€)
Language Slovene
Time Zone CET (GMT+1)
Telephone Code +386

Shops Hours vary throughout the year, with many shops operating on shorter hours in low and shoulder seasons. In high season 8am to 7pm Mon to Fri, and until 1pm Sat.

Money ATMs are widespread and accessible 24hrs a day. Most places will accept credit/debit cards. If you're paying in cash, many businesses won't accept large denominations (over €50) for smaller purchases.

Accessible Travel Generally well-equipped with Ljubljana leading in most areas. Public transport and buildings are fully accessible and car parks have reserved spaces.

Travelling with children Great during the summer months. Most regions have castles that children will love exploring. Some attractions offer free entry for minors. Most restaurants cater for children.

EU Travel Slovenia is an EU member state and located within the Schengen area.

There are no Low Emission Zones currently in place.

●●●●● **Accessibility Score**
View our digital e-guide & find out more at
alanrogers.com/open-to-all

Tourism website slovenia.info

Public Holidays 1 Jan New Year's Day · 8 Feb Prešeren Day · Mar/Apr Easter Sunday · Mar/Apr Easter Monday · 27 Apr Resistence Day · 1 May May Day · May/Jun Whit Sunday · 25 Jun National Day · 15 Aug Assumption · 31 Oct Reformation Day · 1 Nov All Saints · 25 Dec Christmas Day · 26 Dec Independence & Unity Day.

Driving in Slovenia A small but expanding network of motorways. You will need to display a vignette as proof of payment to use motorways. Winter driving equipment is mandatory between Nov and Mar. Headlights must be on at all times. Drink-driving and using a mobile whilst driving are illegal.

Slovenia

View all campsites in Slovenia
alanrogers.com/slovenia

See campsite map page 474

Climate

Cold, sometimes snowy winters and warm summers. Coastal areas enjoy a sub-mediterranean climate.

	Jan	Feb	Mar	Apr	May	Jun	Jul	Aug	Sep	Oct	Nov	Dec
High	4	6	12	18	22	26	28	27	22	16	10	5
Low	-1	-1	2	7	11	14	16	16	12	8	4	0

What Slovenia lacks in size, it makes up for in exceptional beauty. Situated between Italy, Austria, Hungary and Croatia, it has a diverse landscape; mountains, rivers, forests and the warm Adriatic coast.

Mount Triglav is at the heart of the snow-capped Julian Alps, a paradise for lovers of the great outdoors, with hiking, rafting, and mountaineering opportunities. From the Alps down to the Adriatic coast, the Karst region is home to the famous Lipizzaner horses, vineyards and myriad underground caves, including the Postojna and Skocjan Caves.

The tiny Adriatic coast has several bustling beach towns, including Koper, Slovenia's only commercial port, whose 500 years of Venetian rule is evident in its Italianate style. Ljubljana, one of Europe's smallest capitals with beautiful baroque buildings, lies on the Ljubljanica river, spanned by numerous bridges, including Jože Plečnik's triple bridge.

Heading eastwards, the hilly landscape is dotted with monasteries, churches and castles, including the 13th century Zuzemberk castle, one of Slovenia's most picturesque. The old city and castle sit alongside a thriving commercial centre. The Posavje region produces cviček, a famous blend of white and red wines.

Alan Rogers Code: SV4315
300 pitches
GPS: 45.50151, 13.59391
Post Code: SLO-6320

Portoroz, Slovenia

www.alanrogers.com/sv4315
camp.lucija@bernardingroup.si
Tel: +386 56 906 000
www.hoteli-bernardin.si

Open (Touring Pitches):
Mid April - Late October.

Camp Lucija

This is a long narrow site that enjoys attractive views over the bay at the western end. This part of the site is very popular and becomes quite crowded, while in the bar/restaurant area there is music playing for most of the day.

The site is popular with families with young children, and a much-used public cycle/pedestrian path, formally a railway line linking Triest with Porec, runs through it. There are 550 reasonably level pitches (300 for tourers) on grass/gravel, around half of which have 6A electricity. There is a separate terrace for tents. There can be some aircraft noise.

The site is ideally placed for coastal walks. Just 300 m. from the campsite there is a good sports centre with a range of amenities including football, tennis and minigolf. Further afield, day trips to Trieste and the Slovenian coastal towns are possible, while Venice is a long day out. In addition, Lucija's close proximity to the Croatian border makes touring into Istria easy.

Five sanitary blocks (one near reception is heated) all have showers and washbasins. Facilities for disabled visitors. Washing machine. Motorhome services. Shop (Seasonal) Bar/snack bar and restaurant. Playground. Fishing. Bicycle hire. Free WiFi.

Key Features

 Pets Accepted

 Disabled Facilities

 Play Area

 Bar/Restaurant

 Fishing

Scan me for more information.

Alan Rogers Code: SV4110
15 accommodations
250 pitches
GPS: 46.27937, 13.83787
Post Code: SLO-4265

Bohinjsko, Slovenia

Camp Bohinj

www.alanrogers.com/sv4110
info@camp-bohinj.si
Tel: +386 59 923 648
www.camp-bohinj.si

Open (Touring Pitches):
Mid April - End September.

Located on the shores of Bohinjsko Jezero, this tranquil site offers lots of opportunities for nature lovers to explore the Triglav National Park. A stone beach gives lake access where you may enjoy open-water swimming. Kayaks, stand-up paddleboards and mountain bikes are all available to hire on-site. The site takes care of the local environment and recycles waste, uses eco-friendly cleaning products and avoids plastic use wherever possible. Pre-booking a pitch is not possible, so early arrival is reccomended.

A children's play area is found close to the bar/restaurant, allowing little ones to explore whilst the grown-ups enjoy a well-earned break. In the local area, a climb to the peak of Mt Triglav, the highest summit in Slovenia, is a popular activity, but it shouldn't be attempted without the assistance of a local guide which can be arranged from reception. The lake has 2 electric tourist boats which stop at the site and offer panoramic tours of the lake.

Key Features

 Pets Accepted

 Play Area

 Bar/Restaurant

 Bike Hire

 Fishing

Pets permitted. WiFi Available. BBQs Permitted. Toilet facilities with hot and cold showers. Washing machine and dryer (paid) Restaurant/snack bar (seasonal) Kayak and SUP hire. Bike hire. Table tennis. Motorhome service point. Electricity on most pitches in 'Zone A' and limited in 'Zone B'

Scan me for
more information.

Alan Rogers Code: SV4210
55 accommodations
500 pitches
GPS: 46.35607, 14.14992
Post Code: SLO-4248

Lesce, Slovenia

www.alanrogers.com/sv4210
camping@sobec.si
Tel: +386 45 353 700
www.sobec.si

Open (Touring Pitches):
Early April - Early October.

Camping Sobec

Sobec is situated in a valley between the Julian Alps and the Karavanke Mountains, in a pine grove between the Sava Dolinka river and a small lake. It is only 3 km. from Bled and 20 km. from the Karavanke Tunnel. There are around 500 unmarked pitches on level, grassy fields off tarmac access roads, 457 with 16A electricity and 93 premium pitches. 10 Alpine Bungalows and 1 Deluxe Apartment available for hire. Shade is provided by mature pine trees and younger trees separate some pitches. Camping Sobec is surrounded by water – the Sava river borders it on three sides and on the fourth is a small, artificial lake with grassy fields for sunbathing.

Some pitches have views over the lake, which has an enclosed area providing safe swimming for children. This site is a good base for an active holiday since both the Sava Dolinka and the Sava Bohinjka rivers are suitable for canoeing, kayaking, rafting and fishing, whilst the nearby mountains offer challenges for mountain climbing, paragliding and canyoning.

Key Features

 Pets Accepted

 Disabled Facilities

 Play Area

 Bar/Restaurant

 Bike Hire

 Fishing

Five sanitary units with toilets (mainly British style), including child size toilets, controllable hot showers, washbasins, baby changing room, dishwashing area and freezers. Facilities for disabled visitors. Laundry facilities. Motorhome services. Supermarket, bar/restaurant with stage for live performances. Playgrounds. Rafting, canyoning and kayaking organised. Miniclub. Tours to Bled and the Triglav National Park organised. WiFi throughout (free).

Scan me for
more information.

Alan Rogers Code: SV4402
4 accommodations
30 pitches
GPS: 46.25588, 15.09917
Post Code: SLO-3312

Prebold, Slovenia

www.alanrogers.com/sv4402
info@campingpark.si
Tel: +386 41 472 496
www.campingprebold.si

Open (Touring Pitches):
Start April - End October.

Camping Park

Camping Park is set on a grassy field close to the E57, directly beside the Savinja river. It provides 30 pitches (all for tourers, with 10A electricity) and is attractively landscaped with flowers and young trees. Pitching is on one large field, with some shade provided by mature trees and the high hedge surrounding the site. Pitches are not separated, but when it is quiet you can take as much space as you need. It is possible to fish and swim in the river.

The site organises excursions to the nearby Pekel Cave in Sempeter, the Roman Nekropolis, the Lasko, Dobrna and Topolsica health resorts, and to the castles in Celje and Velenje. Somewhat further, but close enough for a day trip, are the Logarska Dolina valley, the Savinjske Alps and the Pohorje mountains.

One traditional style toilet block with modern fittings has toilets, open plan washbasins and controllable hot showers. Laundry facilities. Fridge boxes (free). River fishing and bathing. Large barbecue area. Bicycle hire. WiFi (free). Torch useful.

Key Features

 Pets Accepted

 Fishing

Scan me for
more information.

397

Alan Rogers Code: SV4445
41 accommodations
131 pitches
GPS: 46.57318, 16.17149
Post Code: SLO-9241

Verzej, Slovenia

www.alanrogers.com/sv4445
info@terme-banovci.si
Tel: +386 25 131 440
www.terme-banovci.si

Open (Touring Pitches):
Late March - Mid December.

Camping Terme Banovci

Terme Banovci is a comfortable, quiet, countryside site with 69 touring pitches (set among seasonal and rental units), plus 62 naturist pitches which are located separately. A large, grassy area is set aside for tents. The grassed pitches have ample shade, are accessed by gravel roads and all have 10A electricity. Entry to the indoor (35-38°C) and outdoor (25-27°C) pools with a total surface area of 2,000 sq.m. is free to campers. The pools, with large, outdoor slide and ample space for sunbathing, are all that one expects from a modern, well equipped, thermal spa. The comfortable restaurant is built in traditional style, and drinks and food are available on the terrace beside the pool.

The indoor pool contains thermal mineral water, which is pumped up from a depth of 1,700 m. The water is rich in fluorides and recognised as being beneficial in treating rheumatism and other ailments. The outdoor pool is filled with normal water and is equipped with underwater massage jets, whirlpools, a waterfall and water slide. In addition, there is a children's paddling pool and a separate naturist pool.

Key Features

 Naturist Site

 Pets Accepted

 Disabled Facilities

 Swimming Pool

 Play Area

 Bar/Restaurant

Two well appointed, heated sanitary blocks. Washbasins in cabins. Facilities for disabled visitors. Laundry. Motorhome services. Nordic walking. Volleyball. Tennis. Morning gymnastics. Entertainment programme. Wellness centre with three Finnish saunas. Solarium. Turkish bath. Various massage programmes (at extra cost).

Scan me for
more information.

Alan Rogers Code: SV4430
16 pitches
GPS: 45.76600, 15.06600
Post Code: SLO-8350

Dolenjske Toplice, Slovenia

Camp Dolenjske Toplice

www.alanrogers.com/sv4430
info@kamp-dolenjsketoplice.si
Tel: +386 70 303 111
www.kamp-dolenjsketoplice.si

Open (Touring Pitches):
All year.

Camping Dolenjske Toplice offers just 16 pitches for touring units, all with electricity and water, separated by mature trees forming a high hedge. Unmarked pitching is also provided for tents on an open field among low trees with views on the river.

The site is opposite a health centre which offers thermal spas, saunas, different kinds of massage, herbal baths and supervised gymnastics (20% discount for campers). Alternatively, for those who enjoy canoeing or fishing, the site is right beside the River Krka.

The site's only amenity is one basic toilet block. A useful site for a short stay, especially if you wish to use the spa. Close to the entrance are a restaurant and bar and other amenities are available in the town which is only 300 m. walk. This area is excellent for walking, enjoying the Krka Valley and the Kocevski Rog mountain, or visiting the old towns of Novo Mesto and Bela Krajini.

One basic toilet block with toilets, washbasins and controllable hot showers. Bicycle hire. Fishing. Walking and cycling routes from reception. Campsite guests may use the facilities of the health centre opposite. Torch useful. Free WiFi.

Key Features

 Open All Year

 Bike Hire

 Fishing

Scan me for more information.

Capital Madrid
Currency Euro (€)
Language Spanish and six co-official regional variants
Time Zone CET (GMT+1)
Telephone Code +34

Shops Hours vary throughout the year, with many shops operating on shorter hours in low and shoulder seasons. In high season 10am to 2pm and 5pm to 9pm Mon to Fri, 10am to 2pm Sat. Supermarkets 9am to 9pm Mon to Sat.

Money ATMs are widespread, accessible 24hrs a day and most have multilingual instructions. You should bring cash for emergencies. When paying with a credit/debit card, you will often be asked to show ID such as your passport.

Accessible Travel There is a push to improve accessibility, with Barcelona leading the way. Buildings and transport in other major cities are adapting.

Travelling with children Spain is very family-friendly and has a good range of attractions for all ages. Many restaurants cater well for kids and beaches are safe. Extremely hot during the summer, weather remains warm well into October.

EU Travel Spain is an EU member state and located within the Schengen area.

♻ **LEZ** Low Emissions Zones in all major cities. Registration required.

●●●○○ **Accessibility Score**
View our digital e-guide & find out more at
alanrogers.com/open-to-all

Tourism website spain.info

Public Holidays 1 Jan New Year's Day • 6 Jan Epiphany • Mar/Apr Maundy Thursday • Mar/Apr Good Friday • Mar/Apr Easter Sunday • 1 May Labour Day • 16 Jun Corpus Christi • 15 Aug Assumption • 12 Oct Fiesta Nacional de España • 1 Nov All Saints • 6 Dec Constitution Day • 8 Dec Imaculate Conception • 25 Dec Christmas Day. Other public holidays may be observed at a regional level. Aways check before travelling.

Driving in Spain The surface of main roads is generally good. Certain roads use tolls. You can buy an electronic tag called Via T for repeat trips. If your caravan or motorhome exceeds 12m, you must display one long or two short reflectors at the rear. Drink-driving, using a mobile whilst driving and using the horn in urban areas are illegal.

Spain

View all campsites in Spain
alanrogers.com/spain

See campsite map pages 478, 484, 485

Climate

Temperate in the North with most of the rainfall; dry and hot in the centre; sub-tropical along the Mediterranean.

	Jan	Feb	Mar	Apr	May	Jun	Jul	Aug	Sep	Oct	Nov	Dec
High	10	12	16	18	23	28	32	32	26	19	14	10
Low	1	2	5	7	10	15	18	18	14	9	5	2

One of the largest countries in Europe with glorious beaches, a fantastic sunshine record, vibrant towns and laid back sleepy villages, plus a diversity of landscape, culture and artistic traditions, Spain has all the ingredients for a great holiday.

Spain's vast and diverse coastline is a magnet for visitors; glitzy, hedonistic resorts packed with bars and clubs are a foil to secluded coves backed by wooded cliffs.

Yet Spain has much more to offer – the verdant north with its ancient pilgrimage routes where the Picos de Europa sweep down to the Atlantic gems of Santander and Bilbao. Vibrant Madrid in the heart of the country boasts the Prado with works by Velázquez and Goya, the beautiful cobbled Plaza Major, plus all the attractions of a capital city.

Passionate Andalucía in the sun-soaked south dazzles with the symbolic art of flamenco. It offers the cosmopolitan cities of Córdoba, Cádiz and Málaga, alongside magnificent examples of the past such as the Alhambra at Granada and the awe-inspiring Alcázar, a magical Moorish palace with scents of orange and Jasmine wafting through the air, a must-see in dreamy Seville. On the Mediterranean east coast, Valencia has a wealth of monuments and cultural sites, including the magnificent City of Arts and Science.

Alan Rogers Code: ES91225
32 accommodations
170 pitches
GPS: 42.29033, 2.36242
Post Code: E-17867

Girona, Cataluña-Catalunya

Camping Vall de Camprodon

www.alanrogers.com/es91225
info@valldecamprodon.net
Tel: +34 972 74 05 07
www.valldecamprodon.net

Open (Touring Pitches):
All year.

This large holiday village is attractively situated in a wooded valley with cows grazing to one side, their pleasant bells often to be heard. A stream runs below the site, between it and the road.

There are 200 grass and gravel pitches, some with shade, others without. Some are occupied by seasonal caravans and private chalets interspersed with 170 for touring units, all with 4-10A electricity. There are 32 modern chalets for rent. Only 20 km. away is the mountain and ski resort of Vallter 2000 and to the southwest is the historic town of Ripoll.

Camprodon is a very pleasant old town with a magnificent ancient bridge at its centre.

One centrally placed, fully equipped and well-maintained toilet block. Large en-suite unit for disabled visitors. Baby/toddler baths. Washing machines, dryers and ironing board. Car wash. Shop and excellent bar/restaurant (seasonal). Swimming and paddling pools (seasonal). Play area. Cinema. Adventure play area with zip wire. Fishing and bathing in the river. Tennis. Multisports court. Boules. Miniclub (July/Aug). Riding (July/Aug). Free WiFi over the site. Separate motorhome park outside entrance (fee payable).

Key Features

 Book Online

 Open All Year

 Pets Accepted

 Disabled Facilities

 Beach Access

 Swimming Pool

 Play Area

 Bar/Restaurant

Scan me for more information.

Alan Rogers Code: ES80350
138 accommodations
692 pitches
GPS: 42.18147, 3.10405
Post Code: E-17470

Girona, Cataluña-Catalunya

www.alanrogers.com/es80350
info@campingamfora.com
Tel: +34 972 52 05 40
www.en.campingamfora.com

Open (Touring Pitches):
Mid April - Late September.

Camping l'Amfora

This spacious, friendly site is run by Michelle, Josep and their daughter. It is spotlessly clean and well maintained and the owners operate the site in an environmentally friendly way. There are 830 level, grass pitches (692 for touring units) laid out in a grid system, all with 10A electricity. Attractive trees and shrubs have been planted around each pitch. There is good shade in the more mature areas, which include 64 large pitches (180 sq.m), each with an individual sanitary unit (toilet, shower and washbasin). The newer area is more open with less shade and you can choose which you would prefer.

Three excellent sanitary blocks, one heated, provide washbasins in cabins and roomy free showers. Baby rooms. Laundry facilities and service. Motorhome services. Supermarket. Terraced bar, self-service and waiter-service restaurants. Pizzeria/takeaway. Restaurant and bar on the beach with a limited menu (high season). Disco bar. Swimming pools with 2 long waterslides (seasonal) as also SPA area. Pétanque. Tennis. Minigolf. Play area. Miniclub. Entertainment and activities. Windsurfing. Kite surfing (low season).Sailing, kayak, fishing. Games rooms. Bicycle hire. Internet room and WiFi over site (charged). Car wash. Torches are required in most areas.

Key Features

 Pets Accepted

 Disabled Facilities

 Beach Access

 Swimming Pool

 Play Area

 Bar/Restaurant

 Bike Hire

 Fishing

Scan me for more information.

Alan Rogers Code: ES80400
100 accommodations
1500 pitches
GPS: 42.16098, 3.10777
Post Code: E-17470

Girona, Cataluña-Catalunya

www.alanrogers.com/es80400
info@campinglasdunas.com
Tel: +34 972 52 17 17
www.campinglasdunas.com

Open (Touring Pitches):
Mid May - Mid September.

Camping Las Dunas

Las Dunas is an extremely large, impressive and well organised resort-style site with many on-site activities and an ongoing programme of improvements.

The site has direct access to a superb sandy beach that stretches along the site for nearly a kilometre with a windsurfing school and beach bar. There is also a much-used, huge swimming pool, plus a large double pool for children.

Las Dunas has 1,700 individual hedged pitches (1,500 for touring units) of around 100 sq.m. laid out on flat ground in long, regular parallel rows. All have electricity (6/10A) and 400 have water and drainage.

Five excellent large toilet blocks with electronic sliding glass doors. Toilets without seats, controllable hot showers and washbasins in cabins. Excellent facilities for children, babies and disabled campers. Laundry facilities. Motorhome services. Supermarket, boutique and other shops. Large bar with terrace. Large restaurant & takeaway. Ice cream parlour. Beach bar (seasonal). Disco club. Swimming pools. Adventure crazy golf. Playgrounds. Tennis. Minigolf. Sailing/windsurfing school and other watersports. Programme of sports, games, excursions and entertainment, partly in English. Exchange facilities. ATM. Safety deposit. Internet café. WiFi over site (charged). Dogs taken in one section. Torches required in some areas.

Key Features

 Pets Accepted

 Disabled Facilities

 Beach Access

 Swimming Pool

 Play Area

 Bar/Restaurant

 Bike Hire

 Fishing

Scan me for more information.

CAMPING LAS DUNAS
CAMPING BUNGALOWPARK
www.campinglasdunas.com

COSTA BRAVA
SPAIN

SEASIDE HOLIDAY PARADISE FOR THE WHOLE FAMILY!

alan rogers ● rallies

Why not join a rally?

ABTA
Travel with confidence

Alan Rogers Travel Ltd is a member
of ABTA with membership number
P7119 Y6434.

Alan Rogers has over 50 years experience organising caravan and
motorhome holidays to Europe and we have been arranging highly
successful and enjoyable rallies to the continent for over 15 years.

- **Confidence to book with us**
  Plan, book and travel with confidence knowing you're in safe hands.

- **Free cancellations***
  You have freedom and flexibility to amend or cancel your package
  holiday if the Foreign and Commonwealth office (FCDO) advises
  against travel to your destination.

- **ABTA bonded for piece of mind**
  All of our package holidays are ABTA bonded providing you with
  the financial protection and reassurance to make your next holiday
  booking.

Call our Rally Services team on
01580 214070

Email us on **rallies@alanrogers.com**
or visit our website **rallies.alanrogers.com**

*Covers holiday cancellations in line with FCDO advice at the time you are due to
travel to your holiday destination. T&Cs apply.

Alan Rogers Code: ES81400
165 accommodations
371 pitches
GPS: 41.83631, 3.08711
Post Code: E-17250

Girona, Cataluña-Catalunya

www.alanrogers.com/es81400
info@campingtreumal.com
Tel: +34 972 65 10 95
www.campingtreumal.com

Open (Touring Pitches):
Mid March - End September.

Camping Treumal

This very attractive terraced site has been developed on a hillside around the beautiful gardens of a large, spectacular estate house which is close to the sea. The house is the focus of the site's excellent facilities, including a superb restaurant with terraces overlooking two tranquil beaches, protected in pretty coves.

The site has 542 pitches on well shaded terraces. Of these, 371 are accessible to touring units and there are some 50 pitches on flat ground alongside the sea – the views are stunning and you wake to the sound of the waves. Electricity (6/10/16A) is available in all parts. Cars must be left on car parks or the site roads.

Four well maintained sanitary blocks have free hot water in the washbasins (with some private cabins) and controllable showers, and a tap to draw from for the sinks. No facilities for disabled visitors. Beachside sanitary block. Washing machines. Motorhome services. Gas supplies. Supermarket, bar and takeaway (all season). Restaurant (seasonal). Beach bar. Fishing. Play area. Sports area. Games room. Bicycle hire. Satellite TV. Internet access and WiFi (charged). ATM. Safes. Dogs are not accepted.

Key Features

- Beach Access
- Swimming Pool
- Play Area
- Bar/Restaurant
- Bike Hire
- Fishing
- Sailing

Scan me for more information.

alan rogers

Book directly with over 1,500 campsites throughout Europe

Why book direct?

Book your holiday direct with the campsite owner

Pay the campsite's own 'at-the-gate' prices and standard booking fees*

Make your payment direct to the campsite in the local currency by credit card

If you prefer to 'deal direct' this is the option for you

Discover more at
alanrogers.com/book-direct

Book directly in:

Austria, Belgium, Croatia, Czech Republic, Denmark, France, Germany, Hungary, Italy, Luxembourg, Netherlands, Portugal, Slovenia, Spain & Switzerland.

*Separate fee payable on each campsite booked

Alan Rogers Code: ES80220
125 accommodations
200 pitches
GPS: 41.66202, 2.78043
Post Code: E-17300

Girona, Cataluña-Catalunya

www.alanrogers.com/es80220
campingsolmar@campingsolmar.com
Tel: +34 972 34 80 34
www.campingsolmar.com

Open (Touring Pitches):
Mid March - Mid October.

Camping Solmar

Camping Solmar has been run by the Ribas family for over 40 years and a warm welcome awaits you. The site is located 150 m. from a sandy beach in the busy urban resort of Blanes. The accessible, shaded pitches are 65-85 sq.m. and all have 6A electricity connections. On-site amenities include an attractive restaurant, bar and terrace area, as well as a central swimming pool complex with islands and bridges.

A children's club operates in the peak season (4-12 years) and an outdoor complex of sports facilities is available. A range of fully equipped mobile homes and wooden chalets are available for rent. Regular excursions are available in the town to all the area's main attractions, including Barcelona (65 km) and the Dalí museum in Figueres, whilst the town itself has a wide range of attractions, including some memorable firework displays.

Four toilet blocks are clean and have open style washbasins, controllable showers in cabins and baby baths. Facilities for disabled visitors. Washing machines. Motorhome services. Supermarket. Restaurant. Bar. Swimming pool and terrace complex. Outdoor sports complex. Play areas. Miniclub (June onwards). Evening entertainment (high season). Tourist information and excursions. WiFi over site (charged). Mobile homes and chalets for rent.

Key Features

 Pets Accepted

 Beach Access

 Swimming Pool

 Play Area

 Bar/Restaurant

Scan me for
more information.

Alan Rogers Code: ES83900
431 accommodations
343 pitches
GPS: 41.23237, 1.69092
Post Code: E-08800

Barcelona, Cataluña-Catalunya

Vilanova Park

www.alanrogers.com/es83900
info@vilanovapark.com
Tel: +34 938 93 34 02
www.vilanovapark.com

Open (Touring Pitches):
All year.

Sitting on the terrace in front of the restaurant – a beautifully converted Catalan farmhouse dating from 1908 – it is difficult to believe that in 1982 this was still a farm with few trees and known as Mas Roque (Rock Farm). Since then, imaginative planting has led to there being literally thousands of trees and gloriously colourful shrubs making this large campsite most attractive. It has an impressive range of high-quality amenities and facilities open all year.

There are 343 marked pitches for touring units in separate areas, all with 6/10A electricity, 168 larger pitches also have water and, in some cases, drainage. They are on hard surfaces, on gently sloping ground and with plenty of shade. A further 1,000 or so pitches are mostly occupied by chalets to rent and by tour operators.

Key Features

 Book Online

 Open All Year

 Pets Accepted

 Disabled Facilities

 Beach Access

 Swimming Pool

 Play Area

 Bar/Restaurant

Excellent toilet blocks can be heated and have controllable showers and many washbasins in cabins. Baby rooms. Units for disabled visitors. Serviced and self-service laundry. Motorhome services. Supermarket. Souvenir shop. Restaurants. Bar with simple meals and tapas. Outdoor pools (seasonal), indoor pool (all year, charged). Wellness centre including sauna, jacuzzi and gym. Play areas. Sports field. Games room. Excursions. Activity and entertainment programme for all ages. Bicycle hire. Tennis. ATM and exchange facilities. WiFi throughout (charged). Caravan storage.

Scan me for
more information.

Alan Rogers Code: ES84100
77 accommodations
800 pitches
GPS: 41.16945, 1.47075
Post Code: E-43883

Tarragona, Cataluña-Catalunya

www.alanrogers.com/es84100
info@barapark.es
Tel: +34 977 80 27 01
www.barapark.es

Open (Touring Pitches):
Start April - End September.

Camping Park Playa Barà

Camping Park Playa Barà is a family-friendly campsite located in the town of Roda de Barà approximately 20 km from Tarragona. There are multiple activities on offer, such as swimming in the pool, volleyball tournaments, handball, basketball, tennis, paddle tennis, mini-golf and table tennis. You can also relax in the hot tub or go to the solarium to top up your tan. The campsite's restaurant is ideal for sharing time with the family and enjoying local culinary specialities.

Roda de Barà, the main tourist centre of the Costa Daurada is a town rich in history, with numerous monuments to its glorious past, chief most among these is the Arc de Barà. Of course, you could also visit the beach and enjoy the sand and a range of water-based activities.

4 sanitary blocks are equipped with showers, private washing cubicles and facilities for babies. Washing machines and dryers. Supermarket & Souvenir shop. Bar, Pool Bar, Restaurant, Beach Restaurant and takeaway. Outdoor pools. Spa Area. Daily entertainment program with nightly shows. Tennis & paddle courts, Minigolf. Bicycle hire at reception

Key Features

 Pets Accepted

 Disabled Facilities

 Beach Access

 Swimming Pool

 Play Area

 Bar/Restaurant

 Bike Hire

Scan me for more information.

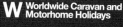

Alan Rogers Code: ES84840
253 accommodations
175 pitches
GPS: 41.15713, 1.44174
Post Code: E-43839

Tarragona, Cataluña-Catalunya

www.alanrogers.com/es84840
info@yellohvillage-gavina.com
Tel: +34 977 80 15 03
www.yellohvillage-gavina.com

Open (Touring Pitches):
Late March - Late October.

Camping Gavina

Yelloh! Village Camping Caravaning Gavina is an attractive, modern, friendly site with superb access to a fine sand beach. It is the sister site to Camping Tamarit (no. ES84830). There are 400 pitches (60 sq.m), of which 175 for tourers have electricity (6A). Set on flat grass and sand, some are separated by tall hedges which provide shade. There is a small tour operator presence.

One side of the site, with large pitches for motorhomes, is open to the 400 m. beach over a very low wall. This is excellent for keen windsurfers and a range of watersports including sailing and water skiing. This beach access does, however, have obvious security implications.

Two good quality, tiled sanitary buildings have free hot water to showers and some washbasins. In one block, showers have no dividers. A room for babies and a unit for disabled campers are in one block. Laundry facilities. Bar/restaurant. Well stocked supermarket. Play area. Tennis. Sports area. Exchange facilities. Safe deposit boxes.

Key Features

 Book Online

 Disabled Facilities

 Play Area

 Bar/Restaurant

Scan me for more information.

Alan Rogers Code: ES85330
283 accommodations
229 pitches
GPS: 41.04136, 0.98139
Post Code: E-43892

Tarragona, Cataluña-Catalunya

Alannia Els Prats

www.alanrogers.com/es85330
reservas@alannia.com
Tel: +34 965 48 49 45
alanniaresorts.com

Open (Touring Pitches):
Start March - End December.

This Costa Daurada beach resort is constantly developing, with excellent facilities. This is a very popular area, close to the Ebro Valley, not far from Tarragona and around 15 minutes drive from Port Aventura theme park.

The complex has a camping area with over 200 pitches ranging in size from 60m2 to 110m2 with a number close to the beach. All pitches are fully equipped with drainage, TV connection, water connection, 220v electrical and internet connection and pets are allowed on some pitches (subject to availability.) A resort area, with approximately 150 cabins, plus studios ensures a fun, relaxing and comfortable family holiday. All cabins have a terrace and some are suitable for pets.

Key Features

 Pets Accepted

 Disabled Facilities

 Beach Access

 Swimming Pool

 Play Area

 Bar/Restaurant

 Bike Hire

Fishing

Three blocks provide clean facilities with controllable showers and some washbasins in cubicles. A fourth, modern unit has WCs and open style washbasins. En-suite unit for disabled visitors. Baby rooms with bath. Washing machines. Motorhome services. Supermarket. Restaurant, takeaway and three bars. Gym and Spa. Three pools (seasonal) one with water jets (aged 16+) a family pool with a waterslide and a shallow children's pool. Children's Play area. Minigolf, paddle tennis court, football and basketball pitch, pétanque and table tennis. Bicycle hire (organised trips). Sailing, windsurfing, canoeing and diving. Activities, excursions and some evening entertainment all season with a full programme in high season. Dogs are accepted in one area. WiFi.

Scan me for
more information.

Alan Rogers Code: ES85400
230 accommodations
700 pitches
GPS: 41.03707, 0.97478
Post Code: E-43300

Tarragona, Cataluña-Catalunya

www.alanrogers.com/es85400
info@latorredelsol.com
Tel: +34 977 81 04 86
www.latorredelsol.com

Open (Touring Pitches):
Mid March - End October.

Camping La Torre del Sol

A pleasant tree-lined approach road gives way to avenues of palms as you arrive at Torre del Sol. This large, well-designed site occupies a good position in southern Catalunya with direct access to a 800m. long soft sand beach.

The site is exceptionally well maintained. There is good shade on a high proportion of the 1,500 individual, numbered pitches, all of which have electricity (700 for touring.) The site boasts three attractive pools with two jacuzzis in the bar and restaurant area. Occasional train noise on some pitches.

Five very well maintained, fully equipped, toilet blocks include units for disabled visitors, babies & children. Washing machines. Gas supplies. Large supermarket, bakery and souvenir shops at the entrance. Full restaurant. Takeaway. Bar with large terrace with entertainment. Beach bar, coffee bar and ice-cream bar. Pizzeria. Open-roof cinema with permanent seating for 520. 3 TV lounges. Soundproofed disco. Swimming pools (two heated). Solarium. Sauna. Two large jacuzzis. Sports areas. Tennis. Squash. Language school (Spanish). Minigolf. Sub-aqua diving. Bicycle hire. Fishing. Windsurfing school. Sailboards and pedaloes for hire. Playground and crèche. Fridge hire. Library. Hairdresser. Business centre. WiFi. Car repair and car wash. No animals permitted. No jet skis accepted.

Key Features

 Book Online

 Disabled Facilities

 Beach Access

 Swimming Pool

 Play Area

 Bar/Restaurant

 Bike Hire

 Fishing

Scan me for more information.

ea, wellness and entertainment Catalunya Sud

E-43892 MIAMI PLATJA (TARRAGONA)
Tel. +34 977 810 486 · info@latorredelsol.com
@latorredelsol_
www.latorredelsol.com

CAMPING
RESORTS

soleil VILLAGE

Alan Rogers Code: ES85370
132 accommodations
387 pitches
GPS: 40.97723, 0.90093
Post Code: E-43890

Tarragona, Cataluña-Catalunya

www.alanrogers.com/es85370
info@eltemplodelsol.com
Tel: +34 977 82 34 34
www.eltemplodelsol.com

Open (Touring Pitches):
Mid March - End October.

Naturista El Templo del Sol

El Templo del Sol is a large, luxurious, terraced naturist site with a distinctly Arabesque feel and superb buildings in Moorish style. The owner has designed the magnificent main turreted building at the entrance with fountains and elaborate Moorish arches.

The site has over 387 pitches of two different sizes, some with car parking alongside and 118 with full services. There is shade and the pitches are on terraces giving rewarding views over the sea. Attractive steps give ready access to the sandy beach. There is some daytime rail noise especially in the lower areas of the site where the larger pitches are located.

The sanitary blocks are amongst the best providing everything you could require. Extensive facilities for disabled campers. Washing machines. Well stocked supermarket. Health shop. Souvenir shop. Bars. Restaurant, snack bar, swimming pools (all open all season). Jacuzzi. Cinema. Games area. Boules. Separate children's pool and play area. Miniclub. Library. Entertainment. Hairdresser. Bicycle hire. ATM. Dogs are not accepted. No jet skis. WiFi over site (charged).

Key Features

 Naturist Site

 Disabled Facilities

 Beach Access

 Swimming Pool

 Play Area

 Bar/Restaurant

 Bike Hire

 Fishing

Scan me for more information.

alan rogers

7th Edition Naturist Guide

- Detailed reviews on over 70 campsites, written by
  our expert campsite assessors.

- Attractive full page layout including contact details,
  GPS coordinates, site description, facilities lists &
  photos presented in an all-new one-campsite-per-page
  view.

- Includes all accommodation types from tent pitches to
  mobile homes, safari tents, chalets and on-site gîtes.

- Full-colour layout, indexed by country, region and
  nearest town, and colour maps.

- Tourist information on featured countries and useful
  advice for travelling abroad.

FKK STRAND

Discover more at
alanrogers.com/naturist

NATURISTS

Featured countries include:
Austria, France, Germany, Great Britain, Italy,
Luxembourg, Netherlands, Norway, Slovenia, Spain

Campsites Region
of Valencia

OPEN

always open **to you**

open **365 days** a year

REGION OF VALENCIA, SPAIN

Welcome

Video

CAMPSITES
REGION OF
VALENCIA

REGION OF
VALENCIA

www.campingscomunidadvalenciana.es

Campsites Guide 2021
Region of Valencia, Spain

DESTINATIONS
MAGAZINE EDITION 8

The magazine from Alan Rogers featuring inspiring holidays for campers, caravans and motorhome owners. It's all about the experience, the atmosphere, the freedom and the fun of a campsite holiday.

Jam packed with holiday ideas for campers, caravanners and motorhomers, Destinations magazine aims to inspire your future trips.

In this edition: an Atlantic road trip through France, HappyLoos from Kildwick Loos, let's talk mental health, undiscovered Catalunya, camping secrets, discover Down Under, exploring Southern Portugal, camping year round, first timers to France, respecting nature and film-inspired holiday locations in Switzerland!

alan rogers

Explore Destinations online at
alanrogers.com/destinations-magazine
or pick up a free copy at the NEC in February and October.

Alan Rogers Code: ES85610
41 accommodations
66 pitches
GPS: 40.27028, 0.30673
Post Code: E-12579

Castellón, Comunidad
Valenciana

www.alanrogers.com/es85610
info@campingribamar.com
Tel: +34 964 76 16 01
campingribamar.com

Open (Touring Pitches):
All year.

Camping Ribamar

Camping Ribamar is tucked away within the National Park of the Sierra de Irta, to the north of Alcossebre, and with direct access to a rugged beach. All the pitches are classified as Premium (90-100sqm) with electricity (6A/10A) and a water supply. A number of bungalows with air conditioning are available for rent.

Leisure facilities here include a large swimming pool plus delightful children's pool and a paddling pool. The main amenities building is adjacent and houses the site's basic bar/restaurant and shop. Twice per week a free shuttle service to the town, available during the winter.

One spotlessly clean toilet block with facilities for babies and campers with disabilities. Laundry facilities. Bar. Restaurant. Shop. Swimming pool. Paddling pool. Multisports terrain. Tennis. Five-a-side football. Basketball. Boules. Paddle court. Bicycle hire. Play area. Library/social room. Chalets to rent. Direct access to rocky beach. Fishing. WiFi (charged). Charcoal barbecues are not allowed.

Key Features

 Open All Year

 Pets Accepted

 Disabled Facilities

 Beach Access

 Swimming Pool

 Play Area

 Bar/Restaurant

 Bike Hire

Scan me for
more information.

419

Alan Rogers Code: ES85700
512 accommodations
404 pitches
GPS: 40.12781, 0.15894
Post Code: E-12595

Castellón, Comunidad
Valenciana

www.alanrogers.com/es85700
camping@bravoplaya.com
Tel: +34 964 31 97 44
www.bravoplaya.com

Open (Touring Pitches):
All year.

Camping Bravoplaya

Camping Bravoplaya is a very large site divided into two by a quiet road, with a reception on each side with friendly, helpful staff. There are three pool complexes (one can be covered in cooler weather and is heated) all of which are on the west side, whilst the beach (of shingle and sand) is on the east. Both sides have a restaurant – the one on the beachside has two air-conditioned wooden buildings and a terrace.

The flat pitches vary in size, some have their own sinks, and most have shade. All have 10A electricity and a few have a partial view of the sea. There are a number of bungalows to rent around the two areas. This is a high-quality site offering a great choice to campers. The site was previously known as Camping Torre la Sal 2

Toilet facilities are of a good standard in both sections, with British style WCs, hot water to some sinks, and facilities for disabled campers. Baby rooms. Washing machines (laundry service if required for a small charge). Motorhome services. Shop, bars, restaurants and takeaway. Modern swimming pool complex complete with flumes (one pool has a bar in the centre). Jacuzzi and sauna (winter). Play park. Large disco. Sports centre. Tennis. Squash. Two football pitches. Pétanque. Outdoor gym. Games room. Bullring. Hairdresser. Varied programme of activities and entertainment. WiFi (charged). Torches are useful.

Key Features

 Book Online

 Open All Year

 Pets Accepted

 Disabled Facilities

 Beach Access

 Swimming Pool

 Play Area

 Bar/Restaurant

Scan me for more information.

A world of sensations

Bravoplaya
CAMPING - RESORT ★★★★★

Open all year

INFORMATION AND RESERVATIONS
camping@bravoplaya.com · Tlf +34 964 31 95 67
Ribera de Cabanes · Castellón · España
www.bravoplaya.com

ADAC Superplatz 2021
★★★★★

ADAC

Alan Rogers Code: ES86110
100 accommodations
80 pitches
GPS: 39.60528, -0.26889
Post Code: E-46530

Valencia, Comunidad Valenciana

www.alanrogers.com/es86110
info@campingpuzol.com
Tel: +34 961 42 15 27
www.campingpuzol.com

Open (Touring Pitches):
Mid February - Mid December.

Camping Puzol

Camping Puzol is a family campsite located on Puzol beach. Only 14 km. From Valencia, the campsite is next to the sandy beach and surrounded by a quiet atmosphere. There are loose gravel pitches with natural shade in summer and sun in winter. All pitches with electricity. There are bungalows to rent.

There is a swimming pool with three slides, the beach is 150 m. from the campsite, there is a cycle route from the campsite to Puzol's town where you will find restaurants, shops and a train station to visit Valencia. Puzol beach has been awarded the Blue Flag. To the North of the beach, there is a wetland called "Marjal del Moro" which has been catalogued as a Special Protection Area for Birds.

There are three sanitary blocks with showers and washbasins. Washing machines. Dryers. Bar and restaurant with a big terrace (open Easter, July and August). 2 swimming pools with slides. A separated area with rental bungalows.

Bar-Cafe. Children's Play Area. Entertainment (only available in High Season)|. Pets allowed on pitch. Rental of Bungalows. Supermarket(Small) Swimming pool. Washing Service. Wi-Fi

Key Features

 Book Online

 Pets Accepted

 Disabled Facilities

 Beach Access

 Swimming Pool

 Play Area

 Bar/Restaurant

Scan me for
more information.

Alan Rogers Code: ES86240
60 accommodations
87 pitches
GPS: 39.32296, -0.30957
Post Code: E-46012

Valencia, Comunidad Valenciana

Devesa Gardens

www.alanrogers.com/es86240
contacto@devesagardens.com
Tel: +34 961 61 11 36
www.devesagardens.com

Open (Touring Pitches):
All year.

This campsite is owned by the La Marina Group, and the huge investment made is showing as the comprehensive renovation programme continues. It is situated between the Albufera lake and the sea, with rice fields on both sides.

The 87 level touring pitches are on sand and gravel, all with 16A electricity hook-ups (2-pin sockets). There are no water connections on pitches at the moment. They are separated by fir hedges and young trees, but there is shade from more mature trees.

A modern amenities complex is at the heart of the site and includes a swimming pool, extensive play facilities for children and a large auditorium. Bungalows for rent are located in a separate area from the touring pitches.

Key Features

 Open All Year

 Pets Accepted

 Disabled Facilities

 Beach Access

 Swimming Pool

 Play Area

 Bar/Restaurant

 Bike Hire

Three heated sanitary blocks, one modern, two old and requiring updating. Facilities for disabled visitors and families. Washing machine and dryer. Bar. Restaurant and takeaway. Supermarket. Entertainment(High Season) Outdoor swimming pool (lifeguard in Apr-Oct, open to public). Riding school. Bullring. Tennis courts. Play area with bouncy castle. Children's club and entertainment. Mini farm. Boat trips. Bicycle hire. WiFi throughout (free). Pets allowed on pitch.

Scan me for
more information.

Alan Rogers Code: ES86250
70 accommodations
56 pitches
GPS: 39.55218, -1.47456
Post Code: E-46317

Valencia, Comunidad Valenciana

www.alanrogers.com/es86250
info@kikoparkrural.com
Tel: +34 962 13 90 82
www.kikoparkrural.com

Open (Touring Pitches):
All year.

Kiko Park Rural

Approaching Kiko Park Rural, you will see a small hilltop village set in a landscape of mountains, vines and a jewel-like lake. Kiko was a small village and farm, and the village now forms the campsite and accommodation. Amenities are contained within the architecturally authentic buildings, some old and some new.

The generous touring pitches (mainly hardstanding and with 6A electricity and water) have high hedges (as does the site) for privacy. Generous planting has been made, which already affords some privacy, and hundreds of trees provide shade. The restaurant serves extremely good food in a pleasant, spacious setting overlooking the pools and their surrounding immaculate lawns.

Three toilet blocks are well equipped (but have short timers for lighting and showers), including facilities for disabled campers. Motorhome services. Gas supplies. Pleasant bar. Excellent restaurant (seasonal, also supplies basics, eggs, bread etc). Takeaway (Easter-Oct). Swimming and paddling pools. Very good playground. Bicycle hire. Entertainment in high season. Many adventure activities can be arranged, including white-water rafting, gorging, orienteering, trekking, bungee jumping and riding. Large families and groups catered for.,Pets allowed in bungalows. Pets allowed on the pitch.

Key Features

 Open All Year

 Pets Accepted

 Disabled Facilities

 Swimming Pool

 Play Area

 Bar/Restaurant

Scan me for
more information.

Alan Rogers Code: ES86150
31 accommodations
170 pitches
GPS: 38.93160, -0.09680
Post Code: E-46780

Valencia, Comunidad Valenciana

Kiko Park

www.alanrogers.com/es86150
info@kikopark.com
Tel: +34 962 85 09 05
www.kikopark.com

Open (Touring Pitches):
All year.

Kiko Park is a smart site nestling behind protective sand dunes alongside a Blue Flag beach. There are sets of attractively tiled steps over the dunes or a long boardwalk near the beach bar (good for prams and wheelchairs) to take you to the fine white sandy beach and the sea.

From the central reception point (where good English is spoken), flat, fine gravel pitches and access roads are divided to the left and right. Backing onto one another, the 170 large pitches all have electricity and the aim is to progressively upgrade all these with full services. There are plenty of flowers, hedging and trees adding shade, privacy and colour.

A pleasant, outdoor swimming pool with adjacent children's pool has a paved area with a bar in summer. The restaurant (lunchtimes only out of season) overlooks the marina, beautiful beach and sea. A wide variety of entertainment is provided all year and Spanish lessons are taught along with dance classes and aerobics during the winter.

Key Features

 Open All Year

 Pets Accepted

 Disabled Facilities

 Beach Access

 Swimming Pool

 Play Area

 Bar/Restaurant

 Bike Hire

Four heated shower and toilet blocks, including facilities for babies and for disabled visitors (who will find this site flat and convenient). Outdoor swimming pools. ATM. Laundry. Restaurant, bar and beach-side bar. Supermarket. Motorhome services. Gas supplies. Playground. Watersports facilities. Diving school in high season. Paddle Sup. Entertainment for children. Pétanque. WiFi. Car rental. Bicycle hire. Pets allowed on pitch

Scan me for
more information.

Alan Rogers Code: ES87435
540 accommodations
594 pitches
GPS: 38.17790, -0.80950
Post Code: E-03330

Alicante, Comunidad Valenciana

Alannia Costa Blanca

www.alanrogers.com/es87435
reservas@alannia.com
Tel: +34 965 48 49 45
www.alanniaresorts.com

Open (Touring Pitches):
All year.

Alannia Costa Blanca (formerly Marjal) is a fully equipped site situated 15 km. inland on the southern Alicante coast, close to the towns of Crevillente and Catral, and the Parque Natural de El Hondo. The 1,200 hardstanding pitches range in size from 90-95 sq.m, and all have electricity (16A), water, drainage, TV and high-speed internet connections (charged).

On-site amenities include a tropical-themed swimming pool complex and a state-of-the-art wellness centre. There is full disabled access, including at the swimming pool and staffed gym. There is accommodation to rent, including 46 Balinese-style bungalows adapted for disabled visitors. The site is ideal for both family holidays in summer and for winter sun-seekers.

Six modern, spotlessly clean toilet blocks have washbasins and free showers in cabins. Facilities for children, babies & disabled visitors. Well equipped shop. Bar, restaurant and takeaway (all year). Swimming pool complex with outdoor pool (Mar-Sept), heated indoor pool (all year), sauna and Hammam. Fully equipped gym. Wellness centre. Hairdresser. Play areas. Games rooms. Library. Multisports courts. Minigolf. Tennis. Football. Entertainment and activity programme (inc Spanish lessons). Kids club. Bicycle hire. Car hire service. Doctor and vet. Free WiFi areas. Mobile homes and chalets to rent.

Key Features

 Book Online

 Open All Year

 Pets Accepted

 Disabled Facilities

 Beach Access

 Swimming Pool

 Play Area

 Bar/Restaurant

Scan me for more information.

OPEN ALL YEAR ROUND
ALICANTE / TARRAGONA

Alannia
RESORTS

alanniaresorts.com
Tel. +34 965 484 945
reservas@alannia.com

Alan Rogers Code: ES87420
91 accommodations
450 pitches
GPS: 38.12965, -0.64958
Post Code: E-03194

Alicante, Comunidad Valenciana

www.alanrogers.com/es87420
info@campinglamarina.com
Tel: +34 965 41 92 00
www.lamarinaresort.com

Open (Touring Pitches):
All year.

Camping La Marina

Very efficiently run by a friendly family, Camping Internacional La Marina has 450 touring pitches of three different types and sizes ranging from 50 sq.m. to 150 sq.m. with electricity (10/16A), TV, water and drainage. Artificial shade is provided and the pitches are well maintained on level, well-drained ground with a special area allocated for tents in a small orchard.

The lagoon swimming pool complex is fabulous and has something for everyone (with lifeguards). William Le Metayer, the owner, is passionate about La Marina and it shows in his search for perfection. A magnificent, modern building which uses the latest architectural technology, houses many superb extra amenities. A member of Leading Campings group.

The sanitary blocks offer modern facilities and are regularly cleaned. Heated in winter, they include private cabins and facilities for disabled visitors & babies. Laundry facilities. Motorhome services. Gas. Supermarket. Bars. Restaurant and café. Ice cream kiosk. Swimming pools (seasonal). Indoor pool. Fitness centre. Sauna. Solarium. Jacuzzi. Play rooms. Extensive activity and entertainment programme including barbecues and swimming nights. Sports area. Tennis. Huge playgrounds. Hairdresser. Bicycle hire. Road train to beach. Exclusive area for dogs. Internet café (charged) and free WiFi.

Key Features

 Open All Year

 Pets Accepted

 Disabled Facilities

 Beach Access

 Swimming Pool

 Play Area

 Bar/Restaurant

 Bike Hire

Scan me for more information.

Alan Rogers Code: ES87810
192 accommodations
290 pitches
GPS: 36.73925, -3.94971
Post Code: E-29793

Málaga, Andalucia

Camping El Pino

www.alanrogers.com/es87810
info@campingelpino.com
Tel: +34 952 53 00 06
www.campingelpino.com

Open (Touring Pitches):
All year.

El Pino is in the Axarquia region of the Costa del Sol, east of Malaga and is surrounded by avocado groves. The old but well-maintained site enjoys some fine views of the surrounding countryside. There are now 290 pitches here, mostly well shaded, and a further 57 mobile homes and chalets to rent. Most pitches have electrical connections and vary in size from 60-100 sq.m. The site is open all year and has some good facilities including a swimming pool, supermarket and bar/restaurant. The nearest beach is 800 m. distant – a bus service runs there from the site.

The site can be found close to Torrox Costa, an area claiming to have the best climate in Europe. The old village of Torrox has traces of its Arabic origins, with narrow, winding streets and whitewashed houses. Torrox Costa is quite different and has been extensively but attractively developed with a lighthouse at one end and a fine sandy beach, the Playa Ferrara.

Key Features

 Open All Year

 Pets Accepted

 Disabled Facilities

 Beach Access

 Swimming Pool

 Play Area

 Bar/Restaurant

Five toilet blocks with hot water and individual cabins. Facilities for disabled visitors. Laundry facilities. Bar, restaurant and shop (all year). Swimming pool with children's pool (seasonal). Play area. Pétanque. Table tennis. WiFi throughout (free). Mobile homes and apartments to rent. Communal barbecue - only gas or electric barbecues permitted on pitches. Pets Allowed.

Scan me for more information.

Alan Rogers Code: ES90850
80 accommodations
230 pitches
GPS: 37.67664, -4.93329
Post Code: E-14100

Córdoba, Andalucia

Camping Carlos III

www.alanrogers.com/es90850
camping@campingcarlosiii.com
Tel: +34 957 30 03 38
www.campingcarlosiii.com

Open (Touring Pitches):
All year.

This rural site lies 30 km. south of the centre of Córdoba, just off the main Córdoba - Sevilla road and maybe a good alternative to staying in the city. A very large, busy site, especially at weekends, it has many supporting facilities including a good swimming pool and a pool, play area and animal corner for children.

With the catering services open all year, the site has a more open feel than the bustling municipal site in Córdoba. The touring areas are canopied by trees which offer considerable shade for the 230 separated pitches. On sandy, gently sloping ground, around two-thirds have 5/10A electricity.

Modern toilet blocks provide a mix of British and Turkish WCs, with hot showers in the block near reception. Laundry service. Motorhome services. Bar/restaurant, shop (all year). Swimming pools (seasonal). Aviary. Boules. Minigolf. Paintball. Play area. Hairdresser. WiFi (charged). Accommodation to rent. Charcoal barbecues are not permitted.

Key Features

 Open All Year

 Pets Accepted

 Disabled Facilities

 Beach Access

 Swimming Pool

 Play Area

 Bar/Restaurant

Scan me for more information.

Alan Rogers Code: ES88535
300 pitches
GPS: 36.29998, -6.12935
Post Code: E-11140

Cádiz, Andalucia

www.alanrogers.com/es88535
booking.conil@ohairesorts.com
Tel: +34 956 44 33 39
www.ohairesorts.com

Open (Touring Pitches):
Start July - End December.

Ohai Conil Outdoor Resort

Located in the heart of nature, next to Cala del Aceite beach, Ohai Conil Outdoor Resort is just a 3-minute walk to the attractive beach. The site features padel courts, table tennis and a water park with 2 swimming pools.

A varied programme of entertainment for all ages is provided during high season, including kids clubs and activities for younger children, teenagers and adults. Dogs are allowed throughout the whole year.

Four sanitary blocks are equipped with showers, private washing cubicles and facilities for babies. Washing machines and dryers. Small shop. Bar. Restaurant and takeaway. Waterpark and two swimming pools. Activity and entertainment programmes (during school holidays). Bicycle hire, horse ride (close to the campsite), water activities close to the campsite. WiFi in the whole campsite free of charge.

Key Features

 Book Online

 Open All Year

 Pets Accepted

 Beach Access

 Swimming Pool

 Play Area

 Bar/Restaurant

 Bike Hire

Scan me for more information.

Alan Rogers Code: ES90860
18 accommodations
129 pitches
GPS: 39.48900, -6.41280
Post Code: E-10005

Cáceres, Extremadura

www.alanrogers.com/es90860
info@campingcaceres.com
Tel: +34 927 23 31 00
www.campingcaceres.com

Open (Touring Pitches):
All year.

Cáceres Camping

Cáceres Camping is quite a small site, located to the west of the interesting city of Cáceres, a World Heritage site. There are 129 pitches here, and, unusually, each has a chalet providing a shower, washbasin and toilet. The pitches are of a reasonable size (80 sq.m) and are well shaded.

A range of leisure facilities is provided, including a swimming pool and a separate children's pool. Cáceres is a city with much interest and fascinating history. Cave paintings on the city outskirts date back 30,000 years! The city is the capital of High Extremadura and, close by, the Montanchez mountain range offers many opportunities for walking and cycling.

Individual sanitary units on pitches (shower, washbasin, WC). Laundry facilities. Bar, restaurant, cafeteria and takeaway meals. Supermarket. Swimming pool. Bungalows and rooms to rent. WiFi (free).

Key Features

 Open All Year

 Pets Accepted

 Disabled Facilities

 Swimming Pool

 Bar/Restaurant

Scan me for more information.

Alan Rogers Code: ES90960
18 accommodations
44 pitches
GPS: 39.32190, -4.64950
Post Code: E-13110

Ciudad Real, Castilla-La-Mancha

www.alanrogers.com/es90960
info@campingcabaneros.com
Tel: +34 926 77 54 39
www.campingcabaneros.com

Open (Touring Pitches):
All year.

El Mirador de Cabañeros

With panoramic views all around of the Sierra de Valdefuertes mountains, Camping El Mirador de Cabañeros is set in the Cabañeros National Park. This is a well cared for, landscaped site with 44 terraced pitches on gravel, all with 6A electricity.

Although pitches are level once sited, the approach is via a steep slope which may cause difficulties for larger units. Run by a very helpful and friendly family, this site is in a very peaceful location where you can just sit and relax or visit the many attractions that the National Park has to offer. It is an ideal base for walking and birdwatching.

One spotlessly clean central toilet block with solar heating includes open washbasins and cubicle showers. Facilities for disabled visitors and babies. Laundry. Motorhome services. No shop but basics from reception. Bar and restaurant (high season, w/ends in low season). Covered swimming pool (all year). Games room. Play areas. Outside fitness area.

Key Features

 Book Online

 Pets Accepted

 Disabled Facilities

 Swimming Pool

 Play Area

 Bar/Restaurant

Scan me for more information.

433

Alan Rogers Code: ES90955
10 accommodations
112 pitches
GPS: 40.50108, -1.59486
Post Code: E-44367

Teruel, Aragon

www.alanrogers.com/es90955
jorge@lascorralizas.com
Tel: +34 627 40 81 82
www.lascorralizas.com

Open (Touring Pitches):
All Year.

Camping Las Corralizas

This site is immersed in a magnificent forest of centenary pine trees, within the Montes Universales. A natural site built with respect for the environment so visitors can truly enjoy the peace and tranquillity the site has to offer. There is a good selection of pitches, some natural unconventional and others that are flat fully serviced suitable for motorhomes.

There are 10 fully equipped wood cabins to hire that are beautifully integrated within the forest. A chance to see deer in their natural habitat and many other species of wildlife. Communal BBQ area with tables and washing up facilities close by make this a comfortable location for family entertaining. The sanitary facilities are well placed throughout the site for easy access for all campers.

There is an on site restaurant, bar and cafeteria. Good location for mountain biking, children's playground, communal BBQ area. Disabled facilities, washing and clothes drying, toilets, showers, dishwasher, free WIFI, postal service and internet connection.

Key Features

 Pets Accepted

 Disabled Facilities

 Play Area

 Bar/Restaurant

Scan me for more information.

Alan Rogers Code: ES90910
23 accommodations
162 pitches
GPS: 40.04218, -3.59947
Post Code: E-28300

Aranjuez, Madrid

www.alanrogers.com/es90910
info@campingaranjuez.com
Tel: +34 918 91 13 95
www.campingaranjuez.com

Open (Touring Pitches):
All year.

Camping Aranjuez

Aranjuez, supposedly Spain's version of Versailles, is worthy of a visit with its beautiful palaces, leafy squares, avenues and gardens. This useful, popular and unusually well-equipped site is therefore excellent for enjoying the unusual attractions or for an en-route stop. It is 47 km. south of Madrid and 46 km. from Toledo.

The site is alongside the River Tajo in a park-like situation with mature trees. There are 162 touring pitches, all with electricity (16A), set on flat grass amid tall trees. The site is owned by the owners of la Marina (ES87420) who have worked hard to improve the pitches and the site in general.

Two of the three modern sanitary blocks are heated and all are well equipped with some washbasins in cabins. Laundry facilities. Gas supplies. Shop, bar and restaurant (all year) with attractive riverside patio (also open to the public). Takeaway. TV in bar. Swimming and paddling pools, (seasonal). Tennis courts. Central play area. Pétanque. Bicycle hire. Canoe hire. Activities for children (high season). WiFi over site (charged).

Key Features

 Open All Year

 Pets Accepted

 Disabled Facilities

 Swimming Pool

 Play Area

 Bar/Restaurant

 Bike Hire

 Fishing

Scan me for more information.

Alan Rogers Code: ES90290
11 accommodations
124 pitches
GPS: 41.49531, -5.00522
Post Code: E-47100

Valladolid, Castilla Y Leon

www.alanrogers.com/es90290
info@campingelastral.es
Tel: +34 983 77 09 53
www.campingelastral.es

Open (Touring Pitches):
All year.

Campingred El Astral

The site is in a prime position alongside the wide River Duero (safely fenced). It is homely and run by a charming man, Eduardo Gutierrez, who speaks excellent English and is ably assisted by brother Gustavo and sister Lola.

The site is generally flat with pitches separated by thin hedges. The 150 touring pitches with electricity (6/10A), six with 10A electricity, water and wastewater, vary in size from 60-200 sq.m. with mature trees providing shade. The toilet block has been designed with environmental sustainability in mind, including solar heated water. This is a friendly site, ideal for exploring the area and historic Tordesillas.

One attractive sanitary block with fully equipped, modern facilities designed to include energy-saving measures and to be easily cleaned. Showers for children and baby room. Facilities for disabled visitors. Washing machines. Motorhome services. Supermarket. Bar and restaurant, frequented by locals, plus a takeaway service all (seasonal). Swimming pool with disability lift, plus paddling pools (seasonal). Playground. Tennis (high season). Minigolf. No charcoal barbecues (July-Sept). WiFi throughout (charged).

Key Features

 Book Online

 Open All Year

 Pets Accepted

 Disabled Facilities

 Swimming Pool

 Play Area

 Bar/Restaurant

Scan me for more information.

Alan Rogers Code: ES92420
5 accommodations
200 pitches
GPS: 40.93125, -4.09243
Post Code: E-40004

Segovia, Castilla Y Leon

www.alanrogers.com/es92420
informacion@campingacueducto.com
Tel: +34 921 42 50 00
www.campingacueducto.com

Open (Touring Pitches):
Start April - End September.

Camping El Acueducto

This family run site is located 3 km. from the centre of the interesting city of Segovia with views across the open plain to the mountains beyond. The 200 grass pitches (50 with 6A electricity, water and drainage) are mostly of medium size and arranged off a central avenue. A few pitches near the gate have room for larger motorhomes.

An uncomplicated site, reception is small but efficient and the owner is helpful and speaks English. Segovia is deeply and haughtily Castilian, with plenty of squares and mansions from its days of Golden Age grandeur, when it was a royal resort.

Two traditional style toilet blocks provide simple, clean facilities. Laundry room with washing machine. Motorhome services. Small shop for essentials. Bar (July/Aug). Two swimming pools (July/Aug). Large play area. Bicycle hire. WiFi in reception (charged). Car wash. Gas and electric barbecues only.

Key Features

 Pets Accepted

 Disabled Facilities

 Swimming Pool

 Play Area

 Bar/Restaurant

 Bike Hire

Scan me for more information.

437

Alan Rogers Code: ES92512
70 pitches
GPS: 41.74581, -2.48451
Post Code: E-42005

Soria, Castilla Y Leon

www.alanrogers.com/es92512
camping@fuentedelateja.com
Tel: +34 975 22 29 67
www.fuentedelateja.com

Open (Touring Pitches):
Start March - End October.

Camping Fuente de la Teja

This small, family-owned campsite to the south of Soria has 70 pitches of which 50 are available for touring units. They are on rough-cut grass with water and electricity (6A) supplied to each. There is a degree of shade from mature trees which also define each pitch.

The site is certainly acceptable as a night stop, with good access from the main road and it is only 2 km. from the town of Soria, with its many shops, restaurants and bars. An outdoor swimming pool is available for use during July and August. It becomes very busy here in the high season.

The single toilet block includes hot showers and washbasins (cold water only). Very limited facilities for babies and disabled visitors. Laundry facilities in a separate area. Small shop selling basic items such as bread and milk. Bar/restaurant (often used by locals). Outdoor swimming pool (July/Aug). Play area. Free WiFi near reception.

Key Features

 Pets Accepted

 Swimming Pool

 Play Area

 Bar/Restaurant

Scan me for more information.

Alan Rogers Code: ES90210
29 accommodations
330 pitches
GPS: 42.34125, -3.65762
Post Code: E-09193

Burgos, Castilla Y Leon

www.alanrogers.com/es90210
info@campingburgos.com
Tel: +34 947 48 60 16
www.campingburgos.com

Open (Touring Pitches):
All year.

Camping Fuentes Blancas

Fuentes Blancas is a comfortable municipal site on the edge of the historic town of Burgos and within easy reach of the Santander ferries. There are around 330 marked pitches of 70 sq.m. on flat ground, 330 with electrical connections (6A) and there is good shade in parts.

The site has a fair amount of transit trade and reservations are not possible for August, so arrive early. Burgos is an attractive city, ideally placed for an overnight stop en route to or from the south of Spain. The old part of the city around the cathedral is quite beautiful and there are pleasant walks along the riverbanks outside the campsite gates.

Clean, modern style, fully equipped sanitary facilities in five blocks with controllable showers and hot and cold water to sinks (not all are always open). Facilities for babies. Washing machine/dryer. Motorhome services. Small shop (May-Sept). Bar/snack bar with terrace, social room with TV and DVD and restaurant (all year). Swimming pool (1/7-30/8). Playground. Entertainment for children and adults (July/Aug). WiFi over part of site (charged). English is spoken.

Key Features

 Open All Year

 Pets Accepted

 Swimming Pool

 Play Area

 Bar/Restaurant

 Bike Hire

Scan me for more information.

Alan Rogers Code: ES89360
92 accommodations
358 pitches
GPS: 42.11398, -8.82601
Post Code: E-36393

Pontevedra, Galicia

Camping Bayona Playa

www.alanrogers.com/es89360
campingbayona@campingbayona.com
Tel: +34 986 35 00 35
www.campingbayona.com

Open (Touring Pitches):
Early April - Mid September.

Situated on a narrow peninsula with the sea and river estuary all around it, this large and well maintained campsite is great for a relaxing break. The 450 pitches, 358 for touring, benefit from the shade of mature trees whilst still maintaining a very open feel. All have 5A electricity and 50 are fully serviced. It is busy here in high season so advance booking is recommended. Sabaris is a short walk away and Bayona is a 20 minute walk along the coast, where you can find a variety of shops, supermarkets, banks, bars and eating places. Maximum unit length is 7.5 m.

Three well maintained modern toilet blocks (one open low season), washbasins and shower cubicles. No washing machines but site provides a service wash. Facilities for visitors with disabilities. Large well-stocked supermarket and gift shop (June-Sept). Terrace bar, cafeteria, restaurant. Excellent pool complex with slide (small charge, redeemable in shop and restaurant). Play area. Organised activities July/Aug. Windsurfing school. Cash machine in reception. WiFi near reception area.

Key Features

 Pets Accepted

 Disabled Facilities

 Beach Access

 Swimming Pool

 Play Area

 Bar/Restaurant

 Fishing

 Sailing

Scan me for more information.

Alan Rogers Code: ES89300
4 accommodations
74 pitches
GPS: 42.76198, -9.07270
Post Code: E-15291

A Coruña, Galicia

www.alanrogers.com/es89300
contacto@campingsanfrancisco.com
Tel: +34 881 02 89 26
www.campingsanfrancisco.com

Open (Touring Pitches):
Mid June - Start September.

Camping San Francisco

Situated 200 m. from the beach, this small and attractive touring site with 104 small pitches occupies a clearing on a hillside that is undoubtedly a magnet for Spanish holidaymakers. Advance booking is recommended.

The 74 neatly laid out and numbered touring pitches are on level grass, divided by trees but with little shade. All have 10A electricity and are fully serviced. The surrounding countryside is scenic and unspoilt by development and the superb white sandy beaches and rocky coves provide endless hours of fun or relaxation for the whole family. Bars and restaurants, together with a few small shops, are all within 300 m. of the site but for everything else, the small town of Muros is only 3.5 km.

One modern spotlessly clean toilet block is centrally positioned with all necessary facilities. Family shower room with facilities for disabled visitors provided in both male and female areas. Washing machines and dryers. First-aid point. Well stocked shop (fresh bread from July). Café/bar. Restaurant with terrace. Play area. Tennis. Multisports court. Free WiFi throughout.

Key Features

 Beach Access

 Play Area

 Bar/Restaurant

Scan me for more information.

441

Alan Rogers Code: ES89420
11 accommodations
120 pitches
GPS: 43.34908, -8.33567
Post Code: E-15179

A Coruña, Galicia

Camping Los Manzanos

www.alanrogers.com/es89420
informacion@campinglosmanzanos.com
Tel: +34 981 61 48 25
www.campinglosmanzanos.com

Open (Touring Pitches):
Mid April - End September.

Los Manzanos has a steep access drive down to the site, which is divided by a stream into two sections linked by a bridge. Pitches for larger units are marked and numbered, 85 with electricity (12A) and, in one section, there is a fairly large, unmarked field for tents.

Some aircraft noise should be expected as the site is under the flight path to A Coruña (but no aircraft at night). The site impressed us as it was very clean, even when full, which it tends to be in high season. Some interesting huge stone sculptures create focal points and conversation pieces.

This site is to the east of the historic port of A Coruña, not far from some ria (lagoon) beaches and with good communications to both central and north Galicia – it is only an hours drive from Santiago de la Compostela, for example.

One good toilet block provides modern facilities including free hot showers. Small shop with fresh produce daily (limited outside June-Sept). High-quality restaurant/bar (July/Aug). Swimming pool with lifeguard, free to campers (seasonal). Playground. Barbecue area. Bungalows to rent. WiFi in the reception area.

Key Features

 Pets Accepted

 Disabled Facilities

 Beach Access

 Swimming Pool

 Play Area

 Bar/Restaurant

Scan me for more information.

Alan Rogers Code: ES89440
60 pitches
GPS: 43.47993, -6.70261
Post Code: E-33718

Arbón, Asturias

www.alanrogers.com/es89440
campinglacascada@hotmail.com
Tel: +34 985 62 50 81
www.campinglacascada.com

Open (Touring Pitches):
Easter - Mid September.

Camping la Cascada

Located in a clearing of the attractive Arbon Valley, this friendly, family-run site offers the chance to experience the delights of rural Spain. There are 74 very small pitches (60 for touring units), all sited on gently sloping grass with electricity (4A), long leads are required. The beaches and small villages of Costa Verde are only 12 km. away and the site has information about this spectacular region. Access to the site is not difficult but a 3,500 kg. weight restriction on the small bridge at the site entrance makes it unsuitable for larger units.

The focal point of this small and well-maintained site is its traditional style restaurant. It is open during July and August and serves a variety of home-cooked, locally grown produce. The unheated, fenced swimming pool is open all season and provides a good sunbathing area. Open from Easter to the end of September, this is a quiet site but it can get busy in high season and advance booking is advised.

Well maintained toilet block. No specific facilities for visitors with disabilities. No washing machine. Shop, bar and snacks (all season). Restaurant (July/Aug). Swimming pool with sun terrace (all season). Play area. Fishing. Covered communal barbecue area. WiFi near bar area.

Key Features

 Pets Accepted

 Beach Access

 Swimming Pool

 Play Area

 Bar/Restaurant

 Fishing

Scan me for
more information.

443

Alan Rogers Code: ES89450
6 accommodations
210 pitches
GPS: 43.07202, -6.19889
Post Code: E-33840

Somiedo, Asturias

www.alanrogers.com/es89450
campinglagosdesomiedo@hotmail.
com
Tel: +34 985 76 37 76
www.campinglagosdesomiedo.com

Open (Touring Pitches):
Start June - End September.

Camping Lagos de Somiedo

This is a most unusual site in the Parque Natural de Somiedo. Winding narrow roads with challenging rock overhangs, hairpin bends and breathtaking views (for 8 km) finally bring you to the campsite at an elevation of 1,200 m. This is a site for 4x4s, powerful small campervans and cars – not for medium or large motorhomes, and caravans are not accepted. It is not an approach for the faint-hearted!

The friendly owners make you welcome at their unique site, which is tailored for those who wish to explore the natural and cultural values of the park without the usual campsite amenities. There are 210 pitches (just four with electric hook-up), undefined in two open meadows.

There are British style toilets and free hot water to clean hot showers and washbasins. Facilities for babies and children, and for disabled visitors. Washing machine. Combined reception, small restaurant with takeaway, bar and reference section. Shop for bread, milk and other essentials, plus local produce and crafts. Horses for hire, trekking. Lectures on flora, fauna, history and culture. Fishing (licence required). Barbecue area. Small play area. Gas supplies. Traditional thatched cabins for hire. Public telephone. No Internet access or mobile signal.

Key Features

 Disabled Facilities

 Play Area

 Bar/Restaurant

Scan me for more information.

444

Alan Rogers Code: ES89625
9 accommodations
77 pitches
GPS: 42.88983, -4.50459
Post Code: E-34840

Cervera de Pisuerga, Cantabria

Fuentes Carrionas

www.alanrogers.com/es89625
info@campingfuentescarrionas.com
Tel: +34 979 87 04 24
www.campingfuentescarrionas.com

Open (Touring Pitches):
Early April - Early November.

Fuentes Carrionas is a smaller campsite located in Cervera de Pisuerga and has 77 touring pitches offering various locations on the site. They also have 9 attractive, fully equipped wooden lodges to hire. The site is in a great natural location with plenty of activities close by including, horse riding, fishing, a sports area and tennis courts.

The site offers a modern, clean, main facilities area with hot showers, toilets and sinks. A good communal BBQ area with seating is available or you are permitted to use a gas BBQ at your pitch, if you fancy a break from cooking there is a nice on-site restaurant offering good local produce. All campers have free access to the outdoor pool which is close by and there are some marked out cycle and walking routes accessible directly from the site.

On site restaurant and small shop providing basic essentials. Disabled toilet. Communal BBQ area with seating, washing machine, dryer and dishwasher. Dogs are permitted. There is access to a sports field close by offering football, basketball and tennis. Walking and cycle routes direct from campsite. Children's play area 100m from the site.

Key Features

 Pets Accepted

 Play Area

 Bar/Restaurant

Scan me for more information.

Alan Rogers Code: ES89640
12 accommodations
102 pitches
GPS: 43.22594, -4.29034
Post Code: E-39510

Cabuérniga, Cantabria

www.alanrogers.com/es89640
info@campingcabuerniga.com
Tel: +34 942 70 62 59
www.campingcabuerniga.com

Open (Touring Pitches):
All year.

El Molino de Cabuérniga

Located in a peaceful valley with magnificent views of the mountains, beside the Saja river and only a short walk from the picturesque and unspoiled village of Sopeña, this gem of a site is on an open, level, grassy meadow with trees. Wonderful stone buildings and artefacts are a feature of this unique site.

There are 102 marked pitches, all with 6A electricity, although long leads may be needed in places. This comfortable site is very good value and ideal for a few nights (or you may well choose to stay longer once there) whilst you explore the Cabuérniga Valley which forms part of the Reserva Nacional del Saja.

A superb, spotless sanitary block provides spacious, controllable showers and hot and cold water to washbasins. Washing machines and free ironing. Unit for disabled campers. Baby and toddler room. Bar serving breakfasts and 'bocadillos' (sandwiches) includes small shop section. Wonderful playground in rustic setting – supervision recommended. Fishing. Bicycle hire. Attractive stone cottages and apartments to rent. No electric barbecues. WiFi throughout.

Key Features

 Open All Year

 Pets Accepted

 Disabled Facilities

 Beach Access

 Play Area

 Bar/Restaurant

 Fishing

Scan me for
more information.

Alan Rogers Code: ES89930
19 accommodations
100 pitches
GPS: 43.41750, -3.44528
Post Code: E-39770

Laredo, Cantabria

www.alanrogers.com/es89930
recepcion@campingplayaregaton.
com
Tel: +34 942 60 69 95
campingplayaregaton.com

Open (Touring Pitches):
Mid March - End September.

Camping Playa del Regaton

Situated a short distance from the bustling seaside town of Laredo and easily accessible from Santander and Bilbao, Camping Playa del Regaton is an ideal stopover for those en route to the ferries. The site has direct access to the beach and the estuary of the Ria del Ason and is an important marsh area for migrating birds.

Of the 125 small pitches, 100 are for touring and have 6/10A electricity and a sink. All are on level grass, with mature trees providing separation and a degree of shade. The site is popular with Spanish holidaymakers. The owners and their staff are keen to ensure you enjoy your stay. Limited English is spoken outside the high season.

One fully equipped heated toilet block. Baby bath. Facilities for disabled visitors and families. Washing machine and dryer. Small shop (all season) sells most essentials. Café/bar with snacks (July/Aug). Play area. Children's club in high season. Games room. Free WiFi throughout. Bicycle hire. Dogs are accepted if less than 12 kg. and only on certain pitches.

Key Features

 Pets Accepted

 Bar/Restaurant

Scan me for more information.

Alan Rogers Code: ES90350
38 accommodations
75 pitches
GPS: 43.39918, -2.69610
Post Code: E-48360

Bizkaia, Pais Vasco-Euskadi

www.alanrogers.com/es90350
recepcion@campingportuondo.com
Tel: +34 946 87 77 01
www.campingportuondo.com

Open (Touring Pitches):
End January - Mid December.

Camping Portuondo

This site has an attractive restaurant, bar and terrace taking full advantage of the wonderful views across the ocean and estuary. Set amongst gardens, the 75 touring pitches are mainly for tents and small vans, but there are eight larger pitches at the lower levels for medium-sized motorhomes. Access to these is a little difficult as the road is very steep and there is no turning space.

The site is mostly terraced, with tent pitches split, one section for your unit, the other for your car and there is some shade. Most are slightly sloping and all have 6A electricity (some may need long leads). In high season (July/August) it is essential to ring to book your space.

Two toilet blocks include mostly British WCs and a baby room. One block with facilities for disabled visitors. A reader reports poor cleaning and maintenance during their visit. Washing machines and dryers. Motorhome services. Shop (seasonal). Bar and two restaurants, all open to public (seasonal, closed Mondays in low season). Takeaway (seasonal). Swimming pools (seasonal). Free WiFi over part of the site. Barbecue area. Torches may be useful.

Key Features

 Pets Accepted

 Disabled Facilities

 Beach Access

 Swimming Pool

 Play Area

 Bar/Restaurant

 Fishing

Scan me for more information.

Spain

Alan Rogers Code: ES90490
53 accommodations
145 pitches
GPS: 43.18067, -1.45139
Post Code: E-31714

Erratzu, Navarra

www.alanrogers.com/es90490
campingbaztan@campingbaztan.com
Tel: +34 948 45 31 33
www.campingbaztan.com

Open (Touring Pitches):
Mid March - Start November.

Camping Baztan

When driving through the small town of Erratzu, extreme caution is required due to the narrowness of the streets and it is not advised at all for large units.

This site's rural setting and the mountain views make this a retreat for those who enjoy camping in quiet surroundings. It consists of a main building housing reception, a shop, a bar and a small restaurant beneath 14 tidy apartments. There are also timber cottages for rent.

Tarmac roads lead to the 145 grass touring pitches which are supplied with water and electricity (10A). Twenty pitches are available for tents. Shady and of a good size, most of the pitches are level. In the early and late season, the campsite is open but a telephone call is necessary to gain access. You may be the only occupants.

The single sanitary block is clean and has facilities for disabled visitors. Shop and bar (all season). Restaurant/takeaway (seasonal). Swimming pool (seasonal). Squash court. In April, May and September to November the site is only open at weekends. If you wish to stay on weekdays, entry can be obtained by dialling a number displayed at the reception (sanitary block will be open). Free WiFi throughout.

Key Features

 Pets Accepted

 Disabled Facilities

 Beach Access

 Swimming Pool

 Play Area

 Bar/Restaurant

Scan me for more information.

449

Alan Rogers Code: ES90480
53 accommodations
150 pitches
GPS: 42.97315, -1.35182
Post Code: E-31694

Espinal, Navarra

Camping Urrobi

www.alanrogers.com/es90480
info@campingurrobi.com
Tel: +34 948 76 02 00
www.campingurrobi.com

Open (Touring Pitches):
End March - Start November.

This large site is in a beautiful location with mountain views. At the entrance is a lively bar, a reasonably priced restaurant and a well-stocked shop. The site is popular with Spanish families and there are many mobile homes, so it can be busy at holiday times and weekends. However, there is plenty of room on the 150 unmarked grass pitches for touring, 82 of which have electricity points (6A) and there are plenty of water taps.

Water activities of all types are catered for, with both a swimming pool and an area of the river sectioned off for safe bathing and paddling. This is a suitable site for families. With many walks and bicycle tracks, there is plenty of scope for discovering this delightful area.

Key Features

 Pets Accepted

 Disabled Facilities

 Swimming Pool

 Play Area

 Bar/Restaurant

 Fishing

Clean sanitary blocks include facilities for disabled visitors (key from reception). Laundry facilities. Motorhome services. Shop, bar and restaurant (all season). Swimming pool. Games room with TV (Spanish). Minigolf. Tennis. Playing field. Play area. Gas and charcoal barbecues only on pitches but not in Aug/Sept (communal area provided). WiFi throughout (free).

Scan me for more information.

Alan Rogers Code: ES90640
24 accommodations
150 pitches
GPS: 42.61940, -0.30408
Post Code: E-22639

Huesca, Aragon

Camping Gavín

www.alanrogers.com/es90640
info@campinggavin.com
Tel: +34 974 48 50 90
www.campinggavin.com

Open (Touring Pitches):
All year.

Camping Gavín is set on a terraced, wooded hillside and you will find a friendly welcome. The site offers 150 touring pitches of 90 sq.m. and with 10A electricity available to all. In some areas the terracing means that some pitches are quite small. The main site buildings have been constructed using natural stone. There are also 13 bungalows and 11 superb, balconied apartments.

A good restaurant, bar and supermarket are open all year (except November). At about 900 m. the site is surrounded by towering peaks at the portal of the Tena Valley. One can enjoy the natural beauty of the Pyrenees and venture near or far along the great Pyrenean footpaths.

Key Features

 Book Online

 Open All Year

 Pets Accepted

 Disabled Facilities

 Swimming Pool

 Play Area

 Bar/Restaurant

 Bike Hire

Excellent shower and toilet facilities in three main buildings with subtle, tasteful décor include facilities for babies, children and disabled visitors. Laundry facilities. Motorhome services. Well stocked supermarket. Bar, restaurant and takeaway. Swimming pools (seasonal) and paddling pools (all year). Tennis. Playground and indoor play area. Bicycle hire. Individual barbecues are not permitted at some times of the year. Communal, covered barbecue area. WiFi in reception area (free).

Scan me for more information.

Capital Stockholm
Currency Swedish Krona (SEK)
Language Swedish
Time Zone CET (GMT+1)
Telephone Code +46

Shops Hours vary throughout the year, with many shops operating on shorter hours in low and shoulder seasons. In high season 9am to 6pm Mon to Fri, and until 1pm Sat.

Money ATMs are widespread, accessible 24hrs a day and have multilingual instructions. Most places accept credit cards, Visa and Mastercard widely accepted, Amex less so. Electronic and mobile payments are common and there is a trend towards cashless payments.

Accessible Travel One of the best equipped European countries for disabled visitors. Most transport, public spaces/buildings offer adapted facilities

Travelling with children Sweden is great for all ages with good transport links and accommodating locals. Most museums are free for minors. Restaurants often offer a kids menu.

EU Travel Sweden is an EU member state and located within the Schengen area.

Low Emissions Zones in all major cities. Registration required.

All of Sweden's major cities have implemented LEZs but only Stockholm's scheme affects passenger cars.

●●●●● **Accessibility Score**
View our digital e-guide & find out more at
alanrogers.com/open-to-all

Tourism website visitsweden.com

Public Holidays 1 Jan New Year's Day • 6 Jan Epiphany • Mar/Apr Good Friday • Mar/Apr Easter Sunday • Mar/Apr Easter Monday • 1 May Labour Day • May Ascension • May/Jun Whit Sunday • 6 Jun National Day • Jun Midsummer Day • 5 Nov All Saints • 25 Dec Christmas Day • 26 Dec Boxing Day.

Driving in Sweden Dipped headlights are obligatory year-round. Away from large towns, petrol stations are rarely open 24hrs, but most have self-serve pumps. There are no services or emergency phones on motorways. Come prepared if driving in winter months. Beware of large animals in the road. Drink-driving and using a mobile whilst driving are illegal.

Sweden

View all campsites in Sweden
alanrogers.com/sweden

See campsite map page 486

Climate

Extremely cold in the north, mild across the rest of the country. Cold, short winters and summers similar to those in UK.

	Jan	Feb	Mar	Apr	May	Jun	Jul	Aug	Sep	Oct	Nov	Dec
High	1	1	4	10	16	20	23	21	16	10	5	2
Low	-3	-4	-2	1	6	11	14	13	9	5	1	-2

With giant lakes and waterways, rich forests, majestic mountains and glaciers, and vast, wide-open countryside, Sweden is almost twice the size of the UK but with a fraction of the population.

Southern Sweden's unspoiled islands with their beautiful sandy beaches offer endless opportunities for boating and island hopping. The coastal cities of Gothenburg and Malmö, once centres of industry, now have an abundance of restaurants, cultural venues and attractions.

With the Oresund Bridge, Malmö is just a short ride from Copenhagen. Stockholm, the capital, is a delightful place built on fourteen small islands on the eastern coast. It is an attractive, vibrant city with magnificent architecture, fine museums and historic squares. Sparsely populated northern Sweden is a land of forests, rivers and wilderness inhabited by moose and reindeer.

Östersund, located at the shores of a lake in the heart of the country, is well known for winter sports, while Frösö Zoo is a popular attraction. Today Sweden is one of the world's most developed societies and enjoys an enviable standard of living.

Alan Rogers Code: SW2735
130 accommodations
336 pitches
GPS: 58.90427, 11.20012
Post Code: S-452 97

Strömstad, Västra Götalands Län

www.alanrogers.com/sw2735
info@dafto.se
Tel: +46 52 626 040
www.dafto.se

Open (Touring Pitches):
All year.

Daftö Resort

This extremely high quality, family campsite, with a strong pirate theme, is beautifully situated on the west coast, 5 km. south of Strömstad. A very large site, terraced in parts, has both shady and open areas. In total there are 650 pitches with around 300 for touring, all with electrical hook-ups (10A, CEE plugs). In addition, there are 130 modern, very well equipped cabins of various sizes and styles. Daftö Resort, with its DaftöLand adventure park (concessions for campers), has activities for all including boating, beach volleyball, walks and yoga, and all manner of theme-based activities for children including theatre, competitions and treasure hunting.

Footpaths take you into the forest where not only mushrooms and blueberries but deer and elk can be found. Bicycles and boats can be rented on-site and boat trips and seal safaris are arranged. The facilities are of very high quality with everything you could possibly want in four clean and attractive blocks.

Five toilet blocks of excellent quality with washbasin cubicles, showers, family rooms, a children's bathroom, sunbeds, saunas and makeup rooms. Wellness centre and hairdressers. Units for disabled visitors. Kitchen with cookers, microwaves, sinks and industrial grade dishwashers. Extensive laundry facilities. Motorhome services. Large supermarket. Fully licensed restaurant. Heated pool (peak season). Games and TV rooms. Themed minigolf. Bicycle hire. Children's club. Boat hire, excursions and seal safaris. Internet and WiFi. Conference room. B&B. DaftöLand adventure park.

Key Features

 Open All Year

 Pets Accepted

 Disabled Facilities

 Beach Access

 Swimming Pool

 Play Area

 Bar/Restaurant

 Bike Hire

Scan me for more information.

Alan Rogers Code: SW2750
63 accommodations
200 pitches
GPS: 59.36765, 12.13962
Post Code: S-672 91

Årjäng, Värmlands Län

Sommarvik Camping

www.alanrogers.com/sw2750
booking@sommarvik.se
Tel: +46 57 312 060
www.sommarvik.se

Open (Touring Pitches):
All year.

Sommarvik Camping (also known as Årjäng Camping & Stugor) is in beautiful surroundings with some of the 350 pitches overlooking the clear waters of the Västra Silen lake in peaceful countryside. The 350 numbered pitches are arranged in terraces on a hillside interspersed with pines and birches, with 200 set aside for touring, all with 10A electricity hook-ups; 40 also include water and drainage.

A large restaurant offers a full range of meals, soft drinks, beers, wines and takeaway meals. Close to reception, a heated swimming pool with a paddling pool, terraces and sun loungers has fine views down to the lake. The pool and most activities on-site attract daily charges. The lake with its sandy beach is popular and safe for children.

Five sanitary units provide shower cubicles (hot showers on payment), washbasins, toilets, family bathrooms, facilities for disabled visitors and baby changing. All are clean and acceptable but may be stretched in high season. Campers kitchens. Laundry facilities. Motorhome services. All activities and amenities are open seasonally. Small shop. Bar, restaurant and takeaway (15/6-15/8). Heated outdoor swimming and paddling pools. Good play areas (one with a pirate ship). Bicycle hire. Internet access. 'Quick stop' pitches for overnight stays. Youth hostel and conference centre. WiFi (charged).

Key Features

 Open All Year

 Pets Accepted

 Disabled Facilities

 Swimming Pool

 Play Area

 Bar/Restaurant

 Bike Hire

 Sailing

Scan me for
more information.

Alan Rogers Code: SW2760
24 accommodations
180 pitches
GPS: 59.54625, 13.34132
Post Code: S-665 91

Kil, Värmlands Län

www.alanrogers.com/sw2760
info@frykenbaden.se
Tel: +46 55 440 940
www.frykenbaden.se

Open (Touring Pitches):
All year.

Frykenbadens Camping

Frykenbadens Camping is a well cared for campsite in a quiet wooded area on the southern shore of Lake Fryken, taking around 180 units on grassy meadows surrounded by trees. One area nearer the lake is gently sloping, the other is flat with numbered pitches arranged in rows, 150 with electricity (10A) and 11 with hardstanding.

Reception, a good shop, restaurant and takeaway are located in a traditional Swedish house surrounded by lawns sloping down to the shore, with minigolf, a play barn and playground, with a pet area also close by. Frykenbadens Camping is a quiet, relaxing place to stay, away from the busier and more famous lakes.

Tables and benches are near the lake, where swimming and canoeing are possible. A good value restaurant is at the adjacent golf club which can be reached by a pleasant walk. Fryken is a long, narrow lake, said to be one of the deepest in Sweden, and it is a centre for angling.

The two sanitary blocks are of a good standard and heated in cool weather with showers on payment, open washbasins, a laundry room and a room for families and disabled visitors. Well equipped campers' kitchen. Motorhome services. Shop. Pub serving food. Minigolf. Play barn and playground. Boules. Lake swimming. Canoes, rowing boats and bicycles for hire. WiFi (charged).

Key Features

 Open All Year

 Pets Accepted

 Disabled Facilities

 Play Area

 Bar/Restaurant

 Bike Hire

 Fishing

 Sailing

Scan me for more information.

Alan Rogers Code: SW2836
137 accommodations
450 pitches
GPS: 61.00853, 14.53178
Post Code: S-792 25

Mora, Dalarnas Län

www.alanrogers.com/sw2836
info@moraparken.se
Tel: +46 25 027 600
www.moraparken.se

Open (Touring Pitches):
All year.

Mora Parkens Camping

Mora, at the northern end of Lake Silijan, is surrounded by small localities all steeped in history and culture. On the island of Sollerön, south of Mora, is evidence of a large Viking burial ground. Traditional handicrafts are still practised in the region. Mora is lively, friendly and attractive.

The campsite, which is good for family holidays, is only ten minutes' walk from the town. The camping area with its 600 pitches (around 450 for touring and 313 with 10/16A electricity) is large, grassy, open and flat. It is bordered by clumps of trees and a stream. The staff are pleasant and helpful.

Travel to Nusnäs, an old village with documents going back to the Middle Ages, and see the production of the brightly coloured wooden horse, Dala. Every household should have two for luck. Winding country roads lead you through rich farmland to the pretty half timbered houses in Bergkarlås/Vattnås.

Four fully equipped toilet blocks. Campers' kitchen. Laundry. Shop (Seasonal). Restaurant/bar. Sauna. Fishing. Minigolf. Playground. 10-pin Bowling alley and Shuffleboard lanes. Canoe hire. WiFi over site (free).

Key Features

 Open All Year

 Pets Accepted

 Disabled Facilities

 Swimming Pool

 Play Area

 Bar/Restaurant

 Bike Hire

 Fishing

Scan me for more information.

457

Alan Rogers Code: SW2780
40 accommodations
650 pitches
GPS: 59.25538, 15.18978
Post Code: S-702 30

Örebro, Örebro Län

www.alanrogers.com/sw2780
camping@gustavsvik.se
Tel: +46 19 196 900
www.gustavsvik.se

Open (Touring Pitches):
All Year.

Gustavsvik Camping

Gustavsvik is one of the most modern and most visited camping and leisure parks in Sweden. This resort-style site is ideally situated almost halfway between Oslo and Stockholm or Gothenburg and Stockholm, at the junction of the E18 and E20 roads. This large campsite provides 650 marked and numbered pitches partly shaded by birch and beech trees, all with at least 10A electricity connections, and others with 16A, TV connection, water and drainage. There are also three partly shaded areas for tents.

'The Lost City' is an impressive paradise for swimming (extra charge and weekend booking essential). The leisure park includes adventure golf, a mini zoo, playgrounds, pools and a water slide and a swimming lake, plus a private fishing lake. The site includes luxury cottages to rent with 'stay and swim' packages available.

Three heated toilet blocks including washbasins with dividers, free hot showers, family rooms, facilities for children and disabled visitors. Very well equipped kitchens with free hot water. Dining area. Washing machine and dryers. Motorhome services. Shower room for pets. Well stocked shop. Restaurant and pub (July/Aug). Takeaway. Swimming pool complex. TV room and playroom. Three playgrounds. Arcade with games room. Adventure golf. Football. Trim trail. Fishing lake. Mini zoo. Bicycle hire. Internet room. WiFi (free).

Key Features

 Open All Year

 Pets Accepted

 Disabled Facilities

 Swimming Pool

 Play Area

 Bar/Restaurant

 Bike Hire

 Fishing

Scan me for more information.

Alan Rogers Code: SW2825
45 accommodations
170 pitches
GPS: 59.28140, 15.90510
Post Code: S-732 92

Arboga, Västmanlands Län

Herrfallet Camping

www.alanrogers.com/sw2825
reception@herrfallet.se
Tel: +46 58 940 110
www.herrfallet.se

Open (Touring Pitches):
All year.

Open all year, Herrfallet Camping is situated on a peninsula and designated nature reserve, on Lake Hjälmaren, one of Sweden's large lakes. There is a small beach on the site and the atmosphere is friendly and 'green'. There are 170 pitches of which 165 with electricity hook-ups (10/16A). A few of these overlook the lake, where you can hire boats, canoes, pedal boats and go fishing (free of charge). You can explore the peaceful surroundings by bicycle, which you can hire at reception.

There are 40 large cottages of an excellent standard with many situated close to the beach where you can swim in the clear water. The most special of these cottages is a 'honeymoon house' with its own beach, jetty and boat. Five smaller hiker cabins are suitable for couples looking for a short stay. The site's fully licensed restaurant organises special events, such as barbecue parties and troubadours.

Three sanitary blocks, one basic for the summer season, two with central heating. Open washbasins, showers (charged). Three family bathrooms (charged). Provision for disabled visitors. Fully equipped kitchen and laundry facilities (charged). Baby room. Motorhome services. Sauna cottage with shower and relaxing room. Sami style hut for barbecue parties. Well stocked shop (Seasonal). Restaurant and bar (Seasonal). Takeaway. Pedal car, pedal boat, bicycle, canoe and boat hire. Fishing (free). Minigolf. Football field. Fitness trail. Playground. TV room. WiFi (free).

Key Features

 Open All Year

 Pets Accepted

 Disabled Facilities

 Play Area

 Bar/Restaurant

 Bike Hire

 Fishing

 Sailing

Scan me for
more information.

Alan Rogers Code: SW2842
20 accommodations
380 pitches
GPS: 59.29560, 17.92315
Post Code: S-127 31

Skärholmen, Stockholms Län

www.alanrogers.com/sw2842
bredangcamping@telia.com
Tel: +46 89 770 71
www.bredangcamping.se

Open (Touring Pitches):
Mid May - Mid September.

Bredäng Stockholm

Bredäng Camping is a busy city site, with easy access to Stockholm city centre. Large and fairly level, with very little shade, there are 380 pitches of which 204 have electricity (10A) and 115 have hardstanding. A separate area has been provided for tents. Reception is open from 08.00-22.00 in the main season (12/6-20/8), reduced hours in low season, and English is spoken.

A three-day public transport card is available from the Tube station. The nearest Tube station is five minutes' walk; trains run about every ten minutes between 05.00 and 02.00, and the journey takes about twenty minutes. The local shopping centre is seven minutes away and a two-minute walk through the woods brings you to a very attractive lake and beach.

Key Features

 Pets Accepted

 Disabled Facilities

 Beach Access

 Play Area

 Bar/Restaurant

Four heated sanitary units of a high standard provide British style WCs, controllable hot showers and some washbasins in cubicles. One has a baby room, a unit for disabled visitors and a first aid room. Cooking facilities are in three units around the site. Laundry facilities. Motorhome services and car wash. Well stocked shop, bar, takeaway and fully licensed restaurant (Open 1 May - 15 Sept). Hostel. Cabins. Sauna. Playground. Minigolf. Frisbee Golf. Outdoor Gym. WiFi throughout (free).

Scan me for more information.

Alan Rogers Code: SW2690
125 accommodations
1350 pitches
GPS: 57.27436, 17.04851
Post Code: S-38773

Byxelkrok, Kalmar Län

www.alanrogers.com/sw2690
info@bodasand.se
Tel: +46 48 522 200
www.bodasand.se

Open (Touring Pitches):
Start May - Mid September.

Camping Böda Sand

Camping Böda Sand is beautifully situated at the northern end of the island of Öland and is one of Sweden's largest and most modern campsites. Most of the 1,350 pitches have electricity (10/16A) and TV connections, 1,100 have water and wastewater drainage.

The pitches and 125 cabins to rent are spread out in a pine forest, very close to a fabulous 20 km. long, white sand beach. Here you will also find a restaurant, kiosks, toilets and beach showers, and a relaxation centre with an indoor/outdoor pool. The reception, the toilet blocks and the services at this site are excellent and comprehensive.

Entertainment and activities both for children and adults are very extensive, with a comprehensive range to choose from every week during high season.

Seven heated sanitary blocks provide a good supply of shower cubicles, washbasins, some washbasin suites and WCs. Facilities for babies and disabled visitors (key at reception). Well equipped laundry rooms. Excellent kitchens with cookers, ovens, microwaves, dishwashers (free) and sinks. Motorhome services. Supermarket and bakery (seasonal). Pizzeria, café, pub and restaurant (May-Aug). Takeaway. Bicycle hire, pedal cars and pedal boat hire. Minigolf. 9-hole golf course. Play area. Indoor/outdoor swimming pool (on the beach). Trim trails. Family entertainment and activities. WiFi (charged).

Key Features

 Pets Accepted

 Disabled Facilities

 Beach Access

 Swimming Pool

 Play Area

 Bar/Restaurant

 Bike Hire

 Sailing

Scan me for more information.

461

Capital Bern
Currency Swiss Franc (CHf)
Language German, French,
Italian and regional variants
Time Zone CET (GMT+1)
Telephone Code +41

Shops Hours vary throughout
the year, with many shops
operating on shorter hours in
low and shoulder seasons. In
high season 10am to 6pm Mon
to Fri, and until 4pm Sat.

Money ATMs are widespread,
accessible 24hrs a day and have
multilingual instructions. Most
restaurants and shops accept
Euros, change given in Swiss
Francs at daily exchange rate.

Accessible Travel Like Sweden,
Switzerland ranks highly when it
comes to ease of access for the
less abled. Transport and public
spaces offer adapted facilities
and most walking trails are
wheelchair-friendly.

Travelling with children
Switzerland is a great
destination for families. Most
restaurants offer a kids menu.
Children aged 6 or under travel
free on trains.

EU Travel Switzerland is not an
EU member state but is located
within the Schengen area.

There are no Low
Emission Zones currently
in place.

●●●●● **Accessibility Score**
View our digital e-guide & find out more at
alanrogers.com/open-to-all

Tourism website myswitzerland.com

Public Holidays 1 Jan New Year's Day · Mar/
Apr Good Friday · Mar/Apr Easter Monday
· May Ascension · May/Jun Whit Monday ·
May/Jun Corpus Christi · 1 Aug National Day
· 1 Nov All Saints · 25 Dec Christmas Day ·
26 Dec Boxing Day. Other public holidays
may be observed at a regional level. Always
check before travelling.

Driving in Switzerland An annual road tax
is levied on all cars using Swiss motorways,
and the 'Vignette' windscreen sticker must be
purchased at the border or in advance, plus
a separate one for a towed caravan or trailer.
Many mountain resorts are vehicle-free. You
are encouraged to use Park 'n' Ride schemes
and access the resorts using cable cars. Drink-
driving, using a mobile whilst driving and sat
navs that warn of speed cameras are illegal.

Switzerland

View all campsites in Switzerland
alanrogers.com/switzerland

See campsite map page 487

Climate

Mild and refreshing in the north. South of the Alps it is warmer, influenced by the Mediterranean.

	Jan	Feb	Mar	Apr	May	Jun	Jul	Aug	Sep	Oct	Nov	Dec
High	3	4	10	16	19	22	25	23	19	14	8	4
Low	-1	-2	2	6	9	13	15	14	11	7	3	0

A small, wealthy country best known for its outstanding mountainous scenery, fine cheeses, delicious chocolates, Swiss bank accounts and enviable lifestyles. Centrally situated in Europe, it shares its borders with four countries: France, Austria, Germany and Italy, each one having its own cultural influence on Switzerland. Switzerland boasts a picture-postcard landscape of mountains, valleys, waterfalls and glaciers.

With its snowy peaks and rolling hills, the Bernese Oberland is the most popular area; Gstaad is a favourite haunt of wealthy skiers, while the mild climate and breezy conditions around Lake Thun are perfect for watersports and other outdoor activities.

German-speaking Zurich is a multicultural metropolis with over 50 museums, sophisticated shops and colourful festivals set against a breathtaking backdrop of lakes and mountains. The southeast of Switzerland has densely forested mountain slopes and the wealthy and glamorous resort of Saint Moritz.

Geneva, Montreux and Lausanne on the northern shores of Lake Geneva make up the bulk of French Switzerland, with vineyards that border the lakes and medieval towns. The southernmost canton, Ticino, is home to the Italian-speaking Swiss, with the Mediterranean style lakeside resorts of Lugano and Locarno.

Alan Rogers Code: CH9140
120 accommodations
150 pitches
GPS: 47.13333, 8.58998
Post Code: CH-6314

Unterägeri, Zug

www.alanrogers.com/ch9140
info@campingunteraegeri.ch
Tel: +41 41 750 3928
www.campingunteraegeri.ch

Open (Touring Pitches):
All year.

Camping Unterägeri

Camping Unterägeri is located next to Lake Agerisee in a quiet, semi-rural area screened by trees and hedges. It provides 270 pitches, 150 for touring, all with a 10A electricity supply. There are 120 seasonal pitches spread throughout the site. The touring pitches are grassy, level and some have hardstandings. The town is a short walk away, as is Lake Agerisee.

The site is popular with campers who enjoy hiking, mountain biking, and cycling, and with those who just wish to relax in a lake and mountain setting. Swimming in the lake is popular and the campsite has its own beach.

Three clean sanitary blocks (two open all year and heated in winter) are spaced across the site and have facilities for disabled visitors. Good dishwashing area. Washing machines and dryer. Small shop for essential and fresh bread (Easter-Oct). Restaurant and bar (main season only). Playground. Fishing. Boat launching. TV room. Dogs are not accepted. WiFi (free).

Key Features

 Open All Year

 Disabled Facilities

 Play Area

 Fishing

Scan me for more information.

Alan Rogers Code: CH9045
5 accommodations
69 pitches
GPS: 47.05000, 7.11000
Post Code: CH-3235

Erlach, Bern

Camping Erlach

www.alanrogers.com/ch9045
info@camping-erlach.ch
Tel: +41 32 513 01 00
www.camping-erlach.ch

Open (Touring Pitches):
Easter - Mid October.

Gemeinde Camping Erlach is a lakeside site within walking distance of the small town of Erlach. With only 69 touring pitches of small to medium size, it fills up quickly during June, July and August, especially at weekends. Some pitches have hardstandings suitable for motorhomes and there are a number of tent-only pitches available. Many pitches have lovely views over the Bielersee, and the marina, with numerous lake cruise options, are only a few minutes walk away.

Although technically in the Bern canton, it is close to Neuchâtel, which can be reached by many excellent ferries that stop near the site. The trip takes an hour each way, and the charming sandstone elegance of the old town of Neuchâtel has much to offer visitors, from the 16th-century fountains by Laurent Perroud to the museums of art and history.

Key Features

 Pets Accepted

 Disabled Facilities

 Play Area

 Bike Hire

 Fishing

The modern, heated sanitary block is of a high standard with free showers. Facilities for disabled campers. An older block is unisex and has limited facilities. Washing machine and dryer. Motorhome services. Shop. Restaurant/bar with shaded terrace overlooking the lake. Fishing. Boules area. Play area. Pedalo hire. WiFi (free). Pods available for hire.

Scan me for
more information.

Alan Rogers Code: CH9172
270 accommodations
60 pitches
GPS: 47.64458, 8.86020
Post Code: CH-8264

Eschenz, St Gallen

www.alanrogers.com/ch9172
info@huettenberg.ch
Tel: +41 52 741 23 37
www.camping-huettenberg.ch

Open (Touring Pitches):
Early April - End October.

Camping Hüttenberg

Camping Hüttenberg is located in eastern Switzerland, in the middle of the beautiful Lake Constance and Rhine landscape. Family-owned and run, this peaceful site is situated on the edge of the forest with wonderful views of Lake Constance and the Rhine. 270 permanent pitches. 60 touring pitches, with views of the Lake and Rhine or near the swimming pool. 10amp electric. Bungalows, PODhouses, and Tent Bungalows for hire.

An ideal starting point for hiking and cycling with the numerous well-marked routes and trails nearby. In the vicinity, plenty to see such as the historic town of Stein am Rhein, Steckborn, Diessenhofen, old town of Schaffhausen, Munot, Rhine Falls, flower island Mainau, Säntis, Conny-Land amusement park.

Three modern sanitary facilities. Private bathrooms. Two wheelchair-accessible facilities. Two baby changing rooms. Dishwasher. Washing Machine. Tumble Dryer. Camper Kitchen with cooker, fridge/freezer. Motorhome service station. Campinggaz. Self service shop. Bistro with sun terrace. Youth Room with TV, games console, table football, darts. Swimming Pool. Children's Paddling Pool. Table tennis. Trampolines. Playground. Table minigolf. Public Barbeque. Pets allowed on campsite only. WiFi.

Key Features

 Pets Accepted

 Disabled Facilities

 Swimming Pool

 Play Area

 Bar/Restaurant

 Bike Hire

Scan me for more information.

Alan Rogers Code: CH9860
48 accommodations
250 pitches
GPS: 46.46408, 9.93240
Post Code: CH-7504

Pontresina, Graubünden

www.alanrogers.com/ch9860
mail@camping-morteratsch.ch
Tel: +41 81 842 62 85
www.camping-morteratsch.ch

Open (Touring Pitches):
All year.

Camping Morteratsch

Camping Morteratsch is a well-equipped mountain site in stunning scenery near St. Moritz. Close to Pontresina, it lies next to the road leading to the Bernina Pass and Tirano in Italy and nestles in the valley floor between fir-clad mountains. There are about 250 pitches for touring units and tents in summer, about half with electricity. Some are in small clearings amongst tall trees and some in a larger open space. They are neither numbered nor marked, and their size is dictated by the natural space between the trees.

Being in a mountain valley, the grass is thin over a stony base with tarmac roads running through. Four small streams run through this long, narrow site with lovely views on each side. A modern reception building houses a comprehensively stocked shop, bistro, TV lounge with kitchen, enormous drying room, and WiFi point.

Three fully equipped toilet blocks can be heated. Family bathroom suites are available. Four-person sauna. Suite for disabled visitors. Washing machines, dryers, and ski kit drying room. Dog wash. Uniquely, there is a facility for refilling most types of propane cylinders. Well stocked shop. Simple bistro within the shop. Grill and snack bar in a teepee (June-Aug plus winter schedule). Guest room with TV, tables, and chairs, and self-service kitchen. Communal fondue room. Internet, telephone, and free WiFi. Bicycle hire. Fishing. Playground. Torch and long leads useful.

Key Features

 Pets Accepted

 Disabled Facilities

 Play Area

 Bike Hire

 Fishing

Scan me for more information.

Alan Rogers Code: CH9950
40 accommodations
210 pitches
GPS: 45.99592, 8.90838
Post Code: CH-6933

Muzzano, Ticino

www.alanrogers.com/ch9950
camping.muzzano@tcs.ch
Tel: +41 91 994 77 88
www.tcs.ch

Open (Touring Pitches):
All year.

TCS Camping Lugano

Camping Lugano is a modern south-facing site leading onto Lake Lugano. It must rank as one of the better sites in Switzerland for a complete family holiday. There are 250 numbered pitches (around 200 for touring units) all with 10A Europlug and 26 have water and drainage. Trees in most parts of the site offer shade to those who prefer less direct sunshine. Cars must be left in the car park, which makes the site less cluttered and safer for children. The site is only a short distance from the airport, so there will be some daytime aircraft noise. Roads have been re-laid and a marina has been built giving full access for watersports enthusiasts.

Well placed for exploring Lugano, southern Switzerland, and northern Italy, or simply for enjoying the facilities of the site. A good, large swimming pool (supervised when busy) and a children's pool have been added and one can also bathe from the sandy beach.

Key Features

 Open All Year

 Pets Accepted

 Disabled Facilities

 Swimming Pool

 Play Area

 Bar/Restaurant

 Sailing

The original toilet block (refurbished) and a modern one include a baby room and a suite for disabled visitors are heated in cool weather. Washing machines and dryers. Motorhome services. Gas supplies. Shop. Bar/restaurant with pleasant terrace (Mar-Nov). Swimming pools (May-mid Oct). Day and TV rooms. Playground. Bouncy castle and children's train (in season). Children's games room. One tennis court. Volleyball court. Football pitch. Fridge hire. Multisports area. Marina. Raft with slide on the lake. WiFi (free). Communal electric barbecue. Accommodation for rent.

Scan me for more information.

Alan Rogers Code: CH9460
250 pitches
GPS: 46.58807, 7.91077
Post Code: CH-3822

Lauterbrunnen, Bern

Camping Jungfrau

www.alanrogers.com/ch9460
info@camping-jungfrau.ch
Tel: +41 33 856 20 10
www.campingjungfrau.swiss

Open (Touring Pitches):
All year.

This friendly and ever-popular site has a very imposing and dramatic situation in a steep valley with a fine view of the Jungfrau at the end. It is a busy site and, although you should usually find space, do not arrive too late in the high season. A fairly extensive area is made up of grass pitches and hardcore access roads. All 391 pitches (250 for touring) have shade in parts, electrical connections (13A) and 50 have water and drainage also.

Over 35% of the pitches are taken by seasonal caravans, chalets to rent and two tour operators. Family-owned, with friendly managers, you can be sure of a warm welcome and English is spoken. You can laze here amid real mountain scenery, though it does lose the sun a little early.

Three fully equipped modern sanitary blocks can be heated in winter and one provides facilities for disabled visitors. Baby baths. Laundry facilities. Motorhome services. Well equipped campers' kitchen. Excellent shop. Self-service restaurant with takeaway (all year). General room with tables and chairs, TV, drinks machines, amusements. Playgrounds and covered play area. Excursions and some entertainment in high season. Mountain bike hire. ATM. Drying room. Ski store. Free shuttle bus in winter. Internet point. WiFi throughout (free).

Key Features

  Open All Year

  Pets Accepted

  Disabled Facilities

  Play Area

  Bar/Restaurant

  Skiing

  Bike Hire

  Fishing

Scan me for more information.

Alan Rogers Code: CH9665
127 accommodations
80 pitches
GPS: 46.30399, 7.79474
Post Code: CH-3942

Raron, Valais

www.alanrogers.com/ch9665
info@camping-simplonblick.ch
Tel: +41 27 934 32 05
www.simplonblick.ch

Open (Touring Pitches):
All year.

Camping Simplonblick

Camping Simplonblick is a fairly small, traditional-style campsite close to the beautiful Valais mountains. The site makes a great base for cycling or walking in this popular region. Pitches are generally level, on grass and there are a number of mobile homes available to rent. The playground, giant chess, and the modernised pool should keep younger guests entertained.

The imposing, nearby Aletsch glacier is reputedly the longest in Europe at around 14 miles in length and shouldn't be missed if you're a keen hiker. If you've got a head for heights then you could take a walk across the Charles Kuonen Hängebrücke. The bridge is one of the longest free-hanging pedestrian bridges in the world and the longest in Europe at just under half a kilometer long. It crosses the Grabengufer ravine at a height of 85 meters and with a width of 65cm, if you suffer from vertigo, you might want to give this one a miss. Numerous skiing options are available with the popular resort of Crans-Montana around a 40-minute drive away.

Outdoor heated swimming pool with a small slide. Gas and charcoal BBQs permitted. Dogs permitted. Laundry with washing machines and dryers. Snack bar (high season only) Bar. Small shop with fresh bread available. Gas exchange. Trampoline. Playground. Table tennis.

Key Features

 Book Online

 Open All Year

 Pets Accepted

 Swimming Pool

 Play Area

 Bar/Restaurant

 Bike Hire

 Scan me for more information.

Alan Rogers Code: CH9425
3 accommodations
84 pitches
GPS: 46.67999, 7.81728
Post Code: CH-3800

Interlaken, Bern

www.alanrogers.com/ch9425
info@camping-alpenblick.ch
Tel: +41 33 822 77 57
www.camping-alpenblick.ch

Open (Touring Pitches):
All year.

Camping Alpenblick

Alpenblick is an all-year site, located at the heart of the Bernese Oberland just 100 m. from Lake Thun. Many improvements, including an excellent toilet block, have been made in recent years. A Swiss chalet-style building houses the reception, shop and a bar/restaurant that is very popular with campers and local residents alike. There are around 100 touring pitches and a further 80 residential pitches. The touring pitches all have 10/16A electrical connections and a number of good hardstanding pitches are available for motorhomes.

Campers here may request a special tourist card with many benefits including free local bus transport. This is, of course, a superb area for cycling and walking. The lake is very popular for all manner of watersports and cruisers depart from a point very close to Alpenblick. The site's restaurant specialises in local food such as 'schnitzelbrot' and dining on the terrace is possible in good weather.

Sanitary block with hot showers, some washbasins in cubicles and a family shower room. Facilities for disabled visitors. Laundry facilities. Shop (Seasonal) with daily delivery of bread. Bar, restaurant and takeaway (all year). Bar and barbecue for socialising and events. Playground. Boules. Basketball. WiFi throughout (charged).

Key Features

 Open All Year

 Pets Accepted

 Disabled Facilities

 Beach Access

 Play Area

 Bar/Restaurant

Scan me for more information.

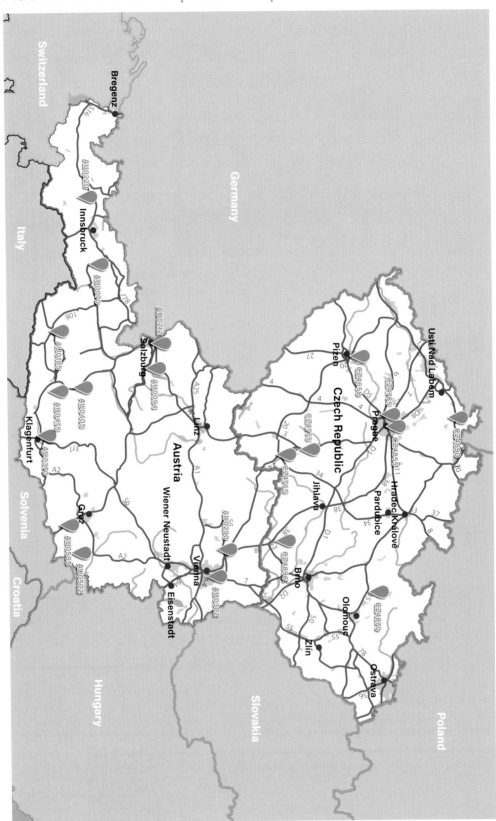

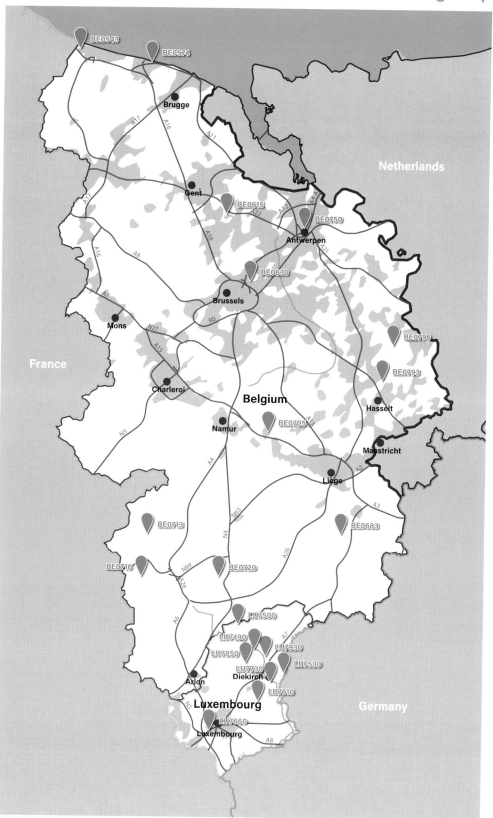

Croatia & Solvenia Map

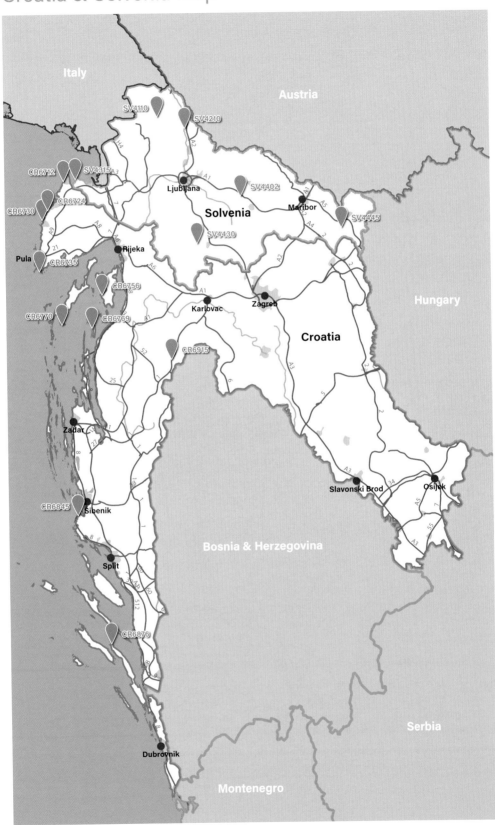

Italy

Austria

SV4110

SV4210

CR6712

SV4315 A3

Ljubljana

SV4402

Maribor

A5

SV4445

CR6724

CR6730

Solvenia

SV4430

Pula

CR6735

Rijeka

CR6756

Hungary

Karlovac

Zagreb

CR6770

CR6769

Croatia

CR6915

Zadar

Slavonski Brod

Osijek

CR6845

Sibenik

Split

Bosnia & Herzegovina

CR6876

Serbia

Dubrovnik

Montenegro

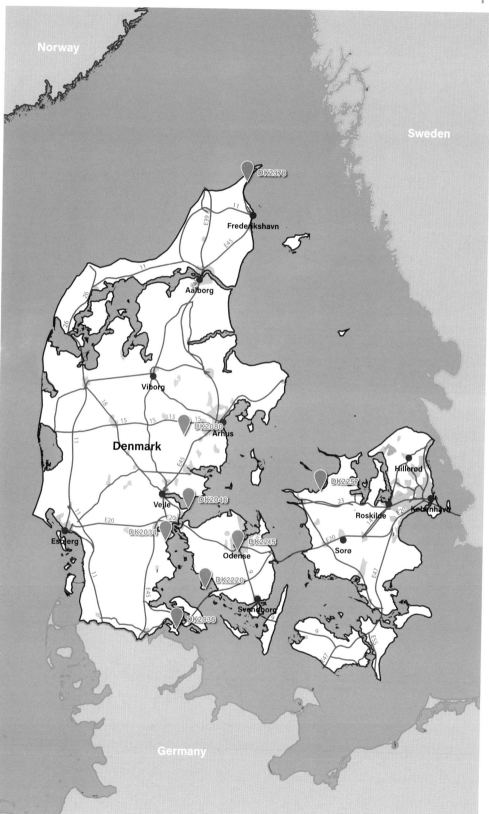

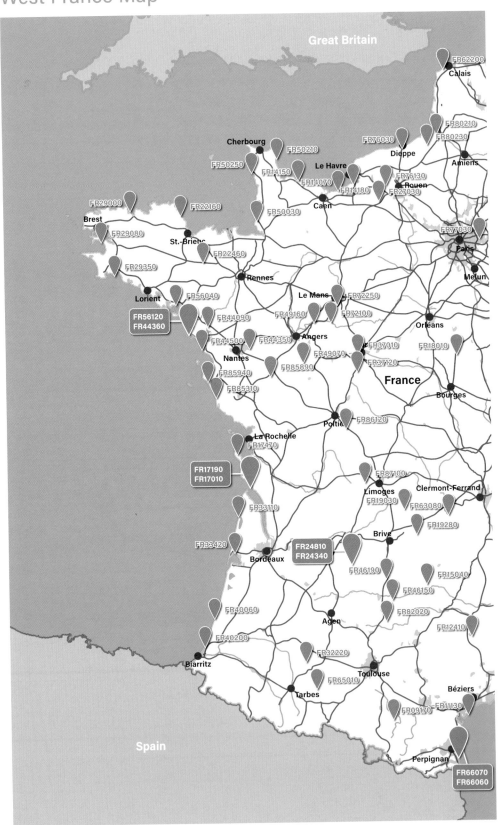

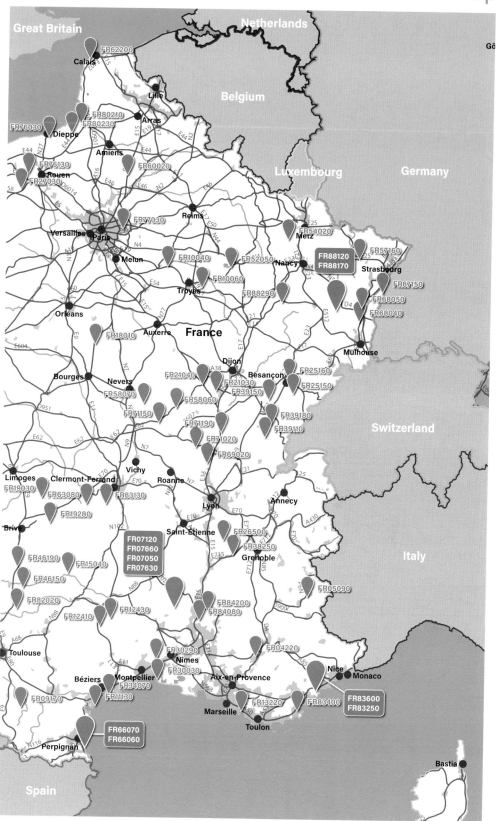

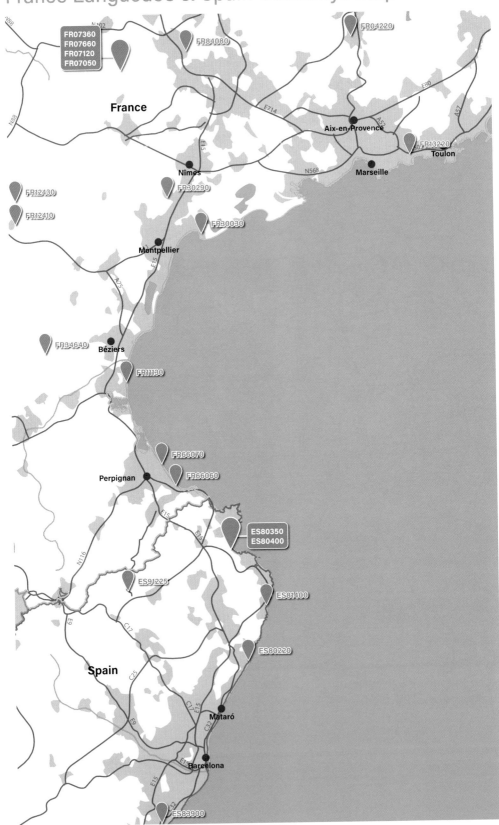

FR07360
FR07660
FR07120
FR07050

FR84080

FR04220

France

Aix-en-Provence

FR13220
Toulon

Nîmes

FR30290

Marseille

FR12430

FR12410

FR30030

Montpellier

FR34640 Béziers

FR11130

FR66070

FR66060

Perpignan

ES80350
ES80400

ES91225

ES81400

ES80220

Spain

Mataró

Barcelona

ES83900

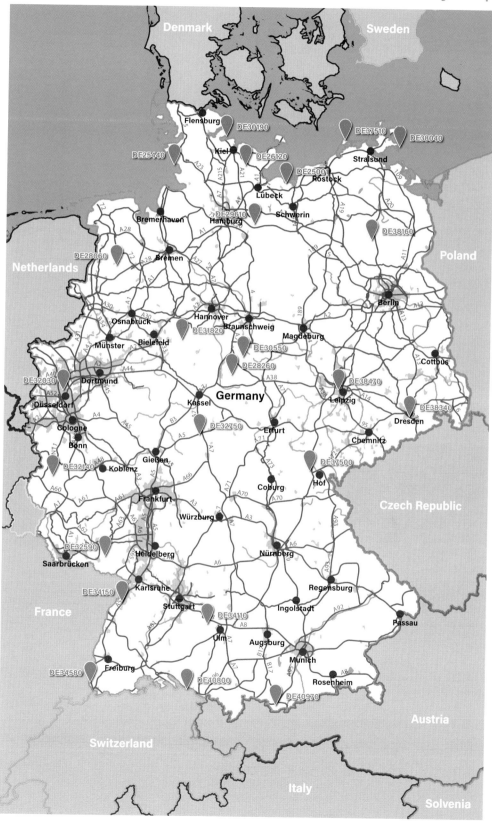

Great Britain & Ireland Map

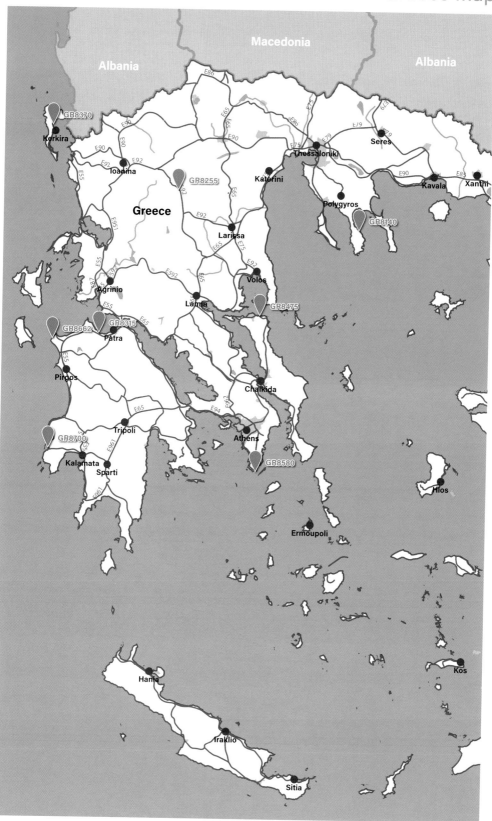

Italy Map

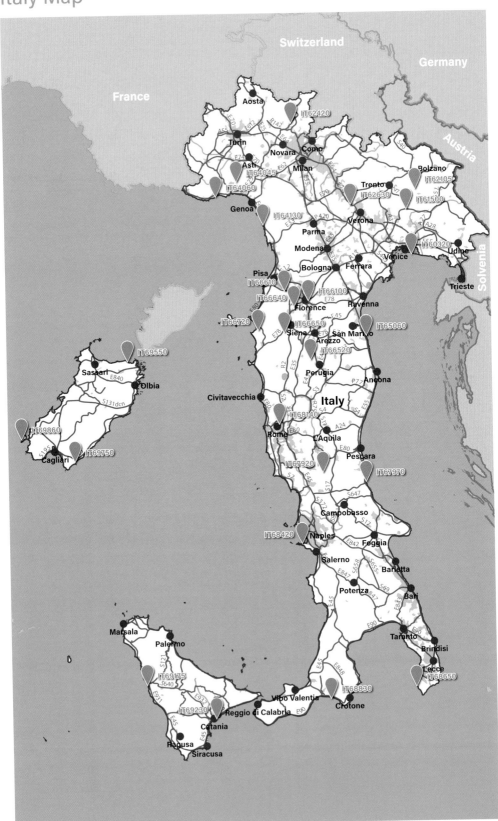

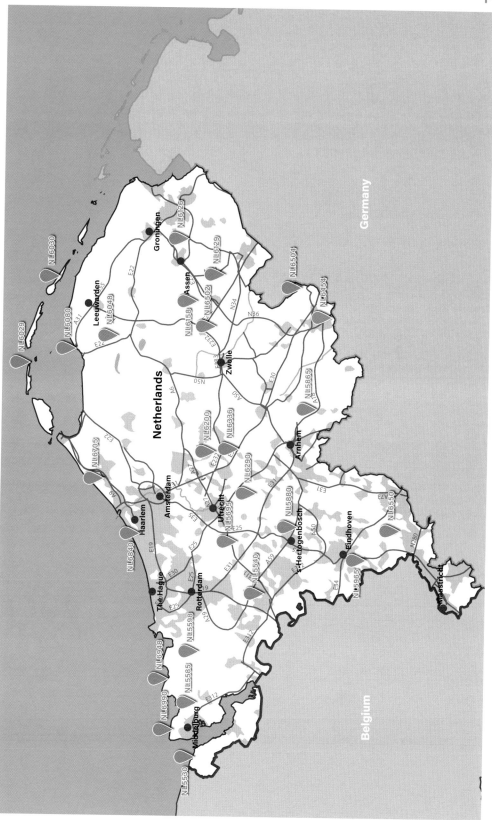

Portugal & Spain Map

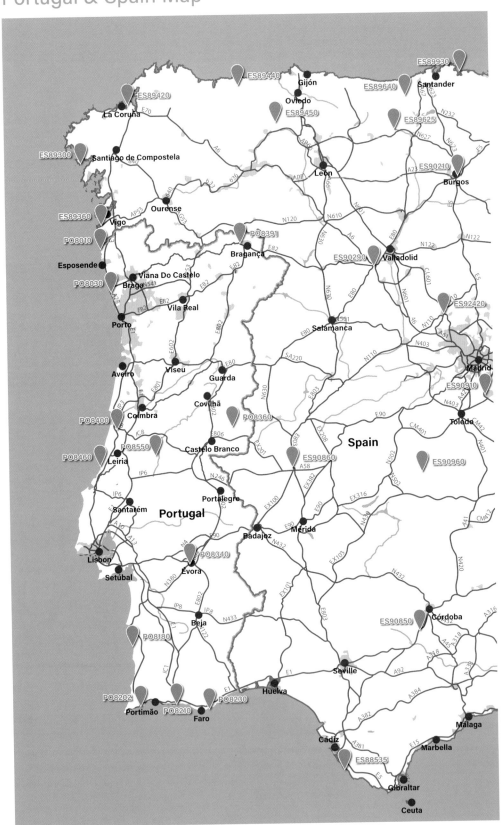

Sweden & Norway Map

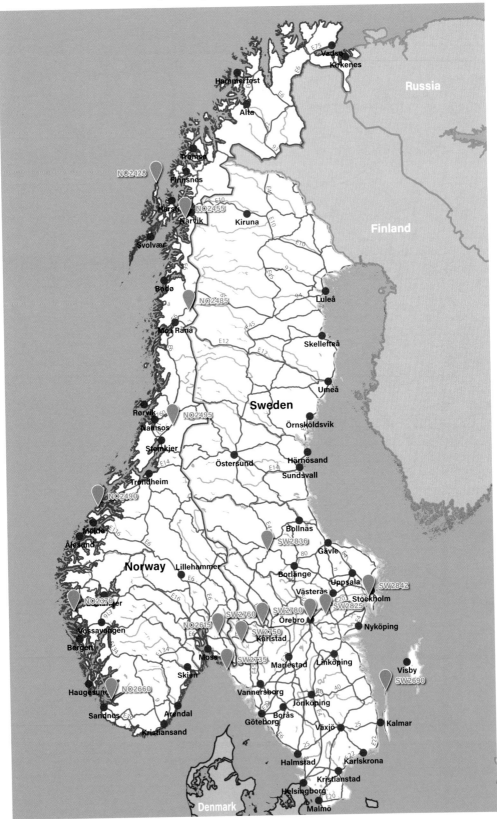

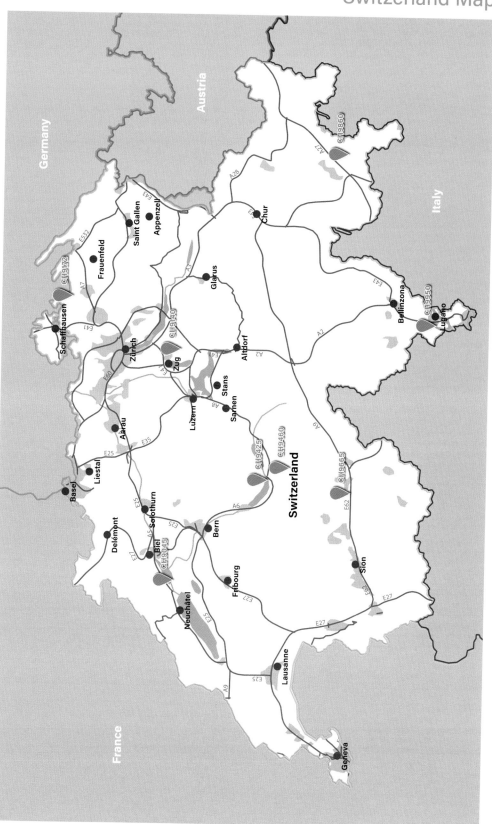

Index By Location

Austria **12**
Carinthia, Döbriach.................................24
Carinthia, Klagenfurt..............................23
Carinthia, Rennweg..................................25
Lower Austria, Tulln 19
Salzburg, Salzburg City 17
Salzburg, St Gilgen/Abersee 18
Steiermark, Bairisch Kölldorf..................21
Steiermark, Leibnitz................................22
Tirol, Lienz-Tristach................................16
Tirol, Umhausen 14
Tirol, Zell-am-Ziller.................................15
Vienna, Wien-Ost.....................................20

Belgium **26**
Flanders, Antwerp....................................30
Flanders, Brabant.....................................33
Flanders, East Flanders............................34
Flanders, Limburg..............................31, 32
Flanders, West Flanders.....................28, 29
Wallonia, Liège...................................36, 37
Wallonia, Luxembourg.......................38, 39
Wallonia, Namur......................................35

Croatia **40**
Dalmatia, Loviste.....................................51
Dalmatia, Primosten................................50
Istria, Medulin...45
Istria, Porec...43
Istria, Rovinj..44
Istria, Umag..42
Karlovac, Rakovica...................................49
Kvarner, Banjol.......................................48
Kvarner, Nerezine....................................47
Kvarner, Punat..46

Czech Republic **52**
Central Bohemia, Prague....................55, 56
North Bohemia, Severocesky....................57
North Moravia, Severomoravsky...............58
South Bohemia, Jihocesky...................60, 61
South Moravia, Jihomoravsky...................59
West Bohemia, Plzeň/Maly Bolevec 54

Denmark... **62**
Islands, Fyn.......................................69, 70
Islands, Sjælland.....................................71
Jutland, Nordjylland................................64
Jutland, Sønderjylland.......................67, 68
Jutland, Vejle 66
Jutland, Århus...65

France.. **72**
Alsace, Bas-Rhin.....................................104
Alsace, Haut-Rhin............................105, 106
Aquitaine, Dordogne.......................153, 154
Aquitaine, Gironde..........................150, 152
Aquitaine, Landes...........................155, 156
Auvergne, Cantal 142
Auvergne, Puy-de-Dôme.................140, 141
Brittany, Côtes d`Armor......................77, 78
Brittany, Finistère.............................74–76
Brittany, Morbihan...........................79, 80
Burgundy, Côte d`Or.......................130, 131
Burgundy, Nièvre............................125, 126
Burgundy, Saône-et-Loire...............127–129
Champagne-Ardenne, Aube 96, 97
Champagne-Ardenne, Haute-Marne........98
Côte d'Azur, Var..............................177–179
Franche-Comté, Doubs.....................134, 135
Franche-Comté, Jura...............132, 133, 136
Languedoc-Roussillon, Aude 169
Languedoc-Roussillon, Gard.............166, 167
Languedoc-Roussillon, Hérault...............168
Languedoc-Roussillon, Pyrénées-Orientales...170, 171
Limousin, Corrèze...........................137, 138
Limousin, Haute-Vienne.........................139
Lorraine, Meurthe-et-Moselle 99
Lorraine, Moselle 103
Lorraine, Vosges.............................100–102
Midi-Pyrénées, Ariège.............................165
Midi-Pyrénées, Aveyron...................160, 161

Midi-Pyrénées, Gers................................159
Midi-Pyrénées, Hautes-Pyrénées 158
Midi-Pyrénées, Lot..........................162, 163
Midi-Pyrénées, Tarn-et-Garonne.............164
Nord/Pas-de-Calais, Pas-de-Calais.............93
Normandy, Calvados..........................84–86
Normandy, Eure..87
Normandy, Manche........................... 81–83
Normandy, Seine-Maritime..................88, 89
Paris/Ile de France, Seine-et-Marne..........94
Pays de la Loire, Loire-Atlantique 109–112
Pays de la Loire, Maine-et-Loire......113, 114
Pays de la Loire, Sarthe..................107, 108
Picardy, Oise..92
Picardy, Somme..................................90, 91
Poitou-Charentes, Charente-Maritime ...121–123
Poitou-Charentes, Vienne 124
Provence, Alpes-de-Haute-Provence.........172
Provence, Bouches du Rhône...................173
Provence, Hautes-Alpes 174
Provence, Vaucluse.........................175, 176
Rhône Alpes, Ardèche......................143–146
Rhône Alpes, Drôme...............................148
Rhône Alpes, Isère..................................149
Rhône Alpes, Rhône................................147
Val de Loire, Cher...................................117
Val de Loire, Indre-et-Loire 115, 116
Vendée, Brétignolles-sur-Mer..................119
Vendée, Saint Jean-de-Monts..................118
Vendée, Saint Laurent-sur-Sèvre.............120

Germany **180**
Baden-Württemberg, Bad Bellingen.........196
Baden-Württemberg, Bühl.......................198
Baden-Württemberg, Laichingen-Machtolsheim ...197
Bavaria (N), Issigau................................193
Bavaria (S), Grainau...............................194
Bavaria (S), Immenstaad.........................195
Hessen, Kirchheim..................................192
Lower Saxony, Clausthal-Zellerfeld..........204
Lower Saxony, Seeburg...........................205
Lower Saxony, Werlte..............................202
Mecklenburg-Western Pomerania, Hohenkirchen ...186
Mecklenburg-West Pomerania, Göhren......188
Mecklenburg-West Pomerania, Prerow......187
Mecklenburg-West Pomerania, Priepert......189
North Rhine-Westphalia, Barntrup...........203
North Rhine-Westphalia, Meerbusch........201
Rhineland Palatinate, Gerolstein-Müllenborn ...200
Rhineland Palatinate, Waldfischbach-Burgalben...199
Saxony, Dresden.....................................191
Saxony, Leipzig.......................................190
Schleswig-Holstein, Basedow...................185
Schleswig-Holstein, Büsum......................182
Schleswig-Holstein, Pion.........................184
Schleswig-Holstein, Waabs......................183

Great Britain **206**
England
Ambleside, Cumbria................................241
Berkshire, South.....................................223
Buckinghamshire, South..........................227
Cambridgeshire, East of England.............228
Castel, Guernsey.....................................210
Co. Durham, Northumbria.......................242
Cornwall, South West.......................211–213
Derbyshire, Heart of England...................234
Devon, South West...........................214–217
Isle of Wight, South................................218
Kent, South East..............................224, 225
Lincolnshire, Heart of England..........232, 233
Mersey, North West.................................236
Norfolk, East of England...................229, 230
Northumberland, Northumbria.................243
North Yorkshire, Yorkshire................237–240
Nottinghamshire, Heart of England.........235
Oxfordshire, South.................................222
Saint Sampson's, Guernsey.....................209
Sark, Channel Islands.............................208
Shropshire, Heart of England...................231
Somerset, South West.............................216

Warwickshire, Heart of England 226
West Sussex, South East 219
Wiltshire, South West 220, 221
Wales
Carmarthenshire, West Wales 246
Ceredigion, West Wales 249, 250
Conwy, North Wales 253
Glamorgan, South Wales 244
Gwynedd, North Wales 251, 252
Pembrokeshire, West Wales 247, 248
Powys, Mid Wales 245
Scotland
Aberdeenshire, Grampian 264
Argyll and Bute, Heart of Scotland 261
Dumfries and Galloway, Lowlands 254, 255
East Lothian, Heart of Scotland 258
Highland, Highlands and Islands 262–269
Isle of Skye, Highlands and Islands 265
North Ayrshire, Lowlands 256
Perth and Kinross, Heart of Scotland 260
Stirling, Heart of Scotland 259
West Lothian, Heart of Scotland 257
Northern Ireland
Co. Down, Newcastle 271
Co. Tyrone, Dungannon 270
Greece **272**
Attica, Sounio 278
Central Greece, Pefki 277
Central Macedonia, Nikiti 276
Ionian Islands, Corfu 274
Peloponnese, Ilia 280
Peloponnese, Kato Alissos 281
Peloponnese, Pylos 279
Thessaly, Kalambaka 275
Ireland **282**
Co. Clare, Corofin 297
Co. Cork, Blarney 291
Co. Cork, Glandore 292
Co. Donegal, Letterkenny 284
Co. Dublin, Clondalkin 285
Co. Kerry, Cahirciveen 294
Co. Kerry, Castlegregory 296
Co. Kerry, Killarney 295
Co. Kerry, Lauragh 293
Co. Mayo, Achill Island 299
Co. Mayo, Ballina 300
Co. Mayo, Castlebar 298
Co. Roscommon, Boyle 301
Co. Tipperary, Roscrea 290
Co. Tipperary, Tipperary 289
Co. Waterford, Dungarvan 288
Co. Wexford, Kilmuckridge 287
Co. Wicklow, Rathdrum 286
Italy **302**
Abruzzo, Marina di Vasto 321
Abruzzo, Opi 320
Calabria, Cropani Marina 324
Campania, Vico Equense 322
Lake Garda, Peschiera del Garda 308
Lazio, Roma 319
Ligúria, Campochiesa di Albenga 306
Ligúria, Sestri Levante 307
Marche, Pesaro 317
Piedmont, Orta San Giulio 304
Piedmont, Spigno Monferrato 305
Puglia, Ugento 323
Sardinia, Aglientu 327
Sardinia, Muravera 328
Sardinia, Sant'Antioco 329
Sicily, Agrigento 326
Sicily, Catania 325
Trentino - Alto Adige, Predazzo 309
Tuscany, Casciano di Murlo 315
Tuscany, Fiesole 313
Tuscany, Marcialla 314
Tuscany, Montopoli 312
Tuscany, Scarlino 316
Umbria, Sant Arcangelo-Magione 318
Veneto, Cavallino-Treporti 311
Veneto, Rocca di Arsiè 310

Luxembourg **330**
Diekirch 332–337
Luxembourg District 338, 339
Netherlands **340**
Drenthe, Dwingeloo 355
Drenthe, Eext 353
Drenthe, Meppen 354
Flevoland, Zeewolde 362
Friesland, Buren 350
Friesland, Harlingen 351
Friesland, Offingawier 352
Friesland, Vlieland 349
Gelderland, Hummelo 359
Gelderland, Maurik 363
Gelderland, Voorthuizen 360
Limburg, Roggel 365
Noord-Brabant, Oosterhout 367
Noord-Brabant, Soerendonk 366
Noord-Brabant, Vinkel 364
Noord-Holland, Alkmaar 348
Noord-Holland, Vogelenzang 347
Overijssel, Enschede 358
Overijssel, IJhorst 356
Overijssel, Lattrop 357
Zeeland, Aagtekerke 343
Zeeland, Kortgene 344
Zeeland, Nieuwvliet 342
Zeeland, Renesse/Noordwelle 345
Zuid-Holland, Nieuwe Tonge 346
Zuid-Holland, Nieuwland 361
Norway **368**
Møre og Romsdal, Averøy 374
Nord-Trøndelag, Snasa 373
Nordland, Andenes 370
Nordland, Ballangen 371
Nordland, Storforshei 372
Rogaland, Jørpeland 376
Sogn og Fjordane, Brekke 375
Østfold, Trogstad 377
Portugal **378**
Beja, Vila Nova de Milfontes 388
Castelo Branco, Idanha-a-Nova 386
Faro, Albufeira 390
Faro, Lagos 391
Faro, Olhão 389
Leiria, Nazaré 383
Leiria, Outeiro do Louriçal 384
Porto, Póvoa de Varzim 382
Santarem, Ferreira do Zêzere 385
Trás-os-Montes, Bragança 381
Viana do Costelo, Caminha 380
Évora, Évora 387
Slovenia **392**
Bohinjsko 395
Dolenjske Toplice 399
Lesce 396
Portoroz 394
Prebold 397
Verzej 398
Spain **400**
Andalucia, Cádiz 431
Andalucia, Córdoba 430
Andalucia, Málaga 429
Aragon, Huesca 451
Aragon, Teruel 434
Asturias, Arbón 443
Asturias, Somiedo 444
Cantabria, Cabuérniga 446
Cantabria, Cervera de Pisuerga 445
Cantabria, Laredo 447
Castilla-La-Mancha, Ciudad Real 433
Castilla Y Leon, Burgos 439
Castilla Y Leon, Segovia 437
Castilla Y Leon, Soria 438
Castilla Y Leon, Valladolid 436
Cataluña-Catalunya, Barcelona 409
Cataluña-Catalunya, Girona 402–408
Cataluña-Catalunya, Tarragona 410–416

Comunidad Valenciana, Alicante.................426, 428
Comunidad Valenciana, Castellón.................419, 420
Comunidad Valenciana, Valencia.................422–425
Extremadura, Cáceres.................432
Galicia, A Coruña.................441, 442
Galicia, Pontevedra.................440
Madrid, Aranjuez.................435
Navarra, Erratzu.................449
Navarra, Espinal.................450
Pais Vasco-Euskadi, Bizkaia.................448

Sweden.................**452**
Dalarnas Län, Mora.................457
Kalmar Län, Byxelkrok.................461
Stockholms Län, Skärholmen.................460
Värmlands Län, Kil.................456
Värmlands Län, Årjäng.................455
Västmanlands Län, Arboga.................459
Västra Götalands Län, Strömstad.................454
Örebro Län, Örebro.................458

Switzerland.................**462**
Bern, Erlach.................465
Bern, Interlaken.................471
Bern, Lauterbrunnen.................469
Graubünden, Pontresina.................467
St Gallen, Eschenz.................466
Ticino, Muzzano.................468
Valais, Raron.................470
Zug, Unterägeri.................464

Index By Alan Rogers Code & Name

Austria **12**
AU0070   Campingdorf Hofer.................15
AU0094   Camping Wolfgangsee.................18
AU0185   Campingplatz Seewiese.................16
AU0212   Camping Stadtblick.................17
AU0220   Camping Ötztal Arena.................14
AU0290   Donaupark Camping Tulln.................19
AU0302   Camping Neue Donau.................20
AU0370   Klagenfurt Wörthersee.................23
AU0405   Camping Ramsbacher.................25
AU0475   Camping Brunner am See.................24
AU0502   Camping Im Thermenland.................21
AU0505   Camping Leibnitz.................22

Belgium **26**
BE0543   Camping Kindervreugde.................29
BE0574   Camping Astrid.................28
BE0615   Camping Groenpark.................34
BE0630   Camping Grimbergen.................33
BE0683   Camping Parc des Sources.................36
BE0705   Camping l'Hirondelle.................37
BE0713   Camping les 3 Sources.................35
BE0716   Camping Maka.................39
BE0720   Camping Tonny.................38
BE0750   City Camping Antwerp.................30
BE0793   Camping De Binnenvaart.................31
BE0796   De Lage Kempen.................32

Croatia **40**
CR6712   Stella Maris Umag.................42
CR6724   Camping Bijela Uvala.................43
CR6730   Camping Amarin.................44
CR6735   Camping Kazela.................45
CR6756   Camping Konobe.................46
CR6769   Padova Camping Resort.................48
CR6770   Camping Baldarin.................47
CR6845   Camp Adriatic.................50
CR6876   Camping Lupis.................51
CR6915   Plitvice Holiday Resort.................49

Czech Republic **52**
CZ4658   Camp Ostende Bolevák.................54
CZ4690   Camping Slunce Žandov.................57
CZ4765   Autocamp Trebon.................60
CZ4775   Autocamping Karvánky.................61
CZ4785   Camp Drusus.................55
CZ4855   Prague Central Camp.................56
CZ4870   Autocamping Morava.................58
CZ4896   Camping Country.................59

Denmark **62**
DK2034   Stensager Camping.................67
DK2036   Gammelmark Strand Camping.................68
DK2046   Camping Trelde Næs.................66
DK2080   Holmens Camping.................65
DK2215   DCU Odense City Camp.................70
DK2220   Helnæs Camping.................69
DK2257   Vesterlyng Camping.................71
DK2378   Bunken Strand Camping.................64

France.................**72**
FR04220   Camping la Rivière.................172
FR05090   Camping Saint James-les-Pins.................174
FR07050   Le Ranc Davaine.................144
FR07120   Nature Parc 'lArdechois.................146
FR07630   Aluna Vacances.................143
FR07660   Domaine de Sévenier.................145
FR09170   Camping La Serre.................165
FR10040   La Noue des Rois.................96
FR10060   Les Rives du Lac.................97
FR11130   La Côte des Roses.................169
FR12410   Camping Saint-Lambert.................161
FR12430   Camping les Bords du Tarn.................160
FR13220   Camping de Ceyreste.................173
FR14070   Camping de la Vallée.................85
FR14150   Camping Port'land.................84
FR14180   Camping la Briquerie.................86
FR15040   Camping Moulin de Chaules.................142
FR17010   Camping Bois Soleil.................123
FR17190   Le Logis du Breuil.................122
FR17470   Le Domaine d'Oléron.................121
FR18010   Camping les Etangs.................117
FR19030   Camping la Plage.................138
FR19280   Camping du Lac.................137
FR21030   Camping les Premier Prés.................131
FR21040   l'Etang de Fouché.................130
FR22160   Camping le Neptune.................77
FR22460   Camping Val de Landrouët.................78
FR24340   Camping le Val de la Marquise.................153
FR24810   Domaine de Fromengal.................154
FR25150   La Roche d'Ully.................134
FR25160   Camping de Besançon.................135
FR26500   Camping du Grand Cerf.................148
FR27030   Camping Saint Nicolas.................87
FR29000   Camping les Mouettes.................75
FR29080   Camping le Panoramic.................74
FR29350   Camping Fouesnant.................76
FR30030   Camping Abri de Camargue.................166
FR30290   Domaine de Massereau.................167
FR32220   Camping Le Siléo.................159
FR33110   La Cote d'Argent.................150
FR33420   Camping la Canadienne.................152
FR34070   Le Sérignan-Plage.................168
FR37010   Camping la Mignardière.................116
FR37120   Camping Parc de Fierbois.................115
FR38250   Camping Lac du Marandan.................149
FR39110   Camping le Moulin.................133
FR39150   Camping les Trois Ours.................132
FR39180   Camping Sous Doriat.................136
FR40060   Camping Club Eurosol.................155
FR40200   Yelloh! Village le Sylvamar.................156
FR44090   Camping le Deffay.................109
FR44350   Camping du Chêne.................112
FR44360   Camping les Paludiers.................110
FR44500   La Guichardière.................111
FR46150   Camping la Truffière.................162
FR46190   Domaine de la Faurie.................163
FR49070   La Vallée des Vignes.................114
FR49160   Les Portes de l'Anjou.................113
FR50030   Château de Lez Eaux.................81
FR50210   Camping le Rivage.................83
FR50250   Camping du Golf.................82
FR52050   Camping en Champagne.................98
FR54020   Camping de la Pelouse.................99
FR56040   Camping de Penboch.................79
FR56120   Camping les Iles.................80
FR57160   Camping les Bouleaux.................103
FR58060   Domaine de la Gagère.................126
FR58070   Camping de Decize.................125
FR60020   Aestiva Camping de Sorel.................92
FR62200   Camping les Erables.................93
FR63080   Camping Le Moulin de Serre.................141

FR63130	Le Repos du Baladin	140
FR65010	Domaine de l'Eglantière	158
FR66060	Camping Le Littoral	170
FR66070	Yelloh! Village Le Brasilia	171
FR67150	Camp Au Clair Ruisseau	104
FR68040	Camping Des Trois Châteaux	106
FR68050	Camping Pierre de Coubertin	105
FR69020	La Grappe Fleurie	147
FR71020	Village des Meuniers	128
FR71150	Camping de Bourbon-Lancy	127
FR71190	Camping de Tournus	129
FR72100	Camping la Chabotière	108
FR72250	Domaine du Houssay	107
FR76030	Camping Vitamin	89
FR76130	Camping de la Forêt	88
FR77030	International de Jablines	94
FR80210	Le Clos Cacheleux	91
FR80230	Camping les Marguerites	90
FR82020	Camping de Bois Redon	164
FR83250	Douce Quiétude	178
FR83400	Holiday Marina Resort	177
FR83600	Camping Holiday Green	179
FR84080	La Simioune en Provence	176
FR84200	Camping le Garrigon	175
FR85310	Camping la Trévillière	119
FR85890	Camping le Rouge Gorge	120
FR85940	Camping Zagarella	118
FR86120	DéfiPlanet de Dienné	124
FR87100	Camping des Alouettes	139
FR88120	Au Clos de la Chaume	102
FR88170	Camping les Pinasses	101
FR88290	Camping Porte des Vosges	100

Germany **180**
DE25001	Camping Ostseequelle	186
DE25440	Campingplatz Nordsee Busum	182
DE26120	Naturcamping Spitzen	184
DE28060	Hümmlinger Land	202
DE28260	Camping Seeburger See	205
DE29610	Camping Lanzer See	185
DE30190	Ostseecamp Lehmberg	183
DE30550	Camping Prahljust	204
DE31820	Teutoburger Wald	203
DE32030	Rheincamping Meerbusch	201
DE32140	Camping Oosbachtal	200
DE32590	Camping Clausensee	199
DE32750	Camping Seepark	192
DE34110	Campingplatz Heidehof	197
DE34150	Camping Adam	198
DE34580	Campingpark Lug ins Land	196
DE37500	Camping Schloss Issigau	193
DE37510	Regenbogen Prerow	187
DE38040	Regenbogen Göhren	188
DE38160	Campingplatz Am Ziernsee	189
DE38340	Camping Dresden-Mockritz	191
DE38470	Campingplatz Auensee	190
DE40800	Schloß Helmsdorf	195
DE40970	Camping Resort Zugspitze	194

Great Britain **206**
England
UK0030	Ayr Holiday Park	211
UK0058	Trewethett Farm (CAMC)	212
UK0320	Looe Country Park	213
UK0681	Mill Park	215
UK0760	Barley Meadow Touring Park	214
UK1415	Alpine Grove Touring Park	216
UK1660	Piccadilly Caravan Park	220
UK1665	Burton Hill Caravan Park	221
UK2070	The Inside Park Touring Park	217
UK2510	Whitecliff Bay Holiday Park	218
UK2571	Bladon Chains (CAMC)	222
UK2700	Hurley Riverside Park	223
UK2755	Cosgrove Park	227
UK2887	Stubcroft Farm Campsite	219
UK3040	Broadhembury Caravan Park	225
UK3055	The Hop Farm Campsite	224
UK3420	Two Mills Touring Park	229
UK3510	Breydon Water Holiday Park	230
UK3560	Highfield Farm Touring Park	228
UK3680	Ashby Park	233

UK3775	Wagtail Country Park	232
UK3803	Grouse & Claret Caravan Park	234
UK3920	Riverside Caravan Park	235
UK4090	Island Meadow Caravan Park	226
UK4411	Ebury Hill C&C Club	231
UK4550	Cayton Village (CAMC)	240
UK4621	Cliff Farm Holidays	239
UK4638	Alders Caravan Park	238
UK4670	Wood Nook Caravan Park	237
UK5360	Willowbank Touring Park	236
UK5520	Skelwith Fold	241
UK5711	Leekworth Camping Park	242
UK5785	Chainbridge Caravan Site	243
UK9770	Vaugrat Camping	209
UK9780	Fauxquets Valley Campsite	210
UK9880	La Valette Campsite	208

Wales
UK5960	Abermarlais Caravan Park	246
UK5982	Trefalun Park	247
UK6000	Gwaun Vale Touring Park	248
UK6005	Brynawelon Camping Park	249
UK6012	Woodlands Caravan Park	250
UK6041	Talybont Farm Camping	245
UK6061	Ty Coch Campsite	244
UK6370	Hendre Mynach Camping Park	251
UK6615	Riverside Touring Park	252
UK6696	Wern Farm Caravan Park	253

Scotland
UK6885	Kings Green Caravan Park	254
UK6940	Loch Ken Holiday Park	255
UK7025	Seal Shore Camping Site	256
UK7046	Beecraigs Camping	257
UK7075	Thurston Manor Leisure Park	258
UK7225	Maragowan (CAMC)	259
UK7310	Twenty Shilling Wood	260
UK7560	Deeside Holiday Park	264
UK7666	Gairloch Holiday Park	266
UK7670	Grantown-on-Spey	263
UK7730	Scourie Caravan & Camping Park	267
UK7735	Sango Sands Oasis Site	268
UK7745	Dunnet Bay (CAMC)	269
UK7750	Staffin Caravan & Camping Site	265
UK7782	Faichemard Farm camping	262
UK7825	Shieling Holidays	261

Northern Ireland
UK7014	Windsor Holiday Park	271
UK8550	Dungannon Park	270

Greece **272**
GR8140	Lacara Camping	276
GR8255	Vrachos Kastraki	275
GR8315	Camping Kato Alissos	281
GR8370	Camping Dionysus	274
GR8475	Camping Pefki	277
GR8580	Camping Bacchus	278
GR8662	Camping Melissa	280
GR8700	Camping Erodios	279

Ireland **282**
IR8635	Rosguill Holiday Park	284
IR8730	Keel Sandybanks	299
IR8750	Belleek Park Camping	300
IR8810	Lough Lannagh Caravan Park	298
IR8825	Lough Key Camping Park	301
IR9100	Camac Valley Camping	285
IR9155	Hidden Valley Camping	286
IR9300	Morriscastle Strand	287
IR9330	Casey's Caravan & Camping Park	288
IR9370	Ballinacourty House	289
IR9420	Streamstown Camping	290
IR9460	Corofin Village Camping Park	297
IR9480	Blarney Camping Park	291
IR9500	Meadow Camping Park	292
IR9550	Anchor Caravan Park	296
IR9570	Creveen Lodge Camping Park	293
IR9590	Fossa Caravan & Camping Park	295
IR9610	Mannix Point Camping	294

Italy **302**
IT60320	Camping Village Cavallino	311
IT61500	Camping Al Lago di Arsiè	310
IT62105	Camping Valle Verde	309

IT62420	Camping Orta	304
IT62630	Camping Bella Italia	308
IT64045	Camping Tenuta Squaneto	305
IT64060	Camping Bella Vista	306
IT64130	Camping Mare Monti	307
IT65060	Camping Paradiso	317
IT66100	Panoramico Fiesole	313
IT66520	Villaggio Italgest	318
IT66610	Camping Toscana Village	312
IT66640	Panorama del Chianti	314
IT66650	Camping le Soline	315
IT66720	Camping Village Il Fontino	316
IT67920	Camping Il Vecchio Mulino	320
IT67970	Camping Il Pioppeto	321
IT68140	Flaminio Camping Park	319
IT68420	Camping Sant' Antonio	322
IT68650	Camping Riva di Ugento	323
IT68830	Villaggio Lungomare	324
IT69175	Camping Valle dei Templi	326
IT69230	Camping Jonio	325
IT69550	Camping Baia Blu la Tortuga	327
IT69750	Tiliguerta Camping Village	328
IT69860	Camping Tonnara	329

Luxembourg **330**

LU7490	Camping Toodlermillen	334
LU7500	Camping Um Bierg	332
LU7530	Camperpark Vianden	336
LU7610	Birkelt Village	338
LU7660	Camping Kockelscheuer	339
LU7730	Camping Bleesbrück	337
LU7850	Camping Fuussekaul	333
LU7930	Camping Du Nord	335

Netherlands **340**

NL5530	Camping Zonneweelde	342
NL5540	De Katjeskelder	367
NL5585	Camping De Paardekreek	344
NL5598	Camping De Grevelingen	346
NL5695	Camping de Grienduil	361
NL5865	Camping De Graafschap	359
NL5880	Camping Dierenbos	364
NL5965	Slot Cranendonck	366
NL6029	Camping Stortemelk	349
NL6030	Klein Vaarwater	350
NL6048	Camping De Potten	352
NL6080	Camping De Zeehoeve	351
NL6126	Camping de Hondsrug	353
NL6129	De Bronzen Emmer	354
NL6158	Camping De Noordster	355
NL6200	Erkemederstrand	362
NL6290	Eiland van Maurik	363
NL6336	Camping Ackersate	360
NL6454	Camping De Twentse Es	358
NL6502	Camping De Vossenburcht	356
NL6504	Camping De Rammelbeek	357
NL6550	Camping De Leistert	365
NL6705	Camping Alkmaar	348
NL6840	Camping Vogelenzang	347
NL6948	De Zeeuwse Kust	345
NL6990	Camping Westhove	343

Norway **368**

NO2370	Botnen Camping	375
NO2428	Andenes Camping	370
NO2455	PlusCamp Ballangen	371
NO2485	Krokstrand Camping	372
NO2490	Skjerneset Bryggecamp	374
NO2495	Vegset Camping	373
NO2615	Olberg Camping	377
NO2660	Preikestolen Camping	376

Portugal **378**

PO8010	Camping Caminha	380
PO8030	Camping Rio Alto	382
PO8180	Camping Milfontes	388
PO8202	Turiscampo Algarve	391
PO8210	Camping Albufeira	390
PO8230	Camping Olhão	389
PO8340	Camping Évora	387
PO8360	Camping Idanha-a-Nova	386
PO8391	Cepo Verde	381

PO8400	Campismo O Tamanco	384
PO8460	Ohai Nazaré Resort	383
PO8550	Camping Quinta da Cerejeira	385

Slovenia **392**

SV4110	Camp Bohinj	395
SV4210	Camping Sobec	396
SV4315	Camp Lucija	394
SV4402	Camping Park	397
SV4430	Camp Dolenjske Toplice	399
SV4445	Camping Terme Banovci	398

Spain **400**

ES80220	Camping Solmar	408
ES80350	Camping l'Amfora	403
ES80400	Camping Las Dunas	404
ES81400	Camping Treumal	406
ES83900	Vilanova Park	409
ES84100	Camping Park Playa Barà	410
ES84840	Camping Gavina	412
ES85330	Alannia Els Prats	413
ES85370	Naturista El Templo del Sol	416
ES85400	Camping La Torre del Sol	414
ES85610	Camping Ribamar	419
ES85700	Camping Bravoplaya	420
ES86110	Camping Puzol	422
ES86150	Kiko Park	425
ES86240	Devesa Gardens	423
ES86250	Kiko Park Rural	424
ES87420	Camping La Marina	428
ES87435	Alannia Costa Blanca	426
ES87810	Camping El Pino	429
ES88535	Ohai Conil Outdoor Resort	431
ES89300	Camping San Francisco	441
ES89360	Camping Bayona Playa	440
ES89420	Camping Los Manzanos	442
ES89440	Camping la Cascada	443
ES89450	Camping Lagos de Somiedo	444
ES89625	Camping Fuentes Carrionas	445
ES89640	El Molino de Cabuérniga	446
ES89930	Camping Playa del Regaton	447
ES90210	Camping Fuentes Blancas	439
ES90290	Campingred El Astral	436
ES90350	Camping Portuondo	448
ES90480	Camping Urrobi	450
ES90490	Camping Baztan	449
ES90640	Camping Gavín	451
ES90850	Camping Carlos III	430
ES90860	Cáceres Camping	432
ES90910	Camping Aranjuez	435
ES90955	Camping Las Corralizas	434
ES90960	El Mirador de Cabañeros	433
ES91225	Camping Vall de Camprodon	402
ES92420	Camping El Acueducto	437
ES92512	Camping Fuente de la Teja	438

Sweden **452**

SW2690	Camping Böda Sand	461
SW2735	Daftö Resort	454
SW2750	Sommarvik Camping	455
SW2760	Frykenbadens Camping	456
SW2780	Gustavsvik Camping	458
SW2825	Herrfallet Camping	459
SW2836	Mora Parkens Camping	457
SW2842	Bredäng Stockholm	460

Switzerland **462**

CH9045	Camping Erlach	465
CH9140	Camping Unterägeri	464
CH9172	Camping Huttenberg	466
CH9425	Camping Alpenblick	471
CH9460	Camping Jungfrau	469
CH9665	Camping Simplonblick	470
CH9860	Camping Morteratsch	467
CH9950	TCS Camping Lugano	468